SAGE was founded in 1965 by Sara Miller McCune to support the dissemination of usable knowledge by publishing innovative and high-quality research and teaching content. Today, we publish more than 750 journals, including those of more than 300 learned societies, more than 800 new books per year, and a growing range of library products including archives, data, case studies, reports, conference highlights, and video. SAGE remains majority-owned by our founder, and on her passing will become owned by a charitable trust that secures our continued independence.

Los Angeles | London | Washington DC | New Delhi | Singapore

The Synergy of Microfinance

The Synergy of Microfinance

Fighting Poverty by Moving beyond Credit

Binod B. Nayak

⑤SAGE   www.sagepublications.com
Los Angeles • London • New Delhi • Singapore • Washington DC

First published in 2015 by

SAGE Publications India Pvt Ltd
B1/I-1 Mohan Cooperative Industrial Area
Mathura Road, New Delhi 110 044, India
www.sagepub.in

SAGE Publications Inc
2455 Teller Road
Thousand Oaks, California 91320, USA

SAGE Publications Ltd
1 Oliver's Yard, 55 City Road
London EC1Y 1SP, United Kingdom

SAGE Publications Asia-Pacific Pte Ltd
3 Church Street
#10-04 Samsung Hub
Singapore 049483

Published by Vivek Mehra for SAGE Publications India Pvt Ltd, typeset in 10/13 Minion Pro by Diligent Typesetter, Delhi, and printed at Sai Print-o-Pack, New Delhi.

Library of Congress Cataloging-in-Publication Data

Nayak, Binod B.
  The synergy of microfinance : fighting poverty by moving beyond credit / Binod B. Nayak.
    pages cm
  Includes bibliographical references and index.
    1. Microfinance—Developing countries. 2. Poor—Services for—Developing countries. I. Title.
    HG178.33.D44N393   332—dc23   2014   2014034736

ISBN: 978-93-515-0042-1(HB)

The SAGE Team: N. Unni Nair, Saima Ghaffar, Nand Kumar Jha and Vinitha Nair

To the fond memories of my grandparents,
parents and uncle;
for my aunt;
and
for
Bandita

Thank you for choosing a SAGE product! If you have any comment, observation or feedback, I would like to personally hear from you. Please write to me at <u>contactceo@sagepub.in</u>

—Vivek Mehra, Managing Director and CEO,
SAGE Publications India Pvt Ltd, New Delhi

Bulk Sales

SAGE India offers special discounts for purchase of books in bulk. We also make available special imprints and excerpts from our books on demand.

For orders and enquiries, write to us at

Marketing Department
SAGE Publications India Pvt Ltd
B1/I-1, Mohan Cooperative Industrial Area
Mathura Road, Post Bag 7
New Delhi 110044, India
E-mail us at <u>marketing@sagepub.in</u>

Get to know more about SAGE, be invited to SAGE events, get on our mailing list. Write today to <u>marketing@sagepub.in</u>

This book is also available as an e-book.

Contents

Prologue

Sound common sense is not to be despised.[1]

Professor Ole Danbolt Mjøs
Chairman, Nobel Peace Committee for 2006 Nobel Peace Prize

Common sense is not so common.

Voltaire

Fighting poverty around the world has remained one of the most complex problems, which has challenged human ingenuity for ages. While it is true that much progress has been made during the last 50 years or so in understanding the multidimensional nature of poverty and how to fight poverty, its alleviation on a mass scale still eludes us. The enormity of the problem that we are up against can be difficult to comprehend sometimes. Suffice it to say that based on UN estimates, the world's population reached 7 billion at the end of October 2011 (Denyer 2011). In this context, it is important to note that various past estimates of world's poor population has been put at about 3 billion (see Chapter 2), constituting about 43 per cent of the total world population. What is more, the estimated 3 billion world's poor live on just about $2.50 or less per day. And of the 3 billion poor, about 1.4 billion are the poorest, constituting 20 per cent of the total world population. The poorest live on about $1.25 or less per day. During the last half century, enormous resources and efforts have been deployed by governments, bilateral and multilateral financial institutions, charitable foundations, and civil society organizations (CSO) to attack poverty at its roots. Even then, poverty around the world remains stubbornly entrenched.

Multidimensional Nature of Poverty Makes It a Challenging Task to Fight Poverty

Traditionally poverty has become synonymous with hunger, lack of shelter, disease and suffering. Anyone who has ever tried to understand the nature of poverty would agree that the causes of poverty appear as a web of tangled knots with many feedback loops. Not only poverty can be its own cause, the feedback loops of poverty can create vicious whirlpools that can throw the poor into 'black holes' of misery, with very little chance of escape. Many of the causes of poverty are so pervasive and entrenched that it is difficult to find ways to attack them at their roots. It all boils down to this—once present in the populace, poverty perpetuates itself by further pauperizing the masses by turning into a vicious cycle. As a result, its alleviation becomes a complex and difficult task.

In Chapter 2, we will briefly discuss about the multidimensional nature of poverty and the combinatorial complexity it gives rise to, which makes it difficult to win the war on poverty. That is not all. Finding practical solutions to fight poverty that are applicable across different societies, cultures, geographical regions and countries in different stages of development are not easy. As a result, building cogent causal models to understand the nature of poverty and finding solutions to alleviate it on a mass scale is an immensely difficult task. That is perhaps less appreciated than anybody would care to acknowledge.

The book is about how lack of access to formal and poor-friendly financial services such as credit, savings, insurance and payment systems for money transfer (MT) have been major impediments to fight poverty effectively. And how microfinance during the last 35 years has been able to design and deliver a menu of poor-friendly financial instruments that cater to the needs of the poor in this regard. The book also explores complementary non-financial services that many microfinance institutions[2] (MFIs) extend to the poor in order to help them fight poverty with greater degree of success.

Microfinance: A New Paradigm in Our Fight Against Poverty

If commonsensical ideas could make profound changes in the way the poor access financial services, then the delivery of microcredit to the poor starting in the mid-1970s has been compared to a 'quiet revolution' (Robinson 2001) in our fight against poverty. Starting with its humble beginnings, formalization of small-value finance in the form of microcredit has been able to deliver credit to the poor on a mass scale. Needless to say, during the last 35 years, microfinance, largely consisting of microcredit, has attained an industry status and many countries are beginning to give it a formal status by passing laws to create an enabling environment for the microfinance sector to grow.

As far as access to financial instruments are concerned, for thousands of years the poor have largely relied on informal credit and savings as financial tools to manage their finances for smoothing consumption and mitigating specific risks, such as health risk. From time to time, they also rely on governmental, donor and charitable assistance, and social capital to mitigate systemic risks such as hurricanes, floods, earthquakes and tsunamis. They also rely on such help during economic downturns such as recessions.

The microfinance revolution started with microcredit. This is because when time is of the essence (particularly in emergencies) it is relatively quicker for a poor person to access funds by borrowing from friends and family and moneylenders. This is also true because poor people, who are constantly strapped for cash, may not have the discipline and the tenacity to save in drips and drabs to have enough funds prior to such emergencies. Besides, whatever savings a household may have built up through thrift can be exhausted by taking care of one emergency or it may not be even sufficient to take care of one such emergency. Under these circumstances, the household has to resort to borrowing. As a result, the poor traditionally have used credit as substitute for savings. Besides, insurance markets have been largely non-existent for the poor. Consequently, to mitigate specific risks, the poor also rely on substituting credit and social capital for insurance.

Instinctively, the poor diversify their sources of borrowing. Even borrowers who have access to microcredit (microloans) usually borrow from other sources such as friends and family and moneylenders. For most poor families, microloans (micro debt) may form only a small part of their overall debt exposure. What is more, in spite of the double-digit growth of microfinance sector during the past years, not every poor household around the world has access to microcredit. In Chapter 3, we will discuss about how the poor have traditionally borrowed and saved. Chapters 4 and 5 of the book are devoted to microcredit.

Widespread access to microcredit around the world has identified how other financial instruments such as formal microsavings and microinsurance are essential to build precautionary liquidity and managing specific risks for poor families. While the poor have been ingenious in saving through thrift and have invented informal ways to save, these instruments are not as efficient as formal savings (see Chapters 3 and 6).

Emergence of insurance as a financial instrument is of recent origin. It is a complex instrument in comparison to microcredit and microsavings. Besides, when one speaks of microinsurance, it constitutes a variety of products, consisting of insurances that cover life, health, accident, property, livestock, crop, weather and natural disaster-related risks. As we shall explore in the book, microinsurance is one of the most complex instruments in the microfinance repertoire, and designing and delivering insurance products that are affordable and user-friendly, and deliver value to the poor has been difficult. Needless to say substituting credit (debt) for microinsurance is not optimal for a poor household. We will explore microinsurance in Chapter 7.

Leaving aside credit, savings and insurance, microfinance also includes other instruments such as microleasing (for lease finance) and improved payment systems for financial transactions including money transfer. Microleasing is a loan substitute. For periodic payments on a microlease (during the leasing period), it allows microbusinesses to use equipments and machinery in their businesses without owning the equipments. While only a handful of MFIs around the world have offered microleasing to the poor in the past, nonetheless it is a powerful financial tool. It is expected that importance of microleasing will increase in the coming years as mature microfinance borrowers would be interested in having access to equipments and machinery to move away from traditional businesses to attain economies of scale. We will discuss about microleasing in Chapter 8.

When it comes to the poor living in remote areas, receiving and sending funds through the existing payment systems could take weeks sometimes. Depositing small sums of money in their microsavings accounts could cost them in terms of transportation charge and even time off from work. In other words, the proverbial 'last mile' has been one of the major bottlenecks in delivering financial services to the poor. One of the most important contributions of microfinance institutions has been to bridge this last mile. The bridging of the last mile has been possible because in delivering financial services, it is the financial institutions (i.e., the MFIs) that come to the door steps of the poor, instead of the poor clients arriving at the door steps of the MFIs. This does increase transaction costs for the MFIs to do business with the poor. Recent innovations in the use of mobile phones for money transfer, paying bills and accessing financial services using platforms such as M-PESA (mobile money) in Kenya is revolutionizing how technology can be used to access financial services by the poor. Similarly, biometric smart card-based technology such as Financial Information Network & Operations (FINO) in India has opened up new channels to provide banking services in remote areas. It is expected that such technology-based platforms could reduce transaction costs and hence cost of accessing financial services by the poor. It is only through improved, poor-friendly and cost-effective connectivity that financial inclusion would take a big step forward. We will discuss about payment systems and money transfer in Chapter 9.

Over the years, there has been increased realization that even with access to all these financial instruments, the poor also need complementary non-financial services including training in such areas as simple arithmetic, literacy including financial literacy, nutrition, hygiene, sanitation, livelihoods and marketing. In fact, institutions such as Grameen Bank and BRAC in Bangladesh, BASIX in India and many other MFIs around the world provide access to these services to help the poor enhance their capabilities to fight poverty. We will discuss about the importance of complementary non-financial services in Chapter 10.

BRAC in Bangladesh is one of the glaring examples how besides providing access to financial services, it provides access to other complementary non-financial services that include such activities as education, health care, water, sanitation, human rights education, legal services, community empowerment, livelihood development and programme to support enterprises. In the area of livelihood development, BRAC provides training in such areas as agriculture, poultry, livestock, forestry and fisheries. All these activities go under the rubric of microfinance plus (Abed et al. 2011).

That is not all. Fighting poverty is not just about access to financial products and complementary non-financial services. In fact, MFIs use novel ways to help the poor in their fight against poverty. Just to illustrate, Grameen Bank expects its clients to memorize 'Sixteen Decisions' about social conduct and follow them resolutely (Dowla and Barua 2006, 55). These decisions were designed to help them overcome social aspects of being poor. We present four of these decisions in the following text:

> Discipline, unity, courage and hard work—in all walks of our lives.
> We shall keep our families small. We shall minimize our expenditures.
> We shall look after our health.
> We shall keep our children and environment clean.
> We shall build and use pit-latrines.

As we shall explore in the book, access to microfinance products and complementary non-financial services offered by the MFIs constitute a major paradigm shift in helping the poor manage their microenterprise and household finances, smooth consumption, mitigate exposure to specific risks, and build social and human capital to monetize their capabilities. However, not all MFIs around the world offer such wide array of products and services. In fact, most MFIs remain minimalist organizations and focus largely on extending microcredit to the poor. This is because for a variety of reasons offering the entire menu of financial instruments and complementary non-financial services has been difficult for the MFIs about which we shall discuss in the book. In other words, MFIs around the world have largely remained mono-product institutions.

Traditionally the poor have relied on credit to substitute for savings and insurance. As we shall discuss in the book, a debt-heavy balance sheet of a poor household could give rise to financial risk, which the household may not be able to cope with because of the lack of a back stop, which is usually the case.

The Synergy of Microfinance

Microfinance (microcredit) grew out of the search to find solutions for the credit needs of the poor. It was based on commonsensical and flexible approach, relying on trial and error method to arrive at product designs that has been already accessed by more than 200 million people around the world by the end of the year 2010 (see Chapter 1).

Microfinance is not pure banking. Fuelled by pragmatic and solution-oriented approaches and an open and flexible platform to experiment with innovative ideas, microfinance has been able to design and deliver commonsensical financial tools and has put down the foundations of financial and social intermediation at the Base of the Pyramid[3] (BOP), which millions of poor families around the world have been able to leverage to join wider socioeconomic networks, which is essential to climb out of poverty (Chapter 12).

The power of microfinance (microcredit) emerges from the fact that the financial tools and complementary non-financial services it delivers are poor-friendly, formal, reliable and are delivered on a level playing field. In delivering microfinance to the poor, it is the bank (i.e., the MFIs), which reaches out to the poor rather than the poor reaching out to the MFIs for accessing banking services. While bridging the last mile has increased the effectiveness of MFIs in delivering financial services to the poor, it does increase administrative expenses for the MFIs.

Microfinance usually caters to a wide range of self-employed individuals and entrepreneurs. More precisely, they are own account workers who are entrepreneurs out of necessity. Most of the businesses they own are low tech and have low entry barriers. Such businesses rarely need skills to own and operate. They are usually undercapitalized and lack economies of scale. Many of these businesses are owned by women (about 74 per cent of microfinance clients are women—see Chapter 1), who work from home (home-based businesses). They multitask, that is, they work on their businesses and in parallel take care of their children, attend to the needs of the elderly and perform household chores. Many of these businesses are clones of each other and hence their margins are usually squeezed. As a result, returns from these businesses are usually low. What these businesses allow is to help poor people diversify their sources of income, which, in turn, reduces income volatility. Needless to say, in spite of poor-friendly access to financial instruments and complementary services, gaining financial self-sufficiency by the poor is hard and fraught with uncertainties and risks. This is accentuated by the fact that the poor lack education and skills, live in areas where there is poor infrastructure, and lack access to public and private institutions such as health care.

All in all, as we shall explore in this book, access to microcredit is no panacea for winning the war against the entrenched multidimensional world of poverty. For example, accumulating impact assessments over the years have yet to corroborate the claim that with access to micro-credit, poor people could move out poverty on a mass scale (Chapter 11). What is more, the emergence of higher levels of delinquency in some markets around the world and the 2010 Andhra Pradesh Microfinance Crisis in India point to the fact that the MFIs have to be on guard regarding their lending practices, which could over-indebt the poor. And the borrowers at the same time have to avoid over-indebting themselves by keeping their overall debt levels under check from all sources, including the moneylenders.

However, in spite of the above cautionary notes, as we shall explore in this book, microcredit remains a major breakthrough in designing and delivering poor-friendly lending services, which has been in high demand (Chapter 11). Given the entrenched multidimensional nature of poverty, access to other financial instruments such as savings, insurance, improved payment systems, leasing and complementary non-financial services (such as livelihood training and marketing) is also vital in creating much needed synergy that can empower the poor to leverage their capabilities to fight poverty. For example, lessons from financial literacy training could sensitize the poor to the importance of other financial instruments such as savings and insurance and downside risks of over-indebting and pitfalls of spurious spending.

The synergy that microfinance gives rise to for the poor takes place on two levels, that is, at the individual level and at the system-wide level. At the individual level, the MFI clients directly benefit by using the formal financial instruments and non-financial complementary services to manage their business and household finances with relative ease. As we shall explore in the book, these instruments have been designed to create value for the poor such that it would help to leverage their efforts to fight against poverty.

At the system level, for example, in spite of poor infrastructure in the communities the poor live, the delivery of microcredit to the poor by bridging the 'last mile' has been able to lay down the foundations of financial intermediation at the BOP, which has inherent value above and beyond the benefits the poor accrue from access to microcredit. The commencement of a credit culture among the poor because of the introduction of microfinance has lasting value, which has inherent value for the entire economy. Moreover, the existence of MFIs, with their upward and downward linkages in the socioeconomic networks of a country, has been able to engender institutional capital for the poor. Chapter 12 discusses about some of the synergies that microfinance creates that has value above and beyond the value it delivers to the poor.

While my interest in microfinance goes back to early 1990s, the present book grew out of my modest attempt to explain microfinance to members of a charitable organization almost 10 years ago, who were mostly professionals consisting of engineers, physicists, biologists, doctors and managers. In spite of the commonsensical nature of microfinance, it was difficult for me to get across many of the ideas underlying the subject. This led me to write a book that could explain microfinance to intelligent laymen who normally have more questions about the subject than they can glean from reports and articles appearing in the news and electronic media.

Writing this book has been a long and lonely journey. But the journey has been a rewarding one for the simple fact that one is constantly in touch with a field that is vibrant with new ideas, products, services and institutions that have become agents of change at the BOP. Last but not the least, opinions expressed and any errors and omissions that may remain in the book are mine.

Notes

1. Quote from the speech given by Professor Ole Danbolt Mjos, Chairman of the Norwegian Nobel Committee, on the occasion of the presentation of 2006 Nobel Peace Prize to Professor Muhammad Yunus and the Grameen Bank in Oslo, 10 December 2006. Available online at http://www.nobelprize.org/nobel_prizes/peace/laureates/2006/presentation_speech.html?print=1 (downloaded on 17 October 2012).

2. See Chapter 4 for a description of MFIs. Throughout the book we use MFIs to denote microfinance institutions in a generic sense.

3. In the literature, the phrase BOP has been used synonymously with the phrase 'bottom of the pyramid' (BOP). The phrase 'bottom of the economic pyramid' was first used by Franklin D. Roosevelt in his 7 April 1932 radio address, 'The Forgotten Man.' Subsequently the phrase 'bottom of the pyramid,' was used by C. K. Prahalad in his book, *'Fortune at the Bottom of the Pyramid,'* which was published in August 2004 by Wharton School Publishing. Available online at http://en.wikipedia.org/wiki/Bottom_of_the Pyramid (downloaded on 5 November 2012).

Acknowledgements

In writing a book, particularly on a subject like microfinance, one is acutely aware of the social and intellectual capital one uses so freely, without proper acknowledgement, is huge–practically difficult to enumerate. People who encouraged and helped me in writing this book include Pulin B. Nayak, Nalini Nayak, Prafulla K. Mohanty, Prasanna K. Mohanty, Babru Samal, Jayashree Samal, Mausumi Nayak McGraw, Darrell McGraw, Nandini Nayak, Shilpa Challa and Sourav Nayak. Pulin Nayak's encouragement, support and advice during the writing of this book was indispensable and Shilpa Challa's help during various phases of the project is greatly appreciated. My publisher SAGE Publications India Pvt Ltd was extremely supportive of the project from the beginning till the end. I would like to thank the anonymous reviewer for the constructive comments on the manuscript. I would particularly like to thank R. Chandra Sekhar, Unni Nair and Saima Ghaffar for their support during the publication of this work. The book could not have been completed without my wife Bandita's encouragement and support during this entire period.

1

Introduction

> Loans to poor people without any financial security had appeared to be an
> impossible idea. From modest beginnings three decades ago, Yunus has,
> first and foremost through Grameen Bank, developed micro-credit into an
> ever more important instrument in the struggle against poverty. Grameen
> Bank has been a source of ideas and models for the many institutions in the
> field of micro-credit that have sprung up around the world.[1]
>
> Press Release, The Nobel Peace Prize for 2006

The above press release for the 2006 Nobel Peace Prize highlights the
stark reality that exists even today, which makes it impossible for
the poor to get loans from the moneylenders without collateral. Besides,
the interest rates on these loans are usurious (see Chapter 3). As we shall
explore in this book, with the advent of microcredit in the mid-1970s in
countries such as Bangladesh, India, Brazil, Bolivia and Indonesia, access
to credit by the poor went through a quiet revolution (see Chapters 4
and 5).

As noted in the Prologue, microfinance is a suite of formal financial instruments consisting of microcredit, microsavings, microinsurance, microleasing and payment systems for MT. The instruments are
designed specifically to cater to the needs of the poor in mind. For example, it takes into consideration their erratic and low levels of income, thin
asset base and lack of employment opportunities in the organized sector.
It also takes into consideration low levels of education and skills and lack
of financial literacy among the poor. Of the five instruments, microcredit
has been around the longest and is most widely used around the world.

As a result, the word microfinance has been used synonymously to mean microcredit.

As we noted in the Prologue, the MFIs besides providing access to these financial instruments also provide access to non-financial complementary services such as training in nutrition, sanitation, hygiene, financial literacy, livelihoods and marketing to expand market access.

The purpose of this chapter is to provide a broad overview of the book. It starts out with a brief discussion of the important achievements of microfinance followed by a discussion of some of the major challenges facing the microfinance industry.

Glimpses into Some of the Important Achievements of Microfinance

It is important that we begin by briefly discussing some of the major achievements of microfinance industry to date. Without such a discussion it is very easy to forget how the poor around the world used to struggle, not only in the past but even today to access poor-friendly and formal financial services such as credit, savings and insurance.

Prior to the arrival of microcredit, the poor largely relied on informal finance, where need for collateral, usurious interest rates, unreliability of access and exploitative nature of moneylenders not only stole their peace of mind, but also impoverished them. While it is true that moneylenders help the poor in the time of emergency, they are, however, not in the business of lending money to alleviate poverty. They are in the business of making money year after year without any regard for improving the financial conditions of their poor clients. What is more, they can go so far as to maximize profit even if they may end up exploiting the poor (see Chapters 2 and 3).

Since its inception in the mid-1970s, the success of microcredit could be gleaned from the following facts. Based on data available from the 'State of the Microcredit Summit Campaign Report 2012' (Maes and Reed 2012), as of 31 December 2010, 3,652 MFIs around the world reported to have provided access to about 205 million poor families, of which about 153 million were women. This implies that women clients constituted about 74 per cent of the total. Of the 205 million clients, about 138 million were among the poorest when they took their first loans, that is, the poorest clients constituted about 67 per cent of the total. Of these poorest clients, about 113 million were women, constituting about 82 per cent of the poorest clients. Assuming five members to a family, microfinance reached (directly or indirectly) almost 1 billion poor people around the world at the end of 2010.

Now moving to highlight some of the major recognitions that have been bestowed on the microfinance industry during the past years, it is important to note that, because of its past successes and future promise in helping the poor to access credit, the year 2005 was declared as the 'International Year of Microcredit' by the United Nations. And in 2006, Professor Muhammad Yunus and the Grameen Bank shared the Nobel Peace Prize '… for their efforts to create economic and social development from below.'[2]

In spite of many successes to its credit, microfinance (microcredit) has been put under the microscope for a variety of reasons about which we will briefly discuss in the next section titled 'Major Challenges Facing Microfinance Industry.' This includes issues such as (1) accumulating evidence regarding microcredit impact pointing to the fact that the benefits of microcredit could be modest in comparison to the outsized claims that it could alleviate poverty on a large scale; (2) emergence of over-indebtedness in some of the selected microcredit markets around the world during the last few years; and (3) with commercialization of microfinance, 'mission drift' has set in, which has emerged as one of the important issues for microfinance industry to manage in a judicious manner (see Chapter 11). For example, the 2010 Andhra Pradesh Microfinance Crisis has raised important issues with regard to how some of the commercialized MFIs put profitability and shareholder value creation well ahead of the absorptive capacity and over-indebtedness of the poor, which resulted in political backlash and meltdown of the microfinance industry in Andhra Pradesh.

In this context, it is important to note that the most recent 'State of the Microcredit Summit Campaign Report 2013' reports a decline in the number of poor families accessing microcredit at the end of 2011, from the previous year, that is, from the 2010 year-end level (Reed 2013). More specifically, while the 2012 report, which outlined that, at the end of 2010, almost 205 million poor families accessed microcredit, the number declined to about 195 million at the end of 2011. Moreover, the total number of poorest clients accessing microcredit registered a decline from about 138 million at the end of 2010 to almost 125 million at the end of 2011.

The report attributes 10 important reasons as to why such a decline took place, the most important being the 2010 Andhra Pradesh Microfinance Crisis in India (see Chapter 11). Some of the other important reasons for the decline were as follows: (1) microcredit markets, which registered high growth rates, such as Bangladesh, are now matured, besides, most of the clients within easy reach in most of these markets are already accessing microcredit; (2) it has been difficult to insulate the MFIs and their clients from the global economic crisis and slowdown; and (3) growing commercialization and negative press related to commercialization have led to the reduction of support by bilateral donors, which would have funded sustainable programmes for poorer clients and clients in remote areas.

In spite of the midlife crisis that the microfinance sector is experiencing, as we shall explore in this book, microcredit remains an essential financial tool for the poor to smooth consumption, mitigate specific risks and monetize their capabilities to generate income streams. As we shall explore in the book, the need for access to other microfinance products, that is, microsavings (Chapter 6) and microinsurance (Chapter 7) by the poor is equally important—even essential. Just to illustrate, the original microcredit model of Grameen Bank, known as Classical Grameen (Grameen I), was rather a rigid credit delivery system that did not incorporate voluntary savings as part and parcel of the original credit extension model. In Chapter 5, we will discuss how the devastating floods of 1998 in Bangladesh necessitated the redesign of Grameen I model (Classical Grameen) to make credit extension more relevant for its borrowers by incorporating voluntary savings at the intrinsic level of the credit delivery model that was named Grameen II. Grameen II model has been very successful in terms of expanding savings by the Grameen borrowers (see Chapters 4 and 5).

As we noted in the Prologue, microinsurance is designed to mitigate specific risks in poor households. It is a complex instrument to say the least, and well-defined financially sustainable business models for microinsurance have yet to emerge from much experimentation that is going around the world in delivering microinsurance to the poor. Moreover, designing affordable microinsurance products that are poor-friendly and deliver value to the poor is not easy. Besides, for a variety of reasons that we will discuss in Chapter 7, there is no natural demand for microinsurance by the poor. Lack of demand is one of the major bottlenecks in attaining financial sustainability in the case of microinsurance. In spite of many obstacles for the spread of microinsurance, major insurance providers around the world along with MFIs are experimenting with a variety of microinsurance product designs and delivery models, which they hope will attain financial sustainability as the poor will learn more about costs and benefits of microinsurance.

The book will also discuss about microleasing (Chapter 8), payment systems and MT (Chapter 9), and the important non-financial complementary services, that include, social intermediation, livelihood promotion and the need for broader market access (Chapter 10).

Microfinance Instruments: Noteworthy Product Innovations

Product innovation plays an important role in microfinance because of unique circumstances of the poor that include such complex issues as erratic income, cash flows that is dominated by small value transactions, lack of education and training, remoteness of localities where they live, lack of infrastructure and connectivity, and lack of asset base (lack of savings and other marketable assets) as a backstop. Under these circumstances, coming up with product designs that are affordable and deliver value but at the same time help MFIs attain sustainability and meet social mission goals concurrently is anything but easy.

It may be true that a simple change in the design of microcredit repayment terms or the introduction of a new savings instrument may not appear like an earth-shaking event, but these simple changes on the margin could help the poor in managing their businesses little easier or to save tiny sums of money for the rainy days. The innovations are important for the industry to constantly keep in step with the unmet and changing needs of the poor. One of the most important aspects of the industry has been that it has not developed a rigid set of rules and remains open to incorporate innovations and accept constructive change with a view to help the poor in their fight against poverty.

Microcredit was the very first product in the microfinance product space. Its success on the ground has been instrumental in propelling microfinance to the limelight and the award of 2006 Nobel Peace Prize to Professor Muhammad Yunus and the Grameen Bank. Some of the noteworthy innovations that microcredit boasts include group lending (joint-liability contracts), social intermediation, flexible repayment terms, progressive lending, compulsory savings and credit life insurance. In order to build capacity to help the ultra poor to access microcredit, programmes such as Targeting the Ultra Poor (TUP) by BRAC in Bangladesh has made a great deal of headway. Such programmes have been replicated in other parts of the world such as India and Haiti. We will discuss and critique many of these innovations in Chapters 4 and 5.

In the arena of microsavings, many of the ideas of commercial banking have been adopted. MFIs such as Grameen Bank offer microsavings in parallel with microcredit, which is well integrated with the credit delivery model. Other models that deliver microsavings to the poor include Village Savings and Loan Associations (VSLAs), Correspondent Banking and E-Money Savings Accounts. Given the fact that in a cash-strapped environment savings in dribs and drabs need a great deal of discipline, innovations such as commitment savings and the 'lend-to-save' model (product P9) of Stuart Rutherford have been used to encourage savings by the poor. Other noteworthy microsavings products that have emerged during the last several years include Grameen Pension Plan, M-KESHO, which offers M-PESA-based savings accounts and 'Jipange KuSave'—implementation of the 'lend-to-save' model on mobile banking. We discuss all these products in Chapter 6.

As we have already noted, designing and delivering affordable and user-friendly microinsurance products that can attain sustainability and create value for the poor is anything but complex. While the poor rely on informal means to insure against risky events, access to microinsurance is paramount because the instruments are targeted to immunize specific risks in a cost-effective manner. Chapter 7 is devoted to microinsurance. Some of the important topics discussed in the chapter include: poverty and heightened vulnerability to risks—why the poor need insurance, what is microinsurance, barriers to adoption of microinsurance by the poor, what are some of the impediments to sustainability of microinsurance,

MFIs as platforms to deliver microinsurance and examples of microinsurance products.

Leases are loan substitutes. The advantages of leases (microleases) stem from the fact that these instruments decouple equipment ownership from equipment use. As a result, a poor person can avail economic benefits of using equipments without its ownership. Microleasing is also a complex instrument to deliver. Chapter 8 is devoted to microleasing. Some of the topics included in the chapter are: the importance of improved access to tools and technology by the poor; what is microleasing; microleasing experience of MFIs in different countries including sustainability of microleasing programmes; MFIs as platforms for microleasing; some of the advantages of lease finance over borrowing and why microleasing remains an underutilized tool.

So far as poor-friendly payment systems for MT are concerned, use of technology such as information and communications technologies (ICTs) has the power to potentially revolutionize the underlying infrastructure on which the payment systems ride to establish connectivity with the poor. It can make the connectivity affordable, efficient and user-friendly. This could lead to expanding the sphere of financial inclusiveness. A case in point is M-PESA (Mobile Money), a small-value MT system that piggybacks on mobile (cellular) phones, which has been used by the poor in Kenya and many other countries in Africa for MT domestically and internationally. The system has also been used for bill payments and transacting with the banks (see Chapter 9). In Chapter 9, we also discuss about other ways to improve payment systems and MT using the traditional systems and also using the technology (ICT)-based payment systems such as FINO.

Over the years, it has been widely recognized that access to financial services (particularly access to only microcredit) does not guarantee that the poor can win the war on poverty. In Chapter 10, we discuss how access to non-financial complementary services can play an important role in helping the poor to enhance their chances of monetizing their capabilities through livelihood promotion and market their products and services to a wider marketplace. Complimentary services can also help them in lessening health risk by providing training in nutrition, sanitation and hygiene. Some of the topics discussed in the chapter include the importance of non-financial complimentary services such as social intermediation to build social capital, livelihood promotion for human capital development and access to wider marketplace for building sustainable microbusinesses.

Microfinance Institutions (MFIs): Driven by Delivery of Poor-friendly Financial Services to the Poor

The book is mostly about microfinance products and non-financial complementary services than about MFIs, self-help groups (SHGs) or other institutional models that help to deliver financial services at the grass-root level (please refer to Chapter 4 for brief descriptions of the MFIs and SHGs). However, throughout the book we make references to MFIs, which remain part and parcel of many of the important aspects of microfinance (microcredit) product delivery, which include product development, setting of microloan terms, loan pricing, loan approval and disbursement, collection of repayments, interest and charges, and overall asset liability management of such institutions. For many MFIs disbursement and repayment of principal, interest and charges take place in weekly meetings with their clients. It is important to note that weekly contact with their clients is an important aspect of MFIs in order to help the poor build social capital, improve their knowledge base and to make sure that the clients remain current on their payments to their respective MFIs. Group meetings are also used as distribution channels.

The MFIs have double bottom-line (DBL) objectives consisting of financial and social bottom-line goals. While financial bottom-line goals are easier to set and communicate, social bottom-line (social mission) goals are less so. One of the important social mission goals is to expand outreach to ultra poor in the communities the MFIs operate. It is also paramount that the MFIs design products and policies and delivery mechanisms that are conducted in a poor-friendly manner. Given the fact that the majority of the MFI clients are women, its products and policies have to take into consideration special needs of their women clients. Unlike financial bottom-line goals, social bottom-line goals are varied, and it is the responsibility of the MFIs to articulate their social mission goals and make sure that the goals are met. Around the world, there has been increasing discontent among the MFI clients that in their quest for sustainability (profitability), many MFIs have forgotten the other half of their objectives, that is, achieving their social mission goals.

There is no denying the fact that the success of microfinance can be attributed to the non-governmental organization (NGO) movement in the developing countries prior to the emergence of microfinance (microcredit). Over the years, NGOs have had endeavoured to bridge the 'last mile' in serving the poor in an ecosystem that even today lacks rudimentary physical infrastructure and many of the necessary public and private institutions that the poor need access. It is also true that it was the NGO movement that was instrumental in identifying the need for financial and other non-financial complementary services for the poor as some of the important missing links in our fight against poverty.

Most MFIs started out as NGOs. In the initial years, the NGO-based MFIs leveraged the infrastructure built by the NGOs to deliver financial and other non-financial complementary services to the poor. As the domain knowledge of delivering financial services expanded and deepened, the MFIs started to create their own institutional niche. The scope of the book does not allow delving into the unique institutional structure that the MFIs have built over the years to fund and deliver financial and other complementary services to the poor.

Slowly but surely the MFIs have been providing financial and institutional infrastructure to establish upstream linkages to integrate with the domestic and international capital markets to channel savings, financial and managerial know-how, and technology in order that the poor could access financial and non-financial complementary services with ease. Establishing such an infrastructure has been one of the most important achievements of microfinance movement. The success of MFI model around the world has been attracting many commercial banks and other non-banking financial institutions (NBFIs) to deliver microfinance to the poor.

Commercialization of NGO-based MFIs

The microcredit portfolios of NGO-based MFIs are largely funded by governmental and donor resources, 'compulsory savings' that is required of the poor clients in order to access microcredit (see Chapters 4–6), equity capital and internally generated resources (retained earnings). Most of the NGO-based MFIs do not provide voluntary savings facilities because regulatory requirements in many countries do not normally allow these institutions to offer such facilities to the poor.

However, budgetary constraints in most developing countries and limited donor funding have had been the major restraining factors in supporting rapid growth of microlending. When this is combined with the fact that total size of equity capital, retained earnings and compulsory savings for most MFIs is relatively small in comparison to the growing demand for microcredit, the microfinance industry increasingly found it necessary to access commercial sources of funding to grow.

Over the years, the commercialized MFIs have been rather success-ful in expanding their lending to the poor. Rosenberg (2010) in his paper *Does Microcredit Really Help Poor People?* discusses about MFIs (reporting to Microfinance Information Exchange [MIX] Market) that were already profitable and needed no further subsidies, accounted for about 71 per cent of all clients. What is more, the MFIs close to achiev-ing sustainability accounted for about 22 per cent of the clients.

Increased funding for many commercialized MFIs has been pos-sible from commercial sources because these MFIs have been able to achieve sustainability (profitability). As a result, many NGO-based MFIs have transformed themselves to become commercial entities. In many cases such conversion has paved the way to receive regulatory approval to provide voluntary savings facilities to the poor. This, in turn, has allowed the MFIs to become true financial intermediaries by tapping into the deposit base of their clients as well as the public at large. In the event voluntary savings can become a stable source of funds for an MFI, both the MFI and its clients benefit because the MFI can potentially diversify its sources of funding (and that too can be at a relatively lower cost), which can contribute towards lower profitability and lower lend-ing rate for the poor clients. Based on October 2011 data, Grameen Bank of Bangladesh did not rely on donor funding or loans, it was entirely funded from the bank's deposits (Chapter 4).

Funding and Asset Growth

MFIs today access commercial funding through a variety of sources that include bank loans, bonds, securitization of microloan portfolios and other instruments. Increasingly more sophisticated financial instru-ments such as microfinance investment vehicles (MIVs) and equity invest-ments in the form of private equity and even initial public offerings (IPOs) have become a reality for the sector (Rhyne 2009). These are important achievements for a sector that not too long ago depended on governmental, donor and charitable funding.

As we shall see, the richness and profit potential of the sector have attracted many types of funders to provide resources for the MFIs. Gone are the days when sustainability (profitability) for the MFIs was considered a mirage. What we are faced with instead is that there are some MFIs that have been even criticized for high levels of profitability without regard for the economic well-being of their poor clients. However, one has to agree that diversifying its funding base from largely governmental, donor and charitable funding to attract commercial funding and tap into the sophisticated capital markets have entirely changed the scenario how microcredit portfolios are funded today.

The funding needs for microfinance (microcredit) have been variously put at about $300 billion. Presumably the number has been perhaps arrived at, based on the following calculations. Assuming there are about 3 billion poor people around the world and five members to a family, the total number of poor families around the world is about 600 million. If one assumes that the total need for microcredit for each family on the average to be around $500, then total funding needs for microcredit would be in the neighbourhood of $300 billion. The $300 billion estimate would vary depending on the size of the actual poor population, number of poor families around the world and the average size of microloans outstanding per family. If we assume that the total number of poor accessing microcredit today to be around 200 million and each borrower on the average has about $500 in microloans, then the total microloan portfolio worldwide could be around $100 billion.

Over the past few years, microfinance around the world has enjoyed a rapid asset growth. Based on estimates, during the period from 2004 to 2008, microfinance assets grew at an average growth rate of 39 per cent (Chen et al. 2010). Such a galloping growth rate resulted in pushing microfinance assets under management to reach over $60 billion by the end of 2008. However, since the financial crisis of 2007–08, good quality total funding data for the microfinance industry around the world has been difficult to find.

While it is true that great strides have been made in channelling funds to grow microfinance assets at a rapid clip, everything is not well with commercialization. In order to highlight some of the issues relating to commercialization, in the following section, under the heading, 'Commercialization and its Discontents,' we will briefly discuss about some of the major challenges facing the commercialization of microfinance industry.

Kiva: 'Microlenders' for Microborrowers—'Birth of Person-to-Person Microfinance'

The power of the Internet has been harnessed by enterprises like Kiva in 'connecting' the interested public ('microlenders') to lend to microborrowers (owners of microenterprises) through intermediaries such as the MFIs. In making such lending to the poor a reality, Kiva stands in the middle to collect and aggregate funds from the public (that can be as small as $25 from an individual lender) and channels such funding to the poor clients through its field partners around the world. In fact, for all practical purposes, Kiva can be viewed as an online approach to enable microlenders to lend to microborrowers, although the lending is not as direct as it may appear.

Moreover, one could also term the funding approach of Kiva as 'crowdfunding.' Just to illustrate the power of such funding, in a recent article titled, 'Crowdfunding development: Kiva's aim is to make microfinance easy' (Duncan 2014), Premal Shah co-founder of Kiva mentioned that since its inception in 2005, Kiva has facilitated over half a billion dollars ($550 million) from one million Kiva lenders to help about one million people around the world.

Kiva was founded in 2005 by Matt Flannery and Jessica Jackley. It is a 501(c) (3) category organization in the US, which are considered non-profit organizations (Flannery 2007). The meaning of Kiva in Swahili is 'unity.' Kiva works with 167 field partners and 450 volunteers in 66 countries to provide funding for microenterprises owned by the poor (Kiva 2012a). Field partners mostly consist of MFIs, social businesses and non-profit organizations. The field partners are entrusted with screening borrowers, providing loan requests to Kiva, disbursing loans to borrowers and collecting debt service consisting of repayments on principal and interest. Since its inception in 2005, Kiva had already lent about $368 million in loans and the funding for these loans were provided by 842,000 microlenders (Kiva 2012a). The total number of borrowers funded through Kiva has already reached about 899,000 (Kiva 2012c). The average size of their loans was about $400.

Kiva does not charge interest on the funds it disburses to field partners. Microlenders that provide funds to Kiva also do not receive any interest from Kiva (2012b). Kiva is supported by grants, loans and donations from its users as well as corporations and institutions. In its website Kiva declares that 'Lending to the working poor through Kiva involves risk of principal.' However, the repayment rate on the loans that Kiva provides to its field partners has been around 98.97 per cent (Kiva 2012c). When Kiva receives funds from its field partners, it repays its lenders. The lenders are encouraged to re-lend the funds to another borrower, donate the funds to Kiva to meet operational expenses or choose to take back the funds lent.

Several important issues have emerged since the inception of Kiva pertaining to the fact that the field partners (such as the MFIs) normally disburse funds to microborrowers well before these borrowers are selected by the microlenders of Kiva to receive funding (Roodman 2009; Strom 2009). If that is the case, the microlenders could write the checks directly to the field partners (i.e., the MFIs) instead of writing checks to Kiva. However, the approach perhaps can be justified on the grounds that Kiva's outreach into microfinance sector in many different countries provides the necessary expertise in recommending to the microlenders (of Kiva) appropriate field partners and microborrowers who they should lend to. Besides, providing funding to these field partners is not enough. One needs to evaluate to what extent these funding have been utilized on the ground effectively. Individual microlenders do not possess the necessary ground knowledge and expertise in evaluating these field partners on an ongoing basis.

Other issues that have been a source of concern include, Kiva field partners have been involved in fraudulent activities (Flannery 2009) and last but not the least, the reported high repayment rates on Kiva loans may be due to the field partners making repayments on behalf of delinquent and defaulted microborrowers to maintain high repayment standards. However, in spite of many of these issues, Kiva has grown in recent years and continues to provide much needed funding for many microenterprises around the world.

In India, Rang De is also an online microlending platform that sources funding (as little as ₹100, equivalent to about $2) from socially minded investors to lend for business and education (Srinivasan 2012). Range De has already raised about ₹50,000,000 (equivalent to about $1 million).

The repayment rate for Rang De is 98.56 per cent. Social investors earn interest at the rate of 2 per cent flat per annum on the funds lent. Interest rates charged to the end user are (Annual Per cent Rate—based on monthly repayment schedule): education loans 9.02 per cent, business loans 15.33 per cent and microventure 17.97 per cent.

Social Performance and Its Measurement

During the last 15 years or so, the microfinance industry has been able to articulate what social performance is and what are some of the widely accepted activities that lead to social value creation. Social performance has been defined as 'the effective translation of an institution's mission into practice in line with accepted social values[3].' And some of the activities that promote social value include provision of financial and non-financial services for greater numbers of poor and excluded people; improving appropriateness of services already being offered; increasing clients' social capital, assets, income and access to services like health care; reducing vulnerability; and improving an MFI's impact on the environment and the community.

Anyone who is even remotely familiar with the field of microfinance could sense that microfinance is not purely banking, nor development banking. The combination of sustainability (profitability) and social mission goals create unique demands on the MFIs that need to be addressed through formulation and implementation of financial and operational policies and procedures and evaluating whether the desired goals have been reached.

The microfinance industry is perhaps among the very few industries in the world that have articulated a vision for Social Performance Measurement (SPM). While the industry has progressively refined its objectives regarding social performance, what is needed is that SPM ought to become a part and parcel of all MFIs, like Financial Performance Measurement (FPM). Anyone looking at the FPM of an MFI also has to look at the SPM in parallel. What is more, FPM of an MFI should not be considered complete without SPM, because MFIs operate in a sector where majority of its clients are poor and vulnerable women.

In Chapter 4 we will discuss a pioneering programme, 'TUP' by BRAC that has been at the forefront of helping the poorest (ultra poor) and through capacity building is helping them graduate from these programmes to become active members of MFIs in order to borrow, save and be self-employed or start a business. The programme has been replicated in India and Haiti. Since these programmes are not sustainable, funding remains an important issue. MFIs use their own sources and donor funding to run such programmes.

The scope of the book does not allow an in-depth discussion of SPM, although we will digress at appropriate places to discuss about social mission and social performance of the MFIs to put into perspective 'mission drift' in the microfinance sector and its implications.

Technology

In the arena of adopting technology to leverage delivery of financial services and non-financial complementary services, the MFIs have been at the forefront. To begin with, in keeping track of literally millions of tiny loans and savings accounts and accounting for disbursements, repayments and other related financial transactions in such areas as credit, savings, insurance, lease finance and MT, the microfinance industry have been proactive in adopting ICT in trying to be cost-effective and efficient in order to attain sustainability. For example, the MFIs have been utilizing ATMs, mobile phones and smart cards such as FINO in trying to minimize transaction costs and offering a variety of financial transactions that the poor could access with relative ease. Systems like M-PESA that started in Kenya and has now spread out to other countries in the world could bring about a major revolution as to how the poor will perform basic financial transactions in the future (see Chapter 9). All in all, with increased use of technology, the MFIs are trying to help the poor transact with ease and reduce transaction costs at the same time. Ease of use and reduction in transaction costs can be a major force in expanding the sphere of inclusive finance in the coming years.

Major Challenges Facing Microfinance Industry

In Chapter 11, we examine some of the major challenges faced by the microfinance industry. For example, if one tries to examine how access to microcredit helps the poor to fight poverty, one wonders how such tiny sums of money, when lent for a rather short periods of time can achieve so much for the poor? Many even question if microfinance is no more than a stop-gap measure—a short-term palliative or even second best solution to the complex problems of poverty (Dichter 2007). And many have wondered how millions and millions of poor could become successful entrepreneurs just by accessing microloans. Many have also criticized microenterprises to be rather rudimentary, lacking economies of scale that can hardly make a dent in our fight against poverty.

Over the years, we have come to realize how access to credit (microcredit) by the poor is not enough (see Chapter 10). As we have already noted, besides microcredit, many MFIs (if not all) provide access to other formal financial instruments, that is, microsavings, microinsurance, microleasing and improved payment systems for remittances. While each of these instruments appears to be conceptually simple, they give rise to a whole host of complex issues in order to be delivered on a mass scale. For example, in order to offer access to microsavings facilities (formal voluntary savings facilities), MFIs that are NGOs or even NBFIs have to be managed professionally as deposit-taking institutions to meet regulatory requirements of their respective countries. These institutions are also required to be supervised by the regulatory authorities. Many of the issues particularly risk-management aspects of deposit-taking institutions that offer savings products to the poor are rather complex. Similarly, as we noted earlier, microinsurance is a complex product to design and deliver in a sustainable manner (see Chapters 6 and 7).

Other complicating factors that drag down the growth and effectiveness of microfinance on the ground have to do with the fact that the poor in general lack education. What is more, a large percentage of the uneducated poor may not be literate either. They also lack good nutrition, shelter, sanitation and hygiene. A combination of these factors increases vulnerabilities of the poor. When one combines lack of health care, education and livelihood training, it would be difficult to imagine how with access to microcredit, microsavings and microinsurance, the poor could lift themselves out of poverty in short order. As a result, many MFIs around the world provide training in literacy including financial literacy, nutrition, sanitation, hygiene, livelihood(s) and marketing (see Chapter 10). They collaborate with the government and businesses to open markets for the products and services produced by the poor. It goes without saying that delivery of non-financial complementary products to the poor may not be easy for most MFIs because they are better equipped to deliver financial services. Therefore, they have to also collaborate with other institutions that specialize in delivering such non-financial complementary services to the poor.

There are other issues that MFIs have to deal with in delivering financial services to the poor. These include lack of good infrastructure and supporting public and private institutions without which delivery of these services can become difficult. For example, a poor person can have access to health insurance through microinsurance, but without suitable access to doctors, drug stores and hospitals in their neighbourhood, receiving the right kind of treatment in a timely manner could be difficult. That is not all. Other complex issues such as apathy, nepotism, corruption, lack of respect for the rule of law and lack of an enabling regulatory environment to support microfinance could make it difficult for MFIs to operate at the grass-root level.

As we noted in the Prologue, recent impact assessments of accumulating evidence regarding microcredit impact point to the fact that the benefits of microcredit could be modest in comparison to the outsized claims made earlier that it could alleviate poverty on a large scale. We also noted that during the last few years there has been emergence of over-indebtedness and higher levels of delinquency in some markets around the world (see Chapter 11). What is more, the 2010 Andhra Pradesh Microfinance Crisis has raised issues with regards to 'mission drift' of MFIs that has put MFI profitability and shareholder value creation well ahead of the absorptive capacity and over-indebtedness of the poor. This resulted in political backlash and meltdown of the microfinance industry in Andhra Pradesh. Under these circumstances, the MFIs need to become responsible lenders and the borrowers need to become responsible borrowers. What is more, the poor need to use microsavings and microinsurance along with microcredit to mitigate risk more actively.

Commercialization and Its Discontents

Commercialization of microfinance has brought with it increased focus on sustainability (profitability). That has led to the so-called mission drift for many MFIs, where sustainability (profitability) has taken precedence over social mission such as improving depth of outreach, delivering complementary services like literacy including financial literacy training, as well as training in such areas as sanitation, hygiene, livelihoods and marketing, and improving an MFI's impact on the environment and the communities the institutions serve.

As many of the MFIs have attained sustainability (profitability), the institutions have come under increased scrutiny for charging high interest rates, over-lending (without regard for absorptive capacity of their poor and vulnerable women clients) and use of coercion to collect debt from delinquent borrowers. There have been cases, where it is alleged that use of coercion has led to suicides by some borrowers (Lee and David 2010).What is more, lack of credit bureaus and lax credit standards has led to multiple borrowing from MFIs by many poor clients, a clear recipe for cash flow inflexibility to service loans and widespread delinquency. In this context, it is important to note that the bulk of the outstanding debt in majority of poor households in the developing countries are held by the moneylenders.

That is not all. Commercialization has also helped the MFIs to diversify their funding base. Some of these institutions with relatively stronger balance sheets and profit potential have been able to go for IPOs to tap into domestic and international capital markets. Examples of such IPOs include the 2007 IPO of Compartamos Banco in Mexico and the 2010 IPO of SKS Microfinance in India. However, these IPOs have been perceived by the critics to have taken commercialization too far by resorting to maximization of profits for their shareholders at the cost of charging relatively higher interest rates and over-lending to their clients (large number of them being vulnerable poor women) to increase market share under saturated market conditions. Such over-lending has been responsible for over-indebtedness of poor households with adverse consequences, which we highlight in Chapter 11. The 2010 Andhra Pradesh Microfinance Crisis in India is a prime example of how mission drift, if taken too far could undermine the entire microfinance sector in a country (Chapter 11).

Social Performance

Traditionally, we are more adept at managing institutions that are driven by a single bottom line, that is, profitability. Moreover, we have a long tradition in measuring financial return and financial performance bottom line. However, setting and measuring social mission goals and arriving at 'social performance bottom line' are less intuitive and more complex. As a result, setting DBL goals and managing MFIs to attain these goals in a seamless manner may sound easier than what they are in reality. However, as we noted in the previous section, much progress has been achieved in conceptualizing, refining and coming up with guidelines as to how to translate an MFI's social mission into practice in line with accepted social values.

What remains to be seen is that the managers of MFIs and the investors in the microfinance industry take social performance bottom line as seriously as the financial performance bottom line. This is imperative because the MFIs directly serve the poor, the most vulnerable section of the society, where errors in judgement could have grave consequences as the 2010 Andhra Pradesh Microfinance Crisis in India has amply shown. Therefore, it is important that social mission, one of the core tenets of microfinance industry, needs to be incorporated at an intrinsic level into rating MFIs.

That is not all. As the MFIs as institutions mature and become larger institutions, issues such as consumer protection, 'truth in lending,' addressing grievances of the poor become recurring events. Unless these are addressed in a seamless manner, they could easily develop into seeds of discontent that could snowball into becoming major issues, which could undermine an MFI or even the entire microfinance industry. Therefore, in evaluating an MFI, it is imperative that investors in the microfinance industry take social performance bottom line as seriously as financial performance bottom line.

The issue of sustainability of programmes that support social mission is an important issue for the MFIs. Lack of standardization of products and services offered by these programmes lead to lack of revenue and business models, which makes it necessary that such programmes have to be supported by donor funding, funding from charitable organizations and funding provided by the MFIs from their own sources. In Chapter 10, we discuss financial costs and benefits of delivering complementary health services by Bandhan, a large MFI in the state of West Bengal in India (Metcalfe et al. 2010). The health services are delivered to Bandhan clients in conjunction with its microfinance programme and it consists of health education, health product distribution and informal linkages with health care providers in West Bengal. The programme was developed and tested in partnership with 'Freedom from Hunger' as part of the Microfinance and Health Protection (MAHP) initiative.

Conclusion

As we shall explore in this book, microfinance takes a focused problem-solving approach to provide formal financial services to the poor, lack of which has been one of the major impediments for the poor in their fight against poverty. Given the multidimensional world of poverty, it is not just credit, but other financial instruments, that is, microsavings, microinsurance, microleasing and improved payment systems for banking services, including remittances are urgently needed by the poor in enhancing their chances to win their battles against poverty. But that is not all, besides the financial services, the poor also need access to other complementary non-financial services such as livelihood and marketing training to build sustainable businesses and access broader markets for their products and services. As we shall explore, the commonsensical tools and the open and flexible platform that microfinance has put together has been able to put down the foundations of financial and social intermediation at the BOP for millions of poor families around the world. As a result, these families have become part of broader social and economic networks, which is essential for them to climb out of poverty.

As we will discuss in the book, based on MFI impact assessments, we have scaled down our expectations of microcredit impact on the ground. What is more, higher levels of delinquency in some markets around the world and the 2010 Andhra Pradesh Microfinance Crisis in India point to the fact that the MFIs have to be on guard regarding their lending practices and the borrowers have to avoid over-indebting themselves, that is, watch their overall debt levels from all sources, including the moneylenders.

The book is largely devoted to microfinance products. It explores how during the last 35 years, fuelled by progressive, pragmatic and solution-oriented approaches, and an open platform to experiment with innovative ideas, the resulting synergy that has emerged and will emerge in the future years is expected to give impetus to making inclusive finance a reality on the ground.

Notes

1. The Nobel Peace Prize for 2006, Press Release, The Norwegian Nobel Committee, Oslo, 13 October 2006. Available online at http://www.nobelprize.org/nobel_prizes/peace/laureates/2006/press.html (downloaded on 28 October 2012).
2. Extract from the Nobel Peace Prize Award announcement, 13 October 2006, as quoted in the speech by Professor Ole Danbolt Mjøs, Chairman of the Norwegian Nobel Committee in Oslo on 10 December 2006. Available online at http://www.nobelprize.org/nobel_prizes/peace/laureates/2006/press.html (downloaded on 28 October 2012).
3. Social Performance Task Force. 'What is Social Performance?' Available online at http://sptf.info/what-is-social-performance (downloaded on 31 October 2012).

2

On Poverty: Who Are the Poor? Why Poverty Persists?

The poor stay poor, not because they are lazy, but because they have no access to capital.[1]

Milton Friedman

...[I]n analyzing social justice, there is a strong case for judging individual advantage in terms of the capabilities that a person has, that is, the substantive freedoms he or she enjoys to lead the kind of life he or she has reason to value. In this perspective, poverty must be seen as the deprivation of basic capabilities rather than merely as lowness of incomes, which is the standard criterion of identification of poverty. The perspective of capability-poverty does not involve any denial of the sensible view that low income is clearly one of the major causes of poverty, since lack of income can be a principal reason for a person's capability deprivation.[2]

Amartya Sen

In his book *The Economics of Being Poor*, Theodore W. Schultz (Schultz 1993, 1), Nobel Laureate in Economic Sciences, makes the following observation: 'In spite of the fact that most people throughout the world are poor, the economics of being poor is not a well-developed part of economics.' Needless to say, causal model(s) of poverty could go a long way in fighting the menace of poverty on the ground; however, multi-dimensional world of poverty has challenged our ingenuity to arrive at causal models with universal applications.

But at the same time, we cannot wait until we learn everything about poverty before attacking poverty. In the following pertinent quote, Jonathan Morduch observes, how bottom-up approaches such as microfinance (microcredit) that were designed to help poor households have improved access to credit, have become powerful tools to understand how these credit instruments work for the poor and how these instruments can be improved. In a similar way, we can not only gain deeper insights into the workings of complex instruments like microinsurance, if the instrument can be carefully rolled out, but it can also provide deeper insights into the nature of poverty.

> The experience with microfinance suggests that there is no need to despair. Muhammad Yunus, for example, did not wait until he had all the answers before he set up the Grameen Bank of Bangladesh. But once it was set up, the introduction of the bank provided a way to learn about credit markets by comparing outcomes in places served by Grameen versus outcomes in control villages (Morduch 1998). As a result, we are now learning about the nature of credit markets in ways impossible before microfinance was established. So too, I expect, with microinsurance. The best hope is that microinsurance implementers will forge ahead with pilot projects, and that, if they are carefully rolled out (with an eye to evaluations), a great deal about risk, vulnerability and poverty can be learned in the process. (Morduch 2006, 343)

As we will explore in the book, our efforts to design financial tools or other complementary services for the poor and delivering them in a poor-friendly manner have the power to help us observe how the poor leverage these tools to smooth consumption, mitigate risk and leverage their capabilities to fight poverty. Such observations can become the basis for designing improved tools for the poor to help them fight poverty.

Given the fact that over 200 million people around the world have already accessed microcredit, the process of designing and delivering these products and subsequent impact assessments have helped us to gain deeper understanding as to how microcredit has been able to help or hurt poor households. The hope is, with other products such as microsavings, microinsurance, microleasing and improved payment systems for MT and financial transactions, a great deal of insights can be gained how the poor use these tools to their advantage. And that, in turn, can help us design improved instruments, build more responsive institutions and policies that the poor would value, and help them in a positive way to improve their economic condition. The process is incremental and each step may be small. But the cumulative impact of such incremental steps can be pronounced. In other words, the recursive nature of these processes can have a profound impact in arriving at improved financial and non-financial products and services over a period of time that could make a major difference in the way how we attack poverty bottom-up.

On the Nature of Poverty

In trying to understand the nature of poverty, the following quote[3] is rather revealing:

> Poverty is hunger. Poverty is lack of shelter. Poverty is being sick and not being able to see a doctor. Poverty is not having access to school and not knowing how to read. Poverty is not having a job, is fear for the future, living one day at a time. Poverty is losing a child to illness brought about by unclean water. Poverty is powerlessness, lack of representation and freedom.

That is not all. Poverty can degrade human beings to unbearable levels. It can inflict severe physical, emotional and mental harms on the poor. Some of the harms it inflicts can be irreversible. We do not even possess tools to measure the level of degradation that can result from such harms. Graphic descriptions of poverty are heart-breaking. Some of us even find it unbearable to witness hunger, disease, death and destruction.

One of the telltale signs of poverty is that, the poor lack assets that can be converted to steady streams of income (Smith 2005). While lack of assets is a sign of poverty, it is also true that lack of assets also becomes one of the important reasons as to why a poor person cannot build assets. One needs money to make money. One needs assets to accumulate assets. Lack of assets that can produce goods and services such as a sewing machine, tools for carpentry or a rickshaw are productive assets that can generate streams of income. Any surplus from such streams of income could be used to accumulate more assets. Besides generating income streams, assets can be used as collateral to access credit which can be used at the time of emergency or for working capital in microbusinesses. As a result, lack of assets becomes an important reason as to why poverty persists. Therefore, the question is: How a person can build assets having practically no assets to start with? In other words, how this vicious cycle can be broken?

Now continuing our discussion of the importance of assets in fighting poverty, one has to agree that good health, that is, physical as well as mental fitness is at the forefront of any person's assets, not just the poor. This is because the poor has to rely on continued good health to earn a living by monetizing their physical as well as mental assets. However, good health for the poor cannot be ensured, because they normally lack access to good nutrition, shelter, hygiene, sanitation and health care. The health risks that the poor face can quickly ruin their finances and impoverish them. But by and large, the poor do not have access to health insurance. At the same time, the poor do not have access to affordable and user-friendly accidental insurance, life insurance, property insurance and flood insurance. Whether one is poor or non-poor, it goes without saying that insurance for specific risks can be a life saver (particularly for poor families who normally lack any backstop mechanism) and insurance payouts could go a long way in helping to compensate for asset depletion.

Similarly, the possession of a skill by a poor person can be an important asset because it can be a potential source of income. But acquiring a skill that is in demand is not easy for a poor person. For example, a poor person cannot learn a skill unless he or she has access to on-the-job training or training in a classroom. But jobs are scarce. Accessing formal training in a classroom is still more difficult. And as a result, we are confronted with the same vicious circularity that traps the poor in poverty for generations. This is because without enhancing their skills, the poor may be confined to old ways of doing things, which may not generate enough income to move them out of poverty.

In the same vein, the lack of literacy, education and training are some of the important reasons why the poor remain underemployed or lack employment at all. The lack of training and education deprives them of taking advantage of opportunities that may come on their way. Even minimal training in literacy, including financial literacy, can make the poor more aware of income opportunities. Most importantly, financial literacy (including adding, subtracting and multiplying numbers) can help them manage their financial affairs better. Similarly, training in rudiments of sanitation, hygiene and nutrition can go a long way in making them healthier and fit for work. Just by boiling drinking water they can avoid a variety of waterborne stomach ailments that plague the poor in the developing countries. By following simple principles of hygiene (such as the use of soaps) and sanitation, the poor can save on health care expenses. More working days and savings on medical expenses mean more money in their pockets. If their children are less sick, they will be less absent from their schools. The benefits of such simple measures can have profound beneficial implications in improving their economic condition. In other words, a penny saved is a penny earned.

As far as building assets by savings is concerned, it is also true that the lack of access to formal savings facilities has been a major constraint for the poor (see Chapter 6) to build financial assets that can be used in the time of emergency. One common misconception is that the poor do not have the wherewithal to save. However, it is through thrift that the poor save tiny sums of money for the rainy days. Particularly, the women amongst the poor instinctively save because they normally have the responsibility to manage the household. Nonetheless, lack of formal savings facilities makes it difficult for the poor to bring about a balance between their assets and liabilities.

As we shall explore in this book, besides access to poor-friendly credit and savings facilities, the poor need access to other financial instruments and complementary non-financial services to manage their household and business finance with ease to be empowered to fight poverty.

On Classifying the Poor

Normally, we tend to jumble up the poor into one single monolithic category. In reality, the poor can be divided into different categories based on such things as asset level, education, training and experience. A poor person who has a roof over his head is very different from someone who makes the footpath his home. Similarly, a poor person who owns assets such as a bicycle, a thatched house, a cow, some hardware or tools, or a small piece of land, belongs to a different category than someone who begs and does not know where the next meal is going to come from.

In 1995, Consultative Group to Assist the Poorest (CGAP) and the Microcredit Summit Campaign Committee formally defined a poor person as someone who lives below the poverty line (Yunus 2003). It also defined the 'poorest' as someone in the bottom-half of those living below the poverty line.

In the following passage, we follow a classification of the poor provided by Brigit Helms in her book *Access for All: Building Inclusive Financial Systems* (Helms 2006). A similar classification of the poor has been widely adopted in the microfinance industry. It divides the poor into three broad categories consisting of (1) destitute—households in the bottom 10 per cent below the poverty line, (2) extreme poor—bottom 10–50 per cent of the households below the poverty line and (3) moderate poor—top 50 per cent of the households below the poverty line. We also add one more group to the above three groups, that is, the group represented by 'vulnerable non-poor,' which will be useful in our discussions of the poor. The group represented by the vulnerable non-poor consists of those poor people who are just above the poverty line, but can quickly move below the poverty line if prevailing economic conditions go against them. The following discussions on poverty groups are based on *Savings Services for the Poor*, edited by Madeline Hirschland (2005).

To begin with, the destitute (the poorest), that is, the bottom 10 per cent below the poverty line is the most vulnerable group amongst the poor. They have practically no asset base that can be used as collateral to access credit. Their income levels are the smallest in comparison to the poor in other categories, and the incomes they earn are highly erratic. This group is incapable of meeting minimum food requirements, shelter and health care. During difficult times, the group depends on governmental and donor assistance. They also rely on help provided by charity. The destitute need the most help, because they are constantly being crowded out by other poor people who are relatively more powerful.

The earnings of the extreme poor group (bottom 10–50 per cent of the households below the poverty line) can be irregular but better than the poorest. As a result, the extreme poor cannot consistently provide themselves with the minimum food requirements, shelter and health care. They also cannot take advantage of the financial services such as microcredit provided by the MFIs. This is because they cannot generate enough income to meet regular payment requirements on microloans. It is only the economically active within the extreme poor group who have the wherewithal to take advantage of such facilities. Microfinance programmes that are targeted to benefit the destitute group by providing subsidized credit, grants and non-financial complementary services are normally crowded out by the members of the extreme poor group.

As the destitute and the extreme poor groups are not capable of taking advantage of the financial services provided by institutions like the MFIs, the MFIs have to make special efforts to reach out to these groups. In fact, for many MFIs, reaching out to the poorest and the extreme poor is part of their social mission. In Chapter 4, we will discuss about TUP, pioneered by BRAC to build capacity such that the ultra poor (consisting of destitute and the extreme poor) can access microfinance.

The members of the moderate poor group cannot adequately provide themselves with minimum food, health care and shelter from their current income (Hirschland 2005). However, all over the world, large numbers of microfinance clients are drawn from this group because the members of this group, in general, have the wherewithal to meet the payment requirements to access microcredit.

The members of this group (top 50 per cent of the households below the poverty line) are reasonably proactive about looking out for opportunities to improve their economic well-being. Normally, they are economically active, well connected and possess skills that can be easily leveraged in running microenterprises. They are also in the look-out for accessing financial services to leverage their capabilities. Although many of them may prefer salaried jobs in the organized sector, there are not too many jobs that they can access to be gainfully employed. What is more, unless they are near a city or town, finding such jobs is difficult. As a result, moderate poor account for a large share of microfinance clientele.

The vulnerable non-poor groups' access to financial services is usually more diversified than the moderate poor groups. This is because some of the group members may be already clients of MFIs, or may have already graduated out of MFIs and have access to credit and other financial services from formal financial institutions such as the commercial banks and credit unions. However, they are vulnerable because they are just above the poverty line and can easily be drawn into the ranks of the poor if exposed to adverse conditions such as an economic downturn, natural calamities or illness in the family.

It goes without saying that the classifications of the poor presented above are not sacrosanct. The underlying intention of providing such a classification is to help us realize that the poor are not a monolithic group and which group members are most likely to join MFIs and which group members would need help in capacity building. Needless to say that, one cannot neatly delineate a boundary between the moderate poor and vulnerable non-poor, nor can one delineate a boundary between the extreme poor and the moderate poor. With ups and downs in the economy and personal circumstances, poor people in one category can end up in another category based on their degree of vulnerability.

Estimates of Number of Poor People in the World

At the outset, it is important to note that estimating the number of poor people in the world is a complex task. Just to illustrate why it is so complicated, it is important to note that the number of poor people just below the poverty line, that is, the number of poor people in the moderate poor category is a volatile number. This is because, if the prevailing economic conditions go against the vulnerable non-poor, the ranks of the moderate poor will swell. However, if economic conditions improve, many of the poor just below the poverty line can move out of the moderate poor category to the vulnerable non-poor category.

With the above qualifications which are somewhat brief, we provide below the World Bank estimates of poor people in the developing countries updated as of February 2010. The estimate which follows is based on 'World Bank Updates Poverty Estimates for the Developing World[4]' in which Chen and Ravallion's 2008 estimates were considered the latest comprehensive estimate of poverty in developing countries. Based on the 2008 estimate, about 1.4 billion people in the developing world were living on US$1.25 or less per day in 2005. Moreover, based on the World Bank Development Indicators, the number of poor people living on US$2.50 or less per day in 2005 was estimated to be about 3.14 billion.[5]

For ease of discussion, throughout the book we will use 3 billion to be the total number of poor people in the world who live on US$2.50 or less per day. We will also use 1.4 billion to be the estimate of the poorest people around the world who live on US$1.25 or less per day.

Why Poverty Persists

At the beginning of the chapter, in the quote from *Development as Freedom* (Sen 1999), Amartya Sen has characterized poverty as 'deprivation of basic capabilities' not just 'lowness of incomes.' He further argues that the enjoyment of 'substantive freedoms' goes to the heart of how an individual takes advantage of his capabilities. Moreover, he also states that, 'The perspective of capability-poverty does not involve any denial of the sensible view that low income is clearly one of the major causes of poverty, since lack of income can be a principal reason for a person's capability deprivation.'

Also quoted at the beginning of the chapter is rather a pithy statement from Milton Friedman, that is, 'The poor stay poor, not because they are lazy, but because they have no access to capital.' What all this points to is that the lack of access to financial capital by the poor can deprive them from enjoying some of the 'substantive freedoms' that the non-poor take for granted. For example, lack of access to capital can deprive a poor person from leveraging her capabilities to improve her economic condition. In fact, Muhammad Yunus has gone so far as to say that access to credit is a human right (Bruck 2006).

Before we delve into the subject of microfinance starting in Chapter 4, it would be useful to illustrate how multidimensional nature of poverty makes it difficult for the poor and the society at large to wage a successful war on poverty. To begin with, we try to illustrate how poverty feeds on itself. One could also say that the longer a person stays poor, the higher the likelihood of her staying poor. Therefore, one of the major causes of persistence of poverty is poverty itself. In attacking poverty, such circularity (feedback loops) complicates the situation in separating the cause from the effect. Therefore, in trying to fight poverty, one has to find innovative ways to break this circularity.

In the following, we enumerate some of the critical impediments that stifle the poor in waging a successful war against poverty. By identifying such impediments and by taking a solution-oriented approach that leads to designing and delivering products (such as financial products) and services (such as training in financial literacy and livelihoods), one can hope that the poor will be able to improve their chances of winning the war on poverty. As we shall explore in this book, microfinance is one such solution-oriented approach that has been taking focused approach to delivering financial and other non-financial complementary services to the poor. And microfinance has been rather successful in delivering credit (i.e., microcredit) to the poor in a sustainable manner. In spite of some of the criticisms that has been levelled against microcredit about which we will discuss in Chapter 11 (Critiquing Microfinance), access to such instruments has made a major difference in helping the poor to avail opportunities for income generation and in the process fight poverty.

Poverty Perpetuates Itself: An Example of Poverty Trap

To illustrate how poverty perpetuates itself, the following quote from *Banker to the Poor* by Muhammad Yunus shows how Sufiya Begum, one of the poor women of Jobra in Bangladesh, was trapped in poverty (Yunus 2003, 48).

> Sufiya Begum earned two cents a day. It was this knowledge that shocked me. In my university courses, I theorized about sums in the millions of dollars, but here before my eyes the problems of life and death were posed in terms of pennies. Something was wrong. Why did my university courses not reflect the reality of Sufiya's life? I was angry, angry at myself, angry at my economics department and thousands of intelligent professors who had not tried to address this problem and solve it. It seemed to me the existing economic system made it absolutely certain that Sufiya's income would be kept perpetually at such low level that she would never save a penny and would never invest in expanding her economic base. Her children were condemned to a life of penury, of hand-to-mouth survival, just as she had lived before them, and as her parents did before her. I had never heard of anyone suffering for the lack of twenty-two cents. It seemed impossible to me, preposterous. Should I reach into my pocket and hand out Sufiya the pittance she needed for capital? That would be so simple, so easy. I resisted the urge to give Sufiya the money she needed. She was not asking for charity. And giving one person 22 cents was not addressing the problem on any permanent basis.

The above paragraph illustrates several things that are instructive: (1) Sufiya Begum, in her hand-to-mouth existence, needed only a tiny sum of money—only 22 cents—to extricate herself from the rigid terms and conditions of the buyer of her goods, who also provided her financing at usurious rates. However, at the same time, she did not have any alternative sources of poor-friendly financing to pay off her debt and proclaim her freedom from a lender who bundled buyer and moneylender into one; (2) she was not earning enough to save up 22 cents to declare her independence from the moneylender; (3) the economic system she was part of did not even realize or perhaps closed its eyes to her needs to provide access to tiny sums of money (microcredit) that is poor-friendly; (4) the real issue was not that just one such poor borrower needed assistance to access a few cents of credit to ameliorate her predicament; literally millions and millions of the poor encountered such stark realities that needed a permanent solution.

In a recent book *Scarcity: Why Having Too Little Means So Much*, the authors Sendhil Mullainathan and Eldar Shafir (2013) highlight how scarcity has the capacity to capture the mind to such an extent that we may end up neglecting important aspects of life, which also needs our careful attention. Pre-occupation with such thoughts has been described as 'tunnelling' in the book, implying that the mind becomes so focused on the issue at hand that many important issues outside the tunnel get neglected. The authors also use another terminology, that is, 'bandwidth' which refers to 'computational capacity' of the brain to include such things as our capacity 'to pay attention, to make good decisions, to stick with our plans and to resist temptations.' In the book, the authors make the claim that scarcity forces us to be inside the tunnel, and taxes our bandwidth so much so that it 'inhibits our fundamental capacities,' such as paying attention to important issues that needs our careful attention. For example, if a poor person tides over an emergency situation by borrowing from a moneylender and gets used to such an idea (even if the interest rates may be usurious), borrowing money becomes the focus in future emergencies, and could deprive the mind to build up savings through thrift over a longer period of time to substitute for such borrowing partially or fully, hence lowering overall interest expenses on household debt, which in turn could help increasing the propensity of the household to save. Such insights are important in designing financial instruments and financial literacy training for the poor in fighting poverty.

As we will explore in the book, microcredit emerged in the mid-1970s as a focused solution to the 'small value' credit needs of the poor which planted the seeds of the microfinance revolution around the world (see Chapter 4).

Lack of Access to Good Nutrition, Shelter and Health Care

'Health is wealth.' But this dictum falls on the wayside when it comes to the poor. Most of the poor are uneducated and not too many of them are aware of healthy practices that can reduce their exposure to diseases. Besides, the fact that the poor normally have low or erratic income can lead to lack of access to good nutrition, shelter and health care. It is not even unlikely that poor families can go hungry because of their poverty. Moreover, due to lack of good nutrition, hunger and proper shelter, they can easily fall prey to diseases. Due to the lack of access to health care, they can become weak and diseased and unfit for work. More often than not, the poor are inflicted with emotional and mental disabilities because of poverty. They can be psychologically depressed to take any initiative. For example, psychological consequences of poverty such as fear, low self-esteem and lack of self-confidence are difficult to diagnose and get rid off. These are some of the reasons why the poor remain trapped in poverty.

Since a high percentage of the MFI clientele are women, and because women in general are more aware of their own and family's health, emphasis on nutrition, sanitation, hygiene and health care aspects in group meetings have the potential to have salutary implications for the overall health of the families of the MFI clients. And if one assumes that the female member of a poor family runs a successful microbusiness, there is much likelihood that a portion of her earnings would go towards improved nutrition, shelter and health care for her family.

It is important to note that some of the MFIs around the world provide complementary services that educate their clients in nutrition, sanitation and hygiene, which can go a long way in motivating the poor to adopt the right kind of practices that has the potential to improve the health of their families. For example, in order to provide poor people with clean drinking water (that could eliminate one of the major sources of waterborne diseases), there are institutions like Integrated Village Development Project (IVDP) in Krishnagiri near Bangalore that provides interest-free microcredit (microloans) to have access to clean water (Murphy 2012). IVDP partners with Unilever to help the poor to purchase the Pureit filter manufactured by Unilever, which is cost-effective and easy to use. In Chapter 10, we will discuss about complementary health services provided by Bandhan, a large MFI in the state of West Bengal in India. The services provided by Bandhan to its clients, in conjunction with its microfinance programme, consist of health education, health product distribution and informal linkages with health care providers in West Bengal. In Chapter 7, we discuss about microinsurance.

Lack of Access to Good Infrastructure

It goes without saying that access to good or even acceptable roads, transportation systems (bus, rail, airports, port systems), electricity, telecommunication systems (radio, telephone, television and others), water supply and so on goes a long way in engendering economic development. Infrastructure developments need large investments. Most developing countries cannot make optimum investments in this arena because of budgetary constraints. And international lending institutions and other donor agencies over the years have provided assistance in various forms in improving infrastructure in the developing countries. In spite of huge investments by the developing countries in infrastructure, the poor, in general, lack access to an acceptable level of infrastructure. As a result, the lack of adequate infrastructure becomes one of the major bottlenecks in improving their economic condition.

As we shall explore in the book, infrastructure provided by ICTs which mobile (cellular) phones, ATMs and smart cards utilize have been leveraged to bring about a revolution in branchless banking for the poor. Mobile phones are already helping the poor establish connectivity with markets, health care providers such as doctors and pharmacies and to receive MTs domestically as well as internationally to name a few. The mobile-phone-based payment system, M-PESA (mobile money), which started in Kenya, has been a pioneer in this field (see Chapter 9).

What is more, the advent of ICT infrastructure in developing countries is making it possible to establish unique identification (UID) for each and every individual where each person's name and UID number can be matched with his or her biometric identifiers. It goes without saying that UIDs will be helpful for the governments in developing countries to provide financial assistance to the poor directly. What is more,

UIDs, like the social security numbers (SSNs) in the USA, can be used by the credit bureaus to track creditworthiness of the poor.

Just to illustrate, Unique Identification Authority of India (UIDAI) issues Aadhaar, a 12-digit UID number on behalf of the Government of India. The UID number is designed to serve as a proof of identity and address anywhere in India.[7] The UID number is designed to facilitate access to banking, mobile phone connections, and other governmental and non-governmental services in India. For example, it is expected that using Aadhaar (UID) issued by UIDAI, the government can make cash transfers to individuals including the poor.

Social, Cultural and Other Forms of Exclusion

According to Elie Wiesel,[6] Nobel Peace Laureate, "Culture may be termed as the soul of economy, just as economy may be defined as the arm of culture. Both can be—must be—nationally inspired and universally applied; in other words, rooted in national aspirations but open to outside ideals." However, more often than not, one finds culture, social status, religion, caste and creed become the basis of stereotyping individuals and dividing people rather than integrating them. What is more, these attributes have been effectively used to exclude people. Such exclusions sometimes can be overt and sometimes subtle. Under these circumstances, the statement that diversity is strength becomes a misnomer.

In other words, diversity can be a source of weakness. It weakens those who are excluded. When sections of the people are denied access to institutions, businesses and opportunities through exclusion, they become economically backward. Economic backwardness leads to impoverishment. Impoverishment, once present in the masses, further restricts access to opportunities to get ahead economically. And again vicious circularity of poverty trap reins.

The list of things that has been used to exclude the poor is long. They include such things as caste, gender, employment, livelihood, property, credit, housing, education and training, health care, democratic participation, public goods, cultural activity and legal recourse (Sen 2000). Such exclusion exacts a big toll on those who are excluded, particularly when one is poor. Under these circumstances, the excluded even do not know whom to complain (even if one complains it falls on deaf years).

Such exclusion can make the poor depressed and sick. More often than not, they blame their destiny and remain entrapped in poverty.

In many societies, women have been effectively excluded to participate in social, cultural and business activities in ways that effectively make them powerless to do anything about it. Just to illustrate, in many societies, when it comes to property rights and financial matters, they are treated as second-class citizens. However, they are expected to take care of the children and the old. They work in the household and even in the field and sacrifice more than the men. In many cultures, they are excluded from getting educated and going outside the household to work. Women, in general, earn less than men. Therefore, in these societies, poverty afflicts the women more than the men. When women are poor, particularly the children and even the entire family suffer along with them.

As we shall see, all over the world, disproportionately large numbers of poor women have become members of MFIs to access financial services to get ahead. This is because access to microcredit without traditional collateral enables them to borrow from the MFIs. Access to credit (for working capital) helps them to be self-employed by running microbusinesses from home. As a result, they can multitask by taking care of the children, the sick and the elderly while attending to their microbusinesses.

Besides, membership in the MFIs has allowed poor women to go outside the home and connect with others. Attending group meetings that are normally used to collect debt service and disburse funds by the MFIs have become powerful platforms that have been also utilized to disseminate ideas about nutrition, sanitation, hygiene and income-generation opportunities to the poor—particularly to poor women. The meetings are also used by the MFI clients to network and share with each other ideas that help in solving their personal and household problems. We will discuss about 'Women as Microfinance Clients,' in Chapter 5.

Underutilization of Networking, Social Connectivity and Social Capital

As we noted in the previous section, social, cultural and other forms of exclusion undermine the capacity of the poor to network with the broader community to harness social capital. Lack of social connectivity isolates them and makes them powerless to take advantage of social capital (see Chapter 10 for a definition and discussion of social intermediation and social capital).

Social connectivity and networks are important support structures for the physical and emotional well-being of its members. It is through networking that we become aware of what is happening around us. This, in turn, allows us to take advantage of opportunities and avoid risks. Without taking full advantage of social capital, the poor people tend to further accentuate their impoverishment.

Social connectivity that fosters social networks leads to value creation. The value contained in social networks is social capital. How do social networks create value? As we shall explore in Chapter 10, social networks have the potential to reduce transaction costs for institutions like the MFIs and also to pool risk for reducing cost of insuring specific risks. When transaction costs and costs of insuring go down, savings by institutions could be shared between the clients and the institutions. Such networks also create value for their members by facilitating special access to public and private institutions.

While the values of social connectivity, social networks and social capital are difficult to measure in dollars and cents, as we shall see in this book, the MFIs use 'solidarity groups' (joint-liability contracts) to reduce credit risk as well as to reduce transaction costs to deliver financial services to the poor. In Chapter 5, we will discuss how 'group lending' has played a major role in the successful delivery of microloans to the poor. However, group lending has its downside. We will discuss downside of group lending in Chapter 5.

Human Capital Formation: Lack of Access to Information, Knowledge, Education and Skills Training

It was Alfred Marshall who observed, 'Knowledge is our most powerful engine of production.' And we are all aware of Francis Bacon's pithy statement 'Knowledge is power.' If we truly believe in these words of wisdom, then one would wonder how the poor could get ahead if they are starved of information, knowledge, education and skills training.

It is a truism that a large percentage of the poor cannot read and write. Similarly, a large percentage of them also do not know simple arithmetic. Not knowing how to add, subtract and multiply, surely would make them powerless in making day-to-day financial transactions. Moreover, not being able to read and write disqualifies a person from applying for jobs and getting ahead when most jobs these days require one to read and write and follow instructions.

Ela R. Bhatt (2006) in her book *We Are Poor but So Many* describes vividly how a populace that is illiterate cannot glean information from billboards, public notices, newspapers, bank documents, legal papers and most importantly advertisements for employment. As a result, the poor, in general, do not have a good grasp of what is happening around them. Consequently, they remain disconnected from reality. Their drift from one menial job to another continues. In a nutshell, disconnectedness becomes a curse.

Due to rudimentary education, poor people even get cheated because they rely on others (say the moneylenders) to tell them how much money they owe. Because many of them are illiterate and do not have the basic understanding of arithmetic, they may not even have the requisite knowledge to question if something may be wrong in such things as financial transactions they enter into. Illiteracy and lack of knowledge of simple arithmetic does put the poor at a disadvantage in accessing financial services. Moreover, information that may be relevant and valuable to them may be held back in order to exploit them, which they may not even realize.

Moreover, a large proportion of the poor are unskilled and uneducated. They also lack opportunities to get trained on the job. Knowledge about livelihoods that the poor can easily pursue may not be available to them either. They also lack access to livelihood training. In this context, the following quote from Amartya Sen's *Development as Freedom* (Sen 1999, 292–93) is appropriate.

> In contemporary economic analysis the emphasis has, to a considerable extent, shifted from seeing capital accumulation in primary physical terms to viewing it as a process in which the productive quality of human beings is integrally involved. For example, through education, learning and skill formation, people can become much more productive over time, and this contributes greatly to the process of economic expansion. In recent studies

of economic growth (often influenced by empirical readings of experiences of Japan and the rest of East Asia as well as Europe and North America), there is a much greater emphasis on "human capital" than used to be the case not long ago.

Based on these observations, one would expect that livelihood and skills training, learning by doing and access to improved technology could enhance the capabilities of the poor to be more productive and better entrepreneurs within their ecosystem. Many MFIs such as BASIX in India and others around the world have been providing livelihood and skills training to their clients to become successful microentrepreneurs. As we shall see, if MFIs offer microleasing, its clients can have the option of accessing tools and machinery (without their ownership), which is one of the important ways to learn skills by working on the equipments. In Chapter 10, we discuss about livelihood training provided to the poor by the MFIs.

Lack of Access to Formal Financial Services

As the poor normally possess assets of little value, it is difficult for them to post collateral for accessing credit from formal banking institutions. Besides, many of the assets the poor possess may not have a secondary market and hence it is difficult to assess their value objectively. Even if the poor possess assets of value, such as a piece of land, they may not possess a clear title to the property. And besides, the assets they own when pledged as collateral fetch only a small fraction of their value as a loan. This is because, in the informal markets that the poor access, moneylenders demand collateral whose value is many times more than the amount of money they lend. And in the event the poor person is not able to repay the loan fully, he or she may forfeit the asset to the lender. Later on, the lenders can make a tidy profit by selling these collaterals.

The poor live in settlements without any formal address. A lot of times they do not own the land on which they live. They work in the informal sector without job security. The businesses they own are informal and there are no records of such businesses. They move from place to place in search of work. Their employment can be seasonal and income highly erratic. No data on their incomes are readily available. Because large numbers of them are illiterate, unskilled and uneducated, and because they lack credit history, accessing formal financial services for most of them becomes next to impossible. Therefore, they rely on the informal financial sector for their financial needs. Subsidized lending and grants from the government and charitable giving do provide help to the poor in times of need, but there is no substitute to access formal financial services such as credit, savings and insurance on an ongoing basis. Needless to say accessing such services should not be intermittent. It should be part and parcel of a poor person's overall financial planning.

There are other factors that make it difficult for the poor to access credit and other financial services. As we noted earlier, the poor do not usually possess legal identification such as SSNs used in the United States. In a large country like India, the establishment of 'UIDAI' is already providing UIDs to the poor and non-poor alike, which can help them in making financial transactions in a secure manner. This would also help MFIs and the microfinance industry to collect credit information about the poor in order to prevent over-lending, which could have adverse implications for the poor as well as the microfinance industry at large (see Chapter 11: Critiquing Microfinance).

Many poor people migrate domestically and internationally for improved economic opportunities. They send money back home for their family members using domestic and international MT facilities (payment systems). These facilities in general are not poor-friendly, expensive, inefficient and unreliable (see Chapter 9). With the arrival of improved MT facilities such as M-PESA (mobile money) using cellular phones, the landscape of MT is rapidly changing. However, lack of education can be an impediment to using mobile phones and hence systems like M-PESA. In Chapter 9, we discuss MT providers in general and about 'Adhikar,' which provides poor-friendly and affordable approach to transfer funds for migrant workers in India.

Lack of Access to Markets

By and large, the poor have limited access to markets to sell goods and services. Lack of good communications and connectivity with the markets makes it difficult for them to have a good understanding of what products and services are in demand and what prices they would fetch. Without a good understanding of the markets in their ecosystem, they limit their chances to optimize on buying inputs and selling their products and services.

Just to illustrate, the poor in the villages who live near a highway have better connectivity with the markets and hence better opportunities at pursuing their livelihoods. They can take public transportation such as buses to the nearest town or city for their inputs or to sell their products and services. Similarly, the poor who live in urban areas (the urban poor) have better opportunities at utilizing their skills to start microbusinesses or to be self-employed. In fact, the urban poor are relatively savvier in taking advantage of financial services provided by the MFIs than the poor in rural areas. This is because they are relatively more knowledgeable about livelihoods, accessing inputs for their businesses competitively and selling their products to the highest bidder.

Today's sellers are tomorrow's buyers. Unless the poor sell their products and services they cannot be consumers of quality products. In his book, *Fortune at the Bottom of the Pyramid: Eradicating Poverty through Profit*, C. K. Prahalad (2005a) has argued for democratizing commerce and co-creating an ecosystem that would allow entrepreneurship on a massive scale where major stakeholders, that is, private enterprises, government, NGOs and the poor can cooperate to eradicate poverty through profits. In his book, he discusses about ICICI Bank in India, which has been involved in collaborating with SHGs to provide financial services to the poor.

The monograph titled, *The Next 4 Billion* by Hammond et al. (2007) is also devoted to showcasing how market opportunities that the poor and the low income people represent can lead to a two-way commerce benefiting businesses as well as the poor. The monograph discusses eight different markets that include health market, information and communications market, water market, transportation market, housing market, energy market, food market and financial services market in which private enterprises could participate for profit to provide products and services for the poor that can benefit the poor as well as the business. As the access to these markets will expand, the poor would have access to superior products and services and at the same time would be in a position to avoid 'BOP penalty,' which forces them to pay higher prices for same products and services in comparison to the non-poor. Examples of superior products for the poor that one could quickly identify include mobile (cellular) phones, access to financial services through microfinance and improved livelihoods[8] by accessing microfinance.

Lack of Access to Legal Process and Justice System

Similar to lack of access to health care, financial services and education, it is also important to highlight the fact that the poor are access constrained when it comes to legal process and justice system. In developing countries, institutions that reach out and protect the rights of the poor are lacking.

To begin with, under the 'Initiative on Legal Empowerment of the Poor,' the United Nations Development Program (UNDP) lists the following as the focus areas for the poor: (1) Property Rights and Tenure Security, (2) Rights to Livelihood and Entrepreneurship, (3) Labor Rights and (4) Rule of Law and Access to Justice.[11] We illustrate below how access to the legal system and economic well-being of the poor are intimately connected. For example, we will discuss how the poor are shortchanged when they cannot have clear title to legal ownership of the land, even when they are the owners of the land.

In his book, *The Mystery of Capital: Why Capitalism Triumphs in the West and Fails Everywhere Else*, Hernando De Soto (2000) shows how the legal system in the developing world fails the poor by not providing user-friendly legal ownership of the land on which they live.

For example, titles to a plot of land in the developing countries are not easily accessible to the poor. As a result, the poor usually have to incur high transaction cost to get the title. High transaction cost results from the fact that the ownership of the land is not clearly defined, or even if it is clearly defined, it is difficult to have access to land records easily. Besides, the land can be litigated and it can take years before the issues can be resolved. The transaction costs include the necessary fees but in many cases it can entail bribes and lost work due to running to various public and private institutions to complete the transaction. Also, the cost of establishing the ownership and consummating the sale can be expensive. The delay in completing such transactions also has an opportunity cost that is difficult to estimate. For example, because the ownership of the land is not clearly defined, the poor are afraid to build on it or to use it in business because of the fear of being evicted. As a result, the land becomes a dead asset for them. Needless to say, the litigated status of the land continues for generations without benefiting its owners (in fact it becomes a drain on their time and money) and the society at large.

Corruption and Poverty

UNDP website[9] on anti-corruption underscores some of the adverse consequences of corruption and how it (1) 'undermines human development and democracy,' (2) diverts 'public resources for private gain,' (3) leads to less resources for building such critical facilities as schools, hospitals, roads and water supply, (4) distorts markets, (5) damages the integrity of the private sector, (6) leads to lack of equal opportunity and (7) access to a fair and just legal system. In an environment where corruption prevails, the poor can be easily exploited because they usually are powerless and vulnerable.

Needless to say that corruption takes its hold by restricting access to individuals who have the power to make decision(s) affecting economic outcome. Delayed decisions penalize owners by reducing the rate of return (ROR) on their businesses. It is not difficult to see that delaying decisions increases associated transaction costs. When transaction costs go up, costs of doing business go up.

When transaction costs of getting things done increase, it is the poor who suffer the most. Whether one is trying to get a title to a land, credit or electricity or water supply connections, corruption increases the cost of such transactions. Prevalence of corruption makes the rich richer and the poor poorer—because the rich with their influence, power and money can buy access, whereas the poor can ill-afford such luxury and as a result economically fall behind.

It is only through increased social connectivity, access to information, knowledge and education the poor can make their voices heard. In such situations, the role of the government, public and private institutions and the civil society at large is to educate the masses how corruption undermines growth and development of a country and how it takes a big toll on the lives of the poor.

One needs to emphasize that the MFIs because of formalized delivery of financial services and openness for scrutiny on such issues as lack of transparency in delivering financial services, charging exorbitant interest rates and resorting to coercion to ensure timely repayment of microloans is a major departure from the way the poor access financial services from the informal sector. As we will discuss in Chapter 11 that in spite of social mission being one of their DBL goals, some of the MFIs in pursuit of higher profitability have succumbed to 'mission drift,' which has been detrimental to the economic well-being of the poor and growth of the microfinance sector.

Conclusion

In this chapter, we briefly touched on some of the important topics that stand in the way of poor people getting ahead economically. Some of the other important topics which we did not include in the above discussions are 'inequality and poverty' and 'environment and poverty.'

In Chapter 3, we will focus on how access to archaic financial instruments (mostly informal credit and savings facilities) that the poor have been accessing through informal institutions such as the moneylenders have been major bottlenecks in managing their cash flow, mitigating exposure to specific risks and taking advantage of opportunities to leverage their capabilities to get ahead. Discussions in Chapter 3 are intended to set the stage for introducing the emergence of microcredit in Chapter 4.

Notes

1. The quote has been widely used in the microfinance literature and can be found by using Google. But I was not able to find the original source of this quote.
2. Amartya Sen. 1999. *Development as Freedom*, p. 87. New York: Knopf.
3. 'Overview: Understanding, Measuring and Overcoming Poverty.' Available online at http://www.colorado.edu/philosophy/heathwood/pdf/worldbank. pdf (downloaded on 7 November 2012).
4. 'World Bank Updates Poverty Estimates for the Developing World.' Available online at http://web.worldbank.org/WBSITE/EXTERNAL/EXTDEC/ EXTRESEARCH/ (downloaded on 8 November 2012).

5. 'Poverty Facts and Stats,' by Anup Shah, last updated on 20 September 2010. Available online at http://www.globalissues.org/article/26/poverty-facts-and-stats (downloaded on 8 November 2012).

6. Elie Wiesel. 1998. *Sustaining Culture and Creative Expression in Development*. Culture and Sustainable Development: Investing in the Promise of Societies, Proceedings of the Conference on Culture in Sustainable Development: Investing in Cultural and Natural Endowments held at the World Bank in Washington, DC, on September 28–29.

7. Allen L. Hammond et al. 2007. *The Next 4 Billion*, p. 5, World Resources Institute and International Finance Corporation.

8. 'National Conference on Emerging Business Opportunities at the Bottom of the Pyramid: Transforming the Indian Rural Economy through Profitability,' Published by Confederation of Indian Industry and The World Bank, 20–21 December 2005.

9. Available online at http://www.undp.org/content/undp/en/home/ourwork/democraticgovernance/focus_areas/focus_anti-corruption.html (downloaded on 11 November 2012).

3
Borrowing and Saving: A Critique

The knowledge that remain in the books but not mastered, the money that has been lent and not under one's control are of little value when their need arise.

Chanakya
Indian Philosopher 350-280 BC

Neither a borrower nor lender be; for loan oft loseth both itself and friend, and borrowing dulls the edge of husbandry.

Shakespeare

Cash today, credit tomorrow.[1]

Anonymous

The plight of the poor to access credit in the developing countries has been told time and time again. For variety of reasons, the poor have not been considered bankable. The age old dictums from Chanakya and Shakespeare quoted above makes one think twice before lending to the poor. The pithy statement, 'Cash today, credit tomorrow,' posted in many grocery stores, tea stalls and convenient stores in the villages and small towns of India tell us rather succinctly, how even provision of small amounts of credit (for a day or two without collateral) is considered risky by the owners of these small shops. The following quote from Marguerite S. Robinson's (2001, 16) book, *The Microfinance Revolution: Sustainable*

Finance for the Poor tells how the informal financial markets squeeze the poor hard by charging exorbitant interest rates.

> Informal commercial lenders typically charge nominal effective interest rates of 10 percent to more than 100 percent a month.

While these interest rates are not normally compounded, and delinquency rates and outright defaults by some borrowers could substantially reduce effective interest rates (EIRs) charged by moneylenders to the poor, nonetheless, after taking these facts into consideration the rates charged are anything but usurious. Moneylenders in the developing countries are not the only ones charging high interest rates. In countries such as the USA, UK, Canada and Australia 'payday lenders' also charge exorbitantly high interest rates. These rates can be in the neighbourhood of almost 400 per cent per annum. We will discuss about payday lenders in the USA later in the chapter.

The rates are exorbitant when one compares non-poor borrowers trying to split basis points before signing a loan document—although it is true that they normally borrow much larger amounts and have the power to negotiate with the banking institutions. The poor are prepared to pay such high rates because they normally do not have any other choice for accessing credit.

Let alone the poor, such high interest rates can easily break the backs of the savviest of the borrowers. It is no wonder that many poor borrowers find it difficult to repay their loans because of the heavy burden that interest on these loans entails, even if the interest on the loans may not be compounded. For example, a poor person borrowing $100 from a moneylender at a 10 per cent interest rate per month will end up paying $100 in just 10 months towards interest. On the contrary, if a non-poor client borrows $100 from a bank at 10 per cent per year, then only after 7.3 years the total interest paid to the bank will be little over $100 (the computation assumes that the banks compound interest on funds lent at the same interest rate). This is the stark difference between a moneylender and a formal banking institution. However, the poor in general cannot access formal banking institutions.

As we shall discuss in Chapter 4, microcredit programmes around the world in general charge interest rates in the range of about 2 to 3 per cent per month. However, there are examples of some MFIs charging much higher interest rates than 2 to 3 per cent per month—although high rates are not the norm. Not only in terms of interest rates, microcredit programmes have revolutionized the entire approach to lending to the poor around the world.

While usurious rates charged to the poor in the informal financial sector ruin the lives of many poor borrowers, the track record of targeted subsidized lending and grants by the governments in the developing countries has not lived up to its expectations either. In most cases, the institutions delivering such grants and loans were entrusted to develop specific sectors of an economy such as agriculture and housing by subsidizing credit to the poor and low-income people. It turns out that, in most cases, such approach degenerated into dispensing subsidies to those who did not deserve such grants and subsidies in the first place.

Besides borrowing from moneylenders and accessing subsidized credits and grants from the government, the poor—particularly the poorest—also rely on charity. There is no denying the fact that charity plays an important role in the lives of the poor. But charity in general is a stop gap approach to the problems the poor face. Charities usually respond to an emergency situation that afflict poor people and help them survive before they can think of the long term. Therefore, charity has never been considered a long-term solution to the financial service needs of the poor on a day-to-day basis.

The Poor Are Ingenious in Managing Their Finances but That Is Not Enough

In order to manage their finances, the poor actively borrow from friends and family and also from moneylenders. The poor also try to access subsidized credit from the government. Contrary to popular belief, they also save being thrifty. However, their savings can be easily wiped out if a family member falls sick or providing for a child school expenses. Therefore, a poor family instinctively diversifies its sources of credit not to be stranded at the time of an emergency.

They also pawn their assets (such as gold ornaments) for cash. (Even in the rich countries such as the USA, poor and even the non-poor, when forced, use pawnshops to get emergency cash.) They also get cash by selling their labour as well as crops ahead of time (in the informal forward market). In order to diversify their consumption, they also swap food grains and other types of produce with each other without going to the market. They tend to diversify their sources of income by working on two different jobs (if such opportunity is available) or by owning a business and working on another job at the same time. During lean times, they may be prepared to migrate for better job opportunities.

Besides, the poor have been rather creative in devising informal associations (clubs) such as Rotating Savings and Credit Associations (ROSCAs) and Accumulating Savings and Credit Associations (ASCAs) to save and borrow in a group environment. As we shall see, the MFIs have borrowed many of the ideas from these informal savings and loan associations in trying to cater to the financial needs of the poor.

Because they are powerless, the informal credit markets have not worked to the advantage of the poor. In the face of uncertainty and risk and with rather minimal backstop, the vulnerabilities of the poor multiply many times more than the non-poor. For example, a poor family could be under severe financial stress, if there is crop failure and it has already promised to sell the harvest ahead of time. In spite of the creative ways they manage their finances, more often than not, meagre and erratic income could force a poor family to borrow.

As a result, the poor normally try to borrow from their friends and family members or from moneylenders in order to smooth consumption and/or mitigate risks such as health risks, crop failure and marriage of their daughters. While the advent of microfinance in the developing countries has brought about a revolution in changing the way how the poor access credit, access to formal savings facilities and insurance on a day-to-day basis, still largely remains limited, although off late, with improved product design these products have been expanding their outreach to the poor around the world.

It is important to note that wherever microcredit is available, the poor have not completely abandoned borrowing from the informal sector. This is because microcredit or other forms of formal finance has to go long ways before it could account for bulk of the borrowing needs of the poor. The 2010 Microfinance Crisis in Andhra Pradesh in India drives home the point that reliability of access to the financial services is paramount whether one is poor or non-poor. In Chapter 11, we will discuss how, on the aftermath of the crisis in lending the MFIs collapsed precipitously in Andhra Pradesh. As a result, the poor borrowers had to make up the difference from other sources. Needless to say, like the non-poor, the poor need access to diversified sources of credit.

The discussions in this chapter could be rather commonsensical and mundane for many. However, without such a discussion, it would be difficult to compare and contrast what microfinance has been able to achieve in comparison to the archaic financial tools that the informal finance offers to the poor around the world.

An Overview of Access to Credit and Savings Facilities by the Poor

In the following text, we discuss some of the important credit and savings channels that the poor have relied on to borrow and save (United Nations 2006). The list is not exhaustive by any means.

Access to Credit

The poor usually access credit using informal channels. Only a small percentage of the poor have access to credit using semi-formal and formal channels. Access to credit through informal channels consists of (1) relatives, friends and neighbours; (2) local moneylenders; (3) savings and credit clubs such as ROSCAs and ASCAs; (4) pawnbrokers and (5) credit providers such as traders and input suppliers. Note that ROSCAs and ASCAs are hybrid organizations. As the names imply, these institutions are used as savings as well as credit institutions.

Access through semi-formal channels consists of NGOs that also act as MFIs, NBFIs, credit unions and credit and savings cooperatives. Finally, institutions providing financial services using the formal channels consist of private commercial banks, state development and agricultural banks, state-owned commercial banks and postal banks. Among the formal banking institutions, the public sector institutions provide subsidized credits and grants to the poor that are mostly funded by the national governments and donors.

In the beginning, it was the NGO-based MFIs that started offering microfinance to the poor. Slowly but surely financial institutions of various kinds such as NBFIs, credit unions, state development and agricultural banks, rural banks, specialized MFI banks and full-service commercial banks have started offering microfinance to the poor (Helms 2006). Moreover, many NGO-based MFIs have been transforming themselves to become regulated commercial financial institutions to offer a wide array of microfinance products (such as savings facilities) in order to become true financial intermediaries.

Access to Savings Facilities

In the 1950s and 1960s, in order to increase agricultural output, providing subsidized credit to small farmers received much attention. However, as far as savings by the small farmers were concerned, very little attention was paid. It is no wonder that Robert Vogel, in 1984, described savings as 'The forgotten half of Rural Finance' (1984).

Even then, in many developing countries the small farmers used state-owned savings banks, development banks and postal banks to establish savings and loan accounts. In a CGAP Focus Note, 'Financial Inclusion 2015: Four Scenarios for the Future of Microfinance,' Littlefield et al. (2006) noted that research by Peachey and Roe (2006) identified over 1.4 billion savings accounts in developing and transition economies. As far as one can tell, the presence of such large numbers of savings accounts did not make any substantial improvement in the way the account holders were able to access other financial services such as credit, insurance and MT.

In the absence of suitable formal savings facilities, the poor over the years found creative ways to save by using ROSCAs and ASCAs. However, as we shall discuss later, these facilities lack the efficiency and flexibility of formal savings facilities offered by formal banking institutions. We will also discuss how the poor in order to access secure and convenient ways to save are prepared to pay hefty fees to savings collectors, consequently earning negative interest rates on their savings (Rutherford 2000).

Because savings in the form of cash are exposed to such risks as theft, or loss of value due to inflation, the poor also save by investing in assets such as gold or silver ornaments, land, cattle and staple food items such as rice that can be stored for longer periods. However, whatever approach the poor take, savings are exposed to risk. For example, cattle and other farm animals could die of diseases. Rice can be eaten away by rodents.

Land can be litigated and could be subject to price risk if one wants to sell it in an emergency. Since ornaments are not standardized and there are no organized markets to trade jewellery, the poor may not fetch the right amount of cash for these ornaments. As a result, the poor instinctively diversify their savings (investments) to mitigate financial risk that these investments may be exposed to. Some of the important ways the poor save (invest) are described below.

Family and Friends: The poor can always keep their small savings in inconspicuous places around the house. But before they know it, these inconspicuous places can become easily conspicuous. And quickly, they lose control over that money. The poor also entrust their hard-earned money for safekeeping with their friends and family. While entrusting one's savings with family and friends may sound like a convenient way to save, it has its disadvantages. For one thing, one does not earn interest on such savings. Besides, by entrusting their savings with family and friends, they lose privacy of their financial affairs and security of such savings. For example, if it is known among the friends and family members that someone has savings, it is not uncommon to ask the person for financial help. And because the poor rely on each other at the time of need, it is difficult not to cater to such requests.

Deposit Collectors: There are instances where the poor use deposit collectors to save, because they do not consider it safe to keep cash at home (Rutherford 2000). Moreover, many do not want to entrust their money with family and friends. The deposit collectors charge a fee to collect deposits on a regular basis and keep it safe from others, including burglars and even spouses who may lay claim on such savings, sometimes forcibly. Most importantly, by saving through deposit collectors, the poor become more disciplined in reaching their savings goals. We will discuss later, how using deposit collectors to save can be very expensive, but even then poor use them because their service offers certain features that they find attractive.

ROSCAs and ASCAs: In simple terms, ROSCAs and ASCAs are informal group-based entities that allow intermediation of funds for its members (Rutherford 2000). ROSCAs allow its members to pool and distribute resources so pooled to each member by turn based on rules agreed to a priori. A member can take out what he or she puts into ROSCA. ROSCAs have finite life and its life span depends on how many members a ROSCA has and how it is structured. Who gets the funds can also be decided based on simple lottery.

There are many variations to the ROSCA theme. The variations revolve around how funds are collected in each period and distributed to its members. 'Bidding' ROSCAs are one of the interesting variations on the ROSCA theme wherein each period members are allowed to bid in order to get the pool of funds collected. Bids are distributed equally among its members. Later in this chapter, we will critique rather briefly why ROSCAs are deficient in meeting varied needs of the poor to save and borrow.

ASCAs on the other hand accumulate funds where some members borrow and others provide the funds (savers or investors in the fund). The savers or investors get a return for the funds so provided. By decoupling savings from borrowing activities, ASCAs become somewhat more flexible. In many ASCAs, the members who borrow pay an interest rate, which is higher in comparison to the interest rates charged to creditworthy borrowers by the commercial banks. However, these rates are usually lower than the rates charged by the moneylenders. This is partly because membership of ASCAs is by self-selection and such membership reduces the credit risk inherent in such lending. In countries like Bangladesh, the interest rates on ASCA funds normally vary between 3 per cent per month to 10 per cent per month. In rare cases, it can be as high as 20 per cent per month (Rutherford 2000, 49). Like ROSCAs, there are wide variations on the ASCA theme that its members could adapt to meet their specific needs.

One of the important advantages of ASCAs is their flexibility to be adapted as a savings club with a given purpose, such as to build up savings as an insurance against fire (Rutherford 2000). Each member of the club saves every week to build up savings, which can be only withdrawn on a proportionate basis in the event of a fire. Because these are single-purpose ASCAs, the funds cannot be used for any other purpose. ASCAs like ROSCAs only recycle the funds provided by the members. They do not borrow from other sources to lend to its members. ROSCAs are time-bound. ASCAs on the other hand can be dissolved and funds returned to the members who provided the funds along with the profits (calculated on a prorated basis).

There is a large body of technical literature on the subject of ROSCAs and ASCAs. Interested readers will find the following two references on the subject to be very useful: (1) *The Poor and their Money* by Stuart Rutherford (2000) and (2) *The Economics of Microfinance* by Beatriz Armendáriz and Jonathan Morduch (2010).

Credit Unions: The credit unions are also known as credit cooperatives. They are member-based organizations like ASCAs—but more formalized (Armendáriz and Morduch 2010). There are large numbers of credit unions in the developing countries that have been serving their poor borrowers for decades (Helms 2006). While most of them are small, some of these institutions can be very large. They are usually non-profit institutions. The membership of these cooperatives has a common bond like working for the same employer or belonging to the same profession.

They provide a wide range of financial services to the poor. In the event of a surplus in earnings, the credit cooperatives return a portion of the surplus in the form of dividends, lower interest rates on loans or increased interest rates on savings, such that the profits are passed on to their members.

Credit cooperatives are usually owned and run by its members. The cooperative members monitor each other. However, in large cooperatives such monitoring becomes impractical. With increased formalization and need for improved asset-liability management, credit unions have been increasingly relying on professional management. The intent in relying on professional management is to be more efficient and to serve their members better. In many countries, credit cooperatives are regulated and supervised to protect its members from financial shenanigans and frauds.

On Critiquing How the Poor Borrow

In the following content, we critique how the poor have traditionally accessed credit from local moneylenders and governmental institutions that provide targeted subsidized lending in the developing countries.

Accessing Credit from Local Moneylenders

The moneylenders have been the lenders of last resort for the poor. It is also true that the moneylenders are not in the business of helping the poor improve their economic condition. They usually concentrate on a limited number of clients and develop a longstanding relationship with them. As a result, it is easier for them to gather intelligence and monitor the credit risk of these clients carefully. They try to recruit most credit-worthy clients and hoard good clients from other moneylenders in the same neighbourhood. In many communities, moneylenders have a great deal of power to exert influence on the financial affairs of their clients. What is more because moneylenders tend to be influential people in a community, they can bring community pressure if their clients are delinquent or default on their loans.

The business of money lending in a given locality consist of a few moneylenders who implicitly come to an understanding as to who their clients are. They guard their interests aggressively. Lack of transparency in the money lending business helps the moneylenders in exploiting the poor. And most poor people being uneducated and powerless and having very limited choice in accessing credit (at the time of an emergency) accept the terms and conditions offered without questioning.

The terms of such lending are not uniform. It varies from one client to the other. By setting different terms for different clients, moneylenders maximize their profit. They take land, ornaments or other forms of collateral to secure their lending, which is usually several times the value of the loan. Collateral demanded by moneylenders makes it difficult for the borrowers to borrow in parallel from other moneylenders during financially difficult times, because poor households normally have limited assets to pledge. In other words, asking for collateral indirectly minimizes the credit risk of moneylenders.

Normally moneylenders diversify their lending and do not limit their exposure to one single borrower. They charge very high interest rates to cover fixed costs, cost of capital, spread for credit risk (although they hold collateral for such risks) and also a spread above the credit spread for profit. In other words, the moneylenders insulate themselves rather well from the risks of lending to the poor.

Although charging usurious rates is illegal in many countries, it is difficult to regulate such lenders because the poor borrowers in general feel powerless to complain about their moneylenders to the appropriate authorities. And they also fear that by complaining about usurious rates being charged, the source of credit from moneylenders would dry up.

What is more, unless the poor make timely payments to their moneylenders, they could forfeit whatever little collateral of value they provided to the moneylenders. Most of the time borrowing from moneylenders impoverishes the poor further because the moneylenders are usually focused on maximizing profit without much concern for economic condition of their clients.

Robinson (2001) in her book *The Microfinance Revolution* concludes that the moneylenders charge much higher interest rates than one would normally charge to operate profitably. The rates the moneylenders charge cannot be justified solely based on high transaction costs and associated risks of such lending. All in all, while moneylenders perform a very useful function by lending money at the crucial juncture of a poor person's life, more often than not, they tend to exploit them based on their vulnerabilities.

Examples of Exorbitant Interest Rates Charged by Moneylenders

Normally a moneylender quotes a periodic rate that is termed as 'flat' rate. Under the flat rate, the rate is applied to the original loan principal to calculate interest to be paid in each period. In other words, as the loan gets repaid, the declining balance of the loan in each period is not factored into the rate calculation. For example, if a borrower borrows $100 for one month and if the interest rate is 10 per cent per month, then at the end of the one-month period, the borrower has to pay the lender $110. However, if the borrower repays the loan after 15 days instead of one month, he/she usually has to make $10 in interest payment. As a result, the yield on the loan for the lender is higher than 10 per cent. However, if the borrower is delinquent and stretches the repayment of the loan including interest payment by say a week, then yield on the loan would go down accordingly. Moneylenders normally do not utilize declining balance method of interest rate calculation, because it is relatively more complex and poor borrowers find flat rates easier to understand.

As we noted at the outset, when the poor borrow from the informal sector, they normally end up paying interest rates in the range of 10–100 per cent per month. When one compounds these rates over a 12-month period, an interest rate of 10 per cent per month comes to about 214 per cent per annum. However, such rates can become miniscule when one compares rates that can reach 20 per cent per day. Robinson (2001) provides examples of daily rates charged to the urban poor in Latin America known as 'five-six' rates. Under the 'five-six' rate, a borrower who borrows $10 in the morning has to pay back $12 in the evening. This translates into an interest rate of 20 per cent per day, and when compounded over a month can reach 23,638 per cent per month! Note that, the compounding assumes that the lender could reinvest the funds at the same rate day after day!

However, the mechanistic use of compounding has very little relationship with reality. In real life, the EIR charged by the moneylenders in the informal sector while usurious, comes down substantially because of several factors (Collins et al. 2009), including (1) the borrowers can be delinquent and can negotiate with the lenders by effectively reducing how much they will be able to pay; (2) some of the borrowers may even ask to forgive a part of the loan and (3) the lenders cannot expand their volume of lending because they lack the ability to check credit and administer lending large volume of funds to large number of borrowers (who borrow small amounts of fund) day after day, hence they focus on limited number of borrowers. Needless to say, the poor borrowers cannot keep on paying such high interest rates for a long period of time. As a result, they hold such loans for short periods of time.

Due to these complicating factors, the moneylenders select their clients carefully, develop longstanding relationship with them and monitor their creditworthiness diligently. All these activities are time-consuming. Besides, moneylenders have to spend time to collect debt service from their delinquent clients. These costs have to be factored into their lending business. In spite of these costs, the EIRs charged by the commercial lenders in the informal financial sector are usurious and the moneylenders make a tidy profit lending money.

In this context, it is important to discuss briefly, the interest rates charged by the MFIs to their clients. Robinson (2001) in her book *The Microfinance Revolution—Sustainable Finance for the Poor* notes that MFIs charge EIRs in the range of 2–5 per cent per month. Based on compounding of interest, a rate of 2 per cent per month would translate to 26.82 per cent per annum. Similarly, interest rates of 3, 4 and 5 per cent per month would result in annual interest rates of 42.58, 60.10 and 79.59 per cent, respectively. However, there are some MFIs that charge interest rates that are even higher than these rates. Sometimes, they can be as high as in the 80–100 per cent range. For example, Banco Compartamos of Mexico had an adjusted interest yield in 2005 of about 86.3 per cent (Rosenberg 2007). When one adds value-added tax of 15 per cent that the clients have to pay, the interest rate on these loans must have reached above 100 per cent per annum. It is important to note that in spite of • lower interest rates charged by the MFIs and their poor-friendly lending terms, these institutions have been criticized for lack of transparency and for charging interest rates, charges and fees that translate to EIRs that are exorbitant.

In Chapters 4, 5 and 11, we will discuss more about MFI interest rates. At this stage, suffice it to say that the interest rates charged by the MFIs are higher in general than the interest rates charged to non-poor borrowers by the commercial banks. But they are much lower than the interest rates charged by the moneylenders.

Interest Rates Charged by the Payday Lenders in the Western Countries

In the context of usurious interest rates charged by the moneylenders in the developing countries, it is important to discuss about usurious interest rates charged by the payday lenders in the Western countries such as the USA, UK, Canada and Australia. In the following text, we discuss how payday lenders in the United States charge exorbitant interest rates to their clients.

The payday loans can be viewed as small cash advances. The exorbitant interest rates charged on these loans can be gleaned from the following example. In the USA, 'a typical $300 two-week loan might carry a $50 finance charge, which amounts to a 435 per cent annual percentage rate (APR) of interest' (De Young and Phillips 2009). Considering exorbitant interest rates charged by payday lenders, such lending has been compared with loan sharking by consumer groups. Assuming someone decides to borrow $300, the borrower provides the lender a post-dated personal check for the amount of $300 or an authorization for automatic withdrawal of the same amount of money from his or her bank account. In return, the borrower receives cash for $250. The remaining $50 goes towards fees.

Access to funds through payday lenders provide short-term liquidity to households that normally receive regular paychecks, possess bank accounts, but might have depleted their other lines of credit (such as credit cards, overdraft facility and loans from pawn shops) or decide not to tap into these credit lines. These loans are sought by individuals and households to avoid overdraft fees and charges, late fees, bouncing of checks, and delay in paying rents and medical bills. In order to get a payday loan, borrowers must have a personal identification, personal checking account and proof of income from employment or payment from Social Security.

The loan is due when the borrower gets the next paycheck. At that point, the lender can cash the check or decide to roll over the loan for two more weeks if the borrower wants more time. Again, the borrowers will have to make a payment of $50 for rolling over the loan. Under these circumstances the borrower gets no new money. Again, based on 'Center for Responsible Lending' website, it is important to note that 91 per cent of the borrowers, who access payday loans, usually take out about five or more such loans in a year. Besides, most payday borrowers go to more than one lender for payday loans. What is more, only 1 per cent of payday loans are made for one-time emergency borrowers.

On the Internet one can find websites offering such loans that can range from $100 to $1,000. From the 'Center for Responsible Lending' website, one can find that low-income consumers, military personnel, 'welfare-to-work' women and people having practically no savings, usually access such loans.[2] During the last 10 years or so, there has been a rapid growth in the payday lending business in the USA. It is possible that the 2007–2008 recession, which was triggered by financial meltdown that froze the credit markets, could have led to growth of payday lending business. Based on most recent statistics (from 'Center for Responsible Lending'), there are about 22,000 payday lenders scattered across 35 states in the USA. Annual loan volume generated by payday lending business is around $27 billion.

On Critiquing Targeted Subsidized Lending to the Poor[3]

After the Second World War, governments in many developing countries placed high priority on bringing about economic development through increased food production. In order to make that a reality, it was assumed that the farmers would need access to capital over and above what they would be able to provide from their own resources. This was predicated by the fact that farming was increasingly becoming capital-intensive with widespread use of improved varieties of seeds, fertilizers, pesticides, irrigation and technology. It was also assumed that the poor farmers would not be able to pay for the full cost of commercial credit, which they would need to borrow in order to adapt new technologies. The justification for such lending was also based on the assumption that the provision of such lending would provide the much needed incentive and impetus for agricultural growth—one of the most important sectors of a developing country's economy.

Unquestionably, the provision of subsidized lending and grants by the governments in the developing countries were based on good intentions. However, considering large budget deficits in most developing countries, sustainability of such lending in the long run was not assured. Besides, the focus of such lending was not based on what implications such subsidized lending would have in the credit markets. Above all, some of the problems that arose in delivering subsidized credit to the poor were not duly anticipated prior to the implementation of such programmes in the 1950s and 1960s. In the following text, we briefly discuss some of these issues that ultimately undermined many of the original intentions of the programme.

By definition, the subsidized loans carry an interest rate that is below the prevailing market rate. Besides, terms of lending on such loans, such as grace period during which no principal is paid (only interest is paid) and final maturity were quite generous. Lending for longer periods with generous grace periods entail higher levels of financial risk. The interest rates on these loans did not adjust for such risk. Without due diligence on credit risk posture of the clients and difficult political, economic and financial realities on the ground, the initial expectations regarding such lending programmes were not realized.

Just to illustrate, in an environment in which the poor were considered not bankable, access to such lending with generous terms and below market interest rates were not only in high demand from the poor, but from the non-poor as well. The reasons were obvious. Such lending was considered 'free' money because savings on interest payments alone were substantial.

Since donor funding was limited and dispensing subsidy required budgetary outlays, which is normally difficult under tight budgetary environment of most developing countries, the loans were rationed based on eligibility criteria. However, in spite of elaborate eligibility criteria to approve these loans for the poor farmers, a large proportion of the loans were cornered by rich farmers and influential people. Consequently, the loans did not reach large sections of the poor farmers as intended.

Besides, the poor farmers had to wait for long periods before getting their loans because of bureaucratic hurdles. In many cases, they had to also pay bribes to have access to such loans. Lost work, lost opportunities (due to delays in getting loans) and bribes to middlemen increased the upfront cost of obtaining these loans. In many cases, by the time the approved loans were disbursed to the beneficiaries, the funds were not enough to meet the funding needs of the projects for which they were approved. As a result, many of these projects were not completed because getting extra funding to complete the projects was difficult. While the poor borrowers were attracted to get these loans because of the stipulated low interest rates and easy terms of lending, in reality the 'all in' effective cost of accessing such loans were much higher.

As the beneficiaries in general did not have other sources of funding (at reasonable interest rates) for completing the loans that were intended for, large numbers of projects remained unproductive or even if productive could not reach their potential. Unproductive projects led to a large number of borrowers defaulting on such loans. For political expediency, loans were also forgiven in many cases. Because the governments were the main source of such lending, large numbers of farmers opportunistically took advantage of the benevolence of the government by defaulting on such loans.

But that set the wrong precedent. Under these circumstances, the discipline of lending and timely repayment of loans broke down. As a result, lending institutions were caught in the middle. As the reader will find in Chapter 11, opportunistic default by many MFI borrowers on the aftermath of the 2010 Microfinance Crisis in Andhra Pradesh in India appears rather similar to such defaults that severely affected credit standing of many of the MFIs.

As far as the banking institutions were considered, the eligibility criteria for extending such loans were based on guidelines that did not make much business sense. The eligibility criteria for accessing such loans were more to do with the poverty level of the poor rather than their repayment capabilities. The criteria normally did not pay much attention to the household cash flow of the poor. In nutshell, eligibility for getting a loan boiled down to the simple fact that if you are poor you are eligible to apply for a loan. In most cases, there was no effective follow-up to find out whether eligible people got the loan and whether the funds were being used as intended. Needless to say that, the effective follow-up for millions of such loans would not have been practical and would have been rather expensive for the taxpayer.

The real problem was that in most developing countries finding hard data on the eligibility of the beneficiaries to receive such loans was difficult. For example, in many developing countries, each citizen does not have a UID, like the SSNs in the United States. As a result, finding reliable household income data about the citizens, particularly whether a household is poor or not is not easy. Defrauding the lending authorities by manufacturing data to prove eligibility was not unusual.

What was also ironic was that in large number of cases, the incentives for the banking institutions were misplaced. For example, the banks were judged by how much subsidized funds they disbursed as opposed to how well they managed their own credit and interest rate risks and how the poor leveraged these funds to improve their economic condition. As a result, the portfolio quality of these banks suffered and large numbers of them became loss-making institutions. Widespread defaults undermined the banking system in many developing countries. As a result, many banking institutions were to be recapitalized because defaults on such lending eroded their capital base.

The targeted subsidized lending also accentuated the risk posture of these banks by concentrating lending in a given sector—such as agriculture. In other words, these banks were putting all their eggs in one basket. The 'portfolio concentration' that ensued from such lending created 'covariant risk,'[4] which these institutions were ill-equipped to manage.

There are other reasons why subsidized lending did not live up to its expectations. The negative real rates (interest rate on loans minus inflation rate) on subsidized loans undermined allocation of loans to worthwhile projects. The criteria for approving loans by the banks were based on whether one is poor or not without regard for the merits of the underlying projects. Influential people, who were not even poor, cornered loans through influence peddling and even bribes.

During this period, the interest rates offered on deposits by the banking sector including the rural banks were lower than the inflation rate.

As a result, savers lost purchasing power on their savings. Consequently, there was no incentive to save. Under these circumstances, injections of relatively large volumes of lending at subsidized rates also did not encourage savings. Such interventions in the credit markets also undermined an orderly development of sustainable financial services for the poor. This has been termed as 'financial repression' by McKinnon (1973).

One of the well-known examples of targeted subsidized programmes that failed to achieve its goals was the Integrated Rural Development Program (IRDP) in India. The programme allocated credit based on 'social targets,' where large percentages of subsidized lending was directed to socially disadvantaged groups such as the 'scheduled' tribe or cast and women. Between 1979 and 1989, almost $6 billion was disbursed on such subsidies. It turned out that the programme suffered from very low repayment rates and only a small percentage of such borrowers came back for second loans. By 2000, recovery rate of IRDP loans was reduced to only 31 per cent (Meyer 2001).

It is important to note that criticisms of grants and subsidized lending in the above discussions should not be construed to mean that they should not be relied upon to help the poor fight poverty. Undoubtedly grants and subsidies have important roles to play in enabling the poorest and the extreme poor access microcredit. This is because, while the moderate poor and vulnerable non-poor have the wherewithal to access microcredit, the poorest and sections of the extreme poor (who are not economically active) need to be part of capacity-building programmes to help them become eligible to access microcredit. Needless to say, donor subsidies have played an important role in building capacity and also helping fledgling MFIs to start them off during the initial period before they can access commercial funding to lend to the poor and offer financial instruments and complementary services.

On Critiquing the Way the Poor Save

In spite of the fact that the poor are always under financial stress, they try to find ways to scrape out tiny amounts of money from their daily cash flow to save for rainy days. This may sound contradictory. If the poor do not make enough money and constantly are in need of borrowing, how can they save? But the truth is that the poor understand the meaning of thrift like nobody else. It is normally the women among the poor, who tend to cut corners to save so that they can pay for the school fees of their children, buy ornaments for their daughter's marriage, and pay for doctor's fees and medicine when the need arises. These savings are not large, but can provide a cash cushion when there is a dire need for funds. Moreover, the poor not only save, they also understand that they need to invest. Little by little, they build up their cash assets to purchase a piece of land or a gadget to help in their businesses. Poor people in India, Bangladesh and other countries buy silver and gold ornaments, which normally act as hedge against inflation.

In spite of the importance of access to formal savings facilities by poor households, for a variety of reasons provision of such facilities did not receive as much attention in the past. There are several reasons why this was so. First of all, there was a general perception that the poor do not have the wherewithal to save. Secondly, the banking sector in the developing countries traditionally did not offer savings and credit facilities to the poor because it is not cost-effective to administer millions of accounts with small balances and millions of small value loans. At the same time, the poor find it time-consuming and expensive to travel long distances to deposit small amount of money in a bank in nearby towns or cities. Besides, widespread lack of literacy and education among the poor become detrimental to opening savings accounts at formal banking institutions. Lack of UIDs, like SSNs in the USA, has not helped the situation any better to open formal savings accounts by the poor without formal identification. Besides, banking sector in each country has strict regulatory requirements that deposit-taking institutions have to meet. Meeting these requirements for the MFIs is not easy.

However, for the poor the need for savings is paramount. This is because for poor borrowers, who largely borrow from the informal sector, cash flow inflexibility increases, as they go deeper and deeper into debt. If they borrow from the MFIs, which as a proportion of their overall household debt may be small, even then it could increase cash flow inflexibility because microcredit requires stricter adherence to repayment schedule under the rubric of group lending as well as overall lending terms. Therefore, it is essential that poor households ought to have easy access to poor-friendly savings facilities to manage their assets and liabilities more effectively. Too much reliance on credit is not the answer to fight poverty. Besides, in the face of over-lending by some of the MFIs, the poor have to be extra careful not to succumb to over-indebting themselves in order to manage their assets and liabilities (see Chapter 11).

On Critiquing ROSCAs[5]

A ROSCA consists of a group of individuals who make contributions (amount of the contribution fixed a priori) to a common fund at predetermined intervals (e.g., on a weekly or monthly basis). And the funds so collected are given as a lump sum to a single individual of the group at the end of each interval. Assuming each individual member makes timely payments to ROSCA during its life, each of its members would eventually have his or her turn to access funds. After each member avails his or her turn to collect funds, the ROSCA comes to an end.

The groups are informal groups formed by self-selection. The members normally come from the same socio-economic and cultural background and are usually from the same neighbourhood. The proximity of the households is an added advantage in forming ROSCAs. Trust for each other is one of the driving forces in the formation of these ROSCAs. One of the important advantages of ROSCAs is that one does not have to warehouse the funds.

What ROSCAs do is to convert small sums of money from its members to a lump sum amount through the participation of its members. Assuming there are 20 people participating in a given ROSCA, the person receiving her funds last will have to wait 20 weeks (assuming the time interval for fixed payments is on a weekly basis). Therefore, the person would have to have the discipline to wait for 20 weeks before she collects her lump sum. Normally, the recipient of the lump sum plans to invest in something of value such as a sewing machine, bicycle or tools, or paying for children's education.

The selection of a member who will receive the lump sum in each period is determined by a method (agreed to a priori) such as a lottery, a predetermined sequence of names or through a process of bidding (bidding ROSCA). Bidding ROSCAs are based on personal needs such as health emergencies and urgent need for funds in a business. Whosoever bids the highest receives the funds. The proceeds from such biddings are shared by the rest of the members. In other words, in the case of bidding ROSCAs, members who do not have immediate need for funds lending to the highest bidder, to earn interest on their savings. This is also advantageous to those members who need money immediately and are willing to pay a premium for the immediate use of funds.

There are several obvious disadvantages to the ROSCA arrangement. First of all, the ROSCAs do not treat their members equitably. For example, the members who receive the funds initially at the beginning of the ROSCA cycle have a clear advantage over other members in terms of the time value of money. The fact that the groups do not charge an explicit interest rate on the use of funds leads to an inequity in sharing the funds because of the time value of money. Besides, the members who remain towards the end may be exposed to credit risk if one or more members become delinquent in their payments to the group.

Some of the other disadvantages of ROSCAs stem from the fact that they are inflexible, that is, the takeout amounts in each period are fixed and the interval between takeouts is also fixed. Similarly, the stipulation that each of its members has to bring in a fixed amount of money every period becomes a burden on the poor members whose incomes are erratic. What is more, increasing the size of the fixed amount brought in each period by its members to increase the size of the takeout could make it difficult for many members to join the group. And if one increases the membership of the ROSCA to increase the takeout, while keeping the fixed amount modest, the members taking out the lump sum towards the end have to wait for a long time.

Bidding ROSCAs by introducing opportunity cost of capital as well as time value of money make the process more sophisticated, but the process is not equitable because the implied rate of interest could be higher or lower depending on the perceived opportunity cost of funds for the bidding members in each period. In general, ROSCAs are less versatile than the MFIs. For example, because ROSCAs do not allow borrowing, it does not allow for takeouts that are more than what the members put in each period. Moreover, ROSCAs come to an end when all the members receive funds as stipulated initially. On the other hand, in the case of the MFIs, its members have an ongoing relationship with the institution, and microsavings are much more versatile instruments in comparison to ROSCAs and ASCAs. The subject of ROSCAs and ASCAs boasts of a large body of literature. Two references provided in endnote 5 provide excellent introductions to the subject.

Deposit Collectors

Saving regularly in a cash flow-constrained environment can be difficult. As a result, the poor who are more often than not under financial stress find it difficult to save. Besides, safe upkeep of their savings is very important for a poor family because losing their savings to fire or theft can be financially devastating.

In his book *The Poor and their Money*, Stuart Rutherford (2000) discusses how the poor prize the convenience and safekeeping of their savings in the hands of the deposit collectors, who provide the poor with an option to save safely and conveniently for a fee that is rather expensive. The fee for accessing such services translates to a hefty interest rate of almost 30 per cent per annum. In return, the poor have the convenience of collection of savings periodically at their doorsteps and the safekeeping of their savings.

Based on the research by Stuart Rutherford, Joanna Ledgerwood (1999) in her book, *Microfinance Handbook* describes how deposit collectors in India facilitate the process of savings by the poor. Normally, the deposit collectors visit savers for collection of deposits every other day. The collectors carry a matrix that has 220 cells. Each time the collector comes to collect funds the saver can cross out as many cells she likes by paying a fixed amount for each cell of the matrix. For example, the payment amounts can be ₹0.50 to 1, 2, 5 or ₹10 per cell. If each cell is worth ₹1 and the client crosses out 5 cells, she pays to the deposit collector ₹5. Once all the 220 cells are filled, the saver can collect her savings from the saving collector. Although she gives the savings collector ₹220, she only collects ₹200; the remaining ₹20 goes towards charges of the savings collector for providing her services.

If one assumes that savings were collected over a 220-day period, the average balance of the savings during the period comes to ₹110. With ₹20 fee, the implied interest rate the savings collector charges for her services is about 18.18 per cent for 220 days. When one annualizes 18.18 per cent (using 365 days in a year), the implied interest rate turns out to be about 30 per cent per annum. The poor saver, who could have received a positive return on her savings from a formal banking institution (if only such access would have been available), ends up paying a hefty fee for the convenience and the safekeeping of the funds that is equivalent to about 30 per cent interest per annum (Rutherford 2000).

The question arises, why would a saver pay to the tune of 30 per cent per annum to save? There are at least three reasons. Firstly, due to lack of formal savings facilities that is poor-friendly, convenient and safe, the poor prize facilities that can provide such services. Secondly, even if such facilities were available, saving requires discipline and the arrival of a deposit collector at one's doorstep does put pressure on the saver to be disciplined to save. This feature is rather similar to 'commitment savings' feature offered by some of the formal banking institutions. Please refer to Chapter 6 for a discussion of commitment savings. Lastly, collection at the doorstep by savings collectors saves time and money for savers; or else they would have to take time off from work to travel to nearby towns or cities to save at formal savings institutions. In some cases, it is even possible that the value of the deposit could be even smaller than the transportation cost of going to the nearby city or town. It is possible that savers could pool savings at home for a period of time before depositing at formal institutions in towns or cities. But that would require discipline and safekeeping of the funds at home.

Deposit collectors do provide a very useful function for the poor; however, the charges they levy are excessive. Not only do they receive about 30 per cent return on the funds provided to them for safekeeping, they can potentially use the 'float' from these savings to invest in secure investments such as money market funds to get an extra return on these funds. Based on huge negative interest rate on savings that the poor are prepared to put up with, one would think that there is perhaps not much competition in providing such services to the poor. Otherwise, implied negative interest rates on such savings would have been much lower.

As we noted earlier, one of the reasons why formal banking institutions have not come forward to provide savings facilities to the poor has to do with the fact that the overhead cost of providing traditional savings accounts to large number of poor clients is expensive. But the above example shows that the poor are even prepared to pay for the convenience and safekeeping of their savings. Besides, the 'matrix' feature of the deposit collectors also makes the point that, even if a poor person may be illiterate, one can always devise user-friendly ways (like crossing a cell of a matrix each time a deposit is made) to help the poor save for the rainy days.

All in all, examples of savings vehicles such as ROSCAs and deposit collectors make the point that commitment feature of these savings instruments are powerful incentives for the poor to save and innovative poor-friendly savings instruments can help them in managing their household and business finances (see Chapter 6).

Why Do the Poor Lack Access to Formal Financial Services?

One of the obvious reasons why formal banking services find it difficult to reach out to the poor is the poor infrastructure in the developing countries. Without good transportation and communication, building brick and mortar branches to deliver financial services in the remote areas becomes rather expensive.

Moreover in extending credit to the poor, the banking institutions find it difficult to gather information about the creditworthiness of the poor. Many developing countries do not have UIDs like SSNs for their citizens. And lack of such unique identification numbers does not help in gathering creditworthiness information about large number of poor clients. The moneylenders on the other hand, concentrate on a few clients in their neighbourhood, diligently gather financial intelligence about their clients, charge exorbitantly high interest rates and take collateral before lending.

For formal banking institutions to replicate the process of due diligence as performed by the moneylenders for large numbers of their clients can be prohibitively expensive. Besides, lack of economies of scale in lending (small value loans) and providing savings facilities (with small savings balances) makes it difficult for the banking institutions to be sustainable. Given the fact that most poor people lack education and some of them may be even illiterate, the overhead cost of providing such services can be prohibitively expensive.

What is more, there are other complicating factors that prevent the banking sector to recover the full cost of doing business with the poor on a risk-adjusted basis. Because of usury laws and ceilings on interest rates, the formal banking institutions are required to charge interest rates that make no business sense. Moreover, in many countries, formal banking institutions are also prohibited from uncollateralized lending (Helms 2006). Above all, it is considered politically incorrect for the formal banking sector to charge higher interest rates to the poor while charging lower interest rates to the non-poor.

In all these discussions we should not forget that the risks of lending (particularly credit risk) to the poor are real. Lack of credit bureaus and difficulty in gathering creditworthiness information about their poor clients makes it difficult for the banking institutions and even the MFIs (who are in close contact with their clients) to assess creditworthiness of their clients. For example, many MFI clients borrow from multiple MFIs without revealing that they are borrowing from other MFIs. As a result, these borrowers overextend themselves and the likelihood that they would be delinquent and ultimately default on their debt increases commensurately (see Chapter 11).

Asymmetric Information and Risks of Lending to the Poor

Before we conclude this section, we briefly mention about a class of problems that give rise to risks that financial institutions, including the MFIs have to confront on a daily basis, which has been detrimental to offering financial services to the poor by banking and other financial institutions. These problems are associated with what has been known as 'asymmetric information.' Asymmetric information gives rise to a class of problems that include, 'moral hazard,' 'adverse selection' and 'agency problem' (Armendáriz and Morduch 2010).

Moral hazard refers to a situation where an agent in a transaction with more information about his or her underlying intentions behaves in a way such that the agent on the other side of the transaction would consider it inappropriate or even immoral—and hence the name moral hazard. For example, in a financial transaction if one of the parties provides misleading or false information with regard to his or her assets, liabilities and risk-bearing capacity, then the other party can potentially incur financial losses. The agency problem described below is a special case of the moral hazard problem.

Targeted subsidized lending by the governmental institutions is subject to moral hazard. For example, in the event of mass defaults on such lending, if the government decides to bail out the lending institutions, it could accentuate the moral hazard problem because it could lead to opportunistic default by the lenders and the borrowers. They can also take risks that were not intended in the loan contract. The motivation for such behaviour has to be personal gain of the clients and the institutions involved. What this implies is that, implicit and explicit guarantees do encourage risk-taking that may not be sustainable in the long run.

As we will discuss in Chapter 11, due to the lack of credit bureaus, MFIs can be subject to moral hazard if clients who borrow from multiple MFIs do not reveal this information to their MFIs. The MFIs without such information can be blindsided in assessing overall risk posture of their lending portfolios and hence pricing their products accordingly.

One finds a typical case of asymmetric information at the time of selling life insurance where the person to be insured has better information about his or her own health than the insurer. For example, a smoker buying life insurance can take advantage of the situation if the insurer cannot assess properly the health risks of the person. Under these circumstances, the risks and hence the costs of providing insurance to its clients by the insurer goes up. As a result, it would have to charge higher premiums to all its clients to mitigate higher level of risk. This would eventually drive out the clients with lesser risk. Such problems of asymmetric information are referred to as 'adverse selection.' That is the reason, insurers are careful in charging clients premiums on a risk-adjusted basis such that low-risk clients are not penalized for the risks arising from high-risk clients.

Under the lender–borrower relationship, adverse selection is a distinct possibility. Given the fact that by lending to poor clients, a lender could be exposed to adverse selection, one wonders, how the local moneylenders thrive and do well in the money lending business. First of all, moneylenders limit their business relationship with limited number of clients. They know their clients well and gather financial intelligence on their clients diligently. They do not reveal to a client, what terms of lending they offer to other clients, the size of their collateral and the interest rate they charge. In other words, they offer differentiated rates and terms based on their intimate knowledge of their clients. In the event a borrower switches to another lender for better terms and lower lending rate, he or she must be prepared to accept denial at the time of asking to borrow again in the future from the same moneylender. Ultimately the poor clients end up accepting such terms because the poor normally do not have many alternative sources to borrow.

Agency problem is also referred to as principal-agent problem. It arises because of asymmetrical information that could exist between the principal and the agent (who is hired by the principal to carry out certain tasks). Its relevance in the case of microcredit has to do with the relationship that exists between an MFI and its clients.

Ideally, the MFIs would like that the proceeds of microloans are properly utilized for the intended purposes they were approved for. And most importantly, the institutions receive timely repayment of loans from their clients. As the MFIs do not, in general, have enough information about each of their borrowers such as their credit histories, the nature and associated risks of the microbusinesses the clients invest in, and the capacity to monitor their progress due to the prohibitive high costs of individualized monitoring, the MFIs are potentially exposed to credit risk. Needless to say, without adequately dealing with such risks, the MFIs cannot aspire to be sustainable. In fact, without adequate credit risk mitigation (non-repayment risk) any lending model would fail to deliver sustainable financial services to the poor.

In order to deal with the credit risk, most MFIs adopt group lending[6] approach where the borrowers in a group try to check on each other and make sure that a single borrower in the group does not hold the entire group hostage due to his or her bad repayment record. The joint-liability approach (contract) has been quite successful in minimizing credit risk for the MFIs. What it normally implies is that the group either disciplines an MFI client who develops a bad repayment record or it bails out the client in case of a genuine difficulty. In a nutshell, the group becomes the shock absorber of such risks. Moreover, the groups facilitate in reducing transaction costs associated with lending. All in all, group lending helps the MFIs in a variety of ways to be sustainable (profitable) and pass on some of the savings to the borrowers by reducing interest rates on microcredit. It is a win-win situation for the poor clients as well as the MFIs.

However, group lending (joint-liability contacts) has its downside. In Chapter 5, we will discuss somewhat in more detail about group lending. For an in-depth discussion of asymmetric information and its implications for lending to the poor, refer to *The Economics of Microfinance* by Beatriz Armendáriz and Jonathan Morduch (2010).

A Bit of History

In Chapter 4, we will introduce the birth of microcredit followed by a broad overview of the subject. The story of the birth of microcredit is intended to motivate the reader to appreciate how access to credit is so very important in the lives of the poor. There is a rich history of trying to provide financial services to the poor on a mass scale. David Roodman (2012) in his book *Due Diligence: An Impertinent Inquiry into Microfinance* provides an excellent account of the rich history of such attempts in the past. In his account, some of the names that stand out include Jonathan Swift, Priscilla Wakefield, Franz Hermann Schulze-Delitzsch, Friedrich Wilhelm Raiffeisen, William Gourlay and Michele Carcano.

In the context of the genesis of microcredit that we are going to discuss in the next chapter, it is important that we briefly mention about 'people's bank' of Schulze-Delitzsch and Raiffeisen's 'village banks.' The first people's banks (that was established in 1850 as a credit cooperative in Germany) extended short-term loans for a period of three to six months. The funds lent were meant for investing in the businesses of its clients. It is important to note that Schulze-Delitzsch cautioned people's bank's clients not to borrow for consumption. Over several decades, people's banks had proliferated in Germany and other countries including Russia. Writing about the personality of Schulze-Delitzsch, Roodman compares him as an 'economic missionary' of his era like Muhammad Yunus of Bangladesh.

Raiffeisen, on the other hand, who started experimenting with credit cooperatives in the 1850s learned from the credit cooperative model of Schulze-Delitzsch and finalized his model around 1864. Raiffeisen's village banks extended loans with maturity of two years or more. Longer maturity of the loans in comparison to the people's bank was introduced in order to cater to the needs of the farmers. Although funding for lending was obtained from the outsiders (based on joint liability), even then the borrowers were asked to save with the bank so that the bank can become independent of outside financing. Around 1880, the village banks started taking off and by 1915, there were almost 17,000 village banks in Germany. Later, during the spread of the cooperative movement, variants of the village banking model spread to Europe, the Americas and Asia. One could say, indirectly, these models were precursors to the microcredit model that envisioned providing access to credit by the poor on a mass scale.

Conclusion

The chapter has tried to show how archaic ways to access financial services (both credit and savings) has been a major bottleneck in the lives of the poor in managing their business and household finances and mitigating exposure to specific risks. Undeniably, lack of access to formal credit and savings facilities do sap poor people's energy to juggle their finances to improve their economic condition. While the informal financial sector has been able to provide access to credit at critical junctures, it has been also a source of exploitation of the poor because of their vulnerabilities. What is more, many of the well-intentioned and targeted subsidized lending programmes that were designed to propel the poor out of poverty did not live up to their expectations. And, the intervention in the credit markets by the governments in the developing countries also undermined an orderly development of sustainable financial services for the poor. It is in this environment in the mid-1970s, microfinance (microcredit) emerged to provide financial services to the poor, which is the topic of the next chapter.

Notes

1. Such statements are posted in some of the small shops in India to discourage customers to ask for credit.
2. 'Payday Lending Basics,' Washington, DC: Center for Responsible Lending. Available online at http://www.responsiblelending.org/payday-lending/tools-resources/payday-lending-basics.html#one (downloaded on 21 November 2012).

3. This section is based on (i) *The Microfinance Revolution—Sustainable Finance for the Poor*, by Marguerite S. Robinson, published by The World Bank, Washington, DC, and Open Society Institute, New York, 2001 and (ii) *The Economics of Microfinance* by Armendaritz de Aghion, Beatriz and Morduch Jonathan, published by The MIT Press in 2010.

4. Covariant risk—because of lack of diversification, the bank loan portfolios were subject to systemic risks such floods, droughts, cyclones, economic down turns and the like.

5. Based on (i) *The Poor and their Money* by Stuart Rutherford, published by Oxford University Press, New Delhi in 2000 and (ii) *The Economics of Microfinance* by Beatriz Armendáriz and Jonathan Morduch by The MIT Press, Cambridge, Massachusetts in 2010.

6. The MFIs also lend to their clients individually where the MFI gets assurances from the client for the timely payment of the loan. Besides the assurances, the MFIs also get some level of security in the form of collateral or a cosigner (who is not a borrower from the MFI) which mitigates credit risk on such loans.

4

How Small Loans Can Make a Big Difference: The Birth of Microcredit and Its Evolution into Microfinance and Beyond

In the past, financial institutions asked themselves, "Are the poor credit-worthy?" and always answered no. As a result the poor were simply ignored and left out of the financial system, as if they did not exist. I reversed the question: "Are the banks people-worthy?" When I discovered they were not, I realized it was time to create a new kind of bank.[1]

Muhammad Yunus

The Norwegian Nobel Committee has decided to award the Nobel Peace Prize for 2006 divided into two equal parts, **to Muhammad Yunus** and **Grameen Bank** for their efforts to create economic and social development from below. Lasting peace cannot be achieved unless large population groups find ways in which to break out of poverty. Micro-credit is one such means. Development from below also serves to advance democracy and human rights.[2]

Press Release, The Nobel Peace Prize for 2006

In our day-to-day lives, we all need 'lump sum amounts' (Rutherford 2000) every so often for payouts—be it in an emergency or making specific payments such as mortgage payment or school tuition. The income of a non-poor household arrives around the year at a steady pace and they usually are able to save enough to meet such payments on a regular basis. In the event, they decide to buy big ticket items such as a car or a house they have access to easy credit from formal banking institutions.

Anyone who is remotely familiar with the lives of the poor knows how, in order to access even small amounts of credit in an emergency, they run from pillar to post hoping that someone, whether their employer, friends, family members or moneylenders, can lend them the requisite amount. It is a haphazard process fraught with uncertainty. Going through the process, where a poor family will get its next loan, is a source of great deal of frustration and even psychological trauma. This is because such need does not just arise once in a blue moon. The need to borrow for a poor household is a recurring phenomenon—because poor households experience cash shortages every so often. And each time the borrower has to approach someone, whether a friend, a family member or a moneylender; he or she has to tell a story why she needs the money; has to be creditworthy in the eyes of her lenders; and should be prepared to post collateral and pay usurious interest rates. The stress of accessing credit takes a big toll on the lives of the poor. Under these circumstances, the household is constantly trying to catch up and lacks the energy and the drive needed to think creatively to get ahead.

As we shall discuss in this chapter, the emergence of microcredit that provided innovative institutional response to the credit needs of the poor has brought about a revolution in the delivery of financial services to the poor. Briefly, microcredit makes it easier for the poor to access credit without collateral. The terms of lending of microloans are poor-friendly and the interest charged on such loans are orders of magnitude lower than the interest charged by the moneylenders. The chapter discusses the birth of microcredit and provides an introduction to microcredit as a financial instrument.

However, at the outset, it is important to note that credit is a double-edged sword. Normally, a poor household's balance sheet is debt-laden by borrowing from moneylenders and other sources. Besides, as we shall briefly discuss in this chapter, accumulating evidence regarding the efficacy of microfinance on the ground point to the fact that benefits of microcredit could be more modest in comparison to the initial expectations (also see Chapter 11). Therefore, leveraging poor people's fragile personal balance sheets (with rather minimal net worth or even negative net worth) with microcredit needs ultra care. In spite of the above cautionary note, as we shall explore in this chapter, microcredit is an essential tool for the poor in smoothing consumption, mitigating risk and monetizing their capabilities to fight poverty.

We begin this chapter with brief introductions to Grameen Bank and BRAC. It is followed by broad discussions on the nuts and bolts of microcredit. The chapter also provides brief discussions on MFIs, SHGs and capacity-building programmes for the ultra poor such as TUP at BRAC in Bangladesh. Chapter 5 is also devoted to microcredit. It discusses, among other things, credit risk reduction through joint-liability contracts, compulsory savings, innovative lending terms, women as MFI clients, and a brief introduction to microcredit products and microloan pricing.

Grameen Bank and BRAC

This section provides glimpses into two pioneering institutions, that is, Grameen Bank and BRAC, which under the able leadership of two pioneers, Professor Muhammad Yunus and Sir Fazle Hasan Abed, respectively, have made lasting contributions to the field of microfinance.

Grameen Bank

Contributions of Professor Muhammad Yunus and Grameen Bank of Bangladesh have been seminal in making microfinance revolution around the world possible, for which, the 2006 Nobel Peace Prize was awarded jointly to Muhammad Yunus and Grameen Bank, 'for their efforts to create economic and social development from below.' Other pioneers and institutions that have made lasting contributions to the field of microfinance include Fazle Hasan Abed and BRAC in Bangladesh, Ela Bhatt and Self-Employed Women's Association (SEWA) in India, ACCION in Latin America, Bank Rakyat Indonesia (BRI) and BancoSol in Bolivia.

While microcredit gained from various models of 'small value finance' that appeared in the informal and formal financial sectors in the past (see Chapter 3), the design and delivery of microfinance was ingenious in making microcredit a success story around the world.

The genesis of Grameen Bank owes much to the vision of Professor Mohammad Yunus who in 1976 discovered how the stool makers of Jobra village near Chittagong University in Bangladesh needed very small (micro) loans to keep their microenterprises running (Grameen Bank 2011). Although skilled and hard-working, these stool makers were barely making a living because they borrowed their working capital (literally very small amounts of money) from moneylenders at usurious rates and were contractually obligated to sell their products at very low prices that did not provide them enough return on their labour, capital and risks they undertook to produce the goods. These artisans were almost like bonded labourers to these moneylenders because they did not have alternative sources to access even small amounts of credit as working capital at reasonable terms and interest rates. Muhammad Yunus's first loan of $27 to 42 village artisans in Jobra was an eye opener as to how small loans can make a big difference in the lives of the poor (Yunus 2003).

Considering all the hurdles that were stacked against formal extension of credit to the poor, Muhammad Yunus initially had to become a guarantor in order for the poor artisans to borrow 10,000 Taka (about $133 assuming 75 Taka to $1) from a commercial bank. It turned out that these borrowers repaid their loans in time and were ready for more loans. Based on this initial experience, Professor Yunus was determined to establish a bank for the poor that would cater to their credit needs.

Having no experience in banking, Muhammad Yunus and his colleagues had to make many innovations to get the bank off the ground. They made their share of mistakes, but the financial, institutional, operational and management innovations they made during the last 35 years have benefited the microfinance industry immensely. While microfinance is no panacea in fighting poverty, the innovative concepts underlying microcredit, that is, starting from designing the credit instrument and building the institutional infrastructure (i.e., the Grameen Bank) to delivering microcredit, started a major revolution in extending financial services to the poor. Many social entrepreneurs inspired by the success of Grameen Bank established and continue to establish MFIs for the poor around the world. In the following text, we summarize some of the noteworthy achievements of Grameen Bank.

Achievements of Grameen Bank:
A Bird's Eye View

Since its inception in 1976, Grameen was formally transformed to a bank in 1983 (Grameen Bank 2011). Today, the Grameen Bank is not only a pioneer in the field, but one of the most successful MFIs in the world. The following bird's eye view of the bank puts in to perspective how it has been thriving as a successful financial institution that combines sustainability and social mission as its main goals.

Based on the information as of October 2011 contained in the website 'Grameen Bank at a Glance,' the bank had already disbursed loans totalling the equivalent of $11.35 billion of which $10.11 billion was repaid (Grameen Bank 2011). Projected disbursement for the year 2011 was $1.6 billion. The loan recovery rate for the bank was about 97 per cent.

Grameen Bank had 8.35 million borrowers as of October 2011 of which 96 per cent were women. It had 2,565 branches. It provided financial and complementary services in 81,379 villages and had a staff of over 22,000. Its members belonged to groups consisting of five individuals. However, the groups are not required to provide any guarantee for loans to its borrowers. There is no joint-liability, that is, the group members are not responsible to pay on account of defaulting member of the group. We will discuss about group lending and joint-liability contracts in this chapter and in Chapters 5 and 11.

Grameen Bank does not rely on donor funding or loans. In October 2011, the bank's outstanding loan portfolio was financed entirely from Grameen Bank's deposits. Total deposits stood at 145 per cent of the outstanding loan portfolio. If deposits and own resources of the bank are combined, the total was 160 per cent of the outstanding loans. Grameen Bank's borrowers accounted for 56 per cent of the deposits. What is more, 20 per cent of the branches had more borrower deposits than loans outstanding and 42 per cent had borrower deposits equivalent to 75 per cent or more of the outstanding loans. This is important because, in an environment where some of the MFIs around the world are being criticized for over-indebting the poor, Grameen borrowers were borrowing as well as building up their savings in parallel. Interest rates on deposits offered to the savers were in the range of 8.5 per cent minimum to 12 per cent maximum.

Grameen Bank had total revenue of $252.05 million in 2010. And total expenditure amounted to $241.29 million. The total profit for 2010 was $10.76 million. The bank declared a cash dividend of 30 per cent. It is important to note that 97 per cent of the banks shareholders are borrowers and 96 per cent of all borrowers are women.

As of October 2011, Grameen Bank interest rate was 20 per cent for income-generating loans. It charged 8 per cent on housing loans, 5 per cent on student loans and no interest (0 per cent interest) to struggling members (beggars). All these rates were calculated based on declining balance method. It disbursed $211 million on housing loans Almost 50,000 received education loans and $3 million in scholarships were also disbursed. There were over 110,000 beggar members of which about 20,000 members had left the programme. After leaving the programme, over 10,000 members had joined the Grameen Bank as mainstream borrowers.

Grameen Bank also offered optional insurance called 'Loan Insurance Programme.' Under this programme, in the event an insured member dies, his or her total outstanding loans are paid off. Husbands of the borrowers can also be insured under this programme. In the event, the husband dies, the outstanding loan amount of the borrower is fully paid off and she can continue to borrow.

One of the popular programmes offered by Grameen Bank is the Pension Benefit Programme. Under the programme, a borrower is required to save a small amount such as 50 Taka (which was $0.66 in October 2011) each month over a 10-year period. At the end of the period, the depositor gets almost twice the amount deposited. At the end of October 2011, the balance under this programme was about $513 million.

Last but not the least, it is important to mention about Grameen Network, consisting of large number of social businesses (see Chapter 12 for a discussion of social businesses), which are independent of Grameen Bank. Some of the names worth mentioning in the networks are Grameen Danone Foods Limited, Grameen Veolia Water Ltd and BASF Grameen Ltd These are the companies that manufacture yogurt with micronutrients, bottled water and mosquito nets, respectively. We will discuss about some of these companies in Chapter 12.

BRAC

BRAC is considered the largest non-governmental development organization in the world. It is a 'holistic' development organization offering an
array of products that complements microfinance products. It has made
lasting contributions to fighting poverty at the grass-root level, including
the ultra poor. As of 2011, it was not yet financially sustainable.

Although in the past, BRAC stood for such acronyms as Bangladesh
Rehabilitation Assistance Committee and Bangladesh Rural Advancement Committee; today, BRAC is no longer used as an acronym.[3] BRAC,
under the remarkable leadership of Sir Fazle Hasan Abed has been helping the poor to fight poverty in Bangladesh, and other countries around
the world, in the following areas: public health—water, sanitation and
hygiene; education; agriculture and food security; microfinance; social
development; construction and maintenance; disaster relief; advocacy
and ICT development. It also operates several social enterprises, which
span such fields as artificial insemination, dairy, poultry rearing, fisheries, feed mills, sanitary napkins and delivery kits, sericulture, solar
energy and tea estate. The BRAC umbrella also includes BRAC Bank
Ltd., BRAC University, BRAC Net, Delta BRAC Housing Finance Corp
Ltd. and Documenta Ltd.

The sheer magnitude of the various operations can be gleaned from
the following statistics. As of June 2012, BRAC was operating in 64 dis-
tricts of Bangladesh covering about 113 million people.[4] It had more than
38,000 teachers, 10,000 health workers and over 45,000 full-time staff,
which added up to more than 93,000 employees. This does not include
BRAC activities in other countries such as Afghanistan, Haiti, Liberia,
Sierra Leone, Southern Sudan and Tanzania.

Based on the statistics provided by BRAC, in 1980 it had an expenditure of $0.78 million, which was funded 100 per cent by its donors.
By 1995, the expanded BRAC had an expenditure of $63.73 million, of
which 54 per cent was funded by its donors. And in 2011, BRAC had
an expenditure of $572 million of which 24 per cent was funded by the
donors.

BRAC launched its microfinance activities in 1974. Currently, its
microfinance programme divides the poor into three distinct groups and
accordingly offers a 'credit ladder' consisting of three programmes called
'Dabi,' 'Unnoti' and 'Progoti.' Dabi is the largest credit programme

offered to the poor. After graduating from Dabi, the borrowers can move to Unnoti and access 'higher range' of microcredit facilities. And Unnoti borrowers, after graduating from the programme, have the option to move to Progoti and access still larger loans for their microenterprises. Besides Dabi, Unnoti and Progoti, BRAC is also actively involved in helping the ultra poor (extreme poor) under the TUP programme, about which we discuss later in this chapter. TUP in many ways is a pioneering programme that has been designed to show that with the right kind of assistance even the ultra poor can succeed in running microbusinesses and in the process can improve their economic status.

As of June 2012, BRAC had 4.39 million borrowers. Cumulative disbursements under the microfinance programme reached little over $8 billion and outstanding loans under the programme amounted to about $715 million. The savings deposits under the programme stood at about $289 million. The average loan size of the programme was about $220.

Based on a brief discussion of Grameen Bank and BRAC achievements, it is difficult to imagine that not too long ago the poor did not have the option to access microcredit without posting collateral and without paying exorbitantly high interest rates. Although, over the last several years, microcredit has been under the microscope for its efficacy on the ground, the scale of operations of Grameen and BRAC does point to the fact that extension of microcredit along with other financial and non-financial services has reached a level of sophistication and success that could not have been imagined even 15–20 years ago.

What Is Microcredit and What Are Some of Its Important Features That Set It Apart from Other Forms of Lending

Under the title 'What is Microfinance?[5]' published in the Microfinance Gateway (CGAP) one finds the following definition of microfinance:

> Microfinance is often defined as financial services for poor and low-income clients. In practice the term is often used more narrowly to refer to loans and other services from providers that identify themselves as "microfinance institutions" (MFIs). These institutions commonly tend to use new methods developed over the last 30 years to deliver very small loans to unsalaried

borrowers, taking little or no collateral. These methods use group lending and liability, pre-loan savings requirements, gradually increasing loan sizes, and an implicit guarantee of ready access to future loans if present loans are repaid fully and promptly.

More broadly, microfinance refers to a movement that envisions a world in which low-income households have permanent access to a range of high-quality financial services to finance their income-producing activities, build assets, stabilize consumption, and protect against risks. These services include savings, credit, insurance, remittances, and payments and others.

While the two above paragraphs provide a broad definition of microfinance, the first paragraph of the two is exclusively devoted to defining microcredit. Even today, microcredit takes up the bulk of the business activities of an MFI. While savings, insurance and payment services for remittances and other financial transactions have gained in importance during the last 10–15 years, these instruments have not reached the same level of penetration as microcredit.

Client Base

Broadly speaking, MFI clients cluster around the poverty line. More specifically the MFIs lend to moderate poor, vulnerable non-poor and also economically active extreme poor because they have relatively more stable cash flow in comparison to the poorest or the extreme poor who are not economically active. As far as rural poor in the remote areas are concerned, they effectively cannot take advantage of microfinance because they are widely dispersed and most MFIs do not have the institutional capacity to reach out to these groups (CGAP 2006). Even if an MFI decides to reach out, the cost of reaching out could be rather high. Without passing on these costs to their poor clients, it would be difficult for the MFIs to be sustainable.

By and large, women constitute the majority of the microfinance clients. There are many MFIs that serve only women. On an aggregate basis 33 per cent of microfinance clients are men.[6] Based on data provided in the 'State of the Microcredit Summit Campaign Report 2012' (Maes and Reed 2012), as of 31 December 2010, 3,652 MFIs reported that they served about 205 million poor clients around the world, of which about 153 million were women. This implies, women clients constituted about 74 per cent of the total. It is important to note, the fact that in accessing microcredit one does not have to post traditional collateral, allowed large number of poor women to access microcredit. This is because, whatever little collateral a poor family has, it is usually the men in most traditional societies, who are allowed to pledge these assets at the time of borrowing.

It is also important to note that the number of people that do not have access to financial services, including banking, is larger than the number of poor people in the world (Helms 2006). What this implies, there are large numbers of people in the low-income but non-poor category who are underserved or un-served by banking and other financial services. The MFIs with appropriate product mix have the potential to reach out to this category to diversify their client base and at the same time attain sustainability.

Purpose of Extending Microloans

Initially, microcredit was envisaged to provide working capital for productive purposes. However, over the years, the menu of activities for which MFIs have been extending microcredits to the poor has become long. This is because like the non-poor, the poor households have varied need for loans. As a result, MFIs today have diversified their product line to extend loans in such areas as housing, education, consumer items such as refrigerators, mobile phones and television sets, emergency health needs and the like. However, by and large microloans are extended for working capital needs or for acquiring fixed assets. Needless to say, given the fact that money is fungible and there is no effective monitoring of lent funds, how the funds are deployed depends to a large extent on the borrower.

Consumer lenders largely focus on lending to salaried individuals (with stable income) to buy consumer items (Rhyne 2009). However, over the years MFIs and consumer lenders have started to compete for the same clientele. This is particularly true in Latin America. It is expected that as the MFIs and purely consumer lenders compete for the same client base, it is possible that microenterprise lending and consumer lending will slowly blur.

Commercialization has brought with it criticism that some of the MFIs in order to increase profitability drift towards extending credits to poor and vulnerable non-poor people who can absorb larger microloans (hence increasing average loan size) to attain economies of scale. Some of them also over-lend to borrowers. Over-lending in many cases has resulted in over-indebtedness among the poor borrowers who are predominantly vulnerable women.

How Microloans Are Used?

Broadly speaking, microcredit involves large-scale extension of small amounts of credit (invariably with short maturities) to poor and low-income clients for working capital needs of their microenterprises or for self-employment. Because money is fungible and microenterprises normally do not have separate legal identity, microenterprise and household finances are usually intermingled. As a result, microloans normally increase household liquidity unless it is used right away in the microenterprise for which it was earmarked. Therefore, a portion of the funds could end up being used for consumption purposes (if such need arises in the short run), until it is replaced by household cash inflows. There used to be a stigma attached to use of such funds for consumption unless it is used for such things as health emergencies, education and repairing one's shelter. Microloans have been used for replacing (restructuring) existing debt that has higher interest rate. Such replacement could result in substantial savings for the poor and could provide extra cash for paying a child's tuition, to build up savings or even to access more loans from MFIs. But over the years, microcredit as a financial product has expanded to provide consumption loans such as loans for education, buying refrigerators, mobile phones and the like.

Size of Loans

While the small size of microloans is one of their important characteristics, loan size is not usually mentioned in the definition of microcredit in order to allow room for flexibility in responding to changing environment in which MFIs operate. In any case, the size of microloans can be as small as $25 and as high as 2.5 times the Gross National Income (GNI) of a country.[7] Size of loans is an important parameter in overall financial management of an MFI. The average loan size has implications for economies of scale and credit risk exposure of microloan portfolios of MFIs that ultimately affects the sustainability (profitability) of MFIs.

Types of Lending: Individualized and Group Lending; Collateral Substitutes

Microlending can be divided into two broad categories (Ledgerwood 1999): lending to individuals and group-based lending. In the case of individualized lending, the MFIs seek assurances from the borrower for timely repayment of interest and principal. Besides the assurances, the MFIs also get other forms of security in the form of collateral or a co-signer (who is not a borrower from the MFI) who provides an extra level of comfort in mitigating credit risk on such lending. Moreover, the MFI staff develops close relationships with its clients before extending microcredit on an individual basis. Repeat loans that progressively increase in size over time are also used as an incentive for timely payment of such loans.

Due to the close monitoring needed in such lending, individualized lending is normally confined among the urban poor. What is more, because the clients of MFIs in the urban areas are normally migrants from other parts of the country, there may be a lack of trust and cooperation among the urban poor. As a result, group-based lending (about which we will discuss briefly below, but more so in Chapter 5) that leverages 'social capital' (see Chapters 5 and 10 for a discussion of social capital) may not be as suitable and successful in urban setting in comparison to individualized lending. Having said that it is important to note that, one also finds individualized lending to be successful in rural areas where the poor are members of credit cooperatives or credit unions. This is partly because of the group-like umbrella credit unions extend to their members.

By and large, MFIs extending individual loans lend to clients who are financially better off than the average poor client. The average loan size for the borrowers who borrow individually is also larger. Moneylenders lend to individuals. If local moneylender model is any guide, individual lending requires closer monitoring, which can be rather time-consuming. Under the individualized lending scenario, one has to understand the financial situation of the clients well before one lends. However, by design, MFIs are in the business of extending microcredit to hundreds of thousands or even millions of clients. Therefore, close monitoring of small loans to millions of borrowers can be prohibitively expensive for the MFIs.

As a result, group lending with joint-liability contracts that substitute 'social capital' as collateral has been used to mitigate credit risk emanating from lending to poor borrowers who normally cannot post traditional collateral. Under the joint-liability contract, the group is collectively responsible for repayment of debt service by its group members. Group-based lending using 'solidarity group' approach evolved at the Grameen Bank through a process of trial and error (Dowla and Barua 2006). Due toits success in keeping repayment rates high, group lending with joint liability contracts has been recognized as one of the most important innovations that made large scale extension of credit to the poor a reality.

However, joint-liability contracts have their downsides. It is important to note that Grameen Bank, innovator of joint-liability contracts, which was used under the Classical Grameen Model (Grameen I) has moved away from using these innovations under the Grameen II model (see Chapter 5), although members still belong to both groups. Considering its importance, we will discuss about group lending in more detail in Chapter 5.

Flexible Repayment Terms

By giving special consideration to household cash flow patterns, the MFIs enable their poor clients to make timely repayments on their microloans. Almost all MFIs allow weekly repayments. There are MFIs that also allow biweekly repayments. Because of shorter time period between repayments, the number of repayments for a microloan is relatively larger and payments in each period are smaller. Smaller payments in each period make it convenient for the poor borrowers to repay their loans with ease. However, the cost of collecting repayments goes up because number of repayments on each microloan is larger, although collecting repayments in group meetings helps to reduce such cost. Many MFIs also make their repayment terms cater to the needs of the farmers whose cash flows are seasonal.

In spite of the flexibilities offered under these repayment terms, the need for strict adherence to repayment schedule or inflexibility in making adjustments to repayment schedule by many MFIs (in the event a borrower is going through financial hardship) makes it difficult for some of the poor borrowers to become members of MFIs. Besides, if a member goes through genuine financial hardship, then other group members have to cover for her under the joint-liability contract. That can be a source of strain for the group member, although, under the joint-liability contract she might have to reciprocate if another member of the group experiences financial hardship. If financial hardship of the family continues (sometimes it does because financial hardships can be bunched), the member could be subjected to the wrath of the group. Besides, if the borrowers of an MFI are exposed to a natural disaster or collectively experience economic hardship due to economic downturn, joint liability can become largely ineffective. As we shall discuss in Chapter 5, under the Grameen II model of microlending, the borrowers are allowed more flexibility in terms of repaying a loan.

Repeat Loans (Progressive Lending)

Another important feature of microcredit includes eligibility of the borrower to have access to repeat loans based on his or her repayment performance. Repeat loans can be bigger in size for clients who have good repayment records. As a result, such loans encourage the borrowers to be current on their payments. What is important to note here is that the MFIs try to establish a relationship with their clients, by catering to their credit needs on a continuing basis. In the process they gain their confidence and their business. They know very well that if their clients do well financially, that bodes well for the MFI in expanding business.

However, repeat loans that can be progressively larger could have a downside in the sense that the borrowers could keep on borrowing from the lender without trying to get out of borrowing. In other words, under these circumstances, a borrower could become dependent on borrowing without paying enough attention to savings.

Under Grameen II model, total lending to borrowers are linked to the savings of the borrower as well as to their repayment history. What is more, borrowers are allowed to borrow and repay to Grameen concurrently within a lending ceiling. Besides, the borrower is also allowed to borrow and save voluntarily at the same time (see Chapter 5).

Compulsory Savings

In order to borrow from an MFI, most MFIs around the world make it compulsory for their borrowers to save. Different MFIs use different approaches to compulsory savings. At the Grameen Bank (under the Grameen I model), the borrowers were required to save a fixed amount weekly (Dowla and Barua 2006). Besides the weekly savings of a fixed amount, the borrowers were required to deposit 5 per cent of the face value of their microloans as a lump sum amount (termed 'group tax') into an account. The 5 per cent group tax used to be deducted from the loan proceeds. The loan deductions and weekly fixed payments towards the compulsory savings were used to create a group fund. The borrowers normally earn an interest on their compulsory savings. For example, Grameen Bank borrowers earned an interest of 8.5 per cent on their compulsory savings in the early 2000s. However, there are MFIs that pay a miniscule interest (even no interest) on compulsory savings.

The management of the group fund (under Grameen I) was under the control of the group. And with the approval of the group, the funds could be lent out to members for a short period of time so long as the loan amount(s) did not exceed 50 per cent of group savings. The funds were largely used for emergency needs of clients, such as health emergencies, payments on children's education and buying food during lean times. The full amount in the fund can be withdrawn in the case of natural calamities. While loans from the group fund were interest-free, the borrowers had to pay a tax of 5 per cent on the borrowed funds. However, the 5 per cent tax was discontinued latter.

By and large compulsory savings is not easily accessible by the poor clients of an MFI. Most of the times, the borrowers cannot withdraw these savings unless they decide to leave the institution. During the initial years at Grameen Bank, if a borrower dropped out of a group, she could not claim her share of the group fund. This arrangement was considered unfair. The practice was changed later. As a result, accumulated savings could be withdrawn after adjusting for outstanding loan amounts if a borrower decides to leave a group. Moreover, for a borrower with good standing, the accumulated savings in the group fund is merged with her personal savings accounts after 10 years. And in the case a borrower decides to leave the MFI, she receives the accumulated savings after adjusting for the loans that were outstanding in her name.

Since group-based microlending is collateral-free (under the traditional definition of collateral), compulsory savings can be viewed as partial cash collateral for such lending. Use of compulsory savings (sometimes referred to as compensating balances) does increase the effective cost of borrowing from the MFIs. On the plus side, it helps its poor clients to use such savings in emergencies and build backstop for mitigating financial shocks. More importantly, it does enable many fledgling MFIs to lend to the poor in order that financial intermediation at the grass-root level could take hold.

As accumulation of compulsory savings in the group fund cannot be easily withdrawn at will by a borrower, it can become an important source of liquidity for an MFI. Over the years, through accumulation, group funds have soared in value for many MFIs. As a result, these funds have been used for a variety of purposes by the MFIs, including investing in secure financial instruments.

Since compulsory savings is an extra burden on borrowers in terms of cash flow and increasing the effective cost of microloans, many MFIs are slowly moving away from compulsory savings. Under the Grameen II model, voluntary savings (microsavings) and microcredit are offered to the poor clients in parallel. In this model, the group fund has been replaced by two individualized savings accounts, that is, personal savings account and obligatory savings account about which we will discuss in Chapter 5.

Although it does increase the effective cost of loans to the borrowers, compulsory savings undoubtedly disciplines MFI clients to build up savings. Considering the fact that savers in developing countries are prepared to save incurring large negative spread (see 'Deposit Collectors' in Chapter 3), the extra cost that compulsory savings entails in terms of higher EIR (on microloans) may be a comparatively small price to pay in order to build up savings and at the same time make it relatively less risky for the MFIs to extend credit to the poor. Given the fact that the borrowers earn interest on their compulsory savings, even if modest, such interest earnings do reduce overall negative cost impact on the borrowers/savers. In the light of MFI clients borrowing from multiple sources (other MFIs and moneylenders), compulsory savings may be a useful backstop for MFI borrowers and the requirement to save could potentially lower unrestrained borrowing by the poor. It also provides MFIs cash collateral and helps to build up liquidity.

Credit Life Insurance

MFIs require borrowers to buy credit life insurance to protect their families from financial burden by extinguishing the outstanding debt in case the borrower of record dies. Credit life insurance not only protects the borrower's family, but also helps the MFIs to collect debt under difficult circumstances. But more importantly, it protects the MFIs from credit risk. The premiums on such insurance do increase effective cost of microloans to the borrowers. It is also important to note that some MFIs also levy an administrative charge to offer credit life insurance. We will discuss credit life insurance at BASIX in India in Chapter 7 (*Microinsurance*).

Market-based Lending

Normally, the MFIs charge market-based interest rates on microloans. In Chapter 5, we will provide a broad outline of how lending rates are set.

The lending policies of the MFIs are not normally influenced by mandated volume and subsidy requirements. They are also not guided by how much to lend to each borrower and what the overall lending volume should be for a region, state or country as a whole. Such lending is also not influenced by guidelines that dictate lending to a specific sector of an economy. As a result, the MFIs avoid portfolios that are concentrated in a given sector or region of an economy exposing them to covariance risk. However, smaller MFIs that are concentrated in a given geographical region are exposed to covariance risk, whereas larger MFIs could diversify across regions to avoid such risk. However, the 2010 Microfinance Crisis in the state of Andhra Pradesh in India unmistakably shows how concentrating lending in a given region (to expand market share for higher profitability) without regard for portfolio concentration could expose an entire industry to covariance risk.

Average of Interest Rates Charged on Microloans: Most MFIs used to specify a flat rate on the disbursed (face) amount of a loan as opposed to the outstanding balance of the loan, which declines as repayment of the principal takes place week after week. That has been changing. More and more MFIs are moving to quote the lending rate based on the declining balance method, which is based on the discounted cash flow (DCF). MFIs around the world normally charge EIRs (see Chapter 5 for a discussion MFI interest rates) that range from 2 to 5 per cent per month. These rates are usually 2 to 4 times the interest rates charged by the commercial banks to the non-poor. However, the rates are much lower than the interest rates charged by the moneylenders.

There are MFIs that charge interest rates that are rather very high. For example, in her article in the Banker, Silvia Pavoni (2010) mentions that Compartamos Banco and Te Creemos in Mexico charge interest rates that are about 72 per cent and 125 per cent, respectively. In the article she also mentions that based on MIX computations (that included 1084 MFIs reporting to MIX), the average interest rate on microfinance loans was about 38 per cent. Moreover, out of the 1084 MFIs included in the computations, about 25 per cent charged interest rates that were less than 22 per cent and the rest charged interest rates that were lower than 44 per cent.

In the paper 'Grameen and Microcredit: A Tale of Corporate Success,' Anu Muhammad (2009) provides 'rate of effective cost of borrowing,' for the clients of Grameen Bank to be about 30.5 per cent and for BRAC and Association for Social Advancement (ASA) to be around 44.8 per cent.

All in all, it would be fair to say that the EIRs charged by the MFIs normally range anywhere from about 20 per cent to about 45 per cent annually. However, it is also true that there are some MFIs that charge much higher interest rates than 45 per cent per annum. We critique the interest rates charged by the MFIs in Chapter 11 (Critiquing Microfinance).

Why Microcredit Is a Powerful Financial Tool for the Poor

To begin with, microcredit has been quite effective in breaking down the barrier that made it almost impossible for the poor to borrow without collateral. Needless to say, lack of access to credit in a poor-friendly manner ties the hands of the poor and prevents them to be proactive in utilizing their capabilities to generate income, help feed their families, fend off specific risks (such as health risks) and in the process aspire to build assets to fight poverty.

Many entrepreneurs rely on their own savings and help from friends and family members to start a business. But in the case of the poor to build up sizable savings being thrifty would normally take a long time. Moreover, it is highly probable that their friends and family members could be themselves poor. And looking for financial help from them in starting and running microbusinesses may not always be a viable proposition. In the event they could borrow from their family and friends, it is difficult to run to them on a recurring basis to borrow to manage their businesses. What they need is an entity that understands their needs (in a business sense and in a business-like manner) and supports them as their businesses evolve. Therefore, access to credit is essential in managing their microbusiness and household finances.

It was in the mid-1970s that NGO-based MFIs changed the rules of the game by lending to the poor without collateral by introducing a variety of innovations such as group lending with joint-liability (as a collateral substitute), innovative repayment terms, progressive lending and the like. When compared with the informal financial sector (i.e., the moneylenders), the relative transparency, efficiency, cost-effectiveness (in terms of EIR on such credit) and predictability in accessing more credit in the future made microcredit truly poor-friendly. What is more, it provided the poor the much needed breathing room in terms of managing their microbusinesses and household finances. Most importantly, it allowed a poor family to access microcredit on a level playing field, because there was no need for collateral.

On the contrary, in order to access credit from the informal markets, the need for collateral and usurious interest rates take a big toll on the financial lives of the poor and make them powerless to think creatively. In fact, they normally cannot think in terms of borrowing from moneylenders to invest in microbusinesses. Microcredit facilitates improved financial management of their debt by repaying high-cost loans to moneylenders that reduces bleeding of cash. In fact, interest savings by substituting microcredit to replace high-cost borrowed funds from moneylenders could easily provide positive cash flow for a microenterprise or household.

For example, assume that a microentrepreneur is compelled to borrow ₹10,000 for one year (in India) and a moneylender lends the money at an interest rate of 5 per cent per month, then the interest expense on the loan per annum would come up to ₹6,000 (assuming interest is not compounded and the borrower makes timely interest payments on the loan). Now, if the borrower can have access to microfinance, and can borrow ₹10,000 from an MFI at an interest rate of say 30 per cent per annum (2.5 per cent per month), then yearly interest payment on the loan would be half, that is, ₹3,000 per annum. If she repays the moneylender by borrowing ₹10,000 from an MFI, she would save ₹3,000 in interest payments in one year, which is ₹250 per month. That is substantial savings (surplus) for a microentrepreneur.

The world of the poor is normally circumscribed by impossibilities. Access to financial capital through microcredit opens the door to more choices and opportunities. That, in turn, helps them to think more in terms of possibilities. With an expanded set of opportunities to choose from, the case can be made that the likelihood of finding a better fit to utilize one's capabilities does improve. In a nutshell, access to financial capital through credit provides them with improved opportunities to monetize their capabilities, which otherwise could have remained dormant.

Access to microcredit is designed to leverage the survival instinct, the inherent strengths and capabilities of the poor to improve their economic well-being (Counts 2008). It is true that most of the microbusinesses that the poor invest are not scalable. However, if they can generate enough income from such businesses to make their ends meet (in the short run at least), these businesses can potentially become stepping stones to bigger and better things. These businesses, even if micro, can teach the poor a thing or two about how to run a business. With experience, an entrepreneur could buy tools to leverage her capabilities (for improved productivity to expand output) and buy inputs at the opportune time to build inventory at a lower cost and in the process improve margins to attain profitability.

Many entrepreneurs fail in several businesses before they find their niche business. The learning process in running businesses is essential to entrepreneurship. Therefore, it is essential for the poor people to have the much needed opportunities to learn about starting and running businesses—even if they fail. The fact that they might fail in a business, instinctively could force them to try their hands on a variety of livelihoods to diversify their sources of income (Banerjee and Duflo 2006). This also helps them to learn by doing a variety of things that has the potential to diversify their sources of income in mitigating income risk. In all this, access to microcredit (as working capital) can be used to bridge cash flow shortfall of their microenterprises as well as their households because microenterprises and the respective households that own these enterprises are not separate legal and financial entities.

Since a poor person's household and the microbusiness(es) she owns are not separate legal entities, microloans de facto increase household liquidity. Because money is fungible, a savvy borrower could take advantage of such opportunity to pay for essential needs such as educational expenses of children or expenses for health needs in the short run. However, there is a downside to increase in short-term liquidity, that is, if the household lacks discipline to use the funds for income generation that could lead to over-indebtedness without commensurate increase in cash inflow. Therefore, it is imperative that the poor have appropriate financial literacy training that helps them to manage their personal balance sheets conservatively. Such training should provide them simple guidelines to manage their assets and liabilities—such as guidelines about savings, debt reduction, insurance and the like.

There are other benefits of being self-employed or starting a new business. At the very least, the fact that the poor can try their hands at starting a new business provides them a new perspective on life. In order to start a business, or even to be self-employed, the poor have to think in terms of the future, in terms of new possibilities. Most importantly, access to microcredit empowers the poor to take risk. That in itself is the first step in making a poor person financially literate. Financial literacy cannot come from textbook lessons alone. One can become financially literate the hard way by starting a business. The risk of losing money is a powerful motivating force in making a person financially literate. Moreover, in order to start a business, a poor person has to think in terms of what products and services to sell, what is the demand for a given product, where to buy inputs cheaply, how to design the product and the like. Understanding these linkages and networking (being part of the social and economic network) is perhaps the greatest education a poor person could have in fighting poverty.

Having access to financial tools such as microcredit, a poor borrower is empowered to solve her financial problem on her own (as opposed being offered a solution). Therefore, access to microfinance (microcredit) enables the poor to be innovative in finding creative solutions to fit their specific needs. On the contrary, by offering off-the-shelf solutions or a one-size-fits-all approach, one tends to straightjacket the recipients to accept solutions that may not meet their unique circumstances. Besides, when the poor come up with their own solutions, they own the problem, and have to work hard to be successful in what they are doing. Because the solutions depend on their own initiatives and the poor want to be successful, they count their pennies because they are starved of financial resources. They have to be leaner and meaner in deploying the borrowed funds. Most importantly, access to microcredit helps to exploit and nurture the initiatives of the poor in a bottom-up manner, which goes a long way in making development work from below.

What follows is a nuanced interpretation as to why microfinance, consisting of microcredit, microsavings and microinsurance, is a powerful financial tool for the poor in fighting poverty and narrowing income inequality between the haves and have-nots. The underlying argument is based on the book *Capital in the Twenty-First Century*, by Thomas Piketty (2014), which highlights how the relationship '$r > g$,' that is, the average return on capital (r) is greater than the growth rate of an economy (g), contributes to widening income inequality between the rich and the poor. It was Milton Friedman who observed that 'The poor stay poor, not because they are lazy, but because they have no access to capital.' Therefore, assuming $r > g$ holds in general, one could posit that poor-friendly access to capital when deployed diligently by the poor could potentially take advantage of $r > g$ to narrow the income inequality between the haves and the have-nots (which could be rather slow and may not be uniform across all the poor people). In other words, the leveraging power of access to microcredit with poor-friendly terms and interest rates, when invested in microenterprises, education and training, retiring high cost debt and even for income smoothing, potentially could fight poverty and narrow income inequality. What is more, access to microsavings (see Chapter 6) could help build (accumulate) capital and access to microinsurance (see Chapter 7) could help preserve capital (and hence help in the accumulation of capital) by lowering capital depletion using insurance cover. It goes without saying that improved earnings, accumulation and preservation of capital in poor households strengthen household balance sheets and have salutary implications for fighting poverty and narrowing income inequality.

Diminished Expectations of Microcredit Impact in Alleviating Poverty on a Large Scale

In the context of discussing the power and virtues of microcredit, it is important to note that the recent microcredit impact assessments using randomized control trials (RCTs) has provided a mixed picture of its efficacy, which are in variance with some of the outsized claims made in the past about microcredit impact (see Chapter11). What is more, increase in delinquency rates in some markets around the world and the 2010 Microfinance Crisis in the state of Andhra Pradesh in India have made it imperative that more caution has to be exercised in extending microcredit to the poor (Chapter 11).

Credit (debt) is a double-edged sword. While borrowing from the MFIs by the poor can be used by them to smooth consumption, mitigate specific risks and leverage one's capabilities to fight poverty, but at the same time, leveraging fragile personal balance sheets of the poor entails risk. Finding the fine balance between too much debt and right level of debt is not easy. Poor household could easily succumb to borrowing more because they are invariably cash-strapped.

Even if credits may be micro, too much microcredit from not only one MFI, but from multiple MFIs (in markets where it is possible) and moneylenders (who charge usurious interest rates) can wreak havoc on the over-indebted poor families. This can be truly problematic if the microbusinesses the poor invest in do not provide adequate returns as expected, or fail. This is particularly true given the fact that microentrepreneurs tend to invest in entities that lack economies of scale and could be clones of each other (see discussions in the next section).

Diminished expectations with regard to microcredit impact point to the fact that borrowers need to be extra careful going out on a limb to borrow from MFIs because accessing credit from MFIs may be relatively easier. In this regard, the use of credit bureaus in monitoring debt levels of the poor borrowers become critical. What is more, through financial literacy training, the poor should be discouraged from over-indebting themselves. Besides, the poor should have access to other essential microfinance instruments such as microsavings and microinsurance and they need to use these instruments concurrently along with credit to manage their assets and liabilities prudently. What is more, they should go through livelihood and marketing training and rudimentary aspects of business finance that could help them in improving their chances of being successful in their businesses (see Chapter 10).

What Kinds of Microbusinesses the Poor Invest and What Kinds of Return One Could Expect from Such Businesses

Given the fact most of the poor entrepreneurs are entrepreneurs by necessity (not by choice), one should not be thinking of them as the legendary entrepreneurs of the Silicon Valley. In becoming microentrepreneurs what they have in mind is to be able to afford food, shelter, health care and other basic necessities of life on a daily basis. In that sense, most of them can be termed as entrepreneurs who work hard to subsist first through self-employment or running microbusinesses. Therefore, one would expect them to invest in businesses that they come across in their neighbourhood, which they could emulate successfully. Establishing niche businesses for them may be difficult, and poor entrepreneurs may be averse to risk in general, investing in businesses about which they do not know much and in which they may not have access to training. As a result, many of the businesses the poor normally would invest could become clones of each other. Under these circumstances, the profit margins on these businesses can get squeezed and could lead to low profitability. Some of these businesses could end up as loss-making entities.

Considering the fact that women constitute about 74 per cent of all microfinance borrowers and most of them do not possess much skill, with a small loan in the range of $100–$200, they may not have other opportunities except for investing in businesses that are home-bound and do not have much profit potential. In many cultures, women are not even allowed to go out of the house to the marketplace on their own. Under these circumstances, women would confine themselves to traditional homebound businesses such as sewing, embroidery work, garments and dress making, toy making and making pickles. Businesses that require more skill such as electrical work, carpentry, masonry and bicycle repair are owned by men. Therefore, it may not be improbable that income generated from such businesses (i.e., which have minimal barriers to entry require low levels of investment capital and lack economies of scale) cannot propel the poor out of poverty quickly. In this context, the following quote from the book *Small Loans, Big Dreams* by Alex Counts (2008, 2) is rather appropriate.

> Microfinance is the rare antipoverty approach based on the poor's strengths rather than their deficiencies. In Third World countries, there is barely a fraction of the jobs required to employ those who want to work, and there is little, if any, social safety net. Most poor people have a stark choice— work for themselves or starve. The vast majority choose self-employment, regardless of how undercapitalized and modest their microbusiness may be, because of the unattractiveness of the alternative. Many of them turn to loan sharks for their capital, and pay rates anywhere from 10 percent per month to 20 percent per day. These enterprises, which range from raising livestock and running a grocery shop to processing food and weaving bamboo mats (and other crafts), are rarely enough to allow the owner to get ahead, or even put three meals on the table per day, but they can keep slow starvation at bay most of the time.

The above paragraph clarifies the image of what it means to be a microentrepreneur or a self-employed poor. The simple fact is that most of the clients of MFIs are already self-employed or run microbusinesses that are usually undercapitalized. These entrepreneurs also lack skills. By accessing microcredit, they gain more breathing room to put their businesses on somewhat of a stronger footing. For example, by accessing microcredit, they can increase the profit potential of their businesses by purchasing inputs in bulk at an opportune time or to buy tools to achieve economies of scale.

A large percentage of the poor depend on farms or microbusinesses for their livelihood (Banerjee and Duflo 2011). Instinctively, they also diversify by working on more than one activity to hedge against being without any income (Banerjee and Duflo 2006). For example, the members of SEWA in India make their living picking rags, making quilts, rolling cigars and farming salt. In big cities, the poor get themselves employed in cleaning houses, cooking and washing dishes.

While all MFIs do not provide livelihood training and skill enhancement, focused approach to providing such training can go a long way in helping the poor to invest in businesses that are not clones of each other. For example, in a big country like India, as the retail market has prospered due to a vibrant middle class, producer companies are increasingly utilizing or even establishing MFIs as intermediaries in the retail supply chains that have the potential to provide a wide variety of livelihoods for the poor.[8] Therefore, while the MFIs in general may not have comparative advantage in providing livelihood training and skills enhancement, they can always strategically collaborate with other public or private institutions to help the poor in finding suitable livelihoods. Vijay Mahajan, founder and Managing Director of BASIX, India has argued that for the success of microfinance as a poverty alleviation tool, it has to transform to livelihood finance (see Chapter 10).

Rates of Return on Microbusinesses

Given the fact that, interest rates charged on microcredit is higher than the rates charged to non-poor by the commercial banks, one wonders whether poor entrepreneurs could still make a profit in such businesses. To start with, such businesses monetize the labour of the microentrepreneur and its employees that are mostly unemployed and unskilled (available surplus labour in the locality) who normally would demand below market wages. As a result one would expect, if there is good demand for the products and services produced by a microbusiness, it could turn profitable.

In the microfinance literature, one finds many of these businesses have high rates of return on capital. For example, a vegetable vendor in India could make 20 per cent return per day if she buys vegetables from the wholesale market and sells the vegetables door-to-door. A cauliflower that may cost ₹3 per head on a farm can fetch ₹10 in the nearby town or city, that is, more than three times the wholesale price. Therefore, vendors may be prepared to pay 5–10 per cent per day to borrow to buy vegetables wholesale to sell retail.

However, these businesses have low volume and are not easily scalable. Besides, as more poor entrepreneurs enter the microbusiness world, some of these 'sweet spots,' eventually disappear. One cannot expect the poor owners of these businesses to overcome poverty quickly. However, in spite of many of the complex issues in starting a microbusiness, one can say that microcredit does provide the poor with ground-level opportunities to discover the latent entrepreneurial abilities that they may harbour, which they could leverage later to get into livelihoods that may be scalable.

In Chapter 11, we describe an RCT-based case study (experiment) in Sri Lanka by Suresh de Mel, David McKenzie and Christopher Woodruff that was designed to answer the question whether small and informal firms (such as the microenterprises) in the developing countries hold the potential for income growth for their owners or do they just represent a source of subsistence income for individuals who cannot find alternative sources of work. Some of the findings of the study were as follows: (1) real return to capital in the microenterprises were 4.6–5.3 per cent per month (i.e., 55–63 per year), much higher than market interest rates; (2) returns varied based on entrepreneurial ability and household wealth, but did not vary with measures of risk aversion or uncertainty and (3) one of the surprising results was that treatment impacts were significantly larger for enterprises owned by males; in fact the researchers found no positive returns for enterprises owned by females.

Later, in trying to rationalize zero per cent return for females in Sri Lanka, David McKenzie in an interview with Tim Ogden (2012) had two important observations: (1) women who were in traditional industries owned by females such as lace-making had the lowest returns and (2) the other reason for low returns can be perhaps attributed to 'intra-household' cooperation. He observed that women who said their husbands supported their business were doing better and there were indications that women did not invest optimally because they feared that, their profits would be captured by others. It is also possible that they did not manage themselves optimally to have enough working capital (see Chapter 11 for a discussion of rates of return on microenterprises owned by women in Ghana).

On Defining Microfinance Institutions

Historically, it was the NGO-based MFIs that spearheaded the microfinance revolution. But today, there are many types of institutions, such as community-based institutions like the SHGs and cooperatives, NBFIs, state-owned banks, rural banks, postal banks, specialized microfinance banks, *downscaled* commercial banks (in the public as well as the private sector) that offer microfinance products and services to the poor. Even consumer lending institutions, especially in Latin America are trying to vie for the microfinance market (Rhyne 2009).

As a result, with so many types of institutional structures in use, it is difficult to define what an MFI is. However, there are several characteristics that are *sine qua non* of MFIs that are summarized below.

- The MFIs provide financial services (credit, savings, insurance, lease finance and MT) to low-income and financially underserved or un-served clients in order that the clients can access these services in a user-friendly manner.
- These institutions have the twin goals of financial sustainability (profitability) and social mission, also referred to as DBL goals.
- Many MFIs are involved in providing non-financial services that complement the delivery of financial services. The non-financial services include such activities as social intermediation, literacy training including financial literacy, livelihood and marketing training, and training in nutrition, sanitation and hygiene.

The DBL goal sets the MFIs apart from large numbers of institutions in the business world that are largely driven by a single bottom line, that is, profitability. While financial return and financial bottom line are easier to define, defining social return and social bottom line is difficult. Considering the importance of the concepts such as 'sustainability' and 'social mission,' to the entire field of microfinance, we digress for a moment to provide broad definitions of these concepts in the following.

By financial 'sustainability,' one implies, '… the ability of a provider to continue and expand its operations without need for further subsidies. It involves two elements: (1) operating revenue (excluding subsidies) is sufficient to cover all financial and administrative costs; and (2) loan delinquency or default does not exceed the levels industry experience has shown to be necessary to avoid eventual collapse of repayment discipline among clients.'[9]

As far as the definition of 'social mission' is concerned, we define it below in the context of 'social performance management.' The Social Performance Task Force (SPTF) defines social performance management to consist of the following (SPTF 2012):

Define and Monitor Social Goals
Ensure Board, Management and Employee Commitment to Social Goals

Treat Clients Responsibly
Design Products, Services, Delivery Models and Channels that Meet Clients'
Needs and Preferences
Treat Employees Responsibly
Balance Financial and Social Performance

Without going into describing each of the above topics, we will briefly discuss about 'social mission.' Interested reader is encouraged to refer to a discussion of these topics in the reference provided above.

In the section 'Define and Monitor Social Goals,' SPTF defines 'social mission' as follows.

> Social mission: the institution's social purpose, which serves the broader purpose of increasing access to financial services for vulnerable or excluded target groups and creating benefits for these clients.

In the section, under 'Essential Practices,' SPTF defines five other items, besides 'social mission.' These are 'target clients,' 'social goals,' 'social indicators,' 'social targets' and 'how to achieve targets,' which frame how an MFI should define and monitor social goals.

As an example, if poverty reduction is one of the social goals, then the institution has to monitor poverty levels of its clients using poverty assessment tools such as per capita household expenditure, food security survey, participatory wealth ranking and other such tools. Needless to say based on its social mission, an MFI would have several social goals, social targets and approaches as to how to achieve these targets and the need for monitoring of the associated social indicators to find out if social targets have been reached or not.

Social performance management, like financial performance management, is one of the cornerstones of management of an MFI. However, the scope of this chapter does not allow an in-depth discussion of this topic.

Why the Poorest Cannot Normally Access Microcredit?

The original intent of microfinance was to serve all the poor irrespective of how poor they are. However, over the years, the MFIs have slowly drifted away from serving the poorest for a variety of reasons. Some of the obvious reasons why the poorest and the extreme poor cannot access microcredit are: (1) their incomes are erratic, as a result they normally cannot meet regular repayment requirements of micro-loans and (2) they usually do not have the savings cushion to meet the initial payments on these loans. Because most of these loans practically have no grace period, the repayment of principal and interest start just after one or two weeks after loan has been disbursed. This puts a heavy burden on the poorest clients such as the destitute and extreme poor, who are not economically active.

Just to illustrate further, SHGs in India require that its clients join savings programmes where they have to prove that they are able to save regularly for a period of six months before they are eligible to take out loans. In such programmes, a weekly savings of ₹20 (less than 50 cents in US dollars) for each client may sound very small, but for a destitute (or even for an extreme poor) whose income may be erratic, making regular weekly payments for six months may not be all that easy. What all this pertain to is that without the wherewithal to save, most of the poorest around the world normally find it difficult to access microfinance.

However, given the fact that reaching out to the poorest is one of the most important social missions of an MFI, many MFIs decide to reach out to the poorest through capacity building. However, capacity build-ing requires deploying financial resources that most MFIs are not fully compensated for. As a result, MFIs in general endeavour to obtain finan-cial resources for capacity building from a variety of sources that include the government, donors and charitable foundations and even the general public. Many large profitable MFIs have the capacity to deploy a part of their profit for capacity building. However, many MFIs, particularly the smaller ones that have not achieved sustainability find it difficult to deploy own resources for capacity building.

The need for capacity building arises because the poorest and the extreme poor who are not economically active are normally not capa-ble of meeting their basic requirements with regard to food (in terms of caloric intake), shelter and health care (Hirschland 2005). As a result, many microfinance practitioners believe that it is appropriate for the government, donors and charitable foundations to provide assistance in these areas. In this connection, the following quote from Marguerite S. Robinson (2001, 20) is appropriate:

> The poorest of the poor should not be the responsibility of the financial sector. The food, employment, and other basic requirements needed to overcome desperate poverty are appropriately financed by government

and donor subsidies and grants. These tools are properly the responsibility of ministries of health, labour, social welfare, and others, as well as donor agencies and private charities.

In this context, it is important to note that TUP programme of BRAC in Bangladesh has made major contributions in building capacity such that extreme poor could become eligible for borrowing from MFIs. We will briefly discuss about TUP programme at BRAC later in this chapter.

On Commercialization of MFIs: Sustainability, Outreach and 'Mission Drift'

We have already discussed briefly in Chapter 1 about commercialization of NGO-based MFIs. The scope of the book does not allow for a broader discussion of some of the complex set of issues related to transformation of NGO-based MFIs to attain commercial status.

Just to reiterate, two important points were made in Chapter 1 about commercialization. First of all, commercialization has been responsible for helping to diversify the funding base, which the MFIs have been able to leverage to expand lending to the poor. As a result, MFIs around the world expanded at a rapid clip up until 2007–08. However, there have been downsides to commercialization, which include among other things, too much emphasis on rapid growth and profitability by some of the MFIs, which led to undesirable consequences such as mission drift. Mission drift made it difficult for these MFIs to achieve their respective social mission goals. In some cases, when mission drift was taken too far without regard for absorptive capacity of poor clients (who are predominantly vulnerable women), it led to over-indebtedness and high delinquency rates among the clients. And in some cases, it went so far as to undermine the microfinance sector in the country (see Chapter 11).

A Brief Introduction to SHGs

In delivering microfinance to the poor, an innovative institutional model that has been widely adopted in India goes under the name of SHGs. SHGs are informal associations consisting of 10–20 women (average size about 14) who normally meet once a month to save small amounts of money in the range of ₹10 to ₹50 (from about 20 cents to about US $1). The groups are usually formed with the support of NGOs, Self-Help Promoting Agencies (SHPAs), public as well as commercial financial institutions such as the commercial banks, MFIs (that not only utilize Grameen style joint-liability groups but also SHGs) and charitable organizations. This section highlights some of the important aspects of SHGs (Ghate 2007).

SHGs are formed through self-selection. Members of an SHG start saving regularly and lending small amounts of money from their savings by charging interest. The interest so earned is ploughed back into the group funds. The groups maintain their group records and learn to manage their respective groups. For all practical purposes, SHGs can be viewed as microbanks.

One of the innovative aspects of the SHG approach is the bank-linkage programme under which the SHGs that have performed satisfactorily in group-based savings and lending, and have maintained proper records for a period of six months, become eligible to be linked with a banking institution.

The linkage programme puts a wide range of financial services at the disposal of the group members. Under this arrangement, an SHG becomes the entity that acts as the intermediary between the bank and the group members. For example, it can borrow from the linked bank and lend the funds within the group. In contrast, under the solidarity group model (joint-liability groups), the MFI tracks how each member in the group is performing although the group members collectively are responsible for ensuring timely debt service payments by its members.

How much a group can borrow from the bank depends on its own funds, which is largely built from the savings of the group members (and interest earned on such savings) and retained earnings from the lending activities within the group. And how much a group can lend depends on the group's own funds and how much it can borrow from the linked bank. One of the major expenses of an SHG is the interest payments on its borrowings from the linked bank.

Two important aspects of the model: (1) savings are built into the system from the beginning (in fact the borrowers have to save before they could borrow), and (2) the members of the SHG are entrusted in managing the SHG. There are several other advantages of the SHG Bank-Linkage

Programme model. For example, over-lending to SHG members are constrained because overall borrowing from the linked bank to lend to the members is a multiple of savings by the group. If savings does not grow, lending is constrained. Indirectly this stipulation is a means test with regards to the capacity of the SHG members to absorb more lending. However, it is also important to note that as time progresses, an SHG that has a good performance record can expect to borrow higher multiples of its own funds (similar to progressive lending) from the linked bank. Another important feature of SHG lending that stands out includes longer microloan maturities (about 2.5 years). As a result, loan cycles are longer. Given the fact that access to microcredit is not enough, one of the clear advantages of the SHG programme has to do with the fact that its members could access a range of livelihood and empowerment services that goes well beyond the delivery of financial services to the poor. The reach (in terms of breadth as well as depth) of the SHG model with the associated Bank-Linkage Programme is truly enormous. One report puts estimates of SHGs and their membership to be 4.5 million and 58 million, respectively.[10] Since the report was published in 2010, one would expect current estimates to be higher.

The SHGs suffer from the disadvantage that it expects its members to take management responsibility of the group too soon. For example, for many MFIs, six months of training in book-keeping may not be enough. What is more, while the savings by the SHG members with the linked bank has been a success, it has many deficiencies. For example, the savings products offered under the MFI model (such as Grameen II—see Chapter 6) are more flexible and more versatile. Moreover, because lending to SHGs is a multiple of their savings, lending cannot grow faster unless savings grow faster and building up savings through thrift is difficult. What is more, because maturities are longer and loan cycles are longer, a potential borrower of the group has to wait until the last member has paid back her loan before they can get repeat loans. Some of these stipulations constrain rapid expansion of lending by the SHGs, which may be a blessing in disguise.

The SHG model has been largely confined to India. For a more in-depth discussion of the differences between SHG and MFI models, the reader is referred to *Indian Microfinance: The Challenges of Rapid*

Growth by Prabhu Ghate (2007). There appears to be a paucity of impact evaluations of the SHG programmes with regard to their sustainability and impact on the borrowers.

BRAC: Targeting the Ultra Poor (TUP)

Prior to the TUP programme, BRAC started its Income Generation for Vulnerable Group Development (IGVGD) programme in 1985 to provide training to vulnerable women to embark on income generation activities (Smillie 2009). The programme also provided training in health care and human rights. During the training period, the trainees were paid with food supplied under the World Food Programme.

After 15 years, that is, by 2000, the IGVGD programme had already served 1.2 million households (Armendáriz and Morduch 2010). Based on an evaluation of the IGVGD programme, BRAC initiated TUP programme in 2002. The programme was built on the lessons learnt from the IGVGD programme. First of all, TUP programme used strict eligibility requirements to target the poor (marginalized women) who needed such assistance. One of the important aspects of the programme is that besides providing health, education (financial literacy), social support and other assistance, BRAC also makes asset transfers in the form of livestock that can generate income for the ultra poor. After remaining in the programme for a period of two years, many of the ultra poor become eligible to access DABI microfinance programme (Whiting 2009). Graduates of the TUP programme not only access microcredit, they also save.

An evaluation of the first phase (2002–06) of the programme (Das and Shams 2011) shows that livelihoods of the participating households in the TUP programme improved 'remarkably.' However, some of the shortcomings of the programme included adoption of evaluation designs that were non-experimental in nature. Based on an evaluation of the second phase of the programme (using RCT approach—for a description of RCT, see Chapter 11), some of the findings that emerged include (1) participating households 'multiplied their asset base from the one initially transferred,' and (2) generated income that reduced their dependency on such activities as working as house maids and begging.

Other improvements that were brought about by participating in the programme included reduction of vulnerability in terms of food security and increased awareness with regard to social and legal issues. However, programme did not make visible impact on education in the short run. This could be because the TUP programme did not directly provide any support for education.

In a nutshell, over the last two decades, BRAC has helped 2.2 million ultra poor families earn income though a value chain approach, which also used safety net food aid (Davis 2012). The programme with an expenditure of $150 per person over a two-year period has helped high percentage of its initial participants (75–98 per cent) to join the 'bottom rung' of the economic ladder. As far as cost benefit of BRAC's TUP programme is concerned, it has been estimated that the benefits are over $5 for every $1 invested (Davis 2012).

In a recent study of BRAC's TUP programme, 'Can basic entrepreneurship transform the economic lives of the poor?' (Bandiera et al. 2012), it was found that participants in the programme after four years registered 92 per cent more time in self-employment, 26 per cent decrease in hours devoted to wage labour, 15 per cent increase in days of work per year, 26 per cent decrease in hours of work per day and 15 per cent increase income per hour of work. What is more, productive asset ownership in the household went up, which showed share of households with livestock went up by 79 per cent and share of households with land increased by 38 per cent. Participation in the TUP programme increased income by 33 per cent after two years and by 38 per cent after four years. Programme also increases consumption by 8 per cent after two years and by 15 per cent after four years. However, consumption gains were uneven. While nobody loses by participating in the programme, income gains were uneven.

Some of the important lessons of the programme were as follows: the programme was quite successful in transforming the occupational choices of the targeted poor, there was a structural change from wage labour to small businesses, which was largely possible because of 'massive assets transfer and intensive training,' and there was change in occupational choice accompanied by 'increase in income, expenditure and food security.' One important lessons of the study was that constraints of capital and skills drive occupational choices of poor women in Bangladesh.

Conclusion

The realization of the fact that formal access to 'small value' loans, that is, microcredit (microloans) on a mass scale can make a big difference in the lives of the poor was one of the seminal ideas in making the microfinance revolution a reality. The push to deliver microcredit on a mass scale has shown how product and institutional design goes to the heart of providing poor-friendly financial services to the poor. If there is at least one lesson that one can take away from the evolution of microcredit industry is that innovative product and institutional design has to be at the forefront of delivering other financial products such as savings, insurance and lease finance to the poor.

While credit is a powerful tool that could help the poor in fighting poverty, it has to be used judiciously and in a balanced manner along with other financial tools such as microsavings and microinsurance. This is particularly true in the context of accumulating evidence that benefits of microcredit could be more modest in comparison to the initial expectations. Therefore, it would be appropriate to be on guard against over-indebtedness of the poor, which could create financial risk that poor families with practically limited backstop may not be able to cope. As the lessons from of TUP programmes show, the poor are constrained by lack of capital and skills. Besides, the poor need training in financial literacy and marketing to improve their chances in fighting poverty more effectively.

Notes

1. Muhammad Yunus with Karl Weber. 2007. *Creating a World Without Poverty: Social Business and the Future of Capitalism*, p. 49. New York: Public Affairs.
2. 'The Nobel Peace Prize for 2006,' Press Release, Oslo, 13 October 2006. Available online at http://www.nobelprize.org/nobel_prize/peace/laureates/2006/press_html (downloaded on 28 November 2012).
3. 'BRAC-FAQ,' Available online at http://www.brac.net/content/faq-0 (downloaded on 2 December 2012).
4. 'BRAC AT A GLANCE,' Issue: June 2012. Available online at http://www.brac.net/content/stay-informed-brac-glance (downloaded on 1 December 2012).

5. 'What is Microfinance?' Available online at www.microfinancegateway. org/p/site/m/template.rc/1.26.12263/#12 (downloaded on 29 November 2012).

6. 'Microfinance Frequently Asked Questions,' CGAP. Available online at http://www.cgap.org/about/faq (downloaded on 29 November 2012).

7. 'What is Microfinance?', Microfinance Information eXchange (MIX), Available online at http://www.themix.org/about/microfinance (downloaded on 8 December 2012).

8. *India Top 50 Microfinance Institutions*, CRISIL Ratings, October 2009.

9. CGAP. 2006. 'Good Practice Guidelines for Funders of Microfinance,' p. 36. 2nd ed., October.

10. CGAP. 2010. 'Andhra Pradesh 2010: Global Implications of the Crisis in Indian Microfinance.' Focus Note No. 67, Washington, DC: CGAP. November.

5

Microcredit: Anatomy of an Instrument That Revolutionized Lending

Money is the sixth sense without which you cannot make complete use of the other five.

W. Somerset Maugham

Give credit where credit is due.

Anonymous

If there is one instrument that has revolutionized the delivery of financial services to the poor, it has to be microcredit. This chapter explores some of the important aspects of microcredit that has been instrumental in its expansion around the world. By and large, during the last 15 years, this expansion has been sustained at a rapid pace, while off late on the aftermath of the 2007–08 worldwide financial crisis, growth rate has moderated. Even then, the fact that as of 31 December 2010, microcredit was accessed by about 200 million poor clients, of which about 74 per cent were poor women and about 67 per cent constituted poorest clients, does portray a picture of microcredit that is valued by the poor.

Many developmental institutions around the world find it difficult to be sustainable, including the MFIs. However, as we noted in Chapter 4, Richard Rosenberg (2010) in his paper *Does Microcredit Really Help*

Poor People? notes that among microfinance providers reporting to MIX market, profitable MFIs that need no further subsidies, accounted for about 71 per cent of all the clients. And MFIs that were 'close to profitability' accounted for another 22 per cent. These are important milestones for an industry that largely lends to clients who are not considered creditworthy. Therefore, it begs the question, what are some of the important aspects of microcredit that helps MFIs to be sustainable (profitable).

Over the last 35 years of its existence, the structure of microcredit as a financial tool has gone through many refinements based on experience gained on the ground. A case in point is the emergence of Grameen II model at Grameen Bank that replaced the original Grameen I model that was inflexible as a lending tool for the poor. As we shall discuss, Grameen II is a more flexible model that is designed to accommodate a borrower experiencing financial hardship. The model incorporates savings at an intrinsic level to bring about an improved balance between borrowing and savings activities of poor households. All in all, this chapter provides glimpses into the design of microcredit, including its pricing.

Group Lending: Innovation That Made Microcredit Viable on the Ground

Lack of ability to post collateral has been one of the major bottlenecks in lending to the poor. The traditional lending models rely on collateral to secure funds being lent. Unless a borrower has collateral and good credit history, accessing credit is rather difficult from formal lending institutions. The group lending approach that used non-traditional collaterals as 'collateral substitutes' did bring about a revolution in lending to the poor. As noted in Chapter 4, although institutions like the Grameen Bank that pioneered group lending have already moved away from group lending (and joint-liability contracts) approach; however, it is still used widely around the world to lend to the poor.

Under the joint-liability contract, the group is collectively responsible for repayment of debt service by its group members. By relying on group-based lending, the MFIs transfer substantial monitoring of their clients in terms of debt service payments to group members. Groups are also required to attend weekly group meetings and repay their loans in these meetings. Group-based lending approach evolved at the Grameen Bank through a trial and error[1] process (Dowla and Barua 2006).

How the Groups Work?

Under Grameen Bank's Classical Grameen Model (also called Grameen I model), each group consists of five members. The group members usually come from similar socio-economic backgrounds. Large groups are avoided because it is difficult for them to be homogenous. Groups that are not homogenous may have members who sometimes dominate the group because of their social status or affluence. Under these circumstances, group cohesion could break down. This can lead to dysfunctional groups. By keeping groups small and homogenous, one could avoid such situations.

Smaller and homogenous groups in general lead to higher-quality group-based guarantee. Higher-quality groups tend to ensure higher-quality social capital. Therefore, smaller homogenous groups are preferable than larger groups where the MFIs might have to resort to sanctions to improving a group's performance. By resorting to sanctions, the clients as well as the MFIs suffer. For example, when sanctions are imposed, the group may ostracize a group member who was bailed out by them. Under these circumstances, the MFIs suffer because sanctions spread negativity. However, the MFIs do resort to sanctions to have teeth in sanctions and to improve timely repayment of loans.

Each group elects a chairperson and a secretary for the smooth functioning of the group. Chairperson of the group collects debt service payments from the members and hands over the collection to the MFI representative in the group meetings that take place every week. Members of every group go through training to understand the rules and regulations of the MFI for its smooth functioning.

Loans are not given to all the members of the group at the same time. In a five-member group, loans are given initially to two members. Depending on their performance, two more members become eligible for receiving loans. The head of the group becomes eligible for a loan at the end. Timely debt service payments by a borrower make her eligible for larger loans depending on how other members in the group are performing. Members of the group are expected to monitor each other to make sure debt service payments take place on a timely fashion. Increasing there is movement towards lending without staggering as to who should receive a loan next in the group.

Groups meet regularly—on a weekly or biweekly basis to coincide with the periodic payments that the clients make to the MFI. It is compulsory for the group members to attend weekly or biweekly meetings. In case of the Grameen Bank, six to eight groups are federated into a centre that holds weekly meetings (Dowla and Barua 2006). Such meetings take place in the communities where group members live. As a result, the MFIs come to the clients rather than clients visiting the institutions. This approach helps to save time and money for the clients. But at the same time, the MFIs also save by pooling financial transactions. Just to illustrate, one of the important purposes of the meetings is to collect debt service, deposits for voluntary savings (note: not every MFI around the world offer savings facilities to their clients), group fund contributions and insurance premium payments. The meetings are also used to discuss individual borrower problems with regard to the utilization of loans. Addressing lending issues in the company of clients has great deal of value for the bank and the clients collectively. Through the group meetings, the MFIs also address major issues of lending and find out if there are any emerging issues.

Social and cultural aspects of being poor are pervasive. As a result, it requires diligent efforts at the grass-root level to change the mindset of the poor to abandon practices that stand in the way of their economic development. Group meetings are a powerful vehicle to bring about changes to the poor people's mindset through discussions with regard to the advantages and disadvantages of social and cultural practices. This can in turn help them make changes to their lifestyle, which could help them in fighting poverty.

Many MFIs use group meetings as a platform to educate the clients and disseminate information regarding literacy, including financial illiteracy, health care, nutrition, sanitation, hygiene, family planning, children's education, agriculture, horticulture, livelihood opportunities and training, marketing, employment opportunities and anything that would benefit their clients. However, it is difficult to measure benefits of group meetings in general. Many critics believe, group meetings are a waste of time and money for the poor.

Group lending helps to contain operating cost of an MFI. One of the advantages of group lending is that it allows for economies of scale. For example, if an MFI staff serves eight groups, where each group consists of five clients, then the staff can take care of 40 clients in one meeting. This is a tremendous cost-saving for an MFI that helps it to reduce transaction cost and in the process save on administrative expenses. Most importantly, because the group members help in debt collection process, and because the joint-liability contracts minimize credit risk exposure of the MFIs, it helps in lowering delinquency rates for the MFIs. As a result, provisioning rate for the MFI could be potentially reduced. That has the direct benefit of lowering the 'interest spread' used in determining lending rate on micro-loans (see 'Microloan Lending Rates: An Introduction').

Group Lending May Not Be Always Effective[2]

For a variety of reasons, group lending may not be as effective as one would like it to be (Armendáriz and Morduch 2010). For example, in an urban setting where the urban poor may come from various regions of a country there may not be the same degree of social cohesiveness as one would find in a rural setting. They may lack same social and cultural background. As a result, group members in urban areas may not know each other well to feel comfortable to join a group. Under these circumstances, group members may not have the same level of commitment behind joint-liability contract.

We have already alluded to pitfalls of over-lending (which can arise to protect market share and achieving higher levels of profitability). Over-lending could reduce group lending ineffective because debt burdens of some of the group members could be prohibitively high (see Chapter 11). Without credit bureaus, group members could borrow from money-lenders and other MFIs without the knowledge of other group members. As MFIs' exposure to group members increase, there is a point at which group members may be reluctant to provide joint-liability cover to bail out MFIs from their insensitivity to contain credit risk without consideration for delicate social contract entailed in group lending.

Group sanctions can be harsh on vulnerable poor women. Psychological pressure of getting isolated because of sanctions can have adverse consequences. As a result, group sanctions give rise to differences of opinion and strained relationships among the group members. Imposing group sanctions can be difficult for a group leader. That is one of the reasons why members of a group may be reluctant to become group leaders because they may end up being unpopular in the group and even in the community.

Increasingly, MFI clients prefer borrowing from MFIs independently without the comfort of security provided by joint-liability contracts. Under Grameen II, Grameen Bank has moved away from joint-liability contract, which was at the heart of group lending. Later in the chapter, we will briefly discuss about Grameen II model and how it is different from Classical Grameen model.

Flexible Repayment Terms: Weekly and Biweekly Repayments[3]

One of the important innovations that have helped microloan borrowers to access and repay these loans with ease has to be weekly or biweekly repayments that keep repayments in each period relatively small and in the process make it easier for the MFI clients to meet their repayment needs with ease.

Loans from development banks normally offer monthly repayment terms with a grace period during which no principal is paid (only interest is paid). After the grace period, the debt service to the lender includes both principal and interest. During the grace period, it is expected that the enterprise reaches its full potential and after the grace period it would be in a better position to meet its debt service needs, which include principal and interest.

Frequent repayments, for example weekly repayments for a loan would increase repayments from 12 repayments (as in the case of monthly repayments) to 50 repayments a year, as is the case for most microloans. As a result, for an MFI say with 100,000 active borrowers, the number of repayments in one year would go up from 1.2 million repayments (if repayments are every month) to 5 million. With 5.0 million repayments, the complexities of dealing with so many repayments go up on a commensurate basis. However, the MFIs by relying on group lending (group disbursement, group collection and other transactions) are in a better position to deal with such a scenario.

For poorer borrowers, weekly repayment terms are normally offered. When repayments are on a biweekly or monthly basis, the repayments are larger and for poorer borrowers it would entail saving from daily earnings before making a larger repayment. However, building savings bit by bit have proven difficult for poorer households. This is because most poor households are constantly inundated with gaps that arise between their income and consumption needs. As a result, they usually borrow informally to bridge such gaps. Under these circumstances, accumulating cash to make lumpy payments would require a degree of discipline that many poor households may lack. Besides, having extra cash around the house may be easily spent on things over which the poor may not have a lot of control. What is more, extra cash around a household in poor communities could encourage kith and kin to lay claim on such cash. Given the fact that poor do not have access to secure voluntary savings, cash can even be stolen from the house. There is evidence of arrears on microloans being shot up when an MFI switched from weekly repayments to biweekly repayments.[4] All in all, given the fact the discipline and enabling environment required for saving through thrift is difficult, making repayments in smaller doses enables the poor to comply with repayment schedule.

Making repayments more frequently helps the MFIs to identify borrowers who are having difficulty with making repayments. That in turn helps the MFIs to work with their clients to smooth out repayment difficulties. In fact, to reduce repayment difficulties, many MFIs collect repayments at the source when their clients get paid. All in all, frequent repayments ensure more contacts with borrowers and opportunities to work with the borrower to mitigate payment difficulties. However, in a recent study, about which we are going to discuss in the following paragraphs, researchers have found that repayment flexibility could lead to reduction in financial stress and other related benefits for poor households.

Given the fact that financial stress could lead to health problems for a borrower, if in order to relieve financial stress policies seek to reduce debt levels, such policies could worsen the economic well-being of poor families. In a field experiment, Field et al. (2012) worked with microfinance clients in India to find out if repayment flexibility on debt contracts could reduce such stress. In the experiment, microfinance clients were randomly assigned monthly or weekly instalment schedule. Cellphones were used to gather survey data on income, expenditure and financial stress every 48 hours over 7 weeks. It was found out that clients repaying on a monthly basis were 51 per cent less likely to report feeling 'worried, tense or anxious' about repaying, in comparison to the clients repaying on a weekly basis. What is more, 54 per cent of the clients making repayments on a monthly basis reported feeling confident about repaying and reported spending less time thinking about their loan in comparison to clients making repayments on a weekly basis. Last but not the least, monthly clients reported higher business investment and income, which implied, flexibility in repayment encouraged them to invest their loans more profitably, helping to reduce financial stress. Based on these results, the authors observe that 'holding availability of credit constant, changing the terms of contract can significantly alter these stress measures.' However, as noted earlier, lengthening repayment interval from weekly to monthly could increase delinquency because pooling cash at home before repaying the MFI could entail risk.

The following example also shows that the need for flexibility in lending terms could help the borrowers to suit the loan for their own need. Dean Karlan and Jacob Appel (2012) in their book *More than Good Intentions* discuss about Erlyn, owner of a '*sari sari*' store (this-and-that store—convenient store) in the Philippines who decided not to borrow from MFIs because the loan terms were not suitable for her. In her case, because of her small floor space she needed to re-stock her store every two months. But microfinance loans in her neighbourhood were extended for six months. That implied she would have to take a larger loan without being able to use the entire loan. Her solution was a local moneylender who was prepared to come to her store and lend her for either 45- or 60-day period. The moneylender also came to her store to collect repayment. Moneylender's interest rates were higher than non-profit lenders, but Erlyn could tailor her loan size and maturity according to her need.

Lack of Grace Period

It appears odd that the poor are not provided with grace period on microloans. In the event a microloan has a grace period, it would allow only interest payment to the MFI during the grace period and after the grace period payment of both principal and interest until the loan matures.

In rationalizing lack of grace period for microloans, it is important to note that microloans usually have short maturities (three months to three years). The loans can be viewed as consumer loans, which usually lack grace period. Initially microcredit was offered for working capital needs of microenterprises, although today microloans can be extended for a variety of purposes, such as mortgages, home improvement, education, emergency and the like. For example, poor people with stable income flows would like to have access to consumer loans, while a financially constrained borrower could benefit from an emergency loan for health emergencies.

Microloans are usually extended without collateral. The loans are based on the payment capacity of the household and usually meant for working capital needs of an existing microbusiness. In extending microloans, ideally the MFI needs to ascertain that the borrower has the capacity to meet debt service requirements.

Considering financial hardships a poor family undergoes, the inclination would be to provide grace period during which the microenterprise could strengthen its business. After the grace period, the business would be in a surer footing to meet debt service payments. However, such a repayment structure could pose risk for poor households because they may not be disciplined enough to build up savings during the grace period to make relatively larger debt service payments once the grace period is over.

Repeat Loans: Progressive Lending[5]

'Progressive lending' implicitly promises borrowers in good standing to keep on receiving progressively larger loans if they are current on their payments to the MFI. By promising larger loans, the MFIs show to the borrowers their willingness to have a long-term relationship with the client and be a partner in their prosperity. Moreover, such an understanding, even if implicit, empowers the borrowers to plan ahead for expanding their businesses. The promise of larger loans provides incentives for the borrowers to be current on the present loan.

It is important to note that progressive lending allows the MFIs to start out with a small loan and see if the borrower is able to repay the loan in time. Therefore, the lender can test the waters before expanding lending to the borrower. The approach not only provides incentives to the borrower to be current on her payments, it caps the risks of lending to poor borrowers who post no collateral. Most importantly, the lenders can elicit timely payment by borrowers by promising larger loans that extinguish their existing debt and lend more funds (new money) to expand their enterprises. Under such lending if the borrower defaults, she loses out on a larger loan. In other words, the opportunity cost of defaulting is higher and hence discourages the borrower to default (Armendáriz and Morduch 2010). However, under progressive lending, there may be the downside risk that the borrowers may become too dependent on borrowing without building savings (reserves) for the household or the business.

What progressive lending policy could indirectly imply is that future loans could not be guaranteed if the borrower becomes delinquent on an existing loan. The fear of losing access to credit becomes an incentive for the borrower to make timely repayments. The MFIs also benefit from such an arrangement because they are able to retain a good borrower, which could maintain or even enhance microloan portfolio quality. Besides, by extending a larger loan helps to increase the average loan size of the portfolio. This in turn could help in lowering administrative expenses. In other words, larger loans entail economies of scale. Economies of scale help the MFIs to attain sustainability (profitability).

Women as Microfinance Clients

Based on the 'State of the Microcredit Summit Campaign Report 2012,' as of 31 December 2010, 3,652 MFIs reported that they served about 205 million poor clients around the world, of which about 153 million were female clients (Maes and Reed 2012). This implies, female clients constituted about 74 per cent of the total. Of the 205 million clients, about 138 million were among the poorest when they took their first loans, that is, the poorest clients constituted about 67 per cent of the total. Of these poorest clients, about 113 million were women, constituting about 82 per cent of the poorest clients. It is also important to note that at the end of October 2011, total membership of the Grameen Bank stood at about

8.35 million of which about 8 million were women, that is, about 96 per cent of the total membership was women (see Chapter 4).

One of the important reasons why women are attracted to borrow from the MFIs has to do with the fact that traditionally women in the developing countries did not have access to credit because borrowing required collateral and it was mostly men as heads of households who owned the assets. As a result, women could not pledge household assets as collateral. When the MFIs started lending without traditional collateral, it was a game-changer. Such lending made it possible for the poor women to access credit.

Given the fact that women in the developing countries network in a community and also work in groups, the concept of group guarantee was amenable to them. As a result, most MFIs around the world find women as suitable candidates for lending. No wonder that women constitute the largest percentage (about 74 per cent) of microfinance clientele around the world. This clearly shows there was a pent up demand for access to credit by poor women, which was not discovered prior to the advent of microcredit.

There are other reasons why MFIs have predominantly female clients. These include (1) women have better payment record in comparison to male borrowers as shown by several studies and (2) borrowing by women contributes more towards non-food and food expenditures in the family. Besides, reduction in fertility rate and illiteracy among women in the developing countries has also been helped by access to microfinance.[6]

Given the fact that lending to women overall has a positive impact on the household, housing loans by the Grameen Bank is exclusively given to women.[7] And in extending the loan, it is ensured that the land on which the house is built has to be in the name of the women in order that she could not be evicted from the house. Such arrangements go to the root of women empowerment. All in all, extension of microcredit predominantly to women assumes that such lending contributes to the DBL goal of sustainability and social value creation.

Access to microlending has been instrumental in providing a formal platform for the poor women to network with each other in a forum that deals with household and business finances and other related issues. It also deals with other practical matters such as sanitation, hygiene, nutrition, health care, education, livelihood and how to find market for their products and services. In the past, poor women in the developing countries, very rarely, if ever, devoted their time to focused discussions on bottom-line issues about their livelihood and family matters. Given the fact that the women look after their family, such discussion in the weekly meetings serves their self-interest well.

The weekly meetings also provide a forum to learn from and share information with each other. The solidarity they build up through networking is social capital at work. They feel empowered because they have an improved understanding of the outside world. By belonging to an MFI and the solidarity group, they develop a separate identity other than the identity traditional societies in developing countries bestow on them.

In the developing countries, poor women are normally less skilled. As a result, they do not have many outside opportunities to work. With access to microloans, they try to generate income from investing their time and money in traditional activities (Armendáriz and Morduch 2010). Besides running their microbusinesses, they also multitask by taking care of the children and the elderly, cooking for the family, which can be rather labour intensive. They are also expected to attend to other household chores, including religious and cultural activities and weekly MFI meetings. In other words, because the businesses require low skill they can attend to other critical activities in the household such as taking care of the children, elderly and the sick, and cooking and other household chores. As a result, income from such businesses remains rather minimal.

We discuss in Chapters 4 and 11 about low returns from women-owned microbusinesses. The discussions in Chapter 11 are based on a RCT study of microenterprises in Sri Lanka by de Mel et al. (2008). The study makes the point that low return of women-owned microenterprises could be explained by the fact that because of their low skill level, women tend to invest in activities such as sewing, lace making, fabric painting, silk flowers, jewellery making and the like. Because such businesses need low skill level and low levels of capital, other women also crowd out such businesses. Consequently, margins are squeezed, resulting in low levels of profitability for the microbusinesses. Besides, because the women are expected to multitask, they are less focused on their businesses and their activities are not optimized, which contributes to low profitability of these businesses. In spite of low profitability, such businesses allow for income diversification, which tends to cushion household income volatility unless the business runs into losses.

In the following text, we provide evidence as to how access to microfinance (microcredit and other non-financial complementary services that go with it), empowered women, brought prestige to them as individuals and helped them to act in their self-interest, which made infanticide of baby girls a thing of the past in Usilampatti in Tamil Nadu, India.

'A Fight to Save Baby Girls in India:' How Improved Economic Prospects for Women by Accessing Microfinance Brought Recognition to Their Economic Status and Helped to Save Baby Girls

What follows is based on the following special report, *A Fight to Save Baby Girls in India*, by Kamala Thiagarajan (2013), which was published in the New York Times of 7 March 2013. It is about Usilampatti in the state of Tamil Nadu in India, home to about 85,000 people. Based on the report, the region in the 1980s was ill-famed for 'gendercide' (infanticide of mostly baby girls) and today because of access to microcredit and complementary services from SHGs, the economic prospects for women has improved considerably and along with it infanticide of baby girls in the region has become a thing of the past.

It was through the efforts of Valli Annamalai, head of the Mother and Child Welfare Project (an initiative of the Indian Council for Child Welfare—an NGO) whose insights and dedication for the project was instrumental in abolishing gendercide in the region. She rightly believed that girls were considered liabilities in households and the only way to stop 'gendercide' was to improve the economic prospects for women.

The magnitude of the problem can be gleaned from the fact that based on statistics, in 1990 there were about 200 infant deaths in the region (all were girls), which were not accounted for (Thiagarajan 2013). The way Valli Annamalai initially approached the problem was to provide care for the children such that the women could return to work—mostly to work in the fields, which could ensure they can be a source of income for the family.

At one point, there were 14 child care centres caring for about 350 children. When the government started providing for child care, Ms. Annamalai focused her attention to protect newborn baby girls (first daughters were usually safe, but subsequent daughters were under threat). She registered every pregnancy to monitor whether it is a baby girl or a boy. They also sought allies in the hamlets to monitor pregnancies. Through such allies, they were able to save baby girls and sent them for adoption. She also counselled parents to keep their daughters. But at the same time, she made arrangements for adoption. During the period from 1991 to 1999, 146 girls were dropped off at the centre for adoption.

However, major changes to the situation in the Usilampatti area was brought about by the presence of 300 SHGs (see Chapter 4), each of which consists of 20–25 members. As a result, group members were able to access microloans. P. Arul Jyothi, age 43 years, one of the members of an SHG, who was married as a teenager, had eight stillborn children and her husband abandoned her. She was depressed and bedridden. She joined an SHG and today leads the SHG. She took five loans from the SHG and has repaid the loans. She invested the loans in selling incense and firewood.

The story of Kalaiselvi Pethusamy, age 45 year, is rather unique. She joined one of the SHGs in 2005. She owned a piece of good agricultural land but did not have the knowledge or the skills needed for agriculture. Over a three-year period, she received training in 'cattle rearing, soil testing, horticulture and floriculture.' She was also sent to observe a successful poultry and cattle farm in Tamil Nadu. She also learned about 'how to irrigate barren, drought-prone land.' From her SHG, she was able to borrow ₹50,000 (about $1,000 assuming an exchange rate of $1 equivalent to ₹50). She invested the sum in five goats. Today, she owns 20 goats. Her land has expanded from 1 to 7 acres. She is repaying the last of her loans of ₹150,000 (about $3,000). A major source of her income comes from selling cow and goat milk and raising poultry. She was invited to a radio station to talk about her success.

As Ms. Thiagarajan notes in the report, according to Ms. Annamalai, since 2001, no baby has been killed or abandoned in the region. Mockapillai, age 47 years, one of the construction workers in the region, who has one daughter and two granddaughters, puts it rather succinctly by comparing the past and the present: "We used to think that if we kill a female baby, we will cry only for a day, if the baby were to survive we would cry all our lives. But now with so many women and girls educated, working and earning well, our attitude has completely changed." For example, Ms. Thiagarajan reports that 16 young girls from the region were trained as nurses and 19 were trained in garments design and stitching during the last year. All in all, the report is a testament to the fact that microcredit along with complementary financial instruments and services has the power to improve economic prospects for the poor that can have salutary implications for the poor and the society at large.

An Overview of Microloan Products

All microcredit products are not the same. Two microcredit products might look almost the same, but slight variations how they have been designed and priced, how they are being delivered, and the underlying financial and other related policies of the MFIs determine how successful these products are on the ground. As we shall see in this section, microcredit products have been going through a great deal of change as the MFIs gain experience in delivering microcredit and other microfinance products to the poor. In this context, the section will briefly discuss Grameen II products which was a redesign of the Grameen I (Classical Grameen) products.

Initially microcredit was envisaged to provide working capital for productive purposes. However, over the years, MFIs have diversified their product line to include consumer loans, mortgages, home improvement loans, water supply, sanitation, energy loans, student loans, emergency loans and the like. For example, poor people with stable income flows would like to have access to consumer loans, while a financially constrained borrower could benefit from an emergency loan for health emergencies.

Lending to microenterprises can be broadly divided into two types: (1) working capital loans and (2) fixed asset loans (Ledgerwood 1999). Working capital loans are used to invest in assets that are consumed by the business within a year. Such loans are also provided for purchasing supplies for microbusinesses such as cloth for making dresses, wood for carpentry or spices for making pickles. The final maturity of working capital loans are normally designed to match the business cycle of an enterprise. They usually have a maturity of three months to a year.

Before discussing about fixed assets loans, it is important to briefly discuss about fixed assets. Fixed assets normally consist of machinery, equipments and property and can include such items as refrigerators, sewing machines, lathe and property whose useful life is longer than one year. Because such items need more monetary outlays, the risk exposure of an MFI is proportionately larger for such loans. As a result, fixed asset loans have longer maturities that vary between one and three years. In many cases, in order to minimize their risk exposure, some MFIs decide to take legal title of the purchased asset as collateral. In Chapter 8, we will explore how microleasing as a financial instrument makes it easier for the poor to use equipments and machinery without their ownership.

There has been criticism that because of microlending, resources have been diverted away from funding loans to small and medium enterprises (SMEs). It is important to note that there are MFIs such as BRAC in Bangladesh that lend to small enterprises. What is more, microleasing that is considered as loan substitutes can be used by small enterprises to lease equipments and machinery.

The evolution of microloan products over the last 35 years has gone through a great deal of change. Needless to say, Grameen Bank was instrumental in coming up with many of the innovative ideas underlying microloans and incubated these ideas over a period of several years. Descriptions of microcredit in Chapters 4 and 5 to a large extent are based on these seminal ideas, which have been referred to as Classical Grameen or Grameen I.

Grameen II

In this section, we will discuss about Grameen II (Grameen Generalized System), which came about as a result of re-designing Grameen I (Dowla and Barua 2006). The genesis of Grameen II could be traced to 1998 floods that devastated Bangladesh. During the floods, two-thirds of the country was submerged under water for 11 weeks (Dowla and Barua 2006). As a result, Grameen Bank started experiencing repayment problems. Almost 20 per cent of the borrowers became irregular in their repayments. This led to widespread delinquencies and defaults in loan repayments. In order to mitigate the system-wide risk that the bank was faced with, it was decided to rethink Grameen's overall financial inter-mediation model, particularly its model of products and services in order to address some of the embedded inflexibilities of the model.

It is difficult to deal with events that give rise to risks that are sys-temic in nature such as droughts, floods, hurricanes and earthquakes that affect an entire area or even a country where MFIs operate. Because MFI portfolios are normally concentrated in a given region, and most of the poor and vulnerable clients find it difficult to recover from such dev-astating natural calamities, it is to be expected that MFIs would experi-ence payment difficulties. While diversification of the client base to other regions can help an MFI to lessen such risk, it is also desirable that MFIs use product designs that deal with such risks not in an *ad hoc* manner. As a result, the Grameen Bank took this opportunity to redesign its loan products based on Grameen I, and Grameen II was born.

Grameen I microcredit products were rigid.[8] For example, Grameen clients had to strictly adhere to the prescribed repayment schedules. This was based on the belief that the products have to be simple in design. Any deviation from such schedule made it difficult for the borrowers to move back again to the original schedule. During the floods, delin-quency rates increased sharply. As a result, large numbers of borrowers fell behind their repayments to the Bank and were not able to get back to the old schedule. The Grameen II design specifically addressed this inflexibility of Grameen I.

Grameen I was not tied to voluntary savings in anyway, except for the fact that the compulsory savings was an important component of the model in order to access microcredit. Grameen I used a common loan ceiling for the entire branch, whereas under Grameen II, each individual borrower has a different loan ceiling that depends on factors such as sav-ings of the borrower, his repayment performance, and the repayment performance of the group, the centre and the branch.

What is more, under Grameen I, loans consisted of many differ-ent products. If a borrower decides to take more than one loan, say a working capital loan for a microbusiness and a second loan for home improvement, then both the loans need to be consolidated to find the total exposure of the MFI to the borrower. This is important to know because there could be borrowers, who would get a housing loan to pay off microenterprise loan. In fact, this problem manifests in a bigger scale, when due to lack of credit bureaus, and lack of sharing of borrower information by the MFIs, a borrower could borrow from one MFI to pay off another MFI.

Under Grameen II, Grameen Bank brought about major changes to its underlying philosophy of financial intermediation. As a result, Grameen switched from group lending and compulsory savings to individualized lending and savings. It merged its loan products into one product called the basic loan. The basic loan was more flexible than the previous loan products. It incorporated temporary reprieve in the form of a flexible loan for borrowers going through financial stress.

It also recognized that a single loan term (of one year) and a single repayment schedule simply did not match the cash flow patterns of poor households. Major changes to loan terms consisted of maturities that varied from three months to three years. What is more, the repayment schedules of loans were designed to be flexible based on discussions with the borrower by taking into consideration a household's cash flow and the business environment the business is operating in. Staggered access to loans by group members under Grameen I was abandoned under Grameen II. Group members were allowed to borrow at anytime irrespective of what other group members were doing.

Loan disbursements were allowed to be flexible and the borrowers can receive loans in tranches. As noted earlier, each borrower has a loan ceiling, and ceiling depends on savings of the borrower, his repayment performance and the repayment performance of the group, the centre and the branch. Loan ceilings can be increased or decreased based on these parameters. Under certain circumstances, a borrower can borrow the amount repaid during the first six months without repaying the loan in full. Loan repayments were still made on a weekly basis.

In the case of payment difficulties, borrowers could reschedule their loans by extending the terms, thus reducing the amount they pay in each instalment. Loan consolidation and rescheduling make it easier for the borrowers to keep on making payments at a reduced rate until they put their financial house in order and can get back on to their earlier borrowing privileges.

The borrowers are required to deposit 5 per cent of the loan amount into two savings accounts divided as follows: (1) 2.5 per cent to a personal savings account with open access and (2) the remaining 2.5 per cent to a savings account with restricted access. Such contributions ensure that outstanding loan will be paid off after the death of the borrower. An extra contribution enables a member to ensure repayment of the outstanding loan upon the death of the spouse. Savings accumulated in obligatory savings accounts are refundable after three years of membership.

For variety of reasons to be discussed in Chapter 6, MFIs normally do not offer voluntary savings facilities to their clients. However, most MFIs require compulsory savings for accessing microcredit. Offer of voluntary savings accounts to their clients by the banking system are strictly regulated in all countries around the world. Unlike most MFIs, Grameen has the legal mandate to offer voluntary savings accounts to members and non-members. Under Grameen II, voluntary savings is offered in parallel with lending and is an integral part of borrowing.

Grameen Bank has regulatory approval to offer voluntary savings accounts to borrowers and non-borrowers. Under Grameen II, borrowers are encouraged to save in the range of 5 Taka to 50 Taka per week. Members with larger loans are encouraged to save more. Interest rates offered to depositors by Grameen varies between 8.5 per cent per annum and 12 per cent per annum.[9] The savings accounts offer a great deal of flexibility in depositing and withdrawing money from the account. What has emerged over the years from offering these accounts is that individualized savings accounts are more effective in building savings. This is because, growth of savings in these accounts becomes an incentive for the saver to keep on saving and watch her savings grow.

Grameen II also encourages its members to save in contractual savings accounts to pay for events such as marriage of their daughters, education of their children, building a house and the like. One of the contractual savings accounts under the rubric of Grameen Pension Scheme (GPS) was designed to build nest-egg for retirement.

Borrowers are required to deposit a fixed monthly amount that helps to build savings over a 5- or 10-year period. The savers in the GPS get good returns on their savings. A borrower who fails to make four consecutive monthly GPS deposits is treated as a defaulter. This is because GPSs are contractual savings accounts and missing deposits for four consecutive months is considered a default.

It is also important to note that borrowers can borrow against their savings. They can access bridge loans to manage short-term gaps that may arise between income and expenditure, instead of using savings that are earmarked for long-term needs. Taking a bridge loan forces a borrower to repay the loan.

Offer of voluntary savings to members and non-members by the Grameen Bank has not only strengthened the personal balance sheets of the poor by bringing about much needed balance between assets and liabilities, it has also strengthened Grameen balance sheet and profitability due to accumulation of these savings, which has provided an important source of low-cost funding for its microloan assets. As we noted earlier, Grameen Bank can provide savings accounts to borrowers as well as non-borrowers. As of September 2011, the balance of deposits consisting of member and non-member deposits stood at about $1.4 billion. The deposits as a percentage of outstanding loans were about 147 per cent, and when one adds own resources of the bank to the deposits they were about 162 per cent of outstanding bank loans. It is important to note that 100 per cent of the loans were financed from the bank's deposits and Grameen today does not rely on donor funding for loans.

In this context, one would wonder if MFI borrowers in Andhra Pradesh in India would have been eligible for flexible repayment terms, the need for coercion by the MFIs would not have been necessary. It is quite possible that a simple change in the repayment terms could have helped to prevent the precipitation of 2010 Microfinance Crisis in Andhra Pradesh.

Microloan Lending Rates: An Introduction

As the microfinance industry has expanded rapidly during the last 15 years or so and as many MFIs have joined the ranks of sustainable (profitable) microfinance entities, interest rates charged by the MFIs have come under the microscope. This has been particularly accentuated by the fact that some MFIs charge interest rates and other charges that result in EIRs that are high—reaching even 100 per cent or more for some but limited number of MFIs. We will critique MFI interest rates in general in Chapter 11 (*Critiquing Microfinance*).

Microloan lending rate is just one number that tells volumes about microloan products offered by an MFI and its posture towards its clients.

The various components used in computing lending rates also tell a great deal about the institution as regards to its DBL posture, that is, its progress towards financial sustainability and social mission, and how successful it has been in its financial and risk management and shareholder value creation aspects.

In the past, the MFIs communicated microloan interest rates as 'flat' rates. But that is changing. Flat rates are applied to the original loan amount or the face value of the loan, even though the loan balance goes down week after week (assuming weekly repayment rate). As a result, the flat rates understate the true cost of the loan by half, assuming the average balance during the life of the loan was half of the face value. For example, if the loan is for $100 and the flat rate is 10 per cent per annum, then assuming the average balance during the life of the loan to be $50, the true cost to the borrower is 20 per cent per annum. The flat rates in general grossly understate the interest rates on the loans. The only advantage perhaps of stating interest rates as flat rates has to do with the fact that it is easier to compute interest payment on the loan by applying the periodic rate (weekly, biweekly or monthly as the case may be) to the original loan amount.

However, in the banking industry, the cost of a loan is disclosed to its clients in terms of EIR which is based on the 'internal rate of return' (IRR) of the cash flow of the loan. The IRR is computed using the DCF of a loan. DCF in turn, depends on the concept of time value of money. The scope of the chapter does not allow for a discussion of these concepts here. The reader can find a discussion of these concepts in any undergraduate text on finance.

It is important that the poor borrowing from an MFI should be provided with EIR, even if they may not be able to understand the complex mathematics that goes into calculating these effective rates. The EIR should also be broken down into interest rate component and a component representing interest equivalent of other charges such as loan processing fee, cost arising out of compulsory savings, payment of premiums towards credit life insurance and the like. As a result, a poor borrower would have a clearer picture of what she is paying towards interest and other charges and fees in each period and over the life of the loan. This would help in helping the client as to what is the true cost of borrowing from her MFI. It is important to note that institutions such as

'MF Transparency' have been at the forefront to promote disclosure of EIRs on microloans by the MFIs around the world.[10]

A Brief Outline of Microcredit Pricing

Like any other financial institution, the MFIs are subjected to market and credit risks such as interest and exchange rate risks and financial risk arising out of loan delinquency and defaults. Under these circumstances, they have to be sustainable, meet their social mission and also grow as financial institutions. Balancing all this to price microloans appropriately becomes rather a difficult task. This is particularly true because MFI lending rates have been perceived to be too high and lacking transparency.

Broadly, in arriving at microloan lending rates, one starts out with the cost of funding a microloan portfolio and adds to its interest spread equivalents of operating expenses, loan loss provisioning and a minimum return on assets (ROA) to be sustainable. On top of this, MFIs can add a spread towards profit margin also. On an EIR basis, loan processing fee and compulsory savings increase the EIR of microloans. The reader is referred to *Microcredit Interest Rates*, published by CGAP (1996) for an in-depth discussion of pricing of microcredit.

In order to arrive at the cost of funds, the CGAP paper cited above states, "For a somewhat more precise result 'weighted average cost of capital' can be projected by distinguishing the various sources that are likely to fund the MFI's financial assets in the future." Normally, microloan portfolios are funded through loans, market borrowing, funding from governmental sources, donor funding, paid-in capital, reserves and retained earnings. Depending on the MFI, compulsory as well as voluntary savings could also provide potentially a funding source.

In this context, it is also important to note that, arriving at the appropriate cost basis for shareholder's equity can be complicated because retained earnings form an important component of equity. Subsidized funds and grant money provided from governmental sources, donors and charitable foundations contribute towards helping the MFIs to grow and in the process contribute towards retained earnings. There are also issues related to how to value 'sweat equity.' Besides, MFIs being DBL-oriented organizations have to consider the important role poor borrowers play in making MFIs sustainable (profitable) by making timely payments on their loans in spite of the fact that interest rates and other related charges on an effective cost basis are considered to be high in comparison to interest rates and charges paid by the non-poor to commercial banks.

With regard to capital, one also needs to mention about capital to risk weighted assets ratio (CRAR), which is applicable to commercialized MFIs (in countries such as India) as a measure of an MFI's capital adequacy. The ratio provides useful information about the institution's solvency. For most commercialized MFIs that are categorized as Non-Bank Finance Companies (NBFCs) in India, the Reserve Bank of India (RBI) requires these institutions to have a minimum CRAR of 12 per cent if they do not accept public deposits and a minimum CRAR of 15 per cent if they accept deposits (Ledgerwood et al. 2006). While this ratio may appear high, considering the variety of risks that the microfinance sector is exposed to, setting relatively higher CRAR has to be considered prudent. However, the need for higher level of CRAR would require either the shareholders to provide more paid-in capital or the MFIs to build their equity base through retained earnings. That would require the MFIs to price their microcredit appropriately to build up retained earnings.

Harper et al. (2011) in their book *Whose Sustainability Counts?* present some of the underlying considerations that go into pricing microcredit for BASIX, India. The presentation in their book was based on their discussions with Vijay Mahajan, Managing Director of BASIX. BASIX is classified as an NBFC in India. Based on the RBI guidelines, BASIX was required to maintain a CRAR of 15 per cent. Based on the assumption that the capital markets in India look for an annual ROR of at least 20 per cent of the capital funding, the loan assets should provide a return of at least 3 per cent (arrived at by multiplying 20 per cent return with 15 per cent CRAR). An after-tax return of 3 per cent will translate to 4.5 per cent return before tax, assuming 33.33 per cent tax rate. Harper et al. in the illustration also assume cost of funds to be 12 per cent, spread equivalent to cover operating expenses to be 10 per cent and allocations to loan loss reserve to be 1 per cent. When one adds all these components including pre-tax ROA of 4.5 per cent, a lending rate of 27.5 per cent is obtained. Therefore, based on these calculations, an MFI would need to charge 27.5 per cent to be sustainable. Harper et al. also

Table 5.1
Components of a Typical Microcredit Lending Rate for NBFCs in India

Funding cost (%)	12.00
Spread for operating cost (%)	10.00
Spread for provision for loan losses (%)	1.00
Return on assets (%)	4.50
Total (%)	27.50

note that for smaller MFIs in India, cost of funding can be 13 per cent and spread to cover operating expenses can reach 12.5 per cent. As a result, the lending rate for the smaller MFIs could rise to around 31 per cent to be sustainable.

It is important to note that assuming operating cost per loan remains fixed, larger the loan size, operating cost divided by loan size goes down. Therefore, higher average loan size would increase profitability of an MFI. Hence, for smaller MFIs, where the average loan size tends to be lower, interest rates have to be higher to break even. Therefore, interest rate ceilings would lower interest income for smaller MFIs in comparison to large MFIs.

Table 5.1 provides disaggregated components of a typical microloan lending rate for relatively larger MFIs (classified as NBFCs) in India as discussed in the above paragraphs.

In this context, it is important to note that, in 'Microfinance India: State of the Sector Report' (Srinivasan 2012), MFI interest rates in India ranged from a minimum of about 17.10 per cent to a maximum of about 32 per cent per annum. We also noted in Chapter 4 that Grameen Bank's lending rate on income-generating loans in October 2011 was 20 per cent.

Conclusion

In spite of scaling back our expectations as regards to what microcredit can achieve on the ground and the recent setbacks to the industry in such areas as commercialization (mission drift), microcredit remains one of the most powerful financial tools that has revolutionized market-based formal lending to the poor. Microcredit in recent times has gone through a sea-change. Some of the important changes to microcredit structure were made at Grameen Bank that included moving away from joint-liability contracts, introduction of flexible repayment terms to help poor clients during financial hardship and introduction of voluntary savings (microsavings) side by side microcredit. These changes have strengthened the microcredit model further. From the discussions in the chapter, it would appear that offering flexibility in terms of repayment terms (in contrast to rigid repayment terms) could pay rich dividends for the poor as well as the MFIs in terms of credit risk. While repeat lending can be a powerful tool to help the poor in growing their businesses, it could have potential downsides in the sense that the borrower could become too dependent on such lending without building her savings (reserves).

Undoubtedly, women around the world have been the biggest gainers from accessing microcredit. What is more, improving economic prospects for women because of microfinance has helped revise the traditional view that women are economic liabilities.

We also discussed in this chapter about pricing of microloans. One can clearly see from Table 5.1 that the two biggest components of microcredit lending rates are funding cost and spread for operating cost. Therefore, providing access to formal savings facilities by the MFIs, besides being financially beneficial for the poor could lower credit risk for the MFIs, and provide a stable source of funding for the institutions from the deposits. It would also diversify sources of funding for the MFIs and lower funding cost in the long run. Moreover, introduction of ICT-based platforms for payment systems such as M-PESA (mobile money) and FINO (see Chapter 9) could also lower spread due to the operating cost in the long run. Lowering of these two spreads could go a long way in lowering MFI lending rates for their poor clients.

Last but not the least, one needs to emphasize that accessing largely mono-product world of microfinance consisting of microcredit only is no panacea for winning the war against the entrenched multidimensional world of poverty. Access to savings, insurance, improved payment systems for MT and other financial transactions, lease finance, and other non-financial complementary services (such as livelihood training and marketing) are also vital for the poor, in order to improve their chances to fight poverty with greater success.

Notes

1. Asif Dowla and Dipal Barua. 2006. *The Poor Always Pay Back—The Grameen II Story*, p. 18. Bloomfield, CT: Kumarian Press Inc.
2. Beatriz Armendáriz and Jonathan Morduch. 2010. *The Economics of Microfinance*, pp. 122–27. Cambridge, Massachusetts: The MIT Press.
3. Beatriz Armendáriz and Jonathan Morduch. 2010. *The Economics of Microfinance*, pp. 148–53. Cambridge, Massachusetts: The MIT Press.
4. Asif Dowla and Dipal Barua. 2006. *The Poor Always Pay Back – The Grameen II Story*, pp. 169. Bloomfield, CT: Kumarian Press Inc.
5. Beatriz Armendáriz and Jonathan Morduch. 2010. *The Economics of Microfinance*, pp. 143–44. Cambridge, Massachusetts: The MIT Press.
6. Beatriz Armendáriz de Aghion and Jonathan Morduch. 2005. *The Economics of Microfinance*. pp. 180–81. Cambridge, Massachusetts: The MIT Press.
7. Asif Dowla and Dipal Barua. 2006. *The Poor Always Pay Back—The Grameen II Story*, pp. 27. Bloomfield, CT: Kumarian Press Inc.
8. Stuart Rutherford. 2005. 'What is Grameen II? Is It Up And Running In Yhe Field Yet?' MicroSave. Available online at http://staging.microsave.net/files/pdf/MicroSave-GB-Briefing-Note-1-Overview.pdf (downloaded on 21 February 2013).
9. Grameen Bank. 2011. 'Grameen Bank at a Glance October 2011.' Available online at http://www.grameen-info.org/index.php?option=com_content&task=view&id=26&Itemid=175 (downloaded on 27 November 2012).
10. See 'www.mftransparency.org.' The institution promotes transparent pricing in the microfinance industry by 'facilitating microfinance pricing disclosure,' 'offering policy advisory services,' and 'developing training and education materials,' for the industry participants.

6

Microsavings: Voluntary Savings for the Poor

For age and want save while as you may;
No morning sun lasts a whole day.[1]

Benjamin Franklin

The great irony in being poor is that you are "too poor to save, but too poor not to save"—you may not be able to save much, but if you do not save at all you have no way of getting hold of those "usefully large lump sums" that you so often need.[2]

Stuart Rutherford

The Poor Richard's Almanac,[3] published by Benjamin Franklin, which dates back to 1732, admonished the poor to be disciplined in saving money for the rainy days. Needless to say, whether one is rich or poor or not so rich or not so poor, there are occasions one needs to have access to 'usefully large lump sums' to manage their finances. Given the fact that the poor cannot aspire to build large savings quickly through thrift, it is important that they need to make a beginning sooner. As we shall explore in this chapter, like formal access to credit, access to formal voluntary savings facilities by the poor is fundamental.

We discussed about accessing microcredit in Chapters 4 and 5. However, credit is a double-edged sword. As the demand for micro-credit has increased around the world, it has shown some of the down-side risks of relying too much on credit. As a result, there is greater realization of benefits of savings for the poor. This is because heavily relying on credit without building up savings gives rise to an unhealthy gap between assets and liabilities in poor households. This is particularly true in an environment where some of the MFIs around the world have been over-lending while access to voluntary savings facilities has not been available widely (see Chapter 11). Besides, access to microinsurance by poor households is not widespread. As a result, in the event of an emergency, the poor households tend to substitute credit for savings, as well as for insurance. Anecdotal evidence suggests that a large percentage of emergency loans from MFIs are taken because of sickness and hospitalization in families. What is more, large percentages of MFI borrowers who are delinquent have someone sick in the family (Microcredit Summit E-NEWS 2008).

As the reader will discover in this chapter, like access to credit, access to voluntary savings facilities by the poor is so fundamental that many working in the microfinance field believe building up savings should come before any poor household borrows from an MFI. This is because experience with building up savings would sensitize a borrower whether the cash flow of the household would be able to support regular debt service payments (mostly on a weekly basis) on microloans. In fact, SHGs in India require their borrowers to save before they can borrow. If nothing else, the requirement does sensitize a borrower as to her capacity to save. That in turn could help her to assess how much she would be able to borrow comfortably.

In comparison to microlending, extension of microsavings by an MFI is relatively more complex endeavour. For example, in order to offer microsavings, MFIs have to meet regulatory requirements and have in-house capability for financial risk management. In spite of these complexities, the microfinance industry around the world has been rather resilient in innovating poor-friendly and cost-effective ways to deliver microsavings to the poor. For example, from insights gained from behavioural economics, there have been innovative products that help the poor to save more using instruments such as commitment savings, 'borrow-to-save' model ('P9') of Stuart Rutherford, VSLAs and the like. We have already discussed in Chapter 5 how Grameen Bank's Classical Grameen Model (Grameen I) that was redesigned to arrive at Grameen II model incorporates microsavings as an integral part of its lending model. Besides, Grameen Bank also introduced commitment savings scheme such as GPS under its Grameen II model that has been quite popular.

In spite of the fact that access to formal savings instruments for the poor has great deal of upside potential and no downside risks (so long as it can be saved securely and keep pace with inflation), access to poor-friendly, secure and convenient savings facilities by the poor remains rather minimal for a variety of reasons about which we will discuss in this chapter.

It is possible that innovative use of technology-based platforms such as M-PESA (e-banking), the marriage of third-party outlets (correspondent banking) along with biometric card-based technology (smart cards) can potentially change how the poor access microsavings. It is expected that as the poor and the MFIs increasingly realize the downside risks of too much dependence on credit, there will be greater push to offer microsavings for the poor, even the poorest who can also benefit from microsavings.

Why the Poor Need Access to Voluntary Savings Facilities

The microfinance revolution started with microcredit. This is because, when time is of the essence (particularly in emergencies), it is relatively easier and quick for a poor person to get hold of 'usefully large lump sums.' Besides, the poor, who are constantly strapped for cash, may not have the discipline and the tenacity to save in drips and drabs to arrive at 'useful lump sum' prior to such emergencies. Besides, whatever savings a household may have built up through thrift, it may be exhausted quickly by taking care of one emergency or it may not be even sufficient enough to do that. Then the household has to resort to borrowing. In spite of these drawbacks, it is important that households need to save because savings buffer against emergencies to buy precious time and evaluate options before a household plunges into borrowing. As a result, in many households, particularly the women, who are entrusted in managing family finances, focus on building savings buffer for emergencies.

The fact that the poor have devised various tools to save and invest and rely on them even if they lack the versatility of formal savings (see

Chapter 3) do suggest that the poor would greatly prize access to formal savings facilities. In this context, it is important to recapitulate how the poor instead of earning an interest on their savings, pay an EIR of almost 30 per cent to deposit collectors for saving. What is more, there have been instances where MFI clients borrow paying relatively high interest rate (of 24 per cent) from an MFI and then save the funds in a savings accounts earning rather minimal interest (of only 4 per cent) just to have lump sum savings at hand for occasions such as marriage of their daughters (Banerjee and Duflo 2011). Under this scenario, the individual resorts to borrowing from an MFI and saving the funds with another bank because her MFI allows her to borrow but does not allow her to save. What is more, the second bank allows her to save, but does not allow her to borrow. Secondly, the borrower is willing to borrow (at a high interest rate) a lump sum amount to save because she avoids time off from work and transportation cost to go to a bank in the nearby town to deposit money in her savings account in dribs and drabs. Most importantly, the discipline required to repay the MFI forces her to save even though she earns a negative interest rate of 20 per cent (–20 per cent) per annum. What this example shows is that the poor value savings so much, so that they force themselves to save by borrowing at a much higher interest rate and earning minimal interest on such savings (instead of earning a positive interest rate).

One of the most important reasons why the poor need savings is to take care of health emergencies. Usually the poor do not have sick leaves and insurance (Chapter 7 is devoted to microinsurance) for health emergencies. They also do not have unemployment benefits. Their microenterprises can run into hard times. Because the poor have very few tangible assets to fall back on, they need to build savings to mitigate financial risk that may arise in the short as well in the long run. They cannot always rely on their family and friends or charity to tide over situations where there is immediate need for cash in emergencies or need for cash on a recurring basis when one is disabled or old.

Access to formal savings can be used for earmarking savings for various future needs such as children's educational expenses, health emergencies, daughters' marriage, religious festivities, building assets such as buying a piece of land or investing in a business. Savings can be lent to others and in the process can build social capital. Social capital is one of the most powerful forms of insurance a poor household can have.

Given the fact that poor households continually rely on borrowing to manage their finances, it is essential that they save in parallel to build up cash assets as a hedge against such liabilities. This is because micro-loans may not be all that small with respect to fragile microbalance sheets of poor households that are usually debt-laden. If a household borrows from other sources, including moneylenders and other MFIs (because there is no need for traditional collateral and no credit bureaus to check credit status of borrowers), cash flow inflexibility can develop if the income of the household becomes erratic. Besides, debt service payments are contractual and cash outflows cannot be postponed. As a result, a delinquent borrower can be subject to pressure from her solidarity group to comply with contractual payments. If a borrower is delinquent for a longer period, it could lead to sanctions from the lender. Needless to say, if a family is prudent and builds savings in parallel with borrow-ing, it provides a modicum of flexibility to deal with emergencies at the minimum.

There are other reasons why the poor would value poor-friendly vol-untary savings provided by the MFIs. For example, they would like to have the privacy and security provided by savings accounts. Besides, the savings accounts can be used for receiving remittances securely from migrant workers and also for remitting funds to kith and kin. As we shall explore in this chapter, savings accounts with commitment sav-ings feature that forces the poor to accumulate 'lump sum' amounts is also prized by them. Besides, in most poor countries, the poor lack social security. As a result, poor families like the illiquidity of accounts such as contractual savings accounts and pension accounts (e.g., Grameen Pension Scheme), which can help them in their old age.

In an important and comprehensive paper on global financial inclu-sion titled, 'The Foundations of Financial Inclusion: Understanding Ownership and Use of Formal Accounts,' Allen et al. (2012) discuss about the growing evidence that financial inclusion has significant beneficial effects for individuals and firms. Access to savings instruments increases savings, female empowerment, productive investment and consump-tion. Some of the important findings of the paper, which is based on a large database on Global Financial Inclusion (Global Findex) Database are as follows: (1) 41 per cent of adults in developing economies bank compared to 91 per cent of adults in high-income countries; (2) adults in middle-income countries (58 per cent) are three times more likely to have an account than adults in low-income countries (19 per cent) and (3) 37 per cent of women in developing economies bank compared to 46 per cent of men. The paper points out that women, youth, the poor and rural residents are the least likely to have formal accounts. The authors also find that 'greater ownership and use of accounts,' is associated with an enabling environment for accessing financial services such as 'lower account costs and greater proximity to financial services.' These are compelling reasons why the poor need to have access to voluntary savings. In this context, we need to mention one more important finding of the paper, that is, offer of low fee accounts, exemption of documentation requirements for opening accounts, use of correspondent banking and making government payments using bank accounts can expand financial inclusion.

Why There Has Been Lack of Voluntary Savings Facilities for the Poor

There has been an implicit assumption that, after taking care of their day-to-day financial needs, the poor may not have enough to save. In fact, being poor and having capacity to save may sound contradictory. That has been one of the reasons perhaps, why there was less emphasis on providing formal savings facilities to the poor and why subsidized loans and grants have been provided to them for economic development.

While the poor may not have the means to save large sums of money, nonetheless, they strive to microsave making thrift as their motto. Without the capacity to save, how else can they borrow from moneylenders and aspire to pay back the loans that carry usurious interest rates. Paying off spiralling debt is not easy by any means when one's income can be erratic. The important point to be made in the present context is that the poor have the capacity to cut corners and muster the discipline to save to repay the moneylenders. Therefore, by providing an enabling environment, poor-friendly savings instruments and financial literacy training they can be expected to save regularly and in the process become financially stronger. For example, with appropriate financial literacy training they could save by repaying high-cost loans from the moneylenders with microloans. Besides, they could cut down on spurious spending. They could also discipline themselves to cut down expenditures on alcohol and tobacco which drain cash from a poor family. Most importantly not indulging in addictive substances can save substantial sums of money from medical expenses in the long run.

Considering the fact that the poor could build savings through thrift, and considering the benefits that the poor could accrue from access to formal savings facilities one wonders why is it that the poor do not have widespread access to formal voluntary savings facilities? The following discussions are designed to highlight some of the causes of lack of such facilities for the poor.

To begin with, developing well-functioning credit market for the poor, that too in remote areas lacking infrastructure is expensive. For example, opening brick and mortar branches and staffing them with professionals to manage small deposit accounts in the millions that normally do not exceed few dollars in savings and entail high administrative cost is not profitable.[4] Besides, even if a commercial bank decides to build brick and mortar offices, there can be only limited number of such offices. That would entail small borrowers to take time off from work and incur transportation cost to go to the bank to deposit tiny sums of money. In fact, the costs associated with taking time off from work and transportation may turn out to be more than the value of the deposit. If the poor decide to pool funds for several days before making a deposit, there is always the possibility that the saved funds could be stolen or could be spent on something that was not envisaged before the deposit is made. As Mas (2009) puts it rather succinctly, "Many financial institutions, especially large commercial banks, find it too costly to reach out to poor customers despite potentially large demand by such customers. Current business models do not handle the 'triple whammy' of low savings balances, small transaction sizes and large numbers of customers."

That is one of the reasons why correspondent banking and e-banking (discussed later in this chapter) are emerging as potential solutions to offer savings facilities to the poor. As we shall discuss in this chapter, the success of these models depends to a large extent on resolving a variety of issues about which we will touch in this chapter. For example, using mobile phone-based M-PESA (mobile money) for savings, one needs to be familiar with using the mobile phone to access savings accounts. As a result there is a technology barrier to use M-PESA. But that is not all. Given the fact that many poor people are not literate, there is a literacy barrier as well before the technology barrier to use e-banking.

Besides, in the developing countries where the government provides low-cost loans to the poor, which can even be forgiven sometimes, there is built-in disincentive to develop a savings culture. While such subsidized lending may be helpful in priming the pump for economic development, they create dependencies and deprive the poor the necessary discipline to build up savings, which is one of the important ways they could build cash assets that can serve as a first line of defence against specific risks. In this environment, even if commercial banking institutions may be desirous of providing savings facilities for the poor, it may be difficult to be sustainable (profitable).

What is more, while providing microsavings facility may appear as one more product line like microcredit, in reality that is not so. This is because institutions that take voluntary deposits from the public are tightly regulated and supervised by the regulatory authorities and bank supervisors in almost all countries around the world. As a result, in order to provide such facilities, the MFIs need to go through transformation to meet strict standards laid down by the regulatory authorities. To meet these standards may not be all that easy considering the fact that many developing countries lack banking and financial risk-management professionals and related systems to extend such facility to large numbers of MFIs, many of which may be located in remote areas. Besides, in offering mobile money facilities such as M-PESA, many countries require service providers for mobile phones to partner with banking institutions.

Last but not the least, there are wide range of savings products that an MFI can potentially offer to the poor. Providing a long menu of products to cater to every need of the poor may not be cost-effective for most MFIs. Many of these products are driven by technology, which an average MFI may not have access to. All in all, many such factors complicate transforming MFIs to become deposit-taking institutions.

MFIs and Other Institutional Models That Offer Voluntary Savings Facilities for the Poor

Most MFIs start out as NGOs and hence do not normally possess the necessary know-how such as financial risk-management capabilities, technology base to offer voluntary savings facilities and expertise in reaching out to the poor to mobilize savings. As a result, these institutions go through transformation so that they get the necessary regulatory approvals before mobilizing savings. All this is to protect the depositors—the poor and the non-poor alike.

In the event an MFI cannot go through transformation to extend savings facilities to the poor, they could perhaps link the borrowers with commercial banks (in the public or private sector), postal banks and cooperatives to help them accumulate savings. In India, under the bank-linkage programme, the SHGs accumulate savings of the poor members before making a deposit in the linked bank (Christen et al. 2005). Pooling (aggregating) savings before making the deposit reduces overhead cost of transaction. The linkage provides small rural depositors' access to secure savings facilities that can earn market-based interest rates on their savings and access to wide range of savings products.

There are many institutional models such as postal banks and cooperatives that have been offering microsavings facilities to the poor such as passbook accounts. However, the poor would like to have access to savings facilities that are more versatile and offer many of the features that non-poor have been availing from commercial banks (such as demand deposits, fixed deposits, contractual and commitment savings accounts) and from employers (such as pension).

The non-poor try to immunize themselves from financial hardship by saving and investing by diversifying across instruments and products. For example, when a child is born many parents start a college fund for the child. This is because getting that 'lump sum' to send a child to college is not easy even for the non-poor. At the place of their employment, they join a pension scheme for old age. Employers provide them with affordable health care. Besides, the employers make contributions towards their pension savings and health care. On top of all this, the non-poor make contributions towards their social security. Above all, they also invest in mutual funds, stocks and bonds and a variety of other instruments. Needless to say, the financial services industry that advises the non-poor actively as regards to how to save and invest has become quite sophisticated over the years.

In the following text, we provide brief descriptions of some of the models that have emerged in the recent past to deliver voluntary savings facilities for the poor. The specific models discussed in the following include: (1) Offering Microsavings by Transformed MFIs, (2) VSLAs and (3) Correspondent Banking. We will also discuss about mobile money service or e-banking (in the context of M-KESHO) in the following section that discusses about specific savings products for the poor (M-KESHO will also be discussed in Chapter 9 in the context of Payment Systems and Money Transfer).

Offering Microsavings by Transformed MFIs

In order to offer microsavings, most MFIs have to be transformed to become regulated deposit-taking financial intermediaries (Ledgerwood et al. 2006). There are basically two reasons why an MFI would like to go through transformation: (1) to access capital in the form of debt as well as equity and (2) to become a regulated deposit-taking financial intermediary.

Commercialization entails transformation of NGO-based MFIs to put these institutions on a more professional footing. One of the important benefits of commercialization is that the MFIs can diversify their funding base to include commercial sources. At a later stage, with approval from regulatory authorities, these institutions can offer savings facilities to poor and non-poor, and the deposits from the savers can form a funding source for the microloan portfolio(s) of the MFIs. As a result, the institutions can be less dependent on donor and governmental funding.

One of the important aspects of commercialization is to attain sustainability (profitability) by an MFI to access debt capital. Only a few MFIs such as Compartamos Banco in Mexico and SKS Microfinance in India have been able to access equity capital after commercialization. While these are landmark achievements for an industry that not too long ago depended on donor funding, governmental assistance and charity, accessing equity capital by the commercialized MFIs, however, have become quite controversial about which we will discuss in Chapter 11.

Commercialization requires a great deal of accountability on the part of an MFI in terms of governance and capital structure. Other important issues that are subject to scrutiny include financial management, product pricing and social mission. As noted earlier, commercialization ultimately leads to a stage where an MFI can transform itself to become a deposit-taking institution. In order to command the trust of the regulatory and banking authorities, including the central bank of the country to which an MFI belongs, the MFI has to be licensed (legally authorized) to take deposits. Taking deposits from the public is perhaps one of the most complex undertakings by an MFI. In that sense, downscaled commercial banks have the advantage of offering savings facilities for the poor, because, they are already licensed to take deposits. As we noted in Chapter 4, the members of SHGs in India have the clear advantage of accessing savings facilities through the bank-linkage programme.

As far as the goals of becoming a regulated deposit-taking financial intermediary is concerned, the MFIs need to create the necessary capacity to meet many of the requirements that regulatory authorities and banking supervisors require of financial intermediaries. This includes such aspects as financial risk management consisting of asset liability management, treasury management, liquidity management and interest and exchange risk management. Needless to say, a transformed MFI that can access commercial funding to lend and can provide savings facilities to the poor goes a long way on its path to becoming a full-fledged financial intermediary.

In an important development in Indian microfinance industry, the RBI granted 'in-principle' banking license to Bandhan (Bandhan Financial Services)[5] in April 2014. The approval is for a period of 18 months. During the 18-month period, Bandhan has to comply with RBI stipulations to secure a permanent license and begin banking activities (ET Bureau 2014). Bandhan is an MFI, which currently operates as an NBFC in Kolkata, West Bengal. In many ways, the announcement can be considered a major achievement for Bandhan and a shot in the arm for the microfinance industry in India, which suffered a major setback after the 2010 Microfinance Crisis in the state of Andhra Pradesh. Bandhan is currently considered the largest MFI in India. On the wake of the RBI announcement, Bandhan plans to open 600–700 new bank branches in

22 states of India where it already has over 2,100 branches (BS Reporter 2014). Undoubtedly, Bandhan's banking license will provide much needed impetus to expand the nascent market for deposits in rural India. It is important to note that Bandhan is currently charging an interest rate of 22 per cent to its clients and it is expected that the banking license would allow it to access the deposit base of its clients to lower its interest rate by 6–7 per cent (Acharya 2014c).

Village Savings and Loan Associations

VSLAs are community-managed informal groups, which was pioneered by CARE in 1991. It was first introduced in Niger. Other agencies such as Plan, Oxfam, Catholic Relief Services and Aga Khan Foundation have successfully adopted VSLA model (MasterCard Foundation). Today, VSLAs serve about 6 million people in 58 countries (Kristof 2012).

A VSLA's main focus is to help the poor to build savings. About 70 per cent of its members are women. VSLAs are self-managed groups. The groups are simple to manage and are stepping stones to join other financial institutions such as the MFIs. The groups do not receive any external capital. The groups also provide access to need-based small loans and emergency loans to their members. Besides helping its members to save, VSLAs help the members to build assets.

After its introduction in Niger in 1991, by 2001 CARE had already helped in the creation of 9,000 VSLAs. The membership in these VSLAs had grown to about 250,000 and total saving in the VSLAs stood at about $14 million. Over the years, CARE was instrumental in adapting the VSLA model for more flexibility in savings and to extend loans of variable amounts and maturity.

Each VSLA consists of anywhere from 15 to 30 members. As in the case of solidarity groups, VSLAs are formed by self selection. New members of the group are trained over several months regarding the purpose of the group and how to elect office bearers. Office bearers consist of a chairperson, treasurer, secretary and two money counters who form the executive committee. Besides, the members of a group select three others who are entrusted with three keys to three locks on the cash box where the group's funds are kept. All financial transactions, that is, disbursements and repayments are carried out in weekly meetings to ensure transparency and accountability.

The groups along with their office bearers decide on such important aspects of VSLAs as terms of savings and loans, interest rates, repayment schedules, penalties for late payments and missed meeting. A new VSLA starts by collecting weekly savings from members. Savings are accumulated in the form of shares. The share price is decided *a priori*. Once enough savings have been accumulated, the group can lend to its members. As can be expected, these are small value loans in the range of $10 to $20. However, interest rates on these loans are rather very high, ranging from 5 to 10 per cent on a monthly basis. These rates are much higher than the rates normally charged by the MFIs. Based on interest earnings and fees collected over one-year period, the members of VSLAs receive a return on their respective savings (shares).

A VSLA also sets up an insurance fund (also called social fund), which is used by its members to access emergency loans or loans during difficult times. In granting a loan, the group decides if it can be an outright grant or an interest-free loan with flexible repayment terms.

After 9–12 months of operation, a VSLA performs an 'action audit' and pays out savings and earnings by the group and dissolves. The audits are usually timed to help group members at the time of heightened cash needs such as at the beginning of the agricultural season. The process also helps some of the members to leave the group and new members to join. However, most disbanded groups again regroup and start another cycle of collecting savings and lending.

The VSLAs have proven to be rather basic but robust informal structures that help in intermediating savings of a group to lend within the group (without any external injection of funds such as borrowing). It also provides insurance cover to members to meet emergency need for cash. VSLA experience by its members helps them to transition to formal institutions such as the MFIs. In that sense, VSLAs complement microfinance.

In a large-scale RCT study (see Chapter 11 for a brief description of RCTs) in Ghana to measure impact of VSLAs, Karlan and Udry (2012) find that participation in VSLA is correlated with wealth, business ownership, having loans and being better integrated in the community by attending village meetings, participation in groups and having friends willing to lend money.

Other findings of the study in Ghana include the following: (1) median weekly contribution for a VSLA member was about $7 and median share amount was about $36, (2) 66 per cent of VSLA members had received share-out and a third of these had received multiple shares-outs, (3) 49 per cent of the members had received a loan—with median loan amount of $22 and (4) 74 per cent of the members had access to social fund (insurance fund) and almost all recipients (87 per cent) had to repay their loans back to the social fund.

Based on the Ghana study, while 75 per cent of the households experienced a shock with large negative effect during a period of 12 months, Karlan and Udry did not find any impact on how households reacted to shocks and the time period they took to recover from shocks. They also did not find any impact in terms of food security, types and amounts of food consumed, impact on health expenditures and use of health services, agricultural inputs and production, business owner-ship and profits, and ownership of productive assets such as livestock and household assets.

However, Karlan and Udry found that households took loans from VSLAs to finance school fees and school expenses. They also found female primary school enrolment increased by 2.5 per cent. They did not find any increase in influence of women on intra-household decisions but women were more likely to speak in village meetings. Overall VSLAs were popular. Karlan and Udry believe that the study period was not enough to observe accumulation of assets.

'Doughnuts Defeating Poverty:' How Tiny Loans from VSLAs Offer Hope to the Poor

The following account of Biti Rose from the village of Masumba in Malawi illustrates how through perseverance, hard work and leveraging $2 loan from her VSLA changed her family fortunes. It is based on an inspiring Op-Ed piece by Nicholas D. Kristof (2012) in The New York Times.

Biti Rose's family consisted of Alfred Nasoni, her husband, and five children. Earlier two children had died because the family could not afford to take them to a doctor. Their eldest son had to drop out of school because the family could not afford $5 school cost for a term. The fam-ily owned 2.5 acre land of which only a part was cultivated because they could not afford seeds for the whole land. However, there is an irony to the whole story. The following quote from Nicholas D. Kristof illustrates some of the stark realities of poverty.

> Yet poverty is sometimes romanticized, and it's more complicated than that. Alfred, 45, told me that even as his children were starving, he spent an average of $2 a week on local moonshine and 50 cents on cigarettes. He added that he also spent $2 or more a week buying sex from local girls—even though AIDS is widespread.

Nicholas Kristof goes on to comment that how 'despair leads people to self-medicate in ways that compound the despair.' But in the midst of this despair, Biti Rose joined a VSLA in 2005. As a member of the VSLA, she deposited equivalent of 10 cents every week along with 19 other members. The money was then lent out to members. CARE trained them to invest in small businesses.

With a loan of $2 from her VSLA, Biti Rose started selling local version of doughnuts. People liked her doughnuts. She initially sold them for 2 cents each. Before long, she was making several dollars of profit every day. Profits from selling doughnuts made Alfred hopeful about the future. He was inspired to start growing vegetables and selling them. In an environment that looked brighter day by day, Alfred curtailed his drinking and buying sex from local girls. With more money in hand, Biti Rose and Alfred bought seeds and fertilizer to cultivate their land plus two extra acre of leased land. They now hire up to 10 farm labourers for their agricultural enterprise. There was a time, their harvest was less than one bag of corn. In 2012, their harvest filled seven ox carts.

The story illustrates how complex network of pathways help a poor family to win the war on poverty. While not all VSLA borrowers can be as successful as Biti Rose, some can. In the context of transformation of Biti Rose's family fortunes, Nicholas Kristof comments that 'something going on here beyond microsavings and entrepreneurship.' He also adds, 'Assistance succeeds when it gives people a feeling that a better outcome is possible, and those hopes become self-fulfilling as people work more industriously and invest more wisely.' Unquestionably, when members of VSLAs see one of them has succeeded, that gives them hope that they too can succeed if they try. This is 'social proof' in disguise. Ultimately, it is hope that energizes a poor person to stand up and attack poverty by capitalizing his or her native intelligence, passion, perseverance and propensity to take risk and other such intangible factors along with access to appropriate mix of capital and skills training (such as financial literacy, livelihood and marketing).

Correspondent Banking and Microfinance

Correspondent banking model was implemented in Brazil in 1970s to extend banking to other regions where the banks did not have a branch (IFMR 2010). Over the years, what these banking correspondents (BCs) had to offer to their clients has expanded rather rapidly. In 1999, through regulatory changes, the correspondent banking in Brazil was further expanded to offer a broader set of services to its clients.

Correspondent banks offer financial services that include opening accounts, taking deposits, withdrawals, loans, and other cash-in and cash-out transactions. Bill payments are one of the major activities of correspondent banking. While in the area of opening new accounts the model has not been that effective, but one could say that correspondent banking has been quite successful in Brazil.

In 2006, RBI, India's central bank, decided to expand financial inclusiveness in the country through extension of banking services by using business correspondents and facilitators (RBI 2006). The approach was designed to provide great deal of independence to banks to use the services of NGOs, SHGs, MFIs and other CSOs as intermediaries in providing financial and banking services to the poor, low-income people and the un-banked. The model also utilizes the help of business facilitators to take the assistance of NGOs, farmers' clubs, cooperatives, community-based organizations (CBOs), IT-enabled rural outlets of corporate entities, post offices, insurance agents, well-functioning 'Panchayats,' Village Knowledge Centres and others to facilitate such activities as identification of borrowers, information and data verification, loan application processing, awareness about products such as savings, debt counselling, money management advice, submission of applications to banks, and support for SHGs and joint-liability groups.

While the business correspondents were allowed to undertake all activities that are under the purview of business facilitators, it undertook such other activities as disbursement of small value credit, debt service collection, collection of small value deposits, sale of microfinance, pension and mutual fund products, third-party products, and receipt and delivery of small value remittances. Business correspondents and facilitators normally receive a fee from the banking institutions for the services rendered.

Presented below are some of the important findings of a study of BCs model in India by Sa-Dhan (2012):

- As of March 2012, there were 96,828 customer service points (CSPs) set up in villages (with no banks) around the country in conjunction with BC model. However, there were widespread criticisms that BC system was not delivering intended results because of various constraints.

- One of the important findings of the study was that BC system faces serious challenges in terms of commercial viability. This is because under the model there is only one product, that is, no frills accounts (NFAs) that are offered to the clients and compensation for the services is rather inadequate to support the system. Under these circumstances the CSPs carry the brunt of the burden. If the current situation prevails, most of the CSPs will be closed down sooner or later.

- The fear of frauds and misappropriation are some of the major factors that were inhibiting introduction of more products by the banks. At the same time low return from the operations inhibits the BCs to build robust systems, procedures and supervisory mechanisms that are appropriate for mini-banks.

- The methodology of selecting BCs needs improvement. The banks select BCs through competitive bidding process and the entity that quotes the lowest is selected. But the process does not assure that the selected entity has done the necessary due diligence in quoting by taking into consideration direct and indirect costs involved in such operations. As a result, the BCs fail to become sustainable in general.

- While there has been a perception that opening CSPs and providing NFAs are signs of financial inclusion, in actuality, there are CSPs where large numbers of NFAs are dormant that range from 88 to 96 per cent. Besides, there are CSPs that are also being closed.

- Financial literacy programme that is key to improving financial inclusion were almost missing. In order to get benefits from the

BCs, the clients need financial literacy training and access to credit.

- It was found that CSPs led by not-for-profit MFIs as BCs were more effective in understanding customer needs. Besides NBFC-MFIs are currently not permitted to be BCs.
- Many banks lack channels for listening to grievances of BC customers.

As can be seen, many of the issues listed above need resolution in order for the BC model to become effective arms of the banks to spearhead financial inclusion. Needless to say, one needs to acknowledge the fact that a full-blown development of correspondent banking model in India has the potential to provide access to savings facilities on a much larger scale.

An Overview of Microsavings Products

The MFIs in general offer three types of products that cater to the short-, medium- and long-term needs of the poor. The specific types of savings accounts offered consist of (1) demand deposit accounts or current accounts, (2) contractual products and (3) time deposits (Hirschland 2005). We will discuss about these products in the following text. Besides these generic products, we will discuss about savings products offered by SafeSave in Bangladesh, GPS and M-KESHO mobile banking (e-banking)-based savings products.

Demand Deposit Accounts

These are bread and butter savings account every poor, including the destitute, should have access to. Given the fact that the income of a poor family is invariably erratic, they would prefer demand deposit accounts where they can save with no minimum amount stipulation and withdraw funds whenever they need. Broadly, demand deposit accounts can be of three types, that is, passbook savings accounts, sight deposits and current accounts (Ledgerwood et al. 2006). In the case of passbook savings accounts, clients receive a book where each deposit and withdrawals are recorded. Clients receive a nominal interest on such accounts because cost of maintaining such accounts are high. In the case of sight accounts, no interest is paid and the client is not restricted by any minimum or maximum amount. Funds can be withdrawn anytime. The transactions can be made using passbooks, ATMs, debit cards or point of sale devices. In the case of a commercial bank, one normally has access to current accounts where the client can transact using checks. In order to offer current accounts, an MFI would need full commercial banking license. It is important to note that offering demand deposits by an MFI can be more complex because, it is much more technology-driven than it appears on the surface and the MFIs should have the wherewithal to invest in such technologies.

Demand deposit accounts are 'costly and demanding to manage' for the MFIs (Hirschland 2005). This is partly because average balances in these accounts are low and number of transactions are usually large. However, it is expected that innovations in mobile money (such as M-PESA) could bring about major changes how MFI clients would transact with their MFIs in the future and reduce transaction cost of depositing and withdrawing money and making bill payments. Such accounts would also be suitable for the poor for receiving remittances and remitting funds.

Contractual Savings Products

Contractual savings is also known as 'accumulated fixed-term deposits' or 'programmed savings' (Hirschland 2005). The product is designed to accumulate fixed amounts of savings (based on saver's choice) at regular intervals for a specified period of time. During the period the saver earns interest. After the maturity date, the savers can withdraw the accumulated savings plus the interest. Early withdrawals are prohibited, although in some cases allowed with penalty. Such instruments have the advantage that the saver can earmark savings for such things as children's education, daughter's marriage and buying equipments for business. The saver can also use such instruments for saving for the old age as in the case of GPS. Some of the reasons why the poor like such savings accounts include: (1) relative illiquidity of such accounts, which forces the savers to keep on saving lest pay a penalty; (2) the accounts can double in say seven years or 10 years depending on the interest rate and (3) the certainty of receiving the funds (in a 'lump sum') at the end of the period. Banking institutions and the MFIs prefer such accounts because the cash flows for these accounts are predictable, and as a result liquidity management (asset liability management) becomes easier for the institutions. Besides, such accounts can also provide a much stable and relatively less expensive funding base for the MFIs. However, such products are not popular with poor who cannot put funds into the account at fixed intervals because their incomes are volatile.

Saving for Retirement: Grameen Pension Scheme

Because the poor are not normally aware of contractual savings, fixed deposits and pension products, they generally do not think in terms of putting aside small amounts to build up a nest egg for their golden years.

Pensions are annuities. They are normally set up using contractual savings accounts and/or fixed deposits to provide monthly payments to savers in old age. One has to set up these accounts ahead of time so that savings along with interest income become substantial to support desired payments in old age. Setting up a pension scheme can be complex and providing payment services in the form of annuity to the poor has to be part and parcel of such a scheme. Over the years, managing pension funds have become sophisticated. The underlying assets of a pension fund are not only invested in fixed-income securities, they are invested in equities, venture capital and other asset classes to have an optimal portfolio for the pensioners. In this regard, the MFIs need to take help from professionals in managing their pension funds.

Among the pension schemes offered by the MFIs, the GPS has become quite successful. The scheme is a contractual savings arrangement where the borrower is required to deposit regularly into an account (Dowla and Barua 2006). For example, all borrowers with loans above 8,000 Taka have to contribute 50 Taka each month to a pension deposit account for five- or 10-year term. Interest rates offered to depositors by Grameen varies between 8.5 and 12 per cent per annum.[6] At the end of the period, the savers are allowed to take the deposits and the accumulated income as a lump sum or as monthly income (annuity).

Because the poor generally lack social security, GPS-like pension schemes are potentially helpful way to build up savings for old age. Such savings would provide financial support to poor households where grandparents, parents and the children live together.

Fixed Deposits (Time Deposits)

Under the fixed deposit scheme (Hirschland 2005), the saver commits a fixed sum of money for a specified period of time. The funds have to be accumulated before committing. Therefore, it would be suitable for the poor who are not able to save specific amounts at specific intervals. It is also suitable for the non-poor savers who save using fixed deposits and receive higher interest rates on their savings because they commit fixed amount of funds for a fixed time. Usually interest rates received on these accounts are higher than the demand deposits and contractual savings accounts.

Again the illiquidity of these accounts forces the poor to remain invested before the funds can be liquidated. Such accounts are suitable for time-bound events such as tuition payments, daughter's marriage and the like. Such accounts can also be used as a savings vehicle to earn interest and to use such interest income as supplement to one's own income.

The non-poor and rich farmers prefer such deposits because they pay higher interest rates and they have the wherewithal to park funds on such accounts for a longer time. Unless the minimum amount needed for fixed deposits are small, the average poor person may not be able to take advantage of such fixed deposits. By keeping minimum amounts small, the average poor can save to build fixed deposits in multiples of the minimum amounts offered for savings. Such savings instruments can be an important source of relatively inexpensive funding for the MFIs.

The asset liability management of such funding sources is easier than demand deposits. In some cases, institutional investors and large savers are attracted to such fixed deposits and provide a boost to low-cost funding for the MFIs. If tax advantages can be provided on interest income earned on such savings, it can become one of the preferred vehicles for the public to save and the MFIs could tap into the domestic savings to fund their microloan portfolios with greater ease.

The fixed deposits could become relatively inexpensive and a stable source of funding for microloan portfolios. Needless to say, the spread earned between interest paid on fixed deposits and interest earned on the microloans would be substantial, enhancing the profitability of the MFIs. Under these circumstances, the MFIs would be in a much better position to bring down interest rates on microloans without jeopardizing sustainability (profitability) of the MFIs. Because of fixed deposits as a stable source of funding, the MFIs would be under less pressure for equity capital and to put MFI profitability and interests of stockholders ahead of the financial sustainability of their poor clients.

However, one needs to add the following observations in this context. The financial management issues (asset liability management and financial risk management issues) emanating from funding microloan portfolios with savings portfolios (demand deposits, contractual savings accounts and fixed deposits) are complex and needs professional management, which many fledgling, smaller and unsophisticated MFIs may lack. Secondly, there is a strong competition for gathering savings by the financial intermediaries to fund their various financial products and as a result these institutions constantly devise savings products (e.g., fixed deposits) with all kinds of bells and whistles and higher interest rates to attract such savings. A few basis points (one hundredth of a percent) higher yield on savings and fixed deposit accounts would move these funds to other institutions where improved return on savings is provided. Therefore, such savings in an MFI can be volatile and asset liability and liquidity management of these institutions has to take this into account.

Commitment Savings Accounts

As we discussed earlier, there are many reasons why a poor household finds it difficult to save. Even if access to formal savings facilities may be available, there are always demanding reasons why a poor family may not be disciplined enough to build up savings even if they might have the wherewithal to save in small doses. Commitment savings by a saver entails restricting his or her rights to withdraw funds from the account until a goal (voluntarily agreed to) has been reached. For example, in the US, 'Christmas Club' accounts have helped people to save over for expenses during Christmas time (Karlan and Appel 2012).

One of the widely known commitment savings products known to the poor is ROSCAs (Mullainathan 2006). As we noted in Chapter 3, in the case of ROSCAs, by participating in a group environment, a saver commits to make contributions to a common fund at predetermined intervals. The total fund so collected, in each interval, is given to one of the members of the group. Ultimately each member of the group has her turn to have access to collected funds (once) during the life of the ROSCA. When all the members have collected their funds, the ROSCA is abandoned. What this shows is that, by joining a ROSCA, a saver is under a group pressure to contribute to the ROSCA and wait for her turn to have access to funds (see Chapter 3). Sometimes, savers join more than one ROSCA to save for different purposes. The commitment to save for a purpose makes them join a ROSCA and the group environment of ROSCA keeps them disciplined to keep on saving.

In an interesting experiment (Ashraf et al. 2006) conducted in Philippines, Nava Ashraf, Dean Karlan and Wesley Yin have shown that commitment features of savings accounts and restrictions on withdrawals appreciably helped increased savings amongst the poor in comparison to the control group. The products were offered to those who were prepared to commit *a priori* to restrict access to their savings. Based on an RCT experiment (refer to Chapter 11 for a description of RCTs), the study found the savers in the treatment group to have increased savings by 81 percentage points than the savers in the control group. The study concludes that the savings response by the treatment group shows 'a lasting change in savings, and not merely a short-term response to a new product.'

SafeSave and Its Products

SafeSave was founded by Stuart Rutherford and Rabeya Islam, a Dhaka housewife with many years of running savings clubs for poor people.[7] SafeSave operates in nine low-income areas of Dhaka, Bangladesh. The goal of the institution is to provide reliable banking services profitably 'to poor and very poor men, women and children, in Dhaka.'

SafeSave makes daily visits to each of its clients. It accepts deposits or loan repayments. The loans have no fixed terms and no fixed repayment schedules. Anyone within walking distance of a branch office can have access to a savings account. Clients are treated as individuals and they are not required to join a group. Children below the age of 16 cannot borrow from SafeSave.

SafeSave offers 'Passbook Savings,' in which savers can deposit as little as one Taka (about $0.012) when a collector visits their house each day.

Savings accounts above a given minimum earn 6 per cent per annum. Clients can withdraw about 500 Taka (about $6) per day at their doorstep. Clients can withdraw 5,000 Taka ($60) per day at a branch office within a guaranteed maximum of 10 minutes. And if they need to withdraw larger amounts, it would take 24 hours to withdraw.

SafeSave also offers long-term 'commitment savings' accounts to save for a defined term of up to 10 years and receive relatively higher rate of interest. Clients can borrow against their long-term savings at a low rate of interest.

Borrowing from SafeSave provides a great deal of flexibility. Loans are quite flexible having no fixed terms and no fixed repayment schedules. There is no minimum loan value. There is a limit of one loan per household. In order to borrow, clients do not have to belong to a group, do not need any guarantors and do not have to attend any meeting. Maximum interest rate on these loans is 3 per cent per month using the declining balance approach. However, for entry level loans, as soon as their outstanding amount falls to 5,000 Taka or below, the interest rate charged is 2.5 per cent per month. For all borrowers, a minimum passbook savings balance of one-third of the loan balance is required as collateral at all times. No other security or personal guarantors are needed for borrowing. Clients must pay interest due each month. Repayment of principal can be flexible. However, in order to increase credit limit steady repayment of principal is required.

Product P9: Product 'P9' is an innovative financial tool, which is a combination of loan and savings at the same time.[8] It was designed by Stuart Rutherford and was first introduced in 2007 by SafeSave's sister organization Shohoz Shonchoy based in Gazipur, Bangladesh.

The product is designed to cater to the variable credit needs of the poor (Rotman et al. 2012). From MFI's perspective, it lends to the borrower with stipulations such that it helps her to build up savings. From a borrower's perspective, the disbursement and the repayments from the MFI are structured in such a way that it also helps to build-up savings.

More specifically, under the P9 model, the clients take an interest-free loan, one-third of which is held back and put in a savings account earning no interest. The clients repay the loans at their own pace. Once the loan has been repaid, they are ready to get a larger loan under the same conditions. As the clients take larger and larger loans, their savings grow until it becomes large enough to cover the value of their next loan. There is no interest on the loan and no interest is paid on savings balances.

A client has to pay a fee to open an account and to receive the disbursed loan. Collectors visit clients at their work or at home to collect whatever they have to repay on the loan. Under P9, clients can set a savings target. If money is withdrawn before the target is reached, the client has to pay a penalty. Under a pilot programme in Bangladesh, P9 model had 790 clients as of February 2012.

There has been an experimental implementation of P9 on M-PESA platform called Jipange KuSave (Rotman 2012) that is designed to provide access to almost 15 million users of M-PESA. It is expected that with such access, large number of M-PESA users in Kenya will have an instrument that allows them to borrow and save in parallel. Without such an instrument mustering strong desire and discipline to save from household cash flow becomes difficult. The fact that savings has been embedded in the borrowing instrument makes it easier for the borrower to build savings while repaying the loan.

M-KESHO: How Mobile Banking Is Emerging as an Important Medium to Provide Mobile Savings for the Poor

The mobile phone revolution has gripped Kenya so much so that about 93 per cent of Kenyans are mobile phone users. What is also noteworthy is that about 73 per cent of Kenyans use mobile money feature provided by M-PESA, which started in 2007 (see Chapter 9 for a description of M-PESA). Simply put, M-PESA provides money storage and transfer facility for its clients. Today, about 23 per cent of Kenyans use mobile money service. These are noteworthy achievements considering the fact M-PESA is only five years old (Demombynes and Thegeya 2012).

M-KESHO was introduced in March 2010. It provides interest-bearing savings accounts (provided by Equity Bank of Kenya) that can be accessed from mobile phones using M-PESA. A Policy Research Working Paper (World Bank) by Gabriel Demombynes and Aaron Thegeya (2012) conclude that while the bank-integrated mobile savings systems such as M-KESHO remains limited to largely better-off Kenyans, the use of 'basic mobile savings,' using mobile money accounts as a depository of funds is quite widespread. While these vehicles were not designed as savings tools, users of these accounts utilize them for storing money although they are not insured and do not earn any interest.

Some of the reasons why people leave their money in M-PESA accounts are: (1) it is safe, (2) easily accessible and (3) it protects the privacy of the account holder. Study by M-PESA regarding these accounts has found that when clients use the basic mobile savings to store funds, it is thought of as reserve funds, and as a result the clients use the funds for specific purposes and try to avoid using for anything else. By segregating the funds in M-PESA, they perhaps treat these funds as commitment savings. Most importantly, because funds stored in M-PESA are hidden, it becomes an easy way to save without the knowledge of others.

One would find it surprising that most of the M-PESA clients do not use M-KESHO as an interest-bearing savings account. The reasons for this may be due to the fact that the interest payment on these accounts is only 0.5 per cent (as of October 2011) for up to 2,000 Kenyan Shillings and an interest rate of 3 per cent for deposits above 10,000 Kenyan Shillings. These interest rates have to be contrasted with the inflation rate of 18.9 per cent (as of October 2011) in Kenya (Demombynes and Thegeya 2012). The negative interest rates are clearly a disincentive for saving one's funds in M-KESHO accounts. Another explanation for slower uptake of interest-bearing accounts has been attributed to two layers of service charges with regard to the usage of funds—first service charge for withdrawing funds from the M-KESHO accounts and then a second service charge to use the funds once the money is in the M-PESA accounts (Demombynes and Thegeya 2012).

It is important to note that 'Jipange KuSave' experiment in Kenya (based on the 'lend-to-save' model of Stuart Rutherford) is being implemented on M-PESA (Rotman 2012). Experience gained so far in the pilot programme has been encouraging. The experiment shows there is demand for financial products that are different from traditional products.

Conclusion

While borrowing has downside risks (see Chapters 4, 5 and 11), building savings has upside potential. Based on discussions in the chapter, it would be prudent if the poor start saving (microsaving) actively in a voluntary savings account even before accessing microcredit. During the period they build-up their savings, they should be taught about upside potential as well as the downside risks of microborrowing, particularly about the pitfalls of over-indebting themselves. In this context, it is also important to emphasize that the role of financial literacy along with lessons in simple arithmetic would go a long way in helping the poor become responsible borrowers.

Today, behavioural economics is being utilized to gain deeper insights into designing microsaving instruments that would provide the necessary incentive to the poor to be disciplined savers. Use of mobile banking to access savings accounts holds a great deal of promise for lowering transaction costs, which could engender wider financial inclusiveness.

As far as MFIs are concerned, the deposit base provided by the savers could provide a relatively inexpensive and stable source of funding for microloan portfolios. This could in turn help to reduce EIRs on microloans. Diversification in access to funding could lead to financially healthier MFIs. All in all, a poor household that saves regularly in a microsaving account can be much stronger financially in comparison to families that are not disciplined about savings and rely solely on credit.

Notes

1. Benjamin Franklin. 1896. *The Autobiography of Benjamin Franklin*. New York: American Book Company.
2. Stuart Rutherford. 2001. *The Poor and Their Money*, p. 43. New Delhi: Oxford University Press.
3. Wikipedia. 'Poor Richard's Almanack.' Available online at http://en.wikipedia.org/wiki/Poor_Richard's_Almanack, yearly almanac published by Benjamin Franklin, appeared continuously from 1732 to 1758.
4. Although, offering large numbers of savings accounts with small balances may not be cost-effective initially, as the size of the savings accounts would grow, the ratio of administrative expenses to total of balances on savings accounts would slowly comedown. Many MFIs besides offering savings accounts to the poor also provide savings accounts to the non-poor. By accepting relatively larger deposits from the non-poor, it could become cost-effective to offer savings accounts to the poor. However, offer of savings facilities by the MFIs require regulatory approval.

5. Suvashree Dey Choudhury and Swati Pandey. 2014. 'RBI Grants IDFC, Bandhan Financial Bank Licenses in Cautious Experiment,' Reuters, April 2, Mumbai. Available online at http://in.reuters.com/assets/print?aid=INDEEA310B520140402 (downloaded on 20 June 2014).
6. Grameen Bank. 2011. 'Grameen Bank at a Glance October 2011.' Available online at http://www.grameen-info.org/index.php?option=com_content&task=view&id=26&Itemid=175 (downloaded on 27 November 2012).
7. http://www.safesave.org/ (downloaded on 10 February 2013).
8. P9 Product Rules. Available online at http://site.google.com/site/trackingp9/home/product-rules (downloaded on 10 February 2013).

7

Microinsurance

> While the uncertainty that pervades our existence may be reduced by the structure we impose, it is not eliminated. The constraints that we impose have, themselves, uncertain outcomes reflecting our both imperfect understanding of our environment and the equally imperfect nature of both the formal and informal mechanisms we use to enforce those constraints.[1]
>
> Douglas C. North

Exposure to uncertainties and risks is one of life's certainties. And when it comes to the poor, risks and uncertainties loom large and could ruin their lives because of their heightened levels of vulnerability. One of the ways the non-poor manage their exposure to risks is by buying insurance against specific risks such as health insurance, accidental insurance, life insurance, property insurance and flood insurance. Whether one is poor or non-poor, it goes without saying that insurance for specific risks can be a life saver (particularly for poor families who normally lack any backstop mechanism) and insurance payouts could go a long way in helping to protect depletion of assets.

As the demand for microcredit has expanded rapidly during the last 35 years, the need for access to microsavings and microinsurance has been acutely felt. In Chapter 6, we discussed how microsavings can play an important role in providing the first line of defence in helping to mitigate emergencies and the risks poor households are exposed to. In this chapter, we will discuss how widespread use of microinsurance could be an important breakthrough to alleviate the impact of downside risks and in the process could lessen asset depletion and indebtedness in poor households.

Microinsurance is a complex instrument to design and deliver in comparison to microcredit and microsavings. In this context, it is important to note that, insurance in general is a financial instrument of recent origin and deals with complex concepts even the educated non-poor may find it difficult to understand. Besides, insurance as a formal financial instrument is not widely available to the poor, and hence they lack experience in using the product. Consequently, they are inhibited from venturing into buying insurance cover without being sure whether the regular payouts towards insurance premiums are worth the contingent benefits. As a result, unlike microcredit and microsavings, there is no natural demand for microinsurance. In fact, there are quite a few impediments to the adoption of microinsurance as a risk mitigating tool by the poor. Finding ways to alleviate such impediments could pay rich dividends in terms of adoption of microinsurance by the poor, which can complement microcredit and microsavings in managing household and business finances for the poor.

Based on current estimates, there are about 140 million microinsurance clients around the world, which constitutes only about 5 per cent of the potential market. And based on estimates by some of the largest insurance providers around the world, the market for commercially viable microinsurance products can be anywhere from about 1.5 billion to 3.0 billion policies, and it is expected that the industry can grow about 10 per cent per year (Koven and Zimmerman 2011).

For example, low-income people of Africa constitute microinsurance market of approximately 700 million. Similarly large countries such as India and China constitute huge microinsurance markets. Given the fact that only 5 per cent of the low-income people around the world use microinsurance today, growth rate of 30–50 per cent is plausible from a smaller base in spite of complex issues the industry is up against (Gray and Bell 2010).

Notwithstanding some of the major impediments the industry is up against in the near future, the intent of the chapter is to show, how increasingly there is an improved understanding of the need for insurance products for and by the poor. National governments around the world consider microinsurance to be a minimum necessity by the poor like microcredit and microsavings. The MFIs clearly see the benefits of access to microinsurance by their clients and are actively involved in collaborating with insurance providers to extend access to microinsurance. This is because appropriately structured microinsurance programmes could reduce vulnerabilities of the poor, which is beneficial for the financial health of the clients as well as the MFIs they borrow from. As we discussed in Chapter 4, it is mandatory for clients of most MFIs to enrol in a credit life insurance programme, which protects both the client and the MFI.

It is important to note that products such as health insurance, accidental insurance, life insurance, property insurance and disability insurance have given rise to huge service providers (in the private as well as public sectors) all over the world, including the developing countries. But by and large, these institutions provide their services to the non-poor. This is because as far as economics and logistics of providing microinsurance to the poor in a poor-friendly and sustainable way are concerned, we have just started to understand many of the complex issues associated with the field. Therefore, the interested reader is referred to 'Protecting the Poor: A Microinsurance Compendium,' edited by Craig Churchill (2006) and published by the International Labour Office (ILO), for a comprehensive view of microinsurance as a risk mitigating tool for the poor. This chapter is designed to provide a broad view of the field.

Poverty and Heightened Vulnerability to Risk: Why the Poor Need Insurance?

The literature on heightened vulnerability to risk in the context of poverty is quite extensive and deep. The following discussion briefly focuses on how poverty heightens vulnerability to risk events and makes it harder for a poor person to escape poverty. The discussion is rather commonsensical and intuitive.

Poverty and Vulnerability to Risk

Whether one is poor or non-poor, exposure to risks can arise from many sources such as illness, accident, old age, fire, harvest failures, earthquakes, cyclones, floods and the like. Severe or chronic illness of the breadwinner in a poor household can create havoc because poor people are usually not employed in the organized sector and do not have sick leaves, health insurance or savings to provide the necessary financial backstop. In the event, the breadwinner of the family succumbs to illness, the household's income declines precipitously. This further accentuates the vulnerability of the family. If the family has no savings, the family has to sell assets to meet these costs. Depletion of savings and assets is surest way to fall into a poverty trap.

Similarly, loss of life in an accident or in a cyclone could set back a poor family for years. Economic downturns that expose the poor to financial hardships can accentuate their vulnerabilities to other risks because they deplete their savings and even assets in order to survive during economic downturns. Besides, protection provided by public sector social programmes such as public health care facilities may not be adequately staffed and assistance available may not be adequate.

As far as health risks are concerned, when it comes to the non-poor, they follow simple guidelines about nutrition (including the use of vitamins), hygiene, sanitation and preventive care. Above all, they use health and accidental insurance at the minimum or they may have adequate savings and assets to cover for such risks. In this regard, the poor normally are at a disadvantage because they have minimal access to the knowledge base regarding good nutrition, sanitation and hygiene (Allianz AG, GTZ and UNDP 2006). They are also not knowledgeable about nutrients and food supplements that could protect them from ill health. As far as over-the-counter drugs are concerned, they practically do not know much about them. What is more, they do not normally immunize their children and themselves at the appropriate time. All these in combination increase their vulnerabilities to health risk. Therefore, educating the poor about nutrition, preventive care and health-related risks can pay rich dividends. For example, boiling water before drinking can reduce exposure to stomach-related ailments, which could save them money in terms of doctor bills, medicines and lost time at work. Many MFIs, such as Bandhan in West Bengal, India, provide health education and distribution of health products to their clients as a complementary service (Metcalfe et al. 2010).

The women and the children amongst the poor are particularly more vulnerable to risks than men because men are usually the main breadwinner in the family in every culture and they tend to have better protection.

And, if someone is poor and old, his or her vulnerabilities multiply several times more because most of them do not have access to pension and social security. Given the fact that in most poor families the women have to work, take care of the children and the management of the entire household, elderly members in the family tend to be neglected. Besides, most poor people are employed in the informal sector where they may not have any other option than to work even if they are ill. Without work they cannot earn. Unless the illness is treated at the right time, it can become chronic and ultimately it may be too late to do anything about it. Moreover, because of access to only rudimentary health care system and lack of access to specialists who could diagnose a disease properly, their vulnerabilities remain high.

What is more, the poor have less-diversified sources of income, which puts them in higher income risk category than the non-poor. For example, if the only source of income for the family is agriculture, drought, floods and any kind of crop infestation could severely reduce the income of not just one family, but most of the families in a given region. Under these circumstances, poor people may not be able to even depend on their neighbours for help. When poor families experience health risks, they may not have adequate savings to visit a doctor immediately. Uncertainty about accessing a loan can have severe consequences for a patient. Many MFIs provide emergency loans under these circumstances.

How the Poor Cope with Risks and Uncertainties of Life?

In order to insure against vulnerabilities, one thing the poor do diligently is to build social capital that they can rely on at the time of need. They always stand ready to help each other within the family, friends and neighbours to lessen the severity of risky events such as taking care of the sick at home. This is because very few of them can afford hospital stay. Helping each other out, on a reciprocal basis, turns out to be a zero-plus game. In the process everyone benefits. However, social capital is no substitute for insurance which covers such things as doctor visits, medicine and hospitalization.

At the time of natural calamities, the poor rely on charitable organizations, governmental organizations and donors to provide food aid, medical and financial assistance and reconstruction loans to rebuild. But such help sometimes arrives too late and exposes the poor to other risks.

However, it needs to be pointed out that some of the risk mitigation mechanisms that the poor substitute instead of buying insurance are not cost-effective and efficient. For example, publicly available health care services for the poor in the developing countries may not be adequate and they may not be staffed by specialists. Karlan and Appel (2012) in their book *More than Good Intentions: Improving the Ways the World's Poor Borrow, Save, Farm, Learn, and Stay Healthy* give examples of health care services in Ghana and India where doctors even do not show up for work.

If a family has a diversified source income, it does help a family to absorb financial shock emanating from health risk. Similarly access to emergency loans from MFIs or any other sources could help a poor family to mitigate specific risks.

Many poor people borrow at usurious rates from moneylenders during sickness in the family, which could get them into a debt trap. If all these options do not work, a poor family may not have other options but to sell assets. However, selling assets under duress does not fetch appropriate price for the assets.

Disciplined households can potentially save for the rainy days. There are instruments such as commitment savings (such as ROSCAs) that a poor family could build up for health risks. But such savings has limited scope because of erratic cash flow of a poor household and their limited capacity to save. What is more, it is very easy to deplete a household's savings after encountering just one emergency. And to build up savings after it has been depleted could take long time. During the intervening period when savings are being accumulated, a poor household is also exposed to other risky events. In reality, even the non-poor cannot build up savings if risks are bunched.

Why the Poor Need Insurance?

Risky events are major causes of asset depletion for a poor household, which ultimately leads to further impoverishment of a poor family. In the absence of health, life and other kinds of insurance, the poor substitute personal savings including sale of assets, credit and social capital, and help from charitable organizations, donors and governmental assistance to mitigate risks and uncertainties of life. However, such help may not fully immunize the poor from likely risks and uncertainties. Therefore, the poor need insurance to minimize asset depletion. However, the household has to make periodic payments towards insurance and buy such insurance ahead of time before the specific risk event occurs. Even if such insurance may provide partial protection against asset depletion, a poor family would still come out ahead.

What Is Microinsurance?

CGAP uses definition by Craig Churchill (2006) to describe microinsurance as 'the protection of low-income people against specific perils in exchange for regular monetary payments (premiums) proportionate to the likelihood and cost of the risk involved.'[2] Microinsurance is characterized by low coverage and low premiums that make it easier for poor households to afford microinsurance. Even if the coverage may be low (only a fraction of the total financial exposure that might emanate from a risky event), it would lessen financial burden of a poor household by that much more.

As an illustration of coverage under microinsurance, the Insurance Regulatory Development Authority (IRDA) of India sets the following limits on microinsurance (Grewal 2012). The current definition of microinsurance by IRDA limits the sum insured to ₹50,000 ($1,000 assuming an exchange rate of ₹50 to $1) for all microinsurance products, with an additional limit of ₹30,000 ($600) for health insurance. While there can be variations on the coverage of different microinsurance policies (which can vary across countries and among insurance providers), IRDA guidelines provide an indication of the coverage that a microinsurance policy could provide.

There are many different models that are used in delivering microinsurance to the poor. However, each and every insurance model has to rely on risk pooling. Therefore, it is important that we provide a brief description of what risk pooling is before we embark on discussing about microinsurance more broadly.

Types of Microinsurance

Microinsurance encompasses a wide variety of insurance products. It offers familiar product such as life insurance, health insurance (that meets claims for such things as primary healthcare, maternity, hospitalization and the like), property insurance (damage or loss of property) and disability insurance. It also includes such insurance products as funeral insurance, livestock insurance, crop insurance, weather insurance and natural disaster insurance. It is important to emphasize that while each one of these insurances comes under the insurance umbrella, each one of it is quite different from the other. The insurance provider has to understand well the associated risks in providing a given insurance product, its clients, the ecosystem they operate in, and knowledge of the regulatory environment of the country to design products that is affordable by the poor while the insurance company remains sustainable (profitable).

It goes without saying that the design of microinsurance products has to take into consideration low income and low net worth of the clients. Because the poor are not familiar with insurance products and the products are rather complex in comparison to financial instruments such as savings and credit, the challenge is to design products in such a way that they are easily understood, trusted and adopted by the insured clients. Sometimes the poor do not understand what they are buying when they buy microinsurance coverage. The fact that some clients may want their premiums back because they did not make any claims during the period they were insured, point to the fact that many of them do not understand the underlying principles of insurance.

Risk Pooling

Risk pooling relies on what is known as the 'law of large numbers,' which can be stated as follows: when a large enough group of individuals distribute (through an averaging process) their exposures to risk which is not uniform across the group (i.e., the risk exposures are independent of each other) then for a relatively small monthly or weekly premium, an individual or family can insure against, for example, hospitalization (which in terms of out-of-pocket expenses can be expensive).[3] The insurance provider pays for the hospitalization partially or fully depending on the insurance policy. And ultimately it comes out of the premiums paid by the group members to the insurance provider. This is possible because the members of the group insured by the insurance provider are not exposed to the specific risk with the same degree of severity at the same time.

Risk pooling works because it is based on an important assumption, that is, risk events experienced by the members of a group (who are insured) are independent of each other. However, this assumption could be violated under a variety of circumstances. For example, epidemic or natural disasters like earthquakes or tsunamis could expose the clients of an insurer to the same risk at the same time. Consequently, risk events experienced by the clients of the insurer are not independent anymore. Under these circumstances, the risk encountered by an insurer is known as covariant risk.

When the risk is covariant, the insurer could experience massive claims. Some of the ways insurers avoid massive claims is by excluding exposures to such risks. Many insurers also reinsure with reinsurance companies to manage their exposure to covariant risk.

Just to illustrate, in the case of health insurance, the risk events (i.e., illness) the clients of insurance providers usually experience are independent unless they are afflicted with an epidemic. As a result, the average health expenses for the group remain closer to the expected number. The year-to-year variations on costs could arise because of inflation and other factors. The insurance provider sets the premium in such a way that when one includes such items as exclusions, deductibles and other restrictive stipulations, the claims can be met by the provider from the premiums paid by the policyholders. The intent is that, not only the insurance provider will be able to meet the claims but it can remain sustainable (profitable).

While discussing about risk pooling, it is important to note that 'moral hazard' and 'adverse selection,' about which we discussed rather briefly in Chapter 3, are important issues an insurance provider has to take into consideration. This is particularly relevant in the case of the poor because of practically non-existent credit history, health records and actuarial data. As a result in pricing insurance premiums, the provider has to make several assumptions, which are later modified based on experience (Harper et al. 2011).

In order to remain sustainable, (profitable) the insurance providers and MFIs err on the side of setting high premiums and bring it down as they gain experience. Unless an insurance provider sets the premium high, moral hazard can create complications. However, high premiums could trigger adverse selection. To counter that, many insurance providers reduce the premiums while keeping the deductibles high. However, that may not be conducive in the sense that it would limit the number of payouts to clients, which a poor household may not find attractive. In spite of low premiums, high deductibles could turn off poor clients to sign up for insurance.

Keeping sustainability in mind, insurance providers deny coverage for events that could give rise to covariant risk, and put caps on claims per occurrence of a risk event and also caps on the sum total of payouts during the period of insurance. Such constraints help to keep the premiums at a reasonable level, which in turn helps to avoid adverse selection by the insurance providers. But again, the clients may not like too much use of such restrictions. They may try out a given insurance for a year or two and depending on the payouts decide not to renew their insurance.

Microinsurance Delivery Models

There are mainly four different approaches to the delivery of microinsurance (Maleika and Kuriakose 2008). These are partner–agent model, full-service model, CBO model and provider-model.

Under the partner–agent model, a partnership is formed between an established insurer and an MFI to deliver microinsurance to the poor. This is largely because microinsurance is a complex product and the MFIs in general do not possess the necessary know-how, capital base, financial risk management capabilities to design, deliver and assume financial risks associated with microinsurance programmes. Most importantly, for risk mitigation purposes, the client base of an MFI may be too concentrated in a given region as opposed to being a diversified group. Therefore, it may be prudent for an MFI to team up with an established insurance provider, which could provide the needed diversification through its existing and diversified client base.

But teaming up with other insurance providers may not be as straightforward as it may sound. This is because the products offered by the insurance provider may not be compatible with the needs of the MFI clients. And in some cases, the products offered may not be affordable to the clients. Therefore, it would be important to find out if the insurance provider is willing to collaborate with the MFI to design microinsurance products that would be suitable for its clientele. This is an important issue because the insurance providers as a group have very little experience to date in providing insurance to the poor. As they become more familiar with the ground rules for delivering such products for the poor, they would be able to design products that are appropriate for their clients.

The most important advantage of the partner–agent model stems from the fact that the insurer takes the risks of insuring (besides the design and development of the microinsurance products), while the MFIs take the responsibility of marketing, delivery and management of the programme. This is quite effective because, the MFIs are close to their clients and they use already established delivery channels to market and distribute microinsurance products. As a result, the approach keeps transaction costs down and microinsurance products become affordable for the poor.

Under the full-service model, MFIs are in charge of design, development, marketing and delivery of the products to its clients. The MFIs also fully absorb all the associated financial risk of the programme. Under this model, the microinsurance provider has full control of the programme but at the same time it has to shoulder all the risks. As noted earlier, most MFIs may not possess the necessary management acumen, financial risk-management expertise and capital structure to extend all but simple microinsurance products. For example, the MFIs rely on full-service model when they deliver such simple products as credit life insurance. In this context, it is important to note that, in many countries MFIs may not even get the approval of the regulators to extend complex microinsurance products to the poor on their own without partnering with established insurance providers.

Under the rubric of CBO, local community organizations such as MFIs, NGOs and cooperatives that function at the grass-root level jointly design, develop and distribute insurance products to gain experience before becoming operational. The approach has not been adopted widely partly because it may be too complex to collect actuarial information, design appropriate products for the clientele of all the participating organizations and share financial risk collectively. The provider model for delivering microinsurance utilizes the distribution network of MFIs and commercial banks to market microinsurance products for the poor. However, the model could result in high transaction cost, which could squeeze margins for the insurance providers. In a focus brief, Rupalee Ruchismita and Sona Varma (2009) mention that partner–agent model has experienced severe implementation issues in India, which has forced some of the microinsurance providers to scale back. They also mention that mutual model appears to be of limited value because the community absorbs all the risk.

Barriers to Adoption of Microinsurance by the Poor

Because the poor by-and-large are not familiar with insurance as a financial product, they need many questions answered before they can build the necessary trust to buy microinsurance for specific risks. The complex nature of insurance as a financial tool (as opposed to borrowing and saving) does not help in trust building. For example, while periodic payments towards insurance premiums are definite, the insurance payouts from the insurance provider are contingent on variety stipulations, which the poor find too complex to understand and hence build trust. Lack of clarity and hence trust about what benefits the poor would accrue from buying insurance has been detrimental to widespread adoption of microinsurance by the poor in managing their household and business finances.

Assuming that a poor client is satisfied that she can trust the insurance provider, the next big test for signing up for microinsurance boils down to the fact whether the insurance is affordable and protection provided is adequate. At the same time, the issue of poor-friendliness of the insurance provider and the MFIs is also important factors in buying microinsurance.

Many poor people think that if they did not receive insurance payout(s) during the year, then the premium payments to the insurance provider should be returned to them. What it implies is that the transition from a world where one gets something (when one pays), to a world where one may not get anything in return for the premiums, is difficult to accept for the poor. Besides, given the fact that households have demanding needs for expenses such as payments for children's education, loan repayments or building savings for their daughter's marriage, these payments appear more important (more real) to them in comparison to making insurance payments for specific risks that lies in the future. Besides, given the fact that household income of poor families can be volatile, it could deter them to sign up for microinsurance, which requires regular payments to insurance provider. What is more, one also needs to remember that poor people in the developing countries usually do not have a family doctor and do not visit a doctor regularly for regular check-up for preventive care. They visit a doctor only when they are exposed to an illness. All these are factors for not signing up for health insurance ahead of time.

The other reason why the poor tend not to sign up for microinsurance has to do with the fact that, even if they sign up for insurance they still have to save and also borrow at the time of an emergency, illness in the family or other specific risks they might be exposed to. In fact, in coping with a risk event such as health risk, the initial expenditures for visiting a doctor, buying medicine and hospitalization has to be paid out from family's savings or borrowed fund and after only submitting the bills to the insurance company the family will receive the reimbursement. Insurance providers usually require forms to be filled out and bills from doctors, pharmacies and hospitals along with the forms to be submitted to receive reimbursement. And the poor are not adept at all these. As a result for the buyers of insurance, who traditionally relied on self-insurance, all these logistics may deter them to sign up for insurance. Besides, microinsurance may not fully replace self-insurance. Therefore, the poor would have to mix and match self-insurance with microinsurance. This could also deter them to buy insurance.

All in all, many of the abovementioned issues have become major bottlenecks in the expansion of insurance markets to the poor. Given the fact that these markets function on the basis of risk pooling, lack of a critical mass of insured clients, would force insurance premiums to be higher, which in turn could deter the poor to buy insurance. As we have seen, in order to avoid low participation rate, participation is mandatory in the case of credit life insurance, which keeps the premiums reasonably low.

Microinsurance: What Are Some of the Impediments to Its Sustainability

To begin with, low premiums on microinsurance imply that the product has to be scalable to be sustainable. As we have seen, it was the scalability of microcredit as a product that has made its sustainability a reality for many MFIs around the world. Microcredit was scalable because there was a natural demand for the product. We have already discussed in the previous section why there is no natural demand for microinsurance. Besides, given the fact that the poor are not knowledgeable enough about how insurance is important for their economic well-being and microfinance industry has been lacking in efforts to educate the poor, generating demand for microinsurance has been difficult.

Moreover, commercial insurance providers that sell microinsurance products (directly or indirectly) to institutions such as the MFIs, NGOs, CBOs, and cooperatives and also to agents and brokers find ratio of high cost to small premiums, lack of awareness about insurance amongst the poor and lack of good infrastructure drives up distribution cost and are some of the most important impediments to becoming sustainable in offering microinsurance to the poor (Micro Insurance Network 2011).

As we have noted earlier, microinsurance has not achieved scale in comparison to microcredit because it is a difficult product to design and deliver. Besides, insurance products are heterogeneous because the underlying actuarial risk assessment for each product is different. Just as an example, health insurance, which is perhaps the most complex to design and deliver, is different from life insurance products. And products such as crop insurance are different from cattle insurance products. Using index-based weather insurance to insure outputs (crops), as opposed to inputs (such as seeds, fertilizers and pesticides) could substantially change the nature of the risk exposure. Therefore, designing insurance products, calculating premiums, deciding on exclusions, setting deductibles, and ultimately selling and servicing insurance products that deliver value to the poor involve complex set of activities.

What is more, lack of access to good-quality client data for risk assessment makes it difficult to price premiums and write policies. For example, in providing access to health insurance, finding the date of birth of a client and hence her age can be difficult. Actuarial profile of the poor is important in designing microinsurance products. Given the fact that the poor lack nutrition, sanitation and hygiene, and do not visit a doctor regularly and pay less attention to health-related issues put them in a different risk category than the non-poor. Besides, because most poor people do not visit doctors for health check-up, they do not have health records. The recent introduction of UIDs for every citizen in a huge country like India and other countries around the world will provide the necessary impetus to building databases consisting of actuarial profile of the poor, including their credit histories.

The issues of moral hazard and adverse selection about which we discussed in Chapter 3 also complicate the situation for insurance providers. Because they cannot assess actuarial risks of their clients does not imply that they cannot set insurance premium somewhat higher and gain experience before lowering the premiums. Given the fact that there is no natural demand for insurance products by the poor, this could deter many poor people to sign up for insurance. This could complicate risk pooling and the ultimate sustainability of insurance providers. That is one of the reasons why credit life insurance offered by the MFIs is not an option. It is compulsory.

However, in spite of many of the abovementioned roadblocks to sustainability, major insurance providers around the world have been expanding their frontier to provide microinsurance to the poor in countries such as India, China and South Africa, and countries in Africa and Latin America. Such expansion into the developing countries has been based on the assumption that in the long run, microinsurance business in these countries is expected to be profitable (Micro Insurance Network 2011).

MFIs as Platforms to Deliver Microinsurance to the Poor

The advantages of MFI platform to deliver microinsurance to the poor are many. The first and foremost being, these institutions have taken great strides in gaining valuable experience and knowledge by bridging the 'last mile' to deliver microcredit to the poor. The existence of such networks provides great deal of opportunity for insurance providers, which they can leverage to design, develop and deliver poor-friendly and sustainable microinsurance products.

While the insurance providers can gain from the existence of MFIs in order to reach out to the poor, the MFIs, on the other hand, can benefit from providing access to microinsurance products to their clients in two ways: (1) by earning fee-based income and (2) by helping to reduce vulnerabilities of their clients in such areas as health, accidents, weather, property, livestock and crop-related risks. Needless to say, buying insurance cover in some of these areas (if not all) can help protect against asset depletion, which in turn could reduce the credit risk of MFI clients. For example, MFI clients can be susceptible to loan non-repayment if someone in the family is sick.

We discussed in Chapter 4, how access to microcredit by the poor is not a panacea in winning the war on poverty. Credit being a double-edged sword, too much reliance on it has its downsides. As a result the mono-product world of microfinance has been in the lookout for balancing its product-mix to avoid situations where the poor are forced to borrow from multiple sources that could result in over-indebting themselves. Unquestionably, along with access to credit for generating income streams, access to poor-friendly microinsurance products can help the poor mitigate specific risks to reduce asset depletion.

Some of the ways the MFIs could help major insurance providers in selling insurance to the poor include (1) bundling microinsurance with microcredit to create demand for insurance, which can help the insurance provider in market expansion and, (2) helping the insurance providers to design, develop and deliver poor-friendly products to their clients and (3) helping the insurance companies to mitigate such risks as moral hazard because of their intimate knowledge of the clientele (many of who may not be able to provide the necessary actuarial data). In a nutshell, collaboration between large insurance companies and the MFIs helps the insurance providers to use MFIs as channels to reach out to the poor. This is important because, usually the large insurance providers are divorced from the needs of the poor at the grass-root level. One of the important benefits of such collaboration for an insurance provider is brand recognition that helps to engender markets expansion, which in turn can help in sustainability (profitability) of the microinsurance business.

Having discussed how MFIs and insurance providers can collaborate with each other in beneficial ways, it is important to note that working as distribution channels for insurance providers may not be all that straightforward as it seems. The cost of distributing and servicing microinsurance products starts with design and ends with the settlement of claims and several other stages in between that include marketing, sales, underwriting and policy administration (Gunaranjan 2008). Undoubtedly, the involvement of MFIs in all the stages could greatly contribute towards providing access to low-cost microinsurance for the poor.

Gunaranjan, the head of insurance business for BASIX[4] (India) in 2008, discusses in a paper about some of the complexities of underwriting policies for BASIX clients. For example, completing insurance policy paperwork for BASIX clients living in remote areas is complicated because of lack of identification and age-related data, since they do not have access to hospitals, schools and public utilities companies that can provide such data. BASIX had to work with insurance providers to find substitutes for such data. In the case of health insurance, insurance providers for BASIX stipulated that hospitals should have 10 beds to be qualified. However, in remote areas of India access to such hospitals may be difficult. BASIX used registered hospitals instead (which did not have 10 beds) in order to offer health microinsurance to its clients. Another area where BASIX showed innovation was that it allowed its clients to make smaller insurance premium payments bundled with repayment of loans. Such innovations (which may not be considered as earth-shaking) have been at the forefront of expanding the scope of microfinance.

Examples of Microinsurance Products

In the following text, we will discuss rather briefly about three microinsurance products, which include credit life insurance, health insurance that include Jamii Bora in Kenya and BASIX in India, and index-based weather insurance for agricultural inputs such as 'Kilimo Salama' (safe agriculture) also in Kenya.

The MFIs traditionally have provided credit life insurance to their clients because it protects the client's family as well as the MFIs by reducing their exposure to credit risk. In this context, we will also discuss briefly about the pricing and sustainability of such programmes based on BASIX's experience.

The motivation for including Community-based Health Insurance (CBHI) scheme at Jamii Bora is to show how an MFI in an urban area of Kenya, which lends to urban poor, including beggars, attempts to solve some of the problems related to accessing health care for its clients. The clients of Jamii Bora find it difficult to access health care because out-of-pocket expenses are relatively larger (Mwaura and Pongopanich 2012). What is striking about the example is that with a modest insurance premium and a small number of insured under the programme, Jamii Bora is able to provide hospitalization care for its clients. One of the impact assessments of Jamii Bora Health Insurance (JBHI) programme discusses only about the insurance programme without analyzing its financial sustainability. However, there is no indication that the programme receives any financial support from other sources.

The next example considers combined credit life and group health insurance programme offered by BASIX, which is one of the pioneers in offering insurance products in India and the world. It was the first MFI around the world that offered 'Weather-Based Crop Insurance.'

Credit Life Insurance

Basic credit life insurance covers only the principal and the interest of an outstanding loan when the borrower dies. Enhanced credit life insurance could also cover other expenses such as funeral expenses, death and disability cover for other members of the family, and fire insurance for client's business. Delivery of credit life insurance is bundled with delivery of credit and in many cases microcredit. In many cases, MFI clients may not even know that they are paying for credit life insurance.

The MFIs offer credit life insurance to their clients because by and large microcredit is extended to the poor without collateral. What is more, most of the MFIs have only a thin capital base, which needs to be safeguarded. Therefore, these institutions protect their microloan assets by buying credit life insurance. But at the same time, for a minimal payment, credit life insurance also protects poor households if the breadwinner dies.

The following example illustrates how credit life insurance premium was set at BASIX (Harper et al. 2011). Working with Aviva, a large insurance provider, BASIX introduced group life insurance in 2002. Due to lack of mortality rate data for its clients, the premium was initially set at ₹8.61 per ₹1,000 insured. The rate was applied to one and half times the loan amount (later it was increased to three times the loan amount). Based on the claims experience, the premium was reduced by 2004 to ₹6.90 per ₹1,000. Based on actuarial evaluation of the claims experience, Aviva further reduced the premium to ₹4.26 per ₹1,000 insured (Harper et al. 2011). In fact, the premium was reduced still further to ₹3.98 per ₹1,000 by 2008 (Gunaranjan 2008). What is more, because of the substantial reduction in premium rate, BASIX decided to extend credit life insurance cover to the spouses of the borrowers. As Gunaranjan notes, sustainable approach to providing access to micro-insurance along with proper administration of the products does add value for the poor borrowers.

However, it is important to note that many consider credit life insur-ance to be an added cost for poor borrowers. It increases the effective cost of microlending to the poor. Besides making payment for credit life insurance, MFI borrowers also make payment towards loan process-ing fee, which also increases effective cost of microloans. Implicit costs associated with compulsory savings also increase effective cost of micro-loans. However, all these added costs need to be compared with usurious interest rates the local moneylenders charge to the poor. What is more, in the event the principal breadwinner of the family dies, the loan(s) still outstanding to the moneylender has to be paid back. Otherwise, the fam-ily would lose their collateral and in some cases might have to liquidate other assets to repay the moneylender.

During the last few years, the microinsurance industry has been able to take advantage of the widespread use of mobile phones by the poor and the unbanked to sell microinsurance products to them. The case in point is the strategic partnership of Grameenphone, Pragati Life Insur-ance and MicroEnsure in Bangladesh to offer life insurance to the poor and the unbanked free of charge, based on their usage of mobile phone. For example, a subscriber of Grameenphone could receive a free life insurance cover of 20,000 BDT (Bangladesh Taka) if airtime used in the previous calendar month ranges between 250 and 349 BDT (excluding VAT). The free life insurance cover has been designed to provide such coverage up to a maximum of 50,000 BDT. To receive free life insurance cover of 50,000 BDT, the airtime used by the client in the previous calendar month has to be 500 BDT or higher.[5] One other example in this arena includes Bharti Airtel, which provides microinsurance products to its mobile phone customers in Africa in strategic partnership with MicroEnsure and local insurance companies. Bharti Airtel, which is a provider of telecommunications services and operations in 20 countries, has entered into strategic partnership with MicroEnsure to offer microinsurance products, which include life, accident, health, agriculture and other forms of cover.[6]

Health Insurance

Because the poor tend to self-insure, helping the poor through health education, nutrition, sanitation and hygiene does help to reduce exposure to health risk. This translates into savings on health care costs. Many MFIs such as Bandhan, BRAC and Grameen Bank encourage their borrowers to follow good sanitation and hygiene. MFIs also help provide immunization to their clients. They also help the poor to have access to potable water. Many MFIs also provide health education in the following areas, that is, alcohol abuse, drugs and HIV/AIDS. We discuss in Chapter 10 the costs of providing health education and health product distribution by Bandhan in West Bengal.

Availability of health care facilities is limited in areas where poor live because the poor do not have the purchasing power to access health care. Lack of good infrastructure also complicates access to health care. For example, without access to reliable electricity and water supply, hospitals cannot even function. Without large number of clients, it is not sustainable for health care providers to open hospital facilities in areas where the poor live. And without these facilities the insurance providers find it difficult to offer microinsurance to the poor. However, it would seem reasonable that once poor people are provided with health insurance, it would be attractive for the health care providers to provide such facilities because the poor now have the purchasing power to spend on health care.

However, in all this, the real bottleneck is that the poor have to be convinced that buying microinsurance cover can add value. One of the ways to motivate the MFI clients to buy microinsurance may be by 'demonstration of benefits through prompt and hassle-free claim settlement procedures,' (Gunaranjan 2008). In fact, in villages where BASIX settled few claims, it was easier for other BASIX clients to be convinced about buying microinsurance. As far as finding the resources to make payment towards premiums are concerned, there are many poor families that spend on 'temptation goods' such as tobacco, alcohol, cigarettes and lottery tickets on an ongoing basis and go on spurious spending during festivities and can be motivated to curtail such spending through financial literacy training.

Jamii Bora: Community-based Health Insurance

Jamii Bora (happy family) is a MFI in Kenya started by Ingrid Munro. The following description of Jamii Bora is based on the transcription of an interview Microcredit Summit Campaign Director Sam Daley-Harris conducted with Jamii Bora founder Ingrid Munro in October 2007 (Microcredit Summit E-NEWS 2008). At the outset, it is important to note that while the institution has done a great deal of pioneering work in delivering microfinance (microcredit) to the poor, it has also worked in such areas as 'get sober' programme for drug addicts and housing projects for the poor people.

Jamii Bora also provides microinsurance for the poor. The reason Jamii Bora decided to provide microinsurance cover to its members was based on the fact that almost 93 per cent of their poor borrowers who were delinquent in making payments on their microloans had someone hospitalized in the family. This is because health-related expenditures for Jamii Bora clients can be very expensive both for public and private facilities, which provide access to hospitals, clinics, diagnostics, medicines and other related costs (Mwaura and Pongopanich 2012).

Initially, Jamii Bora intended to provide health insurance directly to the poor. What they found was, it would cost around $80 per family annually. That was considered too high a premium for the poor members of Jamii Bora. As a result, the institution decided to approach the problem by finding out how much each family would be able to afford to buy health insurance. The amount arrived at was 1,000 Kenyan Shillings (about $12) for each member. Because the members may not be able to pay the premium at a time, it was decided to collect a premium of $0.30 per week.

JBHI programme was established as a CBHI in 2001. Out of a total membership of over 277,000 in the Jamii Bora Trust (JBT), over 32,000 were enrolled in JBHI. Today, the annual health insurance premium is 1,200 Kenyan Shillings ($16) per member (Mwaura and Pongopanich 2012). The insurance can be paid over 50 weeks and the premium per week is $0.40. The insurance covers the member and up to four children less than 18 years of age. In case the family has more than four children, additional insurance has to be paid. The member can also buy insurance for his or her spouse.

JBHI as the insurer, partners with 70 public or faith-based hospitals all over Kenya to provide in-patient services. The insurance programme covers the in-patient treatment costs without any exclusions or cost restrictions. But the insured does have to pay the required co-payments, if any. Members of JBT can also join JBHI. However, it is mandatory for JBT members with loans to pay for health insurance. After repaying the loan(s), a member may decide to continue with JBHI.

The impact assessment by Mwaura and Pongopanich only covers the access aspects of the programme among the urban poor. It does not provide any assessment with respect to the financial sustainability of the programme.

Some of the findings of the impact assessment are as follows: (1) among the insured, about 62 per cent were women and about 38 per cent were men, (2) about 74 per cent of the insured were married and 26 per cent were unmarried, and (3) clients with children join the programme to avoid out-of-pocket expenses.

Overall, the insured members were more likely to be hospitalized than the uninsured and women were more likely to be admitted to a hospital than men. Besides, insured members spent more days in the hospital than non-insured members. Among the insured, those in the lowest income quintile were more likely to use the benefits provided by JBHI as opposed to the highest income quintile members. About 87 per cent of the visits were covered by the services provided by JBHI.

The following quote from Mwaura and Pongopanich (2012) discusses about the success of JBHI health insurance programme for the urban poor in Kenya:

> The JBHI has been implemented for over eight years and it seems to have overcome barriers that most CBHI encounter which lead to their failure. Its membership base has continued to grow annually. The main reason for this

can be explained by its establishment within the JBT microfinance institution. Having the JBHI scheme as a benefit product to JBT members ensures that the members have access to loans and can grow their informal businesses and therefore can afford to pay the weekly premiums.

BASIX: Credit Life and Group Health Insurance

The liberalization of insurance markets in India in 2000 and the requirement that private sector insurers have to serve low-income markets boosted ability of BASIX and other MFIs to expand their insurance offerings to the poor by collaborating with insurance providers such as Aviva, ICICI Lombard and Royal Sundaram. In collaboration with Aviva, BASIX introduced the group life insurance programme in 2002. Credit life insurance is compulsory for microloan borrowers of BASIX. We have already discussed the pricing of credit life insurance premium by BASIX. Besides offering credit life and group-based health insurance, BASIX also offers weather-based crop insurance, livestock and business insurance products.

Its group health insurance programme was introduced in 2005 in collaboration with Royal Sundaram. In the case of health insurance, the coverage was only for hospitalization and it covered a maximum of five days of hospital stay in a year. Initially, the coverage provided for ₹300 (about $6, assuming $1 = ₹50) per day. Later, it was increased to $9 and then to $11 per day as payout for hospitalization. The costs were more than enough to cover hospital stay for one day in local hospitals. Any balance that remained after covering for hospital stay was meant for medicine and loss of earnings. The health insurance also included substantial lump sum benefits in case of an accident (Harper et al. 2011).

The premiums for life insurance and group health insurance have been discussed in the following. Life cover was designed to pay out the outstanding balance on the loan and also to make a lump sum payment to the family. Assuming a BASIX client had a microloan for ₹10,000 (equivalent to about $200, assuming $1 equals ₹50), the premium will be based on an indemnity value that is three times the loan amount, that is, ₹30,000. The premium to indemnify that amount was ₹120, which implied ₹4 in premium for every ₹1,000 life cover. With regard to coverage for group health insurance, the premium was ₹240 plus an annual fee of ₹120. Therefore, the total premium for life insurance (₹30,000 coverage) plus group health coverage comes to ₹480 (less than $10 a year), that is, ₹40 (less than $1) a month (Harper et al. 2011).

As of June 2010, BASIX had provided coverage to 2.55 million clients under credit life as well as group health insurance programme. And as of June 2010, the total payouts (on account of claims) under the life insurance programme were about ₹180 million and under the group health insurance was about ₹71 million. Therefore, total payouts under both the programmes were ₹251 million. Assuming $1 is equivalent to ₹50, total payout for life insurance as well as group health insurance programmes was about $5 million (Harper et al. 2011).

Sustainability of Credit Life and Group Health Insurance Programmes

We have already discussed about many of the bottlenecks in offering microinsurance to the poor, such as lack of good-quality actuarial data, which makes pricing of insurance premiums difficult. Therefore, insurance providers have to rely on risk assessments on an aggregate level such as groups, where buying credit-life insurance is compulsory. Given the fact that the product has to be simple, premiums have to be affordable and the insurance has to deliver value to the poor, it does put a lot of constraints in tailoring an insurance programme for the poor.

Some of the age-old problems of insurance industry such as moral hazard (see Chapter 3) can be roadblocks to sustainability. After its inception in 2005, the credit life and group health insurance programme of BASIX was inundated with 'false and overstated claims' in the years 2007 and 2008 (Harper et al. 2011). As a result, BASIX by 2010 had to employ 80 facilitators to settle such claims. Obviously, this increased administrative expenses.

As a result of false and inflated claims, the insurance providers initially reduced and then eliminated fees as well as commissions that BASIX used to receive from the providers. As we noted above, the total claims that were settled under these two programmes reached about $5 million by June 2010. After elimination of fees and commissions, BASIX was left with ₹10 per month (₹120 per year, about $2.4 per customer) service fee per client plus a small fee for access to BASIX data. While credit life and group health programme was not very profitable for BASIX, institutionally it was concluded that the programmes were an essential component of its lending activity. Therefore, it was decided not to disaggregate the costs for the insurance programme from its lending activities.

In commenting about the sustainability of the credit life and group health insurance programme, Harper et al. note that this programme was offered to the clients as a 'bundle' along with their microcredit programme. In that sense, it was a complement to its lending activities and many customers were not aware that they had bought insurance. In offering the insurance programme, BASIX, over a 10-year period, had to invest money and time in training about 4,000 staff on the rudiments of insurance. This was one of the requirements by the regulators. Besides, BASIX, as an NBFC was not allowed to receive commissions on microinsurance, however, it was allowed to act as insurance agent and can be paid commissions on direct sales to clients but not on group-based microinsurance products. As a result, in order to cover costs, Samrudhi, one of the subsidiaries of BASIX, had to charge the clients a small fee. While during the initial period, BASIX earned generous fees and commissions, with more competition, earnings from fees and commissions were lower. Competition allowed for insurance providers to pick and choose from a pool of large number of MFIs to partner in delivering microinsurance to the poor. All in all, unless services are disaggregated, it is difficult to assess sustainability (profitability) of bundled insurance products such as credit life and group health insurance offered by BASIX. It is important to add that in the wake of 2010 Microfinance Crisis in Andhra Pradesh in India, the financial health of BASIX and other small and large MFIs in Andhra Pradesh did suffer substantially.

Kilimo Salama: Index-based Weather Insurance for Agricultural Inputs in Kenya

We describe below an innovative weather insurance programme in Kenya called Kilimo Salama (safe farming or safe agriculture in Kiswahili), which insures farmers' cost of agricultural inputs such as seeds, fertilizers, herbicides and other farm inputs in the event of drought or excessive rainfall. The programme is collaboration among three entities, Syngenta Foundation for Sustainable Agriculture (SFSA), UAP Insurance and Safaricom (provider of M-PESA). The programme is also supported by IFC. The following discussion of the programme is based on an IFC case study of Kilimo Salama.[7]

One of the major reasons why there is need for such insurance has to do with the fact that farmers in the developing countries are exposed to the risks of unpredictable weather patterns because of climate change.[8] In Kenya, about three-quarters of employment is provided by farming and many farmers' livelihoods are dependent on their harvest to feed the family and generating income from crop sales. As a livelihood, farming in Kenya is very risky because the size of the harvest is largely dependent on the timing and amount of rainfall. What is more, farmers normally do not have access to banking to save and borrow to overcome weather-related shocks. As a result, only 50 per cent of Kenyan farmers invest in improved seeds and fertilizer for cultivation (Abed et al. 2011). This is because the farmers fear that they will lose their harvest along with their investment in seeds and fertilizer if there is too much or too little rainfall.

Traditional insurance that normally indemnifies the insured, covers against crop loss or damage. However, in order to receive a payout for crop loss or damage, a lengthy process is involved, which includes reporting the loss and assessment of the loss, and depending on the assessment the farmer would receive a payout. The process is cumbersome and prone to tampering and fraud by the farmer as well as the insurer.

The product being discussed here is index-based, that is, the payouts are based on comparing historical rainfall patterns in a given region with actual rainfalls to determine if there is too little or too much rain in the region. Kilimo Salama insures the inputs, not the outputs. During the planting season, rainfall is measured using solar-powered weather stations. Obviously, accurate measurement of rainfall is crucial to the overall process of trust building with the farmers. If the actual rainfall deviates too much from the rainfall index, a determination is made if payout has to be made to the farmers. The amount of the payout is based on the amount of deviation from the rainfall index. As a result, insurance payouts are independent of crop damage a farmer may experience. The premium calculation for insuring the inputs has gone through changes, but currently the cost of the insurance premium has been set at 10 per cent of the cost of the inputs.

Currently, Kilimo Salama uses about 50 well-established agricultural input suppliers to distribute the insurance product. The premium is added on top of the input cost to streamline the sale of insurance. But it also helps the farmers to believe that the insurance premium is a part of the input cost, which makes them inclined to part with the extra 10 per cent to insure the inputs. The programme insures inputs purchased for at least one acre of land when a farmer buys the insurance at the time of purchasing the inputs.

The partnership between Kilimo Salama and Safaricom (the largest network operator in Kenya), the provider of M-PESA (see Chapter 9 for a description of M-PESA) makes it easier for the farmers in remote areas to register their inputs and receive payouts. As a result, it becomes easier for the insurance company to reach out to a new client and attain scale. Safaricom uses its mobile banking system M-PESA for collecting premiums and transferring payouts to the insured.

The approach has been streamlined so much so that the farmers pay an extra 5 per cent over the input costs (see the discussion below about the 5 per cent premium) to insure against too much or too little rainfall. Using the camera in a mobile (cell) phone, the barcode in each bag of inputs is registered and a message confirming the registration of the bag(s) under the insurance programme is sent to the handsets. In the event it is determined that the payout has to be made, it is also sent to the handsets. The approach streamlines transactions and hence reduces associated costs. The success of the system depends to a large extent on the streamlining of the transaction process.

Because of innovative design of the programme, it runs rather efficiently without middlemen and very little paperwork. This is important because affordability of insurance premiums, ease of use to transact with the insurance provider and the transparency of the payouts are some of the important aspects that makes or breaks an insurance programme— particularly reaching the critical number of clients that would make the programme sustainable.

However, educating the farmers for signing up for insurance is a challenge. Initially the product was completely paid for by Syngenta Company. However, farmers are distrustful of free offers. Subsequently, the free offer was dropped and a 10 per cent premium was introduced. However, the 10 per cent premium was initially split equally between Syngenta Company and the farmer. Therefore, the farmer had to pay only 5 per cent on the purchase price of the inputs such as seeds and fertilizers.

The latest version of Kilimo Salama called Kilimo Salama Plus also includes coverage for crop outputs. Kilimo Salama Plus insurance covers input cost as well as output based on an estimated value of the harvest. However, the new product is available only in certain areas. In this case, the farmers pay the full price of the premium, that is, 10 per cent.

The product was pilot-tested in 2009 with 200 maize farmers. That year, the farmers experienced one of the worst droughts of their lives. As a result, the farmers received payouts based on the index that ranged from 30 to 80 per cent. In the following season, about 12,000 farmers were covered and only 10 per cent of the farmers received payouts anywhere from 10 to 50 per cent of the insured price of the inputs. These 12,000 farmers were supported by 30 weather stations. It is important to note that about two-thirds of the farmers were recruited through MFIs where enrolment in Kilimo Salama was mandatory. Based on the estimates of Syngenta Foundation, the existing monitoring stations could support up to 50,000 farmers.

IFC case study mentions that currently, Safaricom generates a profit from transaction fees from M-PESA usage, and UAP Insurance is expected to reach sustainability when the programme is scaled up.

In this context, it is important to note that BASIX in India was the first MFI in the world that offered weather-based crop insurance in collaboration with World Bank and ICICI Lombard, an insurance company. The product offered by BASIX was different from Kilimo Salama's product in the sense that it insured output (as opposed to inputs), that is, the crops. As of June 2010, BASIX had about 39,000 policyholders and it had paid out about ₹13,831,121 in claims equivalent to about $277,000—assuming $1 is equivalent to ₹50 (Harper et al. 2011). Independent of BASIX, ICICI Lombard was providing weather-based crop insurance to almost half a million farmers that covered 26 different crops. The insurance was heavily subsidized by some of the state governments in India. For example, in the state of Haryana, the total premium for an acre of land with ₹15,000 of indemnity was ₹1,260 (about $25). However, the farmers had to pay only ₹250 ($5) as premium; the rest was covered by the state government. Insurance companies offered such programmes based on the availability of weather stations as opposed to the needs of the farmers. Under these circumstances, it was difficult to expand the programme. Needless to say, it is difficult to ascertain whether such programmes could be sustainable when subsidies are removed (Harper et al. 2011).

Conclusion

While it is important for the poor households to build assets to fight poverty, protecting the assets from damage, destruction and depletion has to be one of the main pillars of fighting poverty. This is because an occurrence of risky event could destroy or deplete assets and push even the vulnerable non-poor to join the ranks of the destitute. Therefore, investing in insurance (such as health, life, accidents, crop, cattle and weather) should be one of the priorities of poor households to immunize themselves from the vagaries of specific risks.

The reason why microcredit expanded rapidly around the world has to do with the fact that it has a natural demand, it is a reasonably homogeneous product and it can be explained easily to the poor. Besides, the microfinance industry has been able to deliver poor-friendly microcredit products, which have been proven to deliver value in comparison to credit products in the informal sector such as from the moneylenders, pawnbrokers and payday lenders.

Before microinsurance products can be widely adopted by the poor (like microcredit), the product offers have to go through a process of trial and errors. This is a necessity because as discussed in the chapter, the products are complex to say the least, and the poor need education and experience in using these products before they decide to sign up on a continuing basis.

Last but not the least, it may not be too much to say that learning everything about microinsurance before designing and delivering microinsurance products is going to be difficult. As we quoted Jonathan Morduch in Chapter 2, in which he observes that, Muhammad Yunus did not wait until he learned everything about microcredit before rolling out the products, the same ought to be applicable for microinsurance as well (Morduch 2006, 343).

> So too, I expect, with microinsurance. The best hope is that microinsurance implementers will forge ahead with pilot projects, and that, if they are carefully rolled out (with an eye to evaluations), a great deal about risk, vulnerability and poverty can be learned in the process.

Notes

1. Douglas C. North. 2005. *Understanding the Process of Economic Change*, p. 1. Princeton, NJ: Princeton University Press.
2. As quoted in 'Microinsurance Overview.' Available online at http://www. microfinancegateway.org/p/site/m/template.rc/1.11.48248/ (downloaded on 22 January 2013).
3. 'Microinsurance Overview.' Available online at http://www.microfinance-gateway.org/p/site/m/template.rc/1.11.48248/ (downloaded on 22 January 2013).
4. BASIX has been one of the pioneers in microinsurance business in India and perhaps in the world as well. It was the first MFI in the world that provided weather-based crop insurance to farmers in collaboration with World Bank and ICICI Lombard.
5. Based on information contained in the article, 'Grameenphone Launches Insurance Cover for Subscribers.' Available online at http://www.microensure.com/news.asp?id=264 (downloaded on 11 June 2014).
6. Based on information contained in the article, 'Airtel Africa Partners with MicroEnsure for Mobile Microinsurance.' Available online at http://www.microensure.com/news.asp?id=267 (downloaded on 11 June 2014).
7. IFC. 'Kilimo Salama—Index-Based Agriculture Insurance: A Product Case Study.' IFC Advisory Services| Access to Finance, Ideas 42. Washington, DC: IFC (downloaded on 3 February 2013).
8. 'Dissemination of Climate Technologies for Mitigation and Adaptation with the Private Sector: Insurance for Inputs: Kilimo Salama, Kenya.' Partners: The SFSA, Safaricom and UAP Insurance Company. On behalf of BMZ and GIZ (downloaded on 24 January 2013).

8

Microleasing: Improving Access to Tools and Technology

Man is a tool using animal ... without tool he is nothing, with tool he is all.

Thomas Carlyle

Lack of physical assets is one of the tell-tale signs of poverty, which the poor could deploy for generating income streams. Unquestionably they need access to tools and technology to monetize their capabilities. For example, in the developing countries it is not unusual to find poor people not having access to tools such as pump sets, tillers, drills and chainsaws, which they could deploy in their work profitably. More importantly, without the help of tools and technology they will be at a disadvantage to compete in the marketplace.

Tools and technology are usually more expensive because their economic lives are longer. Consequently, acquisition of equipments and machinery for businesses using microloans are usually not suitable. What is more, poor households should not be borrowing relatively large sums of money (which they cannot repay comfortably) for purchasing equipment(s). Besides, before purchasing an expensive piece of equipment they need to have the necessary experience in using the equipment profitably in a business' environment. Moreover, because poor families are usually cash-strapped, by deploying microcredit in acquiring a relatively expensive tool or machinery can make it difficult for the family to have further access to microcredit for working capital needs. Without meeting working capital needs, it may be difficult for the business to meet its production schedules.

This is where lease finance for the poor (i.e., microleasing) can be helpful in having access to tools and technology without their ownership. With access to tools and technology poor entrepreneurs can have a wider choice to invest in businesses, which could have improved economies of scale and better income potential. However, MFI clients do not all necessarily invest the borrowed funds in microbusinesses. But those who do, some of them at least, who have been successful in their businesses, would like to expand their businesses to enhance productivity and hence profitability by acquiring tools and technology. This has to be welcomed because microbusinesses have been criticized for lacking economies of scale. Needless to say, an expanding business can provide opportunities for other poor people to find employment in such businesses.

Recent microcredit impact evaluations have yet to show conclusively that microcredit could move poor people out of poverty on a large scale (see Chapter 11). Therefore, if microleasing can help microbusinesses to expand into small businesses through acquisition of tools and technology, that would be a small but an important step in the right direction in terms of expanding employment opportunities for the poor. In other words, microfinance has to help create an enabling environment in which microentrepreneurs could have the opportunity to move up in the value chain from being the owners of microenterprises to owners of small enterprises.

Having said that, it is important to note that in spite of many advantages microleasing offers in comparison to borrowing, only a handful of MFIs around the world have offered microleasing in order to help microentrepreneurs access tools and technology. We will discuss in this chapter why this has been the case based on actual experience gained on the ground. But at the same time, one would expect that, as largely mono-product world of microfinance comes under criticism for perpetuating microenterprises that are clones of each other leading to crowding out, and squeezing of margins, the microfinance industry would be more inclined to take advantage of every opportunity to help their clients to move up the value chain by acquiring tools and technology to be more productive. It is in this context that microleasing can play an important role in helping the poor to access tools and technology without their ownership.

Importance of Improved Access to Tools and Technology by the Poor

The power of tools and technology in extending the physical and mental capabilities of man cannot be over-emphasized. By rapid adoption of tools and technology in the industrialized countries and constant push to make improvements to existing tools and technology by investing in pure and applied sciences and engineering, these countries have prospered.

There is no denying the fact that technological change plays an important role in the growth and development of a nation. In fact, in a major challenge to neoclassical growth theories, economist Paul Romer proposed an alternative theory of growth, in which technological change was considered endogenous as opposed to being exogenous, as in the case of neoclassical growth models. The New Growth Theory of Paul Romer is also known as the Endogenous Growth Theory.

Based on this theory, improvements to productivity in an economy are linked to a faster pace of innovation and investment in improving human capital. Investments in human capital through knowledge acquisition, skills development, innovation, learning by doing and entrepreneurship drive technological change. And technological change in turn drives productivity growth. Given the fact that productivity growth is crucial to the growth of an economy, technological change is considered an important factor in growth process and hence growth of an economy.

One hears about technological innovations and breakthroughs that were started in the garages in many industrialized countries around the world. However, it is important to note that the average citizen in industrialized countries owns many more tools and equipments in their garages in stark contrast to their counterparts in the developing countries. Finding such simple tools as a screwdriver, plier or even a saw becomes difficult in a poor household. Even a carpenter or an electrician may not have the right tools to do his job properly. With the advent of personal computers, Internet and mobile phones, there has been much discussion of a 'digital divide.' But at a more fundamental level, there is a 'tools and technology divide,' which needs to be bridged if we expect the poor to leverage their physical and mental capabilities to be more productive and generate income streams that can deter perpetuation of poverty.

With access to tools and technology, one would expect that the poor would have opportunities to get trained in the equipment and acquire skills that would make it easier for them to become more productive and hence generate more income in the long run. This is crucial because even if the growth it would engender may be marginal in the beginning, the cumulative impact of productivity growth for an economy in the long run could be substantial because of the compounding nature of growth.

When businesses become clones of each other in the same neighbourhood, it drives down profit margins, which could lead many such businesses to fail. On the other hand, businesses that use improved tools and technology and develop niche products could easily belong to a select group of businesses with healthy profit margins. What is more, because of economies of scale the businesses can make relatively larger profit even if the margins may be narrowed. As the microfinance industry matures, MFI clients with experience may be on the lookout for improved income opportunities by investing in businesses with productive technologies.

In this context, the following observations by Stephen L. Parente and Nobel Laureate Edward C. Prescott (2002, xvi) in their book *Barriers to Riches* are appropriate.

> We found that although the countries have access to the same stock of knowledge, they do not all make equally efficient use of this knowledge because policies in some countries lead to barriers that effectively prevent firms from adopting more productive technologies and from changing to more efficient work practices.

They also observe (Parente and Prescott 2002, 142),

> Our view is that countries are not poor because incentives to develop new technologies are lacking. The technologies have been developed in other countries, and it is just a matter of using the technology that is best, given factor prices, and using that technology efficiently.

Therefore, it may not be far-fetched to say that financial instruments such as microleasing could be helpful, even if in a small way, in the diffusion of technology in poor communities around the world. It may be that the poor may not receive the most up-to-date technology, but any technology that could enhance their productivity, would also help them scale up and make more profits. Once introduced to improved technology, they would learn by doing and ultimately look out for improved technologies. That would make major contributions towards growth and development amongst the poor. In other words, without access to financial instruments such as leasing the poor could be largely mired in low-tech activities and may not be able to reach their fullest potential. This could lead to stagnation and low levels of earnings, which would make it difficult for the poor to transition out of poverty.

What Is Microleasing?

A lease is a contract between a 'lessor' and a 'lessee,' under which the lessee makes regular periodic payments to lease an asset (say an equipment) from the lessor for a specified lease period. The lessor is an entity that owns the equipment—a productive asset—and leases out the asset to the lessee. Lease payments are made on a monthly or quarterly basis over the lease period. The tools and equipments are normally leased for a period of three to five years (Deelen et al. 2003).

Traditionally, lessees in the developing countries have been largely SMEs. The capital requirements of SMEs are usually more. However, microleasing is being increasingly adopted as a loan substitute to provide equipment and machinery for microbusinesses as well. Examples of some of these productive assets include such tools and equipments as sewing machines, power tillers, power looms, refrigerators and mobile phones.

The power of a lease lies in the fact that it decouples the ownership of the equipment from its use. Under this arrangement, the lessor owns the equipments (holds the titles to the equipments) by investing in the acquisition of equipments that are in high demand for leasing. Being the holder of the title, the lessor has stronger legal rights to repossess the equipment. In some Latin American countries, it takes only about a couple of months to repossess the equipment as opposed to a couple of years to recover defaulted loans, which may not be even possible in some cases (Westley 2003).

Because, the lessor finances the entire purchase price of the equipment, the lessee, after leasing equipment for her business still could have the headroom to further avail a microloan for working capital needs. Because, under lease finance, the equipment leased is used as its collateral, the lessee does not have to post any collateral for the lease except for a security deposit. The security deposit can be equivalent to two to three months of lease payment, which *de facto* insures the lessor of lease payments (in case the lessee is delinquent) before the lessor might have to repossess the asset.

The pricing of microleasing premiums is based on the purchase price of the equipment, transportation cost of getting the equipment to the appropriate destination and other expenses such as insurance cost. In calculating the premium, the interest rate used is comparable to interest rate on microloans. But they need not be exactly the same. As we noted earlier, the maximum leasing period is around three years. But in some cases, it could be as high as five years depending on the economic life of the equipment, or it could be lower, say about two years in the case of microleasing of animals.[1] Microleasing has grace period, which is normally one month, but it could only be two weeks in the case of animal leasing. In order to make lease payments poor-friendly, the MFIs price it such that premium payments can be made from operating cash flow of the business without overburdening lessee to dip into his or her savings.

The leases can be broadly divided into two categories: (1) financial leases and (2) operating leases. The financial leases could be further divided into 'hire-purchase,' and 'lease-back' programmes (Dowla 2004; Gallardo 1997; Mutesasira et al. 2001).

Financial Lease

Financial leases are designed such that over the lease period, the lessee pays full price of the equipment plus interest. At the end of the lease period, the lessee could purchase the equipment for a nominal amount normally equivalent to the depreciated asset value. However, the market value of the used equipment could be different from the depreciated asset value. In some cases, the depreciated value could be cancelled based on mutual agreement between the lessor and the lessee.

Financial leases can be thought of as loan substitutes with added bells and whistles, which makes the lease agreement less risky for the lessors. The contracts are designed such that the lessor avoids selling the equipment in the secondary market after the lease period.

In a financial lease, the equipment is normally leased for the entire period of its useful life. The lessee makes the periodic payments on the lease to cover the cost of the equipment and interest payments on the funds used to purchase the equipment. Under the arrangement, the lessee has to amortize all or almost all (95–100 per cent) of the lessor's original cost.

Such leases normally stipulate a buyback option for the lessee that can be exercised at the end of the leasing period. The amount to be paid to own the equipment is also stipulated in the lease contract, based on the residual value (depreciated value) of the asset to be leased.

In order to take care of the damage to the equipment(s), the lessee in most cases is required to makes payments towards insuring the equipment. The lessee is also liable for periodic maintenance of the equipment.

Financial leases are not normally cancelled because the client then can return the equipment (which was bought for her in the first place) and walk out of the agreement.

Hire Purchase

Under the hire purchase programme the lessee initially pays a down payment, such as 30 per cent of the cost of the equipment and then makes monthly instalment payments towards ultimate ownership of the equipment after the instalment period. As the lessee utilizes the equipment and makes monthly instalment payments, she progressively increases the ownership of the equipment every month and owns the equipment after making the last instalment payment.

Sale and Leaseback Programmes

This option is suitable for an existing enterprise that is cash-strapped but has assets such as machinery and equipment, which can become a source of working capital. Under this arrangement, the owner of the enterprise can sell the equipment to the MFI and then leaseback the equipment. As a result, she can generate cash from the sale of the existing equipment and utilize the cash as working capital. She has always the option to use the equipment as collateral for a loan, which may be for a shorter period and may not be suitable for attaining sustainability before applying for another loan.

Operating Leases

Operating leases are similar to rentals. In the case of an operating lease, the lessor leases out the equipment several times during the life of the equipment to several lessees and then at some point decides to sell the equipment in the secondary market to recover the residual value. Depending on the market conditions and the condition of the equipment, the lessor could make a profit on such sales. But at the same time, if the technology becomes obsolete, then the lessor may not be able to sell the asset in the secondary market. Therefore, pricing of operating leases is complex.

The lessors of operating leases cover equipment acquisition cost and the interest on such acquisitions. The lessors of operating leases also bear the cost of insurance and maintenance of equipment they lease out. Such leases do not require the lessee to amortize the full cost of the leased equipment because the lessee is not given the option to buy.

Operating leases can be cancelled. And the lessee has the option to go for a cheaper lease or for leasing equipment(s) with improved features or may decide not to lease at all. Therefore, such leases are suitable for gaining experience before leasing equipment(s) using financial leases.

By offering operating leases, a lessor bears three major risks that are avoided with financial leasing. These risks include damages that may be inflicted on the equipment by the lessee, the risk of leasing the equipment out in the second-hand market and the risk of recovering the residual value. In the event equipment is not leased out, the lessor bears the burden of making payment towards principal and interest. Because operating leases put lot of burden on the lessors, the lessors find it easier to offer financial leases. In this chapter, we will mostly focus on financial leases.

What Kinds of Assets the Lessors Prefer to Lease Out

Lessors prefer assets that have longer economic life and depreciate slowly and fetch good residual value. Lessors also prefer assets that they are knowledgeable about and have access to good suppliers. They also like products for which maintenance service is easily available in case something goes wrong with equipment(s). This may sound like a problem that the lessee should worry about; however, lessors need to focus on these issues at the time of purchasing equipment(s) because unless such problems are dealt with at the beginning, the problems could bunch together to create credit risk for the lessor.

Lessors also try to avoid equipments that require high setup and operational costs. Besides lessors prefer assets that can be sold in the secondary market in the event the lessee defaults on making periodic payments on the lease and the asset is repossessed by the lessor.

When the Grameen Bank started its leasing programme, it did not have a list of equipments and machinery to fund (Dowla 2004). As a result, under the programme any item could be approved for leasing if the appropriate Grameen staff deemed that the client could use the equipment in her business. The programme leased a wide variety of equipments such as power looms, power tillers, battery charges, ball-point pen production machines, refrigerators, pump sets, sugarcane grinders, baby taxis and mini transports. The programme also leased animals. By making it flexible, the clients were empowered to choose the most appropriate equipments for their businesses. However, one of the downsides of such approach was that some of these equipments or machinery could be non-standard and pose a problem to sell in the secondary market.

Other Related Issues

The MFIs need to bear the cost of warehousing the equipments prior to leasing and when they are returned after the leasing period. They have to also bear the associated costs of security and maintenance of these equipments.

In the event a lessee defaults on her lease payments, the lessor takes possession of the leased item and sells it in the secondary market or leases out to another lessee. On the contrary, if a microloan borrower is delinquent in her payments or defaults on her payments, then an MFI's first line of defence is peer pressure. If it does not work, the clients could be subject to sanctions.

Although MFIs should not resort to coercive debt collection tactics, some MFIs in the past have used such tactics resulting in adverse consequences as the 2010 Andhra Pradesh Microfinance Crisis in India has shown (see Chapter 11). Microleasing largely avoids all this because of the lease contract with the lessee, which greatly limits downside risks for the lessors.

Under an operational lease if equipment is repossessed, ascertaining the value of the equipment could be difficult because the equipment has been under use for some time. Besides, because of change in technology the asset may be obsolete. If the value is less than what the lessee owes to the MFI, then the MFI could end up losing money. In the event the client does not have a buyback option, there may not be enough incentives to maintain the equipment. And hence, the leased equipment may not be in a good condition. Under these circumstances, the lessor may have to incur a loss.

Tools and equipments during their use could be damaged, particularly when the lessee is not trained in using the equipments. Some lessor want a damage deposit for such risks and the lessee gets back the deposit in the event the equipment is returned in good condition. If the damage deposit is not enough to repair the equipment, then the lessor could end up losing money. Some lessors take charge of maintaining the equipment during the lease period and charge the lessee for the maintenance cost.

Lessors also sell to the lessees insurance for theft or injuries that could arise out of using leased equipments. Insurance payments could be bundled into periodic lease payment. It protects the lessor as well as the lessee.

Microleasing Experience of MFIs in Selected Countries

As we noted at the outset, in spite of many advantages of microleasing over microcredit, microleasing has not been adopted widely by the MFIs around the world. However, there are MFIs such as Grameen Bank in Bangladesh and African and Latin American MFIs that have used microleasing to help the poor access equipments and machinery.

In this section, we will discuss about microleasing programmes in Bangladesh, Bolivia and Tanzania to provide a flavour of these programmes around the world. Based on the experience gained in these programmes, we will also discuss later what could be some of the important reasons why microleasing has not been adopted widely.

Bangladesh

Among the MFIs, it is again Grameen Bank that was perhaps the first MFI to offer microleasing in 1992. The programme helped the poor to lease and then own (after the lease period was over) such equipments and machinery as power tillers, shallow machines, cellular phones, pump sets, battery chargers, ball-point pen production machines, mini transports and computers (Dowla 2004). One of the important clienteles of the programme was poverty-level weavers that leased power looms from Grameen (Gallardo 1997).

The programme was open to second-time borrowers from the bank's microcredit programme, which benefited from the experience of Grameen's field officers with regard to the suitability of the clients for using microleasing in their businesses. Such screening is important for the success of leasing programmes where field officers asses if the client applying for a lease has the necessary know-how to utilize the equipment profitably. By 1996, the leasing programme at the Grameen had already achieved repayment and default rates that were comparable with Grameen's microcredit programme (Gallardo 1997).

Some of the important parameters used in pricing leases by Grameen consisted of the following: (1) the cost of the equipment being leased; (2) leasing fee, which can be thought of as interest rate on a loan, which was set at 20 per cent and (3) payback period, which was set at three years, although the lease could be paid off in full at anytime. Lease payments were collected on a weekly basis as in the case of its microcredit programme. The programme allowed flexibility in servicing their leases based on their cash flow. For example, farmers who earn their incomes after the harvest were allowed flexible lease payments.

As early as 1994, the Grameen Bank decided to expand its leasing programme (Dowla 2004). At the end of 1997, the bank leased over 8,400 items belonging to about 110 categories. The leasing programme allowed almost 100 male and over 1,100 female clients to own assets through leasing. The average value of the leased assets was about $620, and the share of the leasing programme was about 4 per cent of the total lending portfolio of Grameen.

Grameen leasing operation was suspended between the years 1998 and 2001 (Kennedy 2010). During this period, the bank redesigned its lending products (see Chapter 5). After the introduction of Grameen

II (which replaced Grameen I or Classical Grameen), the leasing programme was renamed to special project loans. The leasing programme was restarted in 2001 when mobile village pay phones were used as productive assets for leasing.

The initial experience in extending microleasing to Grameen clients created the expectation that the businesses owned by these clients have higher likelihood of reaching their sustainability (Dowla 2004). What was also expected that leasing programmes would help in reducing low rates of graduation of successful borrowers as is the case in microcredit programmes.

The argument for such thinking runs as follows: in a group-lending environment, rewarding members in a group who are more entrepreneurial with larger loans may not be suitable because it could jeopardize group cohesion. However, Dowla in his paper discusses findings by Madajewicz, which point to the fact that relatively wealthier borrowers would prefer loans individually in order to avoid joint-liability clause. This is because when the borrowers are wealthier, their incentive to monitor others in a group decreases. As a result, an MFI by providing access to microleasing will help more entrepreneurial borrowers to access relatively more expensive equipments to attain economies of scale. This would also help to keep these successful entrepreneurial borrowers as members of Grameen Bank instead of graduating them from the institution.

Some of the important issues that were identified in the case of the Grameen microleasing programme include, the staff delivering the leasing programme did not follow rules and procedures (Dowla 2004). Other problems associated with the programme included leased vehicles that were involved in accidents did not have up-to-date accidental insurance papers, valid driving license of the operator or road permit. It was also identified that lessees could benefit from training in the equipments before they lease, which would imply, at least some of the lessees did not have appropriate training before leasing the equipments.

Bolivia

ANED in Bolivia has been providing lease finance to microenterprises since 1997 to finance fixed assets (Goldberg 2008). ANED was founded in 1978 to provide credit to low-income rural and urban populace who were traditionally ignored by the banking system. Besides financial leasing, the other major product that ANED offers include financing of working and investment capital. In 2004, it redesigned its leasing programme with support from Inter-American Development Bank.

The impetus for embarking on the leasing programme came from ANED's credit programme, which experienced loan losses (Alvarado and Galarza 2003). The programme was used to acquire fixed assets by its clients. Even though ANED provided incentives for its clients to pay back the loans, significant amounts were not paid back.

Under the leasing programme, ANED started helping microbusinesses to lease fixed assets such as farm equipments, machinery for carpentry shops and bottling plants. It also expanded its leasing programme to include livestock. The farm equipments it leased included such items as tractors, farm ploughs, motorized pumps, farm trucks, cultivators, farm rollers, harvesters and other fixed assets by directly buying from suppliers (Alvarado and Galarza 2003). Expansion of microleasing has helped ANED to reduce its portfolio risk.

In leasing equipments, ANED purchases them directly from the suppliers. In the process ANED clients do not have to go through middlemen to avail such products for leasing. This approach tries to keep the lease payments low for the clients. This is different from the credit-led approach where after taking microloans, small producers may not possess the necessary know-how to access such equipments directly from the suppliers in a cost-effective manner.

In starting off the programme, ANED had to overcome several difficulties that include (1) streamlining the leasing process such that the clients can understand it easily; (2) identifying suppliers who could not only provide the required equipment but could train the clients in the equipments they lease and answer questions—this was important because most of the clients had only basic education; (3) it was difficult to find insurance for the equipment leased by ANED, which increased risk exposure of ANED and (4) the loan officers of ANED found it challenging to divide time between traditional lending programme and the leasing programme. Some of the other challenges that ANED faced include availability of funding to expand the programme, market analysis of products produced by small producers, insurance for leasing products, creating an enabling environment for microleasing to grow and even such issues as reprogramming the accounting software to take into consideration tax aspects of the programme.

These example, even if not elaborate indicate how microleasing could help clients to be more productive, make more profit, employ other poor people and in the process reduce credit risk of an institution. Considering the fact that microcredit has been criticized for lending to microenterprises that lack economies of scale, microleasing programmes could provide MFI clients more focused approach to access tools and technology that could enable them to take advantage of economies of scale.

Tanzania

SERO Lease and Finance Company (SELFINA) in Tanzania provides microleasing to women and businesses with the aim of modernizing their businesses and increasing their efficiency to increase their income potential (Pinder 2001). It also provides loans and bank guarantees.

SELFINA started operation in 1997. From 1997 to 2001, it issued leases and loans amounting to about 1.3 billion Tanzanian Schillings (about $14.9 million based on an exchange rate of 870 Tanzanian Schillings per $1) to 2,300 women. It experienced 97 per cent repayment rate.

As far as leasing business was concerned, SELFINA offered microleasing to women who were in a position to pay 15 per cent of the value of the equipment prior to getting the equipment on lease. The women also needed two guarantors and had to enter into legal agreement with the company. The average value of the lease was 500,000 Tanzanian Schillings (about $575). Leased terms were for 6, 12 or 18 months. Payments on the lease start immediately after one month.

SELFINA provided leasing for the following businesses: catering (coolers, freezers, refrigerators, microwave oven, etc.); tailoring (sewing machines, embroidery sewing machines, chain stitch machines, etc.) and beauty salons (dryers, steamers, etc.). It also provided tools and equipment for carpentry, nursery schools, handlooms and the like. However, based on the data collected about microleasing as well as loans, 48 per cent of its clients leased fridges and freezers, 12 per cent leased sewing machines and 40 per cent took term loans. The value of goods leased was in the range of 63,000 to 2.3 million Tanzanian Schillings (from about $72 to over $2,800).

Based on a case study of the programme, it was found that about 75.5 per cent clients thought that assistance by SELFINA helped to increase their earnings, while 18 per cent thought it did not. However, two-thirds of the clients expressed the opinion that that their earnings improved slightly and 16 per cent of the clients said that earnings improved substantially. About 70 per cent of the clients said they did not experience any problems in keeping up with payments, whereas about 30 per cent experienced hardship in making payments. Only 5 per cent of the clients reported that they were behind in making payments to SELFINA. Complaints of the clients were mostly about the loan programme that included high interest rate loans having no grace period before the payments started. The clients were not satisfied with the customer service and loan processing.

Based on a survey by MicroSave (East Africa), one of the complaints regarding the leasing programme included lack of flexibility in accommodating clients who could not meet lease payments because of sickness in the family or seasonality of their businesses. The clients did not like the quality of the assets leased. Besides, there was no guarantee on asset quality. As a result, the clients had to make lease payments and payment towards asset repair. They also did not like the fact that they were not able to get leases back to back.

As a result, SELFINA clients wanted the institution to find qualified people to assess the quality of the equipment before they are leased out. They also wanted to negotiate a warranty with the suppliers. The clients were prepared to pay for all this. Based on these assessments, SELFINA changed many of its practices.

The above discussion points to the fact that as far as leasing programmes are concerned, they are much different from lending. It requires a great deal of involvement of the MFIs to make the programme successful. In other words, to have a successful microleasing programme, MFIs should have knowledgeable staff familiar with the leasing business. Given the fact that finding knowledgeable staff could be difficult, starting and expanding microleasing programmes could pose problems for the MFIs.

Sustainability of Microleasing Programmes

Among the three microleasing programmes discussed above, only the case study 'ANED, Bolivia: Pioneering Rural Microleasing' (Alvarado and Galarza 2003) provides any financial information regarding the microleasing programme. However, the information provided does not give any clear indication as to whether the programme was sustainable after two years of its operation.

Kevin Kennedy's (2010) extensive review of microleasing programmes around the world in *The Potential of Leasing through Microfinance Institutions in Emerging Markets*, provide example of only one programme in Pakistan 'Network Leasing Corporation Limited' (NLCL), with a modest lease portfolio of $11.6 million (in 2004), which reported consistent profits.

Given the fact that microleasing is a loan substitute, and there are many advantages to providing leasing as a financial product, it would appear that microleasing programmes have yet to find an appropriate product design and enabling environment to attain their potential. In this context, one needs to remember that it took years before microcredit emerged as a product that is not only poor-friendly, and can be delivered to the poor on a mass scale, but also can help the MFIs attain sustainability.

Some of the Advantages of Microleasing Over Microcredit

As the MFIs around the world try to diversify themselves from being mono-product institutions to provide access to other financial products such as microsavings, microinsurance and MT facilities, it has been found that short-term working capital loans are not suitable for acquiring equipment and machinery that have longer economic lives. And the MFIs are usually not equipped to make larger loans with longer maturities for investing in equipment and machinery. At the same time, the poor with fragile balance sheets should avoid undertaking relatively larger loans for investing in equipment or machinery. Under these circumstances, microleasing has a clear advantage over microborrowing. Moreover, because microleasing is a loan substitute, after signing a lease contract, the poor household may still have headroom to take a microloan for working capital needs of her business.

Assuming a poor household might have the wherewithal to invest in tools and technology, it may be still advisable to lease as opposed to buy. Leasing would allow an entrepreneur to try out equipment from various vendors before she finds the appropriate equipment for her job. For example, a microentrepreneur who would like to provide copying and faxing services, would find it advisable to lease these equipment as opposed to buy because the underlying technology keeps on changing and prices of these equipment keep on dropping. Besides, leased equipment allow for gaining valuable experience before an entrepreneur decides to make an investment in machinery of her choice.

Dowla in his 2004 paper on microleasing discusses about anecdotal evidence of 'overlapping,' which is another way of saying that MFI clients borrow from multiple sources, including other MFIs. Overlapping is considered financially risky because it could result in 'loan-pyramiding' schemes that could collapse. He points out that overlapping could result because of credit rationing, which implies that the clients are looking for bigger loans and the MFIs they belong to can only extend relatively smaller loans for working capital needs. Overlapping can have serious consequences as the 2010 Andhra Pradesh Microfinance Crisis has shown (see Chapter 11). One would expect microleasing which is a loan substitute with relatively larger value in comparison to average size of microloans, could reduce overlapping (multiple borrowing). As a result, one would expect that access to microleasing could retain good borrowers.

It is believed that overemphasis on microcredit has shifted our attention away from the 'missing middle,' that is, the level just above the poor, who might be eligible for bigger loans to invest in SMEs (Dichter 2007). Such borrowers could take advantage of economies of scale to generate higher levels of profit and employment for the poor. But at the same time, MFIs have been criticized for 'mission drift' implying some of these institutions lend relatively larger loans to clients who are more creditworthy and in the process make higher levels of profit (through economies of scale). As a result, the poorer borrowers end up being neglected. Under these circumstances, MFIs could perhaps deploy microleasing for relatively better off borrowers which would perhaps avoid criticisms of 'mission drift' as well as the criticism about ignoring the 'missing middle.'

Dowla also discusses findings by Madajewicz, which point to the fact that relatively wealthier borrowers tend to prefer individual loans in order to avoid joint-liability clause. This is because when borrowers are wealthier, their incentive to monitor others in a group decreases. As a result, by offering microleasing, the MFIs could satisfy their relatively wealthier clients.

While most microbusinesses in the developing countries may not be taxable, it is important to note that the tax treatment for leases is favourable because they help to upgrade technology in businesses, increase efficiency, productivity and generate higher levels of income. For example, in most countries around the world, a lessee can offset lease payments against taxable income, whereas borrowers can only expense interest payments on their loans. Moreover, the lessor can claim for the depreciation of the equipment(s) being leased. Microleasing would also allow for diversification of MFI assets without being solely concentrated in microloans.

Why Microleasing Remains an Underutilized Tool by the MFIs?

If nothing else, microleasing programmes require more involvement of the MFIs in comparison to the relatively passive nature of microcredit programmes. But needless to say, when looked from an economic development perspective, it promotes collaboration among enterprises and also could support collaboration with existing supply chains (Othieno). In order to run a successful leasing programme, MFIs would have to collaborate with business development organizations, equipment suppliers, equipment leasing companies, and insurers and businesses that provide training and maintenance services. All this imply that managing a successful microleasing programme may not be easy.

In offering microleasing, the MFIs have to identify suitable clients (from its large client base) who would be prime candidates for microleasing. Besides, after identifying suitable clients, the MFIs have to also identify the kinds of equipments and machinery they would like to lease in consultation with the clients. The officers involved in providing these services have to be knowledgeable about these equipments and machinery. They should be also knowledgeable about (1) suppliers who could provide the equipment and necessary training for the clients; (2) insurers who could insure the equipment and (3) maintenance services to take care of malfunction of equipments. They have to provide assistance to the poor in marketing their products, without which the lessee would not be able to reach her profit potential.

MFIs should be prepared to design payment plans for leased products that are flexible for their clients. In that sense, the MFIs have to employ individuals with a good understanding of lease finance, the business environment in which the poor operate and the businesses for which there is demand for tools and equipment. The personnel have to be well-versed in country's taxation and accounting rules, which can be complex.

For simple things like providing maintenance services in remote areas, the repairmen may have to travel from the nearest town to a village. Downtime due to delay in repairing, could jeopardize profitability of the enterprises. Prolonged downtime of products is not financially beneficial for the poor and hence for the MFIs.

Because the poor are not familiar with lease finance, the demand for leasing is not expected to develop naturally as in the case of microcredit. Like microinsurance, MFI clients have to be educated about benefits of leasing. For example, while microleasing can be a substitute for microcredit and vice versa how one decides whether to buy or lease is not a simple decision. This has to be carefully analysed before one decides whether to lease. Because the poor are not financially savvy, the MFI staff has to invest their time to analyse the situation and provide the right advice.

The setup cost of leasing is more because it involves purchase of equipment to be leased, specific instructions as to the upkeep of the equipment, insurance for the equipment, making arrangement for good repairmen who could fix equipments quickly, particularly in remote areas, to reduce downtime. Most importantly at the end of the lease period, if some clients are not interested in purchasing the leased equipment, they have to be either scrapped or have to be sold in the secondary market. All these entail great deal of management time, employment of right personnel and executing everything back to back.

In many developing countries the legal basis of leasing along with taxation may not be clearly defined. This can create operational issues for the MFIs or for the leasing companies that collaborate with the MFIs. Besides, the funds needed for microleasing are relatively larger. As a result an MFI's exposure to each of its clients is several times more than the average size of microlending. This might be one of the reasons why microleasing has not gained scale around the world. And it is difficult to be sustainable without gaining scale. All in all, microleasing is a more complex instrument than microcredit. It requires greater level of involvement on the part of the MFI for its success.

Conclusion

The mono-product world of microfinance, largely consisting of microcredit, has been criticized for enabling the poor to invest in microbusinesses that lack economies of scale. The other criticism of microcredit is that its clients tend to invest in businesses that are clones of each other. Because cloned businesses crowd out each other, many of these businesses fail. What is more, most MFIs do not normally provide livelihood training to their clients and the clients do not normally have easy access to equipments and machinery. It is in this context that microleasing (a loan substitute) can provide successful microcredit clients to lease equipments and machinery to pursue livelihoods that could provide them improved income opportunities.

Microleasing could become an important instrument for diffusion of technology amongst the poor to facilitate learning by doing, skill improvement and establishment of linkages with equipment manufacturers, input suppliers and ultimately buyers of their products and services. Establishment of such linkages are critical in order for development to take hold.

There is no question that microleasing as a financial instrument has been underutilized because of its specialized nature and it demands a great deal of involvement on the part of the MFIs to offer such instruments. Besides, finding trained personnel proficient in leasing business has been difficult by the MFIs. Many countries also lack legal and tax environment for expanding leasing business.

However, as the microfinance industry matures, relatively passive nature of microcredit business (in comparison to microleasing) has to find other avenues to help the poor to invest in scalable businesses. Microleasing is a financial instrument that can aid the MFIs and its clients in this arena. Prior to the advent of microcredit, delivering microcredit on a mass scale escaped the financial services industry for generations. With ingenious product design and refinements, institutional setup and policies, which also went through many refinements, microcredit expanded rapidly around the world. It is possible that with appropriate product design and institutional setup, microleasing programmes can be an important component for MFIs to help the poor embark on businesses that are sustainable and scalable.

Note

1. In the absence of term lending to the poor under microfinance, leasing with longer lease periods can be viewed as substitute for relatively larger loans and term lending. The machinery or the equipment becomes collateral for such lending.

9
Remittances, Payment Systems and Microfinance

Invisible threads are the strongest ties.

Friedrich Nietzsche

One of the important driving forces why people migrate has to do with availing better economic opportunities. With major revolutions in transportation and communications the world has witnessed during the last 30 years, the number of people migrating domestically and internationally has swelled. Based on UN estimates, more than 215 million people lived outside of their countries of birth (UNCSD Secretariat 2012). What is more, domestic migration is even larger than cross-border migration, which has reached the level of about 740 million. This is partly because there are practically no restrictions on domestic migration and no need for formalities such as passport and visa requirements. Besides, it is also less expensive to migrate domestically. Just to illustrate, there are 'up to 100 million circular domestic migrant workers' in India who decide to leave home for improved income opportunities in other parts of India (Thorat and Jones 2011). These workers contribute as much as 10 per cent to India's national gross domestic product (GDP).

Having migrated, all migrants want to stay connected with their kith and kin, but more importantly they want to send money to their family members and relatives for their upkeep and to take care of emergencies such as health emergencies. As an illustration, in a study conducted for 'Remittance Needs and Opportunities in India,' it was found that the remittances from the migrant workers of Uttar Pradesh state (in India) provided about 80 per cent of the cash income in the sample households (Thorat and Jones 2011). The average annual remittance by these workers was about ₹20,000 (about $400 assuming $1= ₹50).

Needless to say, for poor migrants staying connected back home when their families and friends may be living in areas that are remote and lack good infrastructure may not be easy. However, ICT revolution (piggybacking on microminiaturized digital computer technology) is profoundly changing how the poor stay connected with each other domestically and internationally.

The mobile phones today are revolutionizing how we move voice, music, information, pictures and money, and make bill payments and perform banking transactions. Based on estimates, almost three-quarters of world population today have access to mobile phones (World Bank 2012). More specifically, the number of mobile subscriptions has reached almost 6 billion, which was 1 billion in 2000. Of the 6 billion subscriptions, 5 billion are in the developing countries. Ownership of multiple subscriptions is also increasing. That could push ownership of mobile phones above the world population sooner than later. What is more, in 2011, about 30 billion 'apps,' that is, mobile applications (smart software) were downloaded that are designed to extend the capabilities of the mobile phones to send and receive emails, access news, information, price data, maps and directions, contact one's doctor from remote areas. Using smart technology, mobile phones have been transformed to mobile wallets and to make banking transactions. In this chapter, we will discuss about M-PESA (mobile money, digital money) in Kenya (and other countries around the world) that is revolutionizing how low-income and poor people access financial services using mobile phones. It is expected that, in the coming years, development of 'locally relevant' mobile apps in the developing countries could create opportunities for the poor and low-income people in such areas as communications, business, banking, health care and the like. We will also discuss about another ICT-based system such as FINO that is providing access to microfinance for the poor in India.

This chapter will also discuss about other traditional methods that help to transfer money and provide access to other microfinancial services used by the poor by bridging the proverbial 'last mile.'

Remittances: A Brief Introduction

Migration allows the poor to take advantage of a much broader set of economic opportunities. It also helps to diversify a household's sources of income and hence helps to reduce income volatility. It could also reduce covariant risk in terms of household income. However, migration entails physical, mental and financial hardships that have to be borne by the migrants and their families.

Reliable statistics on migration is difficult to find, particularly when many of the cross-border immigration take place in an illegal manner without documentation. Migration within a country does not need documentation. Hence collection of statistics on migration within a country may also be difficult. Estimates of migration patterns within a country can be discerned from census reports, which only take place every 10 years.

While people initially travel to a distant land for economic reasons and even settle there with their family, they keep their familial, cultural and economic ties with the place they came from even for decades. Needless to say, these ties have been nurtured and enhanced by improvements in transportation (e.g., air), communications (e.g., phones, Internet) and payment systems that are ushering a new era for the migrants to stay connected with their families and friends back home.

People who migrate for better economic opportunities domestically or internationally are adventurous by nature and are willing to take risk to improve their economic status. They not only search for better economic opportunities for them in a distant land, they also try to create better economic opportunities in the communities they came from. Clearly, remittances are an outgrowth of this process and should be leveraged to reap economic benefits.

One can divide remittances broadly into two categories: international and domestic. In each of the categories, one can further divide remittances based on how money is transferred from the source to the destination. For example, funds could be remitted formally or informally. Using formal channels funds can be sent through post offices, inter-bank transfers and non-bank MT institutions. Because poor migrants find it difficult to fill out forms required by post offices and banking institutions, large numbers of such migrants decide to send remittances through informal channels.

Each country has specific informal channels through which people send money. For example, in India, the 'hundi' system has been used for a long time to send money informally. The 'hawala' system, prevalent in the Middle East and South Asia, has been used to transfer funds domestically as well as across countries.

The delivery of remittances through the informal channels can range anywhere from 35 to 70 per cent of the remittances through the formal channels (Nallari and Griffith 2011). There are many reasons why funds flow through informal channels. Some of the important reasons are: (1) existence of black market in foreign exchange that may offer higher exchange rate for the senders; (2) cost of sending funds through informal channels could be lower and (3) informal channels may cater to specific needs of the sender such as delivering funds to the receiver directly at the home address.

Besides, fund transfers carried out by friends and family members are convenient for the poor because they normally send small amounts of money, and sending money through formal channels can be expensive. Moreover, personalized delivery of funds at home is more secure as opposed to delivery of funds in public places. Such transfers also remain confidential. However, it is also true that while informal transfers may be poor-friendly, personalized and cost-effective, it may not be reliable and secure. For example, if the funds are embezzled by an informal MT operator, the poor may not have any recourse.

The funds that are not remitted formally tend to stay outside the formal financial system. For example, such funds are not saved in savings accounts. As a result, these funds are not intermediated or leveraged to the fullest extent to realize its development potential. By and large, remittances through informal channels end up being used for legitimate purposes. However, there is always the danger that such transfers could be used for illegitimate reasons such as money laundering. All in all, the poor and the non-poor alike are interested in MT systems (payment systems) that are user-friendly, reliable, cost-effective and efficient.

Remittances at the Aggregate Level

While average size of international and domestic remittances may be small, the trickle becomes a torrent when the number of migrants remitting funds on a regular basis is in the millions. Estimation of such remittances is a difficult task because large numbers of migrants do not remit funds using the formal channels and hence escape formal recordation. As a result, these transfers are not included in the remittance statistics. One can only provide an estimation of such informal transfers. It is important to note that, international official remittance flow to developing countries reached $406 billion in 2012 (Groves 2012). As noted earlier, informal remittance flows to these countries can vary anywhere from 35 to 70 per cent of official flows.

Similarly estimating total value of domestic remittances by migrant workers is also a difficult task because a substantial part of such remittances flows informally. For example, remittance market in India was estimated to be around $10 billion in 2007–08 (Tumbe 2011). About 70 per cent of the remittances were estimated to be channelled through the informal sector and about 80 per cent of all transfers were directed to rural households. Given the fact almost 80 per cent of the transfers was directed to rural households, institutions such as MFIs could play an important role in MT business.

How Remittances Are Used?

The importance of remittances for the poor stems from the fact that, because the poor migrate to areas with better job opportunities, relatively higher wages (than the home countries they come from), stable macroeconomic conditions and strong currencies, they are able to remit funds months after month which when converted to the local currency provide incomes that are orders of magnitude higher than what they would have earned staying in their home countries.

Because there is improved job security in the new country they migrate to, there is reasonable stability in the flow of such remitted funds. Because remittances are month after month cash injections with less variance, and because normally there are no strings attached as to how such cash should be spent except for daily upkeep of the family, the overall financial status of the poor families back home improves appreciably. Needless to say, the migrant workers have to take a great deal of hardship, and run into financial indebtedness, to remit funds from a foreign land such that their families can have a better life.

Remittances (whether cross-border or domestic) are largely used for consumption. It is also used for meeting working capital needs, savings and investing. Recipients of remittances also use the funds for education and health. Families receiving remittances in general have better access to nutrition, health care and shelter. Remittances also encourage entrepreneurship among the remittance-receiving households (Ratha 2006). There is evidence that remittances have helped the poor in improving literacy and school attendance. It also helps in decreasing infant mortality (Truen et al. 2005).

Given the fact that access to banking and other financial services by the poor is limited in the developing countries, there is less opportunity for remittances to be formally saved. As a result, it is difficult for these families to leverage remittances to access credit for investing in microbusinesses, housing and education, and purchasing health and accidental insurance.

Because the remittances are relatively large cash injections (when compared with the average income level of a poor family back home), they help their families improve their financial status rather quickly. However, given an enabling environment, these families could leverage these funds to improve their financial status appreciably. Therein lies the opportunities for the MFIs to help the remittance receiving households to fight poverty.

Payment Systems and the Poor

Payment systems are sustained by financial transactions. MTs (remittances) rely on payment systems. The MT business deals with a variety of remittance services that include business-to-business, business-to-person and vice versa, government-to-person and vice versa, and person-to-person transfers (Isern et al. 2005). The instruments used to transfer funds from one individual to another or one institution to another are varied. When funds are transacted on a face-to-face basis (in cash form), it can be very expensive. The costs go down further when one uses checks (that can be sent through mail). When credit and debit cards are used, the costs go down still further.

Institutions such as post offices, banking institutions and other related institutions are designed to enable smooth transfer of funds. However, there are several layers of institutions (both public and private) with increasing sophistication that are entrusted with funds transfer within and outside of any country. ICT-based funds transfer requires clearing and settlement, which ultimately leads to final exchange of funds.

What one finds is that, increasingly we rely less and less on cash-based transactions, which is labour intensive, requires care in preventing paper money getting mutilated and protecting it from getting stolen. While it is true that, 'cash is king,' unless money is saved in a safe and secure place that earns a 'reasonable' interest, the poor lose out on taking advantage of 'time value of money.' Without being saved, intermediated and leveraged for the benefit of the poor, one cannot say that the poor have gotten most out of their remittances.

Increasingly the non-poor around the world rely on such instruments as credit and debit cards that are more secure. Credit card provides the cardholder instant credit, and the debit card helps the cardholder access to cash without carrying cash. It is like having electronic wallet. Each of these instruments has its advantages and disadvantages. When it comes to the poor, they largely rely on cash-based transactions. They carry money for whatever transactions they want to make, which is cumbersome. In the process, they could lose their money or it could be stolen. Because the poor invariably rely on cash-based transactions, they largely remain outside the formal payment system.

As noted in Chapter 6, most MFIs around the world are not allowed to offer voluntary savings accounts to the poor because of regulatory requirements. As a result, sending funds electronically through MFIs becomes difficult unless MFI clients have savings accounts of their own. Besides, in order to receive funds, the MFIs have to be approved to receive MTs.

During the last 10 years, mobile phone-based systems such as GCASH in Philippines, M-PESA (mobile money) in Kenya (also available in many other countries around the world, including India and Wizzit in South Africa are some of the important examples of 'electronic wallets,' that use 'digital money' (converted from cash by appropriate service providers) to make and receive payments or even to save.

Similarly 'smart card'-based payment systems for providing financial services are being used around the world to enable financial transactions. One such example is FINO in India. It is provided to financial institutions and to their clients by FINO Ltd. These are relatively more robust and sophisticated systems about which we will also discuss in this chapter. FINO is currently being used in the context of correspondent banking in India (see Chapter 6).

Traditionally, the post offices in the developing countries have been used to transfer funds to the poor. Because the funds are physically carried to one's doorstep by a postman, such transfers are usually expensive. Besides, there may be unnecessary delay in receiving these funds. As a result, the poor person may not have access to these funds at the right time. Besides, in many countries one has to tip the postman delivering remittances, which can eat into small remittances poor people receive. Once the funds are received, safe keep of the funds in the household may not be all that easy. Because the poor normally do not have access to formal savings facilities, the funds are kept in the house or with relatives or friends, which may not be all that safe.

What all this imply is that, in order to send funds to the poor it costs more than sending funds to the non-poor. This is because of improved connectivity and economies of scale helps to reduce charges for sending funds to the non-poor. Therefore, 'poverty penalty' is also a reality in transferring funds.

For example, in India, as far as domestic remittances are concerned, to send ₹500, it costs ₹25 (i.e., 5 per cent of the face amount) using the postal system. As we will discuss later in this chapter, migrant workers in the state of Gujarat, use a service provider called Shramik Sahajog (SS), which can send funds to the state of Odisha for a fee of about 4 to 6 per cent of the amount being sent. The funds reach the destination rather quickly and are delivered at the doorstep for a fee.

International transfers from industrialized countries to developing countries can be quite expensive. For example, to send $200 from the USA to Brazil (during the first quarter of 2012) the cost was on an average about $24 (including the exchange rate margin), which amounts to about 12 per cent of the funds sent ('Remittance Prices World Wide,' The World Bank). Similarly, to send $200 from USA to Mexico, the cost was on an average about $11.55, amounting to about 5.78 per cent of the funds sent.

How MFIs Are Helping to Bridge the 'Last Mile' and Enhance the Developmental Impact of Remittances

The microfinance revolution has been able to bridge the 'last mile' to deliver financial services to the poor by establishing people-to-people (P2P) contact. In fact, success of microfinance revolution is largely predicated by such contact. Without P2P contact, expansion of microfinance, particularly, microcredit would not have been possible at such a rapid pace. It is also expected that P2P contact will be the driving force behind spread of other microfinance instruments such as microsavings and microinsurance.

However, with the advent of ICT-based payment systems such as M-PESA and FINO (to be discussed below), MFIs have increasingly becoming important nodal points in facilitating remittances to their clients, earn fee income on such transfers, and leverage and intermediate these funds for the benefit of their clients.

In spite of regulatory hurdles that the MFIs encounter in the developing countries to offer banking services, they enjoy several advantages over other institutions such as commercial banks that are worth mentioning. For example, at the time of delivery of remittances, identification of the individual receiving funds is critical and the MFIs are in a unique position to provide such identification for the poor. By design, the MFIs rely to a large extent on the principle of 'Know Your Client' (KYC) to minimize credit risk. While many developing countries are instituting UID numbers for their citizens, knowing an individual on one-to-one basis as a member of an organization provides an extra layer of security in delivering remittances. What is more, because of their regular contact with their clients, the time elapsed between the receipt of funds by an MFI and its delivery to the appropriate recipient can be short. In other words, the float can be minimized.

Because the MFIs may have a better understanding of the financial standing of their clients, they are in a better position to recommend them how the remittances they receive can be utilized. In fact, at the time an MFI client receives remittances can be an opportune moment to offer microfinance services to her before the funds are spent. For example,

MFIs could recommend them to use the remittances to buy insurance such as health insurance, save for retirement, start a commitment savings for children and pay down debt or to start a business.

Examples of Payment Systems for Money Transfer and Other Microfinance Services

In this section, we will provide three examples to illustrate how the poor have been benefiting through improved connectivity provided by different types of institutions dedicated to MT. The selection of the three examples is based on the approach these institutions have taken towards MT business.

The first example is Adhikar in India, which besides providing microcredit and microinsurance also provides money remittance service through SS (Workers Cooperation). It relies on P2P contact and the banking system to provide payment services to migrant workers. Because of the P2P contact, SS has been quite successful in transferring funds and offering other microfinance services to the migrant workers. We will also discuss about two other MT systems that include M-PESA (Mobile Money) and FINO, both of which are largely driven by ICT. M-PESA uses mobile phones as the underlying platform to offer financial services to the poor. FINO, on the other hand, uses biometric smart cards (for biometric authentication), hand-held devices and Micro Deposit Machines to provide financial services to the poor, including MT.

Adhikar: Shramik Sahajog (Workers Cooperation)

The mission of Adhikar[1] has been to provide 'effective, flexible and responsible financial' services for the deprived and marginalized communities in the state of Odisha in India. To achieve this, Adhikar provides four different financial services, which include money remittance, microfinance (microcredit and microinsurance), livelihood services and co-operative-based services. It also provides legal counselling for the poor. In the following, we will focus on SS, the money remittance arm of Adhikar.

SS has been well recognized for its remittance services. It has been at the forefront of providing remittance service to Odia migrant workers from the state of Odisha working in Gujarat and Maharashtra. Given the fact that bankers are required to apply KYC policy to everyone, it becomes difficult for poor migrant workers, without formal home address, to avail banking services such as sending money home. Besides, these workers work from dawn to dusk and hence do not have the time to visit their banks during working hours.

Adhikar provides these poor people financial services until midnight. Besides, they collect money from their doorstep and remit the funds to their families back home. This is particularly helpful to those families back home where ailing parents may not be in a position to travel to the bank to receive money that may be 15–20 kilometres away (Oikocredit 2012). Besides being poor-friendly, SS remittance service has been able to provide quick, cost-effective, safe and timely delivery of cash to dependents of migrant workers. It is claimed that the post offices and banks are not able to provide similar services.

In order to send funds through the institution, one has to be a member of SS. There are two types of membership, that is, membership for MT services and membership for MT and other services such as savings and insurance services. There is no membership fee for just availing MT services; however, there is a service charge for sending money. SS charges an entry fee of ₹30 (about $0.60 assuming an exchange rate of ₹50 to $1) for multiple services, which include MT, savings and insurance. Some of the typical charges for MT services by SS are as follows: for remitting funds up to ₹500 the charges are ₹30, and for remitting ₹501 to ₹1,000 the charges are ₹40. Using SS, one can send a minimum of ₹500 to a maximum of ₹25,000 per month. On the average, the charges vary from about 4–6 per cent of the amount remitted plus ₹10 to ₹20 for door-to-door delivery.[2] The delivery of funds to beneficiaries takes about three to four days, whereas remittances through postal system and informal MT organizations could take longer. What is more, charges by informal MT organizations are usually more and they are less reliable.

SS utilizes Remittance Collection Officers (RCOs) to collect remittance money from the workers, based on their availability—mostly during evening hours. Money so collected are processed and accounted for and sent to an appropriate destination using the core banking system. At the destination, the funds are distributed to the beneficiaries by the Remittance Disbursement Officers (RDOs).

The procedures in transferring funds to the beneficiaries are fairly transparent. Suffice it to say that, the institution has an elaborate institutional structure to collect, remit and disburse funds. In order to control fraud, the institution provides a money receipt when cash is received. It provides a return receipt after the recipient receives the funds. Interstate transfer of funds takes place through the formal banking system. The institution is audited on a quarterly basis and there is also an annual statutory audit.

Adhikar extends savings support to its members in collaboration with ICICI Bank. It also provides life insurance policy through Janata Personal Accident Life Insurance Company with coverage of ₹100,000 for accidental death and ₹50,000 for permanent disability.

SS also provides a deposit service for depositing at least ₹100 every month (Thorat et al. 2009). And the deposited funds can be withdrawn only after one year. In order to send funds using the remittance service, the funds have to be new money. The deposit account that has been around for at least one year receives 6 per cent interest per annum.

By providing P2P contact with their clients at the front-end as well as the back-end, SS helps its clients not only in MT, but also in areas such as microsavings, microinsurance and microcredit that include the entire gamut of microfinance services. By providing financial literacy training to the poor, SS also contributes towards helping its clients to become financially more secure.

During the last 10 years Adhikar has made great strides on various fronts, including linking with other financial institutions such as ABN-AMRO, ICICI Bank, SIDBI, UNITUS, AXIS Bank, CITI Bank, NABARD, SBI and OIKOCREDIT. In the year 2009, Adhikar was included among the top 50 MFIs in India by Credit Rating and Information Services of India Ltd (CRISIL 2009).

As can be seen, the model used by Adhikar for MT is labour intensive. Today, even poor migrant workers in India own mobile phones. With introduction of M-PESA and FINO (under the Correspondent Banking model), there may be competition for Adhikar from these sources in the coming years. However, real advantage of Adhikar comes from the fact that it is a door-to-door service, which is convenient and poor-friendly.

M-Banking: M-PESA (Mobile Money)

M-PESA (M stands for Mobile and PESA stands for money in Swahili) hosted by Safaricom, is considered the largest mobile money network in Kenya. Since its inception in 2007, it has expanded rapidly to include almost 15 million customers representing 78 per cent of Safaricom's 19 million customer base (How We Made It in Africa 2012). It was initially developed and run by Sagentia. The pilot programme for M-PESA was jointly funded by the Department for International Development (UK government) and Safaricom, Vodafone's affiliate in Kenya.

M-PESA is a small-value electronic payment system that stores monetary value electronically, which can be accessed from mobile (cell) phones to make payments remotely (Mas and Radcliffe 2010). Being a mobile (cell) phone-based technology, it utilizes Subscriber Identification Module (SIM card) to perform basic banking transactions remotely. SIM cards encrypt unique identification key for the user. SIM cards are used on GSM protocols. GSM phones allow for short messaging service (SMS), which is used by the clients to send messages regarding MT.

In order to use the M-PESA system, the customer has to deposit cash to her M-PESA account at a network of retail stores (also known as agents) to be converted to electronic value. The electronic value is used to make payments using the M-PESA system. The agents are authorized to convert cash to electronic value or electronic value to cash and are paid a fee for each conversion. All transactions take place in the real time and are made using secure SMS and have a ceiling of $500 per transaction.

Survey has shown customers of M-PESA are normally better educated, twice as likely to have bank accounts and wealthier. Government audit of M-PESA accounts has shown that the average balance on M-PESA accounts amounted to only about $2.70. The usage of M-PESA is largely driven by following activities (listed by order of usage), that is, receive money, send money, store money for everyday use, buy airtime for the client, buy airtime for others, store (save) money for emergencies and pay bill. Of all the customers, who were asked to compare M-PESA with other alternatives, 98 per cent consider it to be quicker, 96 per cent consider it to be more convenient, 98 per cent consider it to be safer and 96 per cent consider it to be cheaper (Mas and Radcliffe 2010).

Some of the conclusions of the paper are as follows: (1) M-PESA system has shown that mobile technology can be used as a vehicle to deliver financial services to the poor on a mass scale, (2) usage-based revenue model (prepaid airtime and charges on other transactions) was preferable to float-based revenue models and (3) low-cost transaction platform was preferable because it enables the poor to utilize M-PESA for a broad range of activities.

Increasingly, M-PESA clients use it for bill payments and payments at supermarkets. Equity Bank of Kenya by teaming up with Safaricom offers M-KESHO, which M-PESA customers can use to open savings accounts. Savers can earn interest on amounts as little as 1 Kenyan Shilling. M-PESA also offers microinsurance.

More recently, M-PESA along with the Commercial Bank of Africa (CBA) has been offering M-Shwari, which is a product that can be used to borrow as well as to save using customer's phone. For example, what a customer can do is to borrow 100 Kenyan Shillings or higher amounts into M-PESA accounts, which can be used in business, and for bill payments and other needs. As the borrower pays off the loan, she can also build up savings. She can also move money out of savings account to M-PESA account for expenditure. Inter-account MTs between savings, borrowing and M-PESA accounts provide great deal of flexibility to the borrowers to manage their finances. Total savings under M-Shwari stood at about 4 billion Kenyan Shillings (equivalent to about $47 million) in March 2013.[3]

As we noted in Chapter 6, M-KESHO savings accounts (offered by Equity Bank of Kenya) have not been popular with M-PESA clients. One of the reasons for not using these accounts as interest-bearing savings accounts was perhaps due to the fact that the interest paid on these accounts was only 0.5 per cent for up to 2,000 Kenyan Shillings, and 3 per cent for deposits above 10,000 Kenyan Shillings (as of October 2011). These interest rates were much lower than the inflation rate of 18.9 per cent (as of October 2011) in Kenya. The negative interest rates are clearly a disincentive to save using M-KESHO accounts. One other explanation for slower uptake of interest-bearing accounts has been attributed to some of the complexities of cooperation between Safaricom (parent of M-PESA) and Equity Bank of Kenya, which has led to two layers of service charges being levied on the clients: first service charge to withdraw funds from M-KESHO savings accounts into M-PESA accounts and then the second service charge for making transactions from the M-PESA accounts once the funds are available after transfer. Besides, there has been a lack of vigorous promotion of these accounts among the Kenyans (Demombynes and Thegeya 2012).

It is also important to highlight that some of the complications arising in using M-PESA include the agents of mobile operators not having enough cash at hand when there may be large number of withdrawals. The agents are not equipped as in the case of bank branches to have enough liquidity at hand. One other concern has to do with safety issues related to customers' transactions. There could be hidden charges as well as fraudulent charges that the clients may not be able to find out easily. Besides, at the time of registration, it is difficult to authenticate the identity of the person registering. Many users of the system do not trust the system because they do not fully understand the system. Poor people who are not conversant in using mobile phones and those who are illiterate cannot use M-PESA. Last but not the least, in many countries, regulatory authorities are wary of non-bank entities receiving and making payments on behalf of banks.

Sarah Rotman (2012) in her article 'Savings and Credit on Mobile: The Jipange KuSave Experiment,' discusses about 'rails' that branchless banking community has started to build in some countries to serve the poor. In the article, she discusses about Jipange KuSave experiment in Kenya, a 'lend-to-save' model, which is an adaptation of P9 model of Stuart Rutherford. We have already discussed about P9 model in Chapter 6. The important point to be made here is that, as the mobile money technology matures, innovators, social entrepreneurs and business leaders are thinking in terms of using this technology and the platform to make inclusive finance a reality. And if Jipange KuSave experiment shows any promise, it has the potential to replace mattresses and other esoteric places to hide cash a reality. In other words, it could contribute greatly towards making microsavings an important addition to the mono-product world of microfinance that largely consists of extending credit to the poor.

Financial Information Network and Operations: Money Transfer and Financial Inclusion

FINO Ltd of India provides technological solutions to institutions such as banks, insurance companies, government entities, MFIs and other financial institutions such that they can reach out to millions of unbanked and under-banked households in India in order to make financial inclusion a realty.[4] As of November 2012, FINO had almost 50 million customer base and over 30,000 CSPs in 26 states of India (FINO 2012).

FINO's generalized platform for low-cost branchless banking using biometric smart cards, hand-held devices and databases on servers can perform wide range of financial transactions. These include mobile banking, insurance, MT, financial advisory services and identification services. The system has been used by the MFIs to offer savings accounts and provide remittance services to its customers. It can be used for balance transfers, deposits and withdrawals. Its business model is scalable.

FINO has an alliance with most of the major banking institutions in India. It is also involved in government-funded schemes such as the National Rural Employment Guarantee Act and the Rashtriya Swashthya Bima Yojana through ICICI Lombard. Investors in FINO include ICICI Bank, Intel Capital, IFC, Life Insurance Corporation (LIC) of India and several of India's public sector banks.

FINO's technology allows businesses to roll out multiple business strategies in the area of microfinance. It provides consultancy services to its client institutions to roll out branchless banking products. Its technology platform is smart enough to track if a customer is accessing loans with fake identity. The robustness of the technology elicits trust from its customers and the institutions that use the technology.

FINO works through a network of *bandhus* (bandhu means a friend) to connect with low-income clients (India Knowledge@Wharton 2010). It relies on biometric technology to store each customer's photograph, fingerprint, a unique identification number (UIN) and account details. The field devices are equipped with fingerprint reader and smart card reader and can be connected with back offices of the MFIs via a telephone line. Once the data are downloaded into FINO servers, they are available for accessing using the Internet.

Moreover, using FINO, details of financial transactions can be accessed in an offline mode that reduces the cost of bookkeeping, improved accuracy and most importantly generating management information for monitoring what is happening in the field. The system is very useful for the BC model promoted by ICICI Bank in India (see Chapter 6).

Because the system also reduces fraud, it is considered more secure than other systems used by the poor for financial transactions. The presence of *bandhu*s helps clients who may not be technology-savvy. It also reduces errors in entering transaction details.

FINO can have other benefits. FINO could also serve as a credit bureau for the financial sector. It can be used to track the credit history of a client as they move from one MFI to another. Credit bureaus would cut down costs of tracking customers as and when group lending may be phased out. It could provide credit data to MFIs to reduce defaults. It could also make it easier for the clients to move to access bank lending as they graduate from MFIs. It would also enable the MFIs to offer individual loan products instead of group products. While FINO is not an MFI, it has the capabilities to provide microfinance service through its network. In fact, FINO has already demonstrated its capability to extend microcredit to the poor.

It is true that extension of microcredit to the poor has achieved scale and even a great deal of maturity. Extension of microsavings and microinsurance on the same scale would require a great deal of work in terms of product design, pricing and delivery. It is hoped that FINO-enabled technologies and its versatile platform would make headways in this regard by reducing transaction costs.

It is also possible that FINO could extend microcredit to the poor below 20 per cent interest rate per annum. This may be possible by leveraging '*bandhu*' network to cross-sell multiple products, that is, microcredit, microsavings, microinsurance and other financial products, which could reduce transaction costs. Because introduction of FINO could reduce paperwork, it could in turn help *bandhu*s acquire new customers.

There has been some criticism of FINO system by M.S. Sriram (India Knowledge@Wharton 2010). He contends that in order to add one layer of intermediation, FINO adds four layers of cost that include commission to the bank correspondents, cost of technology that consists of smart cards, point-of-sales terminals, cost of regulation and cost of the carrier such as mobile or VSAT (satellite ground station). He believes that the model will be workable if the model piggybacks on mobile-cashless platform. However, FINO management does not agree with the argument and believes that because micro transactions cost $1 at a bank, 60 cents at an ATM and only 10 cents for BCs, there is enough room that margins can be squeezed by using FINO. However, it is difficult to imagine how

BCs could provide all the services that MFI loan officers provide to their clients on a face-to-face basis such as in group meetings.

Profitability of Mobile Money Providers

Given the fact that platforms such as M-PESA have emerged as providers of mobile money, it would be appropriate to ask the question whether such services are sustainable (profitable). This is particularly important because mobile money platforms have been already operational in limited number of markets around the world.

We discuss about sustainability of mobile money business later in this section. However, it is important to note that based on the 2011/2012 financial results, M-PESA's revenue increased by 43 per cent to reach $203 million. Today M-PESA directly employs 50,000 people. And it had about 40,000 agents (How We Made It in Africa 2012). The magnitude of the operations as well as the size of the revenue show that in only five years (M-PESA was established in 2007), M-PESA has been quite successful in expanding its business, which is critical for attaining sustainability (profitability).

In a survey by Karina Baba, 20 senior managers from major mobile network operators (MNOs) in 15 different markets were asked about their expectations with regard to the performance of their businesses (Baba 2010). The questions they were asked included the following: (1) whether their respective businesses will make money? (2) What is the expected time before their business would make money? (3) What are some of the implications of mobile money business for their core businesses? Some of the findings of the survey were as follows:

- Sixty-four per cent of the respondents said, they had launched mobile money during the previous year. Seventy per cent of the respondents claimed that they had already reached a customer base of over half a million utilizing such features as MTs and bill payments.
- Assuming mobile money as the only source of revenue, 70 per cent of managers said they believe (to certain extent) that mobile money could be a significant source of revenue for the MNOs. They also

agreed to some extent that, the business could also make large profits over time. Sixty-three per cent of the managers expected mobile money as a new source of revenue. Only 50 per cent of the managers expected it is a strategy to acquire new customers.

- Most of the managers expected that mobile money could contribute 30 per cent of the overall revenue of the MNOs in eight years. And they also expected the mobile money business to have positive cash flow within three years.

- Based on the survey, less than 10 per cent of the MNOs believe mobile money does not need to be self-sustainable. Mobile money managers in general wanted to see mobile money to generate direct revenues from providing financial transactions such as remittances and other types of payments as opposed to indirect revenues by selling airtime for mobile money transactions.

- As far as MNOs were concerned, they gave equal importance to restructuring agent commissions and renegotiating technology platform cost in order to improve profitability.

All in all, the managers portrayed an optimistic picture of mobile money business and expect it to be profitable, but did not provide an expected time period during which their respective businesses would attain profitability.

Conclusion

Improved connectivity facilitates financial inclusion. The pithy statement, 'Medium is the message,' by Marshall McLuhan sums up rather succinctly how the medium plays a dominant role not just in communications, but in transforming the society we live in. A case in point includes the continuum of inventions in the communications arena such as telephones, TV, computers, personal computers, mobile phones, Internet (e.g., Google, Facebook), e-mails and iphones. Needless to say, these inventions have transformed our society in ways that was unthinkable before the emergence of these tools. In the same vein, partnership of open and powerful platforms such as M-PESA and FINO with common-sensical microfinance instruments and services potentially could have far-reaching consequences in delivering financial services to the poor to facilitate financial inclusion on a much wider scale.

Notes

1. 'Adhikar: A Bird's Eye View.' Available online at www.adhikarindia.org/index.php (downloaded on 21 March 2013).
2. 'Adhikar: Money Remittance.' Available online at www.adhikarindia.org/MoneyRemittance.php (downloaded on 21 March 2013).
3. Based on information contained in the article, 'Is it a phone, is it a bank?' Available online at http://www.economist.com/node/21574520/print (downloaded on 19 June 2014).
4. About FINO. FINO. Available online at http://www.fino.webithub.com/Press-Kit (downloaded on 25 February 2013).

10
Complementary Non-financial Services

Given the fact the world of poverty is multidimensional, it is not difficult to visualize that income generation, building and protecting assets, and wealth creation cannot take place in an atmosphere where there is lack of literacy including financial literacy, good nutrition, sanitation, hygiene, health care, education, training and adequate infrastructure. As we shall discuss in the following text, in order that microfinance can be an effective tool in the hands of the poor, they need access to complementary non-financial services.

Needless to say, delivering financial services to the poor is a hugely complex task. Therefore, many in the microfinance field wonder whether it is wise for the MFIs to spread out rather thinly in delivering complementary non-financial services to the poor. Besides, lack of well-defined revenue model(s) makes it even more difficult for the MFIs, particularly the MFIs that are not financially strong, to offer such services. This is because attaining the goal of financial sustainability makes it imperative for many MFIs to be minimalist in offering such services. Besides, most MFIs do not have any comparative advantage in delivering such services either, because their main focus is design and delivery of financial services to the poor.

Unquestionably, if an MFI has the resources to provide some of the complementary services then it is well and good. Otherwise, given the importance of such services in leveraging the effectiveness of microfinance instruments, it is important that the MFIs play a catalytic role in the delivery of these services to the poor. In other words, whether such services are delivered by the MFIs or by other private or public sector institutions becomes immaterial. What is needed is that the poor ought to have poor-friendly access to these services in order that they could benefit the most from their access to financial services. This is important because a client who is unsuccessful in her business is a potential credit risk for the MFIs.

The Importance of Complementary Non-financial Services for the Poor

It is assumed that, after getting an income-generating microloan, an MFI client would invest the loan proceeds in a microbusiness or self-employment scheme. And one would expect that the client's business would be profitable sooner or later and make her financially better off. But over the years, evidence has been mounting that access to micro-credit is no panacea for alleviating poverty on a mass scale.[1] In this regard, it is important to note that, Vijay Mahajan, Managing Director of BASIX India, has expressed the following opinion: 'Right from the beginning we've believed that credit, or more broadly microfinance, is necessary, but not sufficient condition,' for alleviation of poverty (Microfinance Gateway 2009).

Every entrepreneur normally would try hard to generate sufficient income to pay for debt services, inputs, supplies and other expenses before she takes a part of the income, say for household expenses. However, there is distinct possibility that the entrepreneur may fail to generate enough income. This may be because the types of income-generating businesses a poor entrepreneur normally invests require low levels of capital, have low barriers to entry and may be clones of other such businesses in the neighbourhood. That could lead to squeezing of margins and profitability and sometimes the business may fail.

Needless to say, this is something every borrower tries to avoid. However, if the microbusiness she invests does not generate enough income, she may not have any other choice but to borrow more to avoid difficult cash flow situation. That could lead to the beginning of a downward spiral.

One of the reasons for such predicament could be that poor people may lack entrepreneurial ability, the necessary business experience and training in running businesses and marketing ability. This could be the case because the poor may not have any other choice but to be self-employed or start a new business. In other words, they end up becoming an entrepreneur out of necessity. Therefore, it would be desirable for the MFIs to create an enabling environment in which its clients might have the option to access appropriate advice in choosing a livelihood and getting trained in adopting the livelihood. Unquestionably, delivering all this to the poor is more complex than it appears on the surface.

There are other reasons why borrowers may fail. For example, they might spend the borrowed funds for business in spurious consumption. This could be a distinct possibility in an atmosphere where the MFIs may be resorting to over-lending by relaxing their credit standards. This would imply that the MFIs did not provide appropriate guidance (such as financial literacy training) to their clients in managing their household finances—such as how much a household could comfortably borrow based on their household income, assets and liabilities. Such training also ought to emphasize the importance of savings and insurance in managing financial risk. If a household's income is erratic (which is true of many poor households), financial literacy training should also emphasize building larger savings cushion than usual to tide over lean times. Such training is also essential because the poor tend to over-indebt themselves and because of lack of credit bureaus for the poor (in most developing countries), there is no deterrence for over-borrowing.

Leaving aside livelihood training and training in financial literacy, other complementary non-financial services, such as training in nutrition, sanitation and hygiene, could greatly reduce a poor household's exposure to health risks. Even drinking boiled water can prevent a variety of stomach ailments and save a family from a great deal of medical expenses. Similarly, using bed nets regularly can go a long way in preventing malaria. Moreover, if in a poor household the breadwinner can be motivated to reduce or even eliminate expenditures on sinful goods such as cigarettes and alcohol that would have salutary implications for the family in terms of cash flow as well as improving the physical health of the breadwinner.

Many MFIs decide to offer complementary services to extreme poor and the poorest (ultra poor) to build capacity such that they can become eligible to borrow from the institution. Such capacity building also goes a long way in meeting their social mission goals. Moreover, offering such services to the ultra poor can also dispel the perception that the MFIs are more institution-centric as opposed to client-centric (Datar et al. 2008). Given the fact that generating revenue from such activities may be difficult, access to grant money can be utilized in providing such services. Many charitable foundations also provide funding for such activities.

As we noted in Chapter 4, BRAC has been a pioneer in providing assistance to the ultra poor under its TUP programme. One of the important aspects of the programme is that BRAC makes asset transfers in the form of livestock that can generate income for the ultra poor along with providing health, education, social support and other assistance. After remaining in the programme for a period of two years, many of the ultra poor become eligible to access DABI microfinance programme (Whiting 2009) under the BRAC umbrella. Graduates of the TUP programme not only access microcredit, they also save.

The debate on 'creative capitalism' that ensued after Bill Gates' speech (Gates 2008) at Davos in 2008 showed the amount of interest it generated in finding ways to 'expanding capitalism into new areas and using it to solve problems that previously were assigned to charity or to government' (Rangan et al. 2007). As far as businesses are concerned, it is not inconceivable to imagine a scenario where the business can play an important role in catalysing better livelihoods for the poor by imaginatively utilizing the productive capacity of the poor. They can provide appropriate inputs and technology along with training in order that the poor can become a part of their value and supply chain. Under the rubrics of corporate social responsibility (CSR) and creating shared value (CSV), many businesses are slowly emerging as important sources of funding, training, technology and marketing assistance to help the poor fight poverty. We will briefly discuss about CSV in Chapter 12 in the context of social business models.

While group lending (joint-liability contracts) unleashed the power of social capital, which the MFIs and SHGs have leveraged successfully in lending to the poor (we discussed about some of the downsides of using joint-liability contracts in Chapter 5), a much broader leveraging of social capital could greatly help the poor in their fight against poverty. For example, unless the poor collectively believe in civic sense, sense of discipline, elimination of social exploitation such as the dowry system and corruption, all efforts to uplift them from poverty can be easily negated. For example, in order for sanitation and hygiene to have beneficial impact, the community in which the poor live has to collectively believe in it. As noted in the Prologue, the Grameen Bank tries to inculcate many of these values among its clients using 'Sixteen Decisions' (Dowla and Barua 2006, 55–62) and expects that its clients follow them diligently. We presented four of these decisions in the Prologue.

If an MFI has donor funding available to provide access to complementary services, then it goes a long way in helping the MFIs to fund these services. However, such funding may not be available year after year. Under these circumstances, the MFIs have to find other ways to fund such activities. MFIs that are already profitable may decide to contribute a part of their profit towards delivering complementary services for the poor. This will help them to achieve their social mission goals. But ultimately, the MFIs have to charge a fee for cost recovery, which even if partial, can provide indications as to the real demand for such services. Without charging a fee for cost recovery, it would be difficult to find out if a given service is of value to their clients or not. At the end of this chapter, we will discuss about sustainability of delivering complementary services to the poor.

The Importance of Social Intermediation in Building Social Capital to Fight Poverty

> Whereas physical capital refers to physical objects and human capital refers to properties of individuals, social capital refers to connections among individuals – social networks and the norms of reciprocity and trustworthiness that arise from them. In that sense, social capital is closely related to what some have called 'civic virtue.' The difference is that "social capital" calls attention to the fact that civic virtue is most powerful when embedded in a dense network of social relations. A society of many virtuous but isolated individuals is not necessarily rich in social capital.
>
> Robert Putnam

In order to understand how social capital helps the poor, we discuss below three interrelated concepts, that is, social networks, social capital and social intermediation. Our focus is to highlight how the use of social intermediation, helps to build social capital such that individuals and groups are empowered to act with self-interest.

Over the last 35 years, microfinance has shown that in order for the poor to access financial services, particularly microcredit, without collateral, these underserved and socially disadvantaged groups would require something extra. That extra has to do with their desire to build social capital (brought about through a process of social intermediation), which microfinance has been able to leverage as collateral substitutes (as joint-liability contracts) to extend microcredit to the poor. It is important to note that the discovery of utilizing social capital in a tangible manner was the result of a trial and error process (Dowla and Barua 2006), where the objective was to minimize credit risk as well as transaction costs of delivering credit to the poor.

While there are some MFIs (e.g., Grameen Bank) that have already moved away or are in the process of moving away from group-based lending, such lending is still practiced by the majority of the MFIs around the world. De-emphasizing group-based lending, particularly joint-liability contracts, does not imply that the role of groups in microfinance is losing its value. In fact, one of the important aspects of microfinance paradigm is the use of group meetings to interact and communicate with the clients and perform variety of tasks that are crucial to the functioning of MFIs. In fact, groups are crucial in reducing transaction costs, which ultimately contributes towards sustainability of MFIs.

Social Networks

Whether we consciously know it or not, we are part and parcel of social networks. Our social identity is largely defined in terms of which groups or networks we belong to. Groups are also networks of people with common goals. We belong to a variety of networks consisting of family members, friends, neighbours and the like. In our professional life, we belong to professional networks and we also create special interest groups (SIGs) to keep abreast of a field of specialization. The recent growth in 'social networks' (e.g., Facebook) tells us in no uncertain terms, the value we attach to such networks to stay connected with others. Social networks empower us in ways that is difficult to comprehend. It provides anchors that bring stability to our existence. We leverage social networks for our benefit in a variety of ways.

Networks are basically flat organizations having minimal hierarchy. One normally becomes a member of a network based on self-selection. A group as a human network helps to build trust and consensus among its members about issues that the group considers important.

Human networks gather and assimilate information and bring about an understanding (by building consensus or deciding on a course of action) to act in a manner, which is of value to its members, other similar groups, the government, the business and the society at large. For example, we become members of social networks such as homeowners' association, parents and teachers association (PTA), and other such associations to build consensus and to decide on a course of action in such areas as garbage disposal, funding for computers in schools and the like. Internet has become the hub of thousands of social networks because besides helping its participants to interact with each other, it facilitates easy assimilation, transformation and dissemination of information.

Perhaps the most important aspect of any human network is that it provides a sense of belonging, a sense of identity for the poor. In the case of the poor, who are socially excluded, belonging to solidarity groups helps them find their identity. They use the network to find solutions to their life's problems, such as learning about home remedies to over-the-counter drugs to referral for doctors. They can also leverage the network to learn about what microbusiness to invest in, where to find supplies for the business inexpensively. Therefore, benefits of belonging to solidarity groups go well beyond microlending. However, there could be downside to group lending (see Chapter 5). For example, in the event a delinquent group member is subject to sanctions, it could have serious consequences for the individual. This is because group sanctions could alienate the individual not only from the group, but also from the community in which he/she lives, which can be devastating. In the case of poor women, such sanctions can have huge emotional and financial impact.

In Chapter 12, we will discuss how there is evidence that Pareto inequality of a populace depends to a great extent on 'network effect' (Buchanan 2002), which arises from how a populace organizes itself into networks (how the populace interconnects with each other in the socioeconomic network) and how wealth spreads around (through transactions) in the network based on economic interconnectivity and transactions among the members of the network. When people transact with each other in a network, wealth spreads around and tends to reduce (even out) unequal distribution of wealth. In other words, isolated groups make less financial transactions with the rest of the economy and hence have lesser chance for reducing unequal distribution of wealth.

Based on this hypothesis, one could conjecture that microfinance by providing poor-friendly access to credit, savings, insurance and improved MT would give rise to more economic interconnectivity, which would lead to more financial transactions by the MFI clients with the rest of the economy. The increased transactions in general would tend to lower unequal distribution of wealth and hence economic inequality. This reduction in inequality may perhaps would take long time to materialize, but it could have important implications for fighting poverty at the grass-root level. In Chapter 12, we will also discuss, rather briefly, how financial development such as introduction of financial intermediaries tends to reduce economic inequality by disproportionately boosting the incomes of the poor.

Social Capital

Capital comes in many forms. Financial capital and human capital are two of the five most common forms of capital one is familiar with (Mahajan 2007a). Other forms of capital include natural, social and physical capital. Natural capital includes land, forest, water, mineral resources, livestock, weather and the like. Physical capital consists of infrastructure such as roads, rail and communication networks consisting of such technologies as telephones, TV, mobile phones, Internet and the like. It also includes office buildings and factories consisting of plants and machinery. Social capital, on the other hand, consists of honesty, trust, reciprocity, reliable performance of duties and the like, which enhances cooperation among individuals and groups. Well-functioning groups, associations and institutions (private or public) embody social capital.

As noted by Robert Putnam, embedding 'civic virtue' in a dense network of social relations goes to the heart of social capital. It would appear that, if not all, most poor societies could greatly leverage the latent power of social capital to build informal and formal institutions to help them improve their economic condition.

Social capital is a subtle concept that is difficult to define rather precisely. It is an intangible wealth that every society enjoys in various forms but very difficult to put a value on. The smooth functioning of societies depends on social capital. And that depends on the quality of interconnectivity within a social network and outside the network, that is, with other social networks. The resulting connectivity, that is, when people come together, has a mind of its own. It is a powerful force. Shankar Vedantam (2007) puts it rather succinctly by describing social capital as follows: "Levels of social capital predict everything from the quality of schools and local government, to the risk that a country will go down in corruption or blow up in civil war."

In a paper titled *Social Capital, Civil Society and Development* Francis Fukuyama (2001, 7) defines social capital as follows:

> The definition I will use in this paper is social capital is an instantiated informal norm that promotes cooperation between two or more individuals. The norms that constitute social capital can range from a norm of reciprocity between two friends, all the way up to complex and elaborately articulated doctrines like Christianity or Confucianism. They must be instantiated in an actual human relationship: the norm of reciprocity exists *in potentia* in my dealings with all people, but is actualized only in my dealings with *my* friends. By this definition, trust, network, civil society, and the like which have been associated with social capital are all epi-phenomenal, arising as a result of social capital but not constituting social capital itself.

One can view honouring social contract within a solidarity group as an instantiation of social capital. Extension of credit to a group (or to its members) and its use by the group or its member depends on trust and socially agreed contract among the group members. The cooperation of poor people in solidarity groups or SHGs to guarantee the loan of a fellow member is an example of social contract, which translates to social capital in the form of 'collateral substitute.' In more concrete terms, group-based contracts (joint-liability contracts) are used by groups to backstop default by fellow group members. The arrangement provides the necessary financial comfort to MFIs to lend to the poor without collateral. And group lending along with 'joint-liability contracts' translate into savings (in terms of dollars and cents) by lowering credit risk and transaction costs. All this help in achieving eventual sustainability (profitability) of MFIs. This, in turn, could translate into lower interest rates on microloans.

In an article in the World Street Journal, 'The Secrets of Intangible Wealth,' Ronald Bailey (2007) discussed how intangible wealth such as social capital plays an important role in developed societies. The article is based on a World Bank research titled, 'Where is the Wealth of Nations? Measuring Capital for the 21st Century.'

The study defined natural capital as the sum of non-renewable resources (including oil, natural gas, coal and mineral resources), cropland, pastureland, forested areas and protected areas. The study also includes produced or built capital that consists of machinery, equipment and structures (including infrastructure) and urban land. When the value of natural and produced resources of the world was added up, the study found that vast majority of the wealth of the world was missing. The sum total of the value of the natural and manufactured resources could not account for the vast majority of the wealth as well as the level of income of the countries under study. As a result, there was a search to find out what are the reasons that account for the high level of wealth in the developed societies? And the following quote from Bailey shows how the study demystified what was missing.

> The rest is the result of 'intangible' factors—such as the trust among people in a society, an efficient judicial system, clear property rights and effective government. All this *intangible capital* also boosts the productivity of labour and results in higher total wealth. In fact the World Bank finds, "Human capital and value of institutions (as measured by the rule of law) constitute the largest share of wealth in virtually all countries."

In this article, what Bailey points out is that after one takes into account all the natural resources and produced capital, 80 per cent of the wealth of rich countries and 60 per cent wealth of the poor countries are of the intangible type. Bailey observes that such things as machinery, building, roads and the like only constitute about 17 per cent of the wealth of the rich countries. What is even more surprising is that 'The natural wealth in rich countries like the USA is a tiny proportion of their overall wealth—typically 1–3 per cent—yet they derive more value from what they have.' In a nutshell what this study points out is that in any society (rich or poor) intangible capital such as civic duty, rule of law and property rights are some of the important ingredients in creating wealth.

In the same vein, in spite of some of the downside risks of group lending, one can say that introduction of such lending has been one of the important steps MFIs around the world have taken to attain sustainability. Similarly, intangible institutional capital that MFIs bring to poor communities also plays an important role in wealth creation. For example, the introduction of formal credit culture, creation of financial networks to lay the foundations of financial intermediation teaching the poor rudiments of financial literacy, and respect for honouring social and financial contracts, may remain invisible, but are important constituents of an enabling environment that ultimately helps in the flow of capital to the poor for wealth creation.

Ronald Bailey (2007) has observed that societies with rich endowment of social capital are prosperous. In other words, financial capital flows to societies that are endowed with social capital. With access to financial and institutional capital, it is easier to leverage the use of other forms of capital such as human, natural and physical capital for growth and development. While MFI institutional model may not be perfect, the presence of MFIs in poor communities have given impetus to the formation of social and institutional capital by establishing solidarity groups and providing upward and downward linkages to social and economic networks. It is expected that as microfinance industry gains experience on the ground, various institutional models delivering microfinance to the poor will go through change.

Social Capital and the 2010 Andhra Pradesh Microfinance Crisis in India

While financial sustainability (profitability) is paramount for an MFI, social mission with social value creation remains equally important for such institutions serving the vulnerable poor clients, who are predominantly women. However, with the advent of commercialization of many MFIs, the pressures of the marketplace have led some of these institutions to succumb to 'mission drift.' And when the desire to grow rapidly to make a quick profit becomes the ethos, without regard for social mission, social mission suffers—that too sometimes miserably.

With above observations, one could perhaps attribute the prevalence of such a culture, which helped to precipitate the 2010 Andhra Pradesh

Microfinance Finance Crisis in India (see Chapter 11). Based on media reports of the crisis, one can surmise a dismal picture of the crisis, where desire to grow rapidly for higher profitability led to over-lending by some of the MFIs in a market that was already saturated by such lending (Lee and David 2010). As a result, many poor clients were over-indebted, which led to repayment inflexibility, delinquency and ultimate default by some borrowers. Under these circumstances, some of the MFIs resorted to coercive tactics to collect debt service payments, which led to alleged suicides by some borrowers.

In an exhaustive article, Yoolim Lee and Ruth David (2010) of Bloomberg Markets Magazine described the crisis as follows: 'As India struggles to provide decent education, health care and jobs to millions still locked in poverty, microlending—the loaning of small sums to the world's neediest people to help them earn a living—has taken a perverse turn.' The article also included the following quote from Malcolm Harper, Chairman of Micro-Credit Ratings International Ltd. in India, who had this to say about the crisis: 'Selling debt to illiterate women in Andhra Pradesh, you've got to be a lot more responsible.'

As microfinance industry expands rapidly around the world, responsible microfinance will have to be the motto, particularly when its poor clients are the most vulnerable sections of any country. While financial sustainability (profitability) is important for any commercial entity for its survival and to access capital on reasonable terms, on the same token, taking profitability and shareholder value creation too far by ignoring the interests of the poor clients could have serious consequences as the Andhra Pradesh microfinance crisis in India has clearly shown. Over-lending to illiterate poor and vulnerable women to increase market share in a saturated market cannot be considered accomplishing an MFI's social mission.

It takes long time to build social capital. It also takes long time to build trust and inculcate respect for honouring social and financial contracts. And there is no question that the 2010 Andhra Pradesh microfinance crisis destroyed, to a large extent, social capital and credit culture that was painstakingly built by the MFIs over long years of their existence. In the words of N. Srinivasan (2010), "More than 15 years of hard work has gone into the sector. For the mindless actions of a few with profit motive, a large number of customers are set to lose linkages to institutions that had helped them over the years."

Social Intermediation

After discussing about social networks and social capital, we define below what one implies by social intermediation. The following definition of social intermediation puts it rather succinctly what is social intermediation.

> Social intermediation has been defined as a process in which investments are made in the development of both human resources and human capital, with the aim of increasing the self-reliance of marginalized groups, preparing them to engage in formal financial intermediation. A short-hand definition would be that social intermediation is financial intermediation with a capacity-building component, aimed at those sectors of society that lack access to credit and savings facilities. (Edgcomb and Barton 1998)

The various chapters of the book have already discussed various socially desirable and valuable endowments that the MFIs have tried to nurture through group meetings and group-based lending. In the words of Joanna Ledgerwood (1999, 77), 'Social intermediation can thus be understood as the process of building the human and social capital required for sustainable financial intermediation with the poor.' It is also important to emphasize that without the financial service component, very few poor people would perhaps come to group meetings on their own and for social intermediation to take place.

Matin et al. (2007) point to the fact that minimalist MFIs may ignore taking advantage of social, network and institutional capital that can be engendered through social intermediation, which the poor can leverage in their fight against poverty. Unless and until one has a handle on these aspects of development, eradicating poverty may be difficult. They give examples of how BRAC capitalizes on process capital on such areas as (1) developing poultry as a viable enterprise, (2) rearing livestock, (3) getting basic health services to reach the poor and (d) building opportunity ladders for the extreme poor. They are of the opinion that innovations in the financial space alone fails to make use of process capital, which could help the poor to be successful in their livelihoods.

All in all, social intermediation through its capacity building component empowers the poor individually or in a group for more self-determination. Without being empowered, it is difficult for individuals to act in their self-interest. Acting with self-interest helps them to focus on things that could benefit them. For example, financial literacy training can help the poor individually and in a group to be sensitized about downside of over-indebting themselves in an environment where MFIs may be on an over-lending binge. They can be sensitized about the benefits of building savings and signing up for insurance such as health insurance.

Human Capital Development: The Importance of Livelihood Promotion for the Poor

> To deal with investment in man the traditional concept of capital had to be extended to make room for human capital. I was perplexed by the omission of human capital in the economic growth models that dominated the literature of economics.
>
> Theodore W. Schultz

> Knowledge is our most powerful engine of production.
>
> Alfred Marshall

One of the major reasons, why the poor command low wages has to do with the fact that most of them are unskilled. Even if access to microcredit empowers them to invest in microbusinesses or to be self-employed, many of them find that easy business opportunities have been already saturated. With limited access to capital, lack of education and training, the poor normally invest in businesses that have low barriers to entry and low returns. With very little backstop, the poor also tend to invest in businesses for which they have proclivity and they believe can succeed. More often than not they end up investing in businesses that tend to be clones of other businesses in the neighbourhood.

'Knowledge is power.' However, when it comes to the poor, they are disempowered because they are largely disconnected from the information sources, education and training that can help them to invest in niche businesses. As we discussed in Chapter 2, people can become more productive over time with the help of education, learning and skills training, which ultimately 'contribute greatly to the process of economic expansion' (Sen 1999). Therefore, the need for access to training and education for the poor cannot be over emphasized.

While many MFIs may not be in a position to deliver livelihood training to the poor, one of the leading practitioners of microfinance, Vijay Mahajan, Managing Director of BASIX, India puts livelihood promotion for the poor as one of the most important objectives of his institution. In fact, he has advocated for transitioning from microfinance to 'livelihood finance' as one of the major goals of BASIX. In the following, we will give several examples how access to capital alone is not enough, and how livelihood training could play a vital role in enabling poor entrepreneurs to increase their chances to succeed in their businesses.

In an article, 'Beyond Microfinance,' Vijay Mahajan (2007a) discusses how graduate students from the Indian Institute of Management, Ahmedabad (IIMA), were involved in helping a poor community of leather workers to improve their business to access broader marketplace. The article is very instructive in showing that even if these traditional leather workers, known as the *raigar*s, had the skills to produce leather products in the traditional way, in order to access a wider market for their products (e.g., to sell their products to consumers in New Delhi), they had to be re-trained. The training included learning to adopt new designs from the National Institute of Design in Ahmedabad and also learning the skills of tanning soft leather. Such training was not easy. It took several months of work by IIMA volunteers to bring these artisans up to speed in producing and marketing these products. What this implies is that access to microcredit may not be enough to ensure that the clients may be successful in their respective businesses.

Many MFIs under the rubric of Enterprise Development Services (EDS) provide livelihood training for the poor. EDS has been also referred to as Business Development Services (BDS) (Ledgerwood 1999). EDS broadly includes skills and basic business training. It also includes product development services. Other important trainings that EDS provides to its clients include help in the areas of production, packaging and marketing. It also provides training in literacy, including financial and computer literacy, bookkeeping, technology transfer and arranging apprenticeships for the poor where they can get hands-on experience.

Because attaining sustainability remains a major issue for many MFIs, it is not essential that such training be provided by the same institution that is already providing microcredit. Besides, considering wide range of areas, in which livelihood training can be imparted, all MFIs may not be in a position to deliver such training to their clients. Therefore, it is imperative that they play a catalytic role in bringing other stakeholders (the government, business and the donors) to come forward to provide resources such that the poor can have access to skills training, technology and hands-on experience in livelihoods that they can pursue profitably.

Governmental organizations in many developing countries do provide access to livelihood training for the poor. For example, National Institute of Fashion Technology, Chennai, India, has been training SHG women in ready-made garment making, leather products and fashion design. Other governmental institutions in India such as Central Institute of Plastic Training and Technology, Tamil Nadu, Livestock Development Agency, Fisheries Training College, Tuticorin, Coir Board of India and similar other organizations train rural men and women in a variety of livelihoods.

In trying to help rural women in more technical areas, Centre for Empowerment of Women, Anna University in India has been training women in using Photoshop, MS-Office, hardware maintenance of fax machines such that they can establish kiosks in rural areas to earn a living. Businesses in India, such as Larson & Toubro (L&T), Tata Industries, Saint Gobain Glass India and hotel industry, have been helping the poor to be part of their supply chain (Confederation of Indian Industries and the World Bank 2005). Some of the training provided by the businesses in India includes masonry, electrical work, carpentry, sanitary work, paper cup making, producing bakery items, milk production, vegetable production, making coir products, industrial tailoring and the like.

In order to provide livelihood training and other ancillary support for the poor, BASIX in India provides three integrated services known as Livelihood triad (Harper et al. 2011): Livelihood Financial Services (LFS), Institutional Development Services (IDS) and Agricultural/Business Development Services (Ag/BDS). Under LFS, BASIX provides access to credit, insurance and savings facilities. It also provides improved transfer of remittances by migrant workers, loans for housing and vocational training, life insurance and insurance for livestock, and microenterprise assets and financial inclusion services that include business correspondent banks.

Under Ag/BDS, BASIX provides productivity enhancement by increasing yield and reducing costs; mitigating risk (other than insurance) such as livestock vaccination; and local value addition through such activities as milk chilling, value chain improvements and diversification from farming to farm-allied and non-farm activities.

Under IDS, BASIX helps to form common interest farmers' groups, savings groups, federations and cooperatives It also helps in skills and entrepreneurial development that include building trust among groups, IT assistance in accounting and management information systems, and organization support for absorbing new technology. Vijay Mahajan (2007b) has called this integrated approach 'livelihood finance'. Later under the heading, 'Sustainability of Providing Non-Financial Complementary Services by the MFIs,' we will discuss about BASIX's experience in generating revenue in delivering livelihood training for its clients.

In providing livelihood training, 100 per cent cost recovery by the MFIs has been an important issue. In order to offer livelihood training on a sustainable basis, Nachiket Mor believes in targeting these services to the second level microentrepreneurs, that is, those microentrepreneurs who have already gained some experience in business. In his paper titled, *Some Thoughts on Access to Markets as a Strategy to Address Poverty*, Mor (2006) discusses about other missing markets besides the financial services. In the paper, he observes that, when credit constraints are removed, individuals would normally choose a set of activities based on their preferences and capabilities. However, it is very likely that in the initial phase the households would continue to be poor. As a result, they would be vulnerable to even moderate levels of economic shocks that they may encounter. This is when the role of the 'missing markets' in such areas as 'skill building, quality control and productivity improvement,' would be useful for MFI clients.

The assumption is that, when credit constraint is removed, the poor clients of the MFIs would invest in microenterprises that would uncover the 'revealed preference' of their clients with regard to what kinds of businesses they are good at. That would provide a powerful signal as to the livelihoods in which the poor clients feel relatively more comfortable in leveraging their capabilities. Mor in his paper mentions how

40 per cent of ICICI Bank's 3 million or so clients in microfinance area were engaged in dairying. With this knowledge, providing 'well-targeted livelihood enhancement interventions,' such as training to increase dairy productivity was considered meaningful.

Later in this chapter, we will discuss briefly about the prospects of sustainability of livelihood promotion programmes at BASIX. As the reader will find, appropriately designed livelihood promotion programmes for the poor hold a great deal promise to be sustainable.

The Importance of Broader Market Access for the Poor

> Democratized commerce has two dimensions. Each of us individuals are consumers and therefore, each of us must have the ability to afford world-class products and services as a consumer and have the ability to shape their own experiences. That is my first point. I also have to improve my livelihoods. That means, I must have access to fair prices for my efforts, for my knowledge, for what I produce, and I must have access to global markets. So there are two sides. One, as a consumer, how do I get across global standards, global products, at affordable prices? And two, as a producer, how do I get a fair price for my efforts, how do I get access to global markets for what I have produced. That means we have to seamlessly integrate villages, small towns, large towns and the whole global marketplace.
>
> C.K. Prahalad (2005a)

It is difficult to imagine how the pace of development for the poor can be accelerated without access to broader marketplace. Needless to say, large numbers of MFIs around the world have been instrumental in establishing formal credit markets for the poor in places where they were nonexistent. Other financial instruments such as savings, insurance and lease finance are slowly emerging such that the poor can access these instruments with ease. However, leaving aside the access to financial services market, access to markets on broader scale is essential for the poor if we expect them to get ahead in terms earning more income.

As producers and consumers, the poor are largely isolated, that is, de-linked from the wider marketplace. The relaxation of credit constraint by accessing financial services market by relying on microcredit can be considered as an essential first step that is already providing much needed impetus to have access to other markets by the poor. This is because, access to financial capital is a powerful force in buying and selling and hence establishing markets. It is also believed that as access to other financial instruments, that is, savings, insurance, lease finance and MT will expand, it would make the poor financially stronger to access other markets. For example, microcredit and lease finance (a loan substitute) can provide access to inputs and equipments, which can be deployed by the poor to become participants in value and supply chains to provide goods and services to the wider marketplace.

There is no denying the fact that expanding market access for the poor is rather a difficult task because markets are interlinked, they feed on each other, and develop through trial and error. And when it comes to the poor, some of the essential markets are missing. For example, it is difficult for the poor to have access to inputs, tools and technology, training, and distribution channels. Therefore, major stakeholders such as the national government, the business community, donors, charitable organizations and CSOs have to make a concerted effort to create an enabling environment, which can hasten access to wider marketplace by the poor.

How the MFIs are Helping the Poor to Expand Market Access

The poor pay a 'poverty penalty' (Prahalad 2005b) when buying and selling. This is because they possess limited market intelligence and bargaining power. They do not have the luxury of shopping around while buying and seeking out different market outlets when selling their goods and services. However, with the advent of microfinance (wherever microfinance is available), it has greatly reduced the poverty penalty in accessing credit. While interest rates in some cases can be rather high, MFI clients in general pay much lower interest rates when compared to rates charged by moneylenders in the neighbourhood. We discussed in Chapter 9 about how transformative technologies such as mobile phones are on the verge of revolutionizing delivery of financial services to the poor. We will see in this section, how access to mobile phones is helping to expand market access by the poor.

Establishing connectivity goes to the heart of market making. Unless two sides shake hands in a deal, a sale is not final. ICT platforms facilitate such handshakes to take place. For example, sellers (selling coffee beans) in a remote area in a developing country can sell their produce to buyers in another country who may be prepared to pay higher price for the product. Mobile phones are being used to provide the necessary platforms in making such markets.

Because of their connectivity with their clients and a deeper understanding of the needs of the poor, MFIs have been leveraged as distribution channels. Businesses that use MFIs as distribution channels to sell their products, can use the poor as a part of their supply/value chain as well. By using the poor as supply/value chains, the businesses create capacity for consumption by the poor. This is because today's seller is tomorrow's buyer. In this context, the following quote from Jeb Brugmann and C.K. Prahalad is relevant:

> There are NGOs that have created large distribution networks that can furnish food, medicine and credit, especially in remote areas. They have developed a deep understanding of local cultures and consumption habits. And they have established credibility and earned people's trust by repeatedly assisting disadvantaged communities in the face of poverty, natural disasters and conflicts. Companies are beginning to work with such organizations to break into new markets. For instance, Telenor has teamed up with Grameen Bank to cellular phones to rural consumers. Telenor has taken advantage of the bank's knowledge of the rural microcredit groups' collection and payment system to set up a joint venture, Grameen Phone, in which it has 62% equity stake. Similarly, World Diagnostics found that, in Uganda, it could best sell its HIV, STD, and malaria test kits through NGO operated health care networks. The NGOs are helping villagers to deal with AIDS, and they have trained medical personnel, set up clinics, and earned the trust of Ugandans along the way. (Brugmann and Prahalad 2007)

Because the MFIs provide access to capital for the poor along with upward and downward linkages to institutions, which can provide access to tools, equipments, training and markets to sell their products and services, it can greatly help the poor in their efforts to succeed in their businesses.

Leveraging Mobile Technology to Improve Market Access by Microentrepreneurs

Anyone who has been in a developing country knows how cellular phones have been a boon for the micro and small businesses. For example, in India, rickshaw and taxi operators market themselves using their mobile phones. Using mobile phones, they multitask throughout the day attending to their business and running errands for their household. Without the mobile phones they would have to wait at a rickshaw or taxi stand for their customers to arrive. Mobile phones free up their time to attend to such tasks as taking their children to school or taking care of their parents at home.

Dean Karlan and Jacob Appel (2012) in their book *More than Good Intentions* provide an example of how mobile phones are helping fishermen in the state of Kerala (India) to match buyers and sellers, which is helping to stabilize the prices of fish in the coastal towns of Kerala.

Prior to the advent of the mobile phones, fishermen used to sell their daily catch in the local markets. Karlan and Appel allude to a research by Robert Jensen of UCLA, who, in 1997, did a survey of 15 coastal towns in Kerala. Based on the research, he found that on a daily basis, in more than half of the markets, there was an imbalance of supply and demand, that is, in some markets there was an oversupply of fish and the vendors have to give away fish and in some other markets there was dearth of fish and prices were much higher. Needless to say, the uncertainty surrounding supply and demand was not conducive for the buyers as well as the sellers.

With the advent of cellular phones in Kerala during the period from 1997 to 2000, the fishermen were able to gather market intelligence using mobile phones in the nearby towns and travelled in their boats to those markets where they could fetch better price. As a result, fish prices stabilized across the markets. This benefited both the buyers (finding fish when they needed) and the sellers (price of fish did not gyrate).

We provide below one more example of how access to mobile phones as a tool in the hands of the low-income people is changing the ecosystem in which they operate their microbusinesses.

Alex Counts (President and CEO of Grameen Foundation) and Lauren Moore (Head of Global Social Innovation, eBay Inc. and President, eBay Foundation) in an article, 'Mobile Phones and the Rise of the Microentrepreneurs' (Counts and Moore 2012) in the Huffington Post Impact (The Blog) discuss how access to mobile phones have been a transformative force in the lives of the low-income people around the world. They allude to the fact that out of about 6 billion mobile phones around the world, about 75 per cent are in the developing countries. As a result the mobile technology not only does open up new prospects for the low-income people to stay connected, but it also enhances their access to markets, financial services and business opportunities.

They give example of Indonesia, where about 75 per cent of the citizens live on less than $2.50 per day. But at the same time 80 per cent of the people in the country have mobile phones and 96 per cent of those users utilize text messaging. People in the rural areas of the country use mobile phones in their businesses. Farmers use the phone to monitor market price of their produce as well as weather conditions. And the unbanked use it for accessing financial services.

Considering the potential advantages of mobile technology for the poor, Grameen Foundation and eBay foundation working together in the summer of 2012 started building solutions to some of the 'market challenges', which the microentrepreneurs faced in Indonesia. The joint effort is designed to help more than 10,000 women microentrepreneurs in the West Java region. These women sell airtime minutes to their customers. It is important to note that a 2010 study found that about 47 per cent of the participants in a mobile microfranchise programme doubled their income by the fourth month of their participation.

The intent of the programme is to develop a mobile transaction platform and mobile marketplace. It is expected that the mobile transaction platform and the marketplace would provide the low-income people wide range of services, which in turn would open up new business opportunities for them. It is expected that the network of women will be expanded from over 10,000 women to about 60,000 women. The microfranchises that sell airtime minutes will be able to provide about 4.5 million customers with mobile marketplace and transaction platform.

In the following, we give two examples of more sophisticated efforts to expand markets for the poor. The first example is from India, called e-Choupal, an electronic marketplace for the villagers in India, developed through the initiatives of ITC Limited, one of the largest diversified businesses in India, and the second example is Aarong, a marketing organization for the handicrafts of the artisans in Bangladesh, developed through the initiatives of BRAC, perhaps the largest non-governmental development organization in the world.

ITC e-Choupal—Web-based Tools for Indian Farmers

ITC e-Choupal (*choupal* literally means 'village meeting place' or electronic village) grew out of the desire to overcome supply chain inefficiencies in ITC's foods business (IBEF 2012). ITC is one of the largest diversified business groups. ITC's supply chain inefficiencies in food business emanated from information asymmetries that existed between buyers and sellers. What is more, poor infrastructure, fragmented land holdings and multiple layers of middlemen also accentuated supply chain inefficiencies. To give an example, it is estimated that such inefficiencies lead to a loss of 30 to 35 per cent of India's perishable food production.

ITC e-Choupal initiative was started in the year 2000. An e-Choupal centre consisting of a personal computer (and other ancillary hardware for information access) installed in the house of a trustworthy member of a village, known as the *sanchalak* (operator), becomes an instrument to enter and retrieve data from the e-Choupal system. Then there are hubs that are set up to collect and sell produce from the farmers. At the hub, there are people known as *samyojaks*, who are ITC representatives responsible for purchasing produce at the hub.

The sanchalaks are approved both by ITC and the villagers. Sanchalaks also take public oath to provide non-discriminatory access to the workstation. The centres are within walking distance (about 5 kilometres) and hubs are located at about 30 kilometres from villages.

ITC with the establishment of e-Choupal has created an online network of almost 4 million farmers in India. Today with about 5,000 information centres, the project spans 30 per cent of all the states of India. It is envisioned that the project will expand its reach to four times the number of farmers and half the states in India.

Some of the important features of e-Choupal are as follows: (1) it provides information to the farmers about market prices, news affecting them and weather forecasts; (2) disseminates information about risk management and best practices in farming; (3) provides information about where to purchase agricultural inputs and consumer goods and

(4) offers marketing opportunities for the sale of agricultural produce. It is important to note that ITC receives a marketing fee from firms that market their products on the e-Choupal network.

The synergy that e-Choupal has been able to bring about as an electronic marketplace has translated to increased profits for the farmers (Prahalad 2005b). Access to e-Choupal helps the farmers to monitor price movements of their produce. Based on price movements, they can either hold back or sell their produce to maximize profit.

Some of the specific advantages of e-Choupal for the farmers are as follows: (1) access to useful information regarding weather forecasts, input prices and procurement prices; (2) transparent procurement process and (3) improved margins during procurement without much hassle. For example, farmers benefit from selling to ITC on fixed prices based on the quality and grade of produce. The farmers get immediate cash payments, including transportation cost. What is more, the sanchalaks and samyojaks receive a commission on the purchase and sale of agricultural inputs and other consumer goods to the farmers.

Based on anecdotal evidence, access to e-Choupal is having measurable impact in terms of what types of crops the farmers plant (Annamalai and Rao 2007). For example, after access to e-Choupal, soy cultivation went up by 50 to 90 per cent in some regions, which was on a decline. What is more, because of e-Choupal, institutions such as Indian Council of Agricultural research have found an important medium to disseminate useful information for the farmers on a much wider scale. Besides, based on testing of crop samples by ITC, information about crop quality is provided to the farmers. The farmers are also provided with advice as to how to improve the quality and yield of their crops.

The e-Choupal platform has helped to reduce transaction costs for the buyers and sellers by about 6 per cent. For ITC the savings on procurement cost is about 2.5 per cent. This is due to reduction in fewer commissions and travel cost disbursements. ITC also envisages to provide credit and insurance to farmers in collaboration with large banks such as ICICI. The lending services have been designed to use the ground knowledge of sanchalaks in providing lending services to the poor.

Because of the introduction of e-Choupal, a variety of jobs such as of *mandi* labourers have been affected. ITC planned to employ them in the procurement hubs. Besides, because of e-Choupal operations, there has been realignment of taxes received by the mandis near the hub for e-Choupal operations, whereas many other mandis have lost tax revenues.

Kuttayan Annamalai and Sachin Rao enumerate many challenges that e-Choupal faces. These include changes in the structure of traditional community-based business model with the introduction of sophisticated electronic marketplace like e-Choupal, which needs to be addressed with sensitivity for all the stakeholders. With access to e-Choupal, the knowledge base of the farmers has been expanded along with their aspirations. They are now much more aware of what inputs they need for producing quality crops with higher yields. And they have been demanding appropriate inputs such as improved quality seeds on a timely basis. ITC is very much aware of e-Choupal's procurement efficiency. As a result, it expects there would be more competition for procurement in the future years.

It is expected that in the future years ITC will leverage e-Choupal platform on a variety of aspects of procurement, which include the following parameters: procurement based on quality of crops, procurement of perishable crops (which would require enforcing standards that would even go down the production process to work with farmers), allowing buyers and sellers to come together under e-Choupal to procure commodities, and using the platform as a much more versatile medium for marketing, distribution and sourcing products from rural areas. ITC also envisions leveraging the power of e-Choupal in such areas as telemedicine, traditional medicine, eco-tourism and traditional crafts.

BRAC Social Enterprises: Aarong

BRAC created *Aarong* (meaning 'village fair') as a social enterprise in 1978. Its creation was based on BRAC's core mission of alleviating poverty and empowering poor people (particularly poor women) to create productive livelihoods (BRAC 2013). Aarong started out by commercializing arts and crafts made by artisans and craftsmen in Bangladesh for generations. Over the years, Aarong has become an effective arm of BRAC to link rural artisans to the marketplace by interpreting their arts and crafts and in the process alleviating poverty and empowering people.

Prior to the creation of Aarong, BRAC explored how to leverage the rich tradition of Bangladesh in making arts and crafts such as bed coverings, table cloths, paintings, pottery, wood carving, embroidery, saris, inlays, *shikas*—hangers made of jute for flower pots, quilts and block printing. Based on initial estimates, it appeared that products such as bed coverings and table cloths could generate surplus. And these items produced by a single skilled woman in a day could generate enough profit that was almost seven to eight times the farm labour rate (Smillie 2009).

However, there were logistical issues related to marketing and selling the items at handicrafts stores. These stores took these items on consignment and the producer was not paid until the items were sold. If the items got sold, the producer was paid by check which took a month to clear. If the items were not sold then the women were left with unsold inventory. Given the fact that the women invested their labour and borrowed funds for inputs in making products, unsold products exposed them to potential losses which they could ill afford. Under these circumstances, BRAC could have become a middleman between the artisans and the handicraft stores; however, that would have entailed cost of carrying inventory and other associated costs (Smillie 2009). One of the issues BRAC had to wrestle with in establishing Aarong was: how BRAC, a non-profit organization could establish Aarong, a for-profit entity. Finally, it decided to establish Aarong in collaboration with Mennonite Central Committee (international development arm of Mennonite Church) who had established, 'Ten Thousand Villages,' in 1946 devoted to retailing products of artisans around the world through catalogue sales and shops in United States and Canada (Smillie 2009).

In 1978, the year Aarong was established it had a loss of about $5,000. However, in the year 1981 it had a surplus after subtracting donor and BRAC's contributions. Ian Smillie in his book *Freedom from Want* notes that in 2004, Aarong's total sales were about $14 million and it returned a surplus of $1.96 million to BRAC.

Starting with a single shop in Mannikganj in Bangladesh, today Aarong has spread out in Bangladesh by establishing 13 Ayesha Abed Foundation centres (with nearly 600 sub-centres). It caters to over 1,000 artisan groups and entrepreneurs and provides livelihood to over 65,000 artisans (80 per cent of which are women) and their families which directly benefits about 320,000 people. Aarong employs over 2,300 people (60 per cent women). It ploughs back its surplus (profits) to BRAC's development programmes (BRAC 2013).

Sustainability of Providing Complementary Non-financial Services by the MFIs

We noted earlier, MFIs normally lack well-defined revenue models for delivering complementary non-financial services. There is also a lack of published accounts that provide in-depth analysis of sustainability of delivering such services to the poor by the MFIs. What is more, the models used by the MFIs to offer such services are not standardized. As a result, financial costs and benefits of these services cannot be easily compared across countries as in the case of largely standardized products such as microcredit.

Bandhan

Bandhan is a large MFI in the state of West Bengal in India (Metcalfe et al. 2010). Bandhan provides health services to the poor, which is delivered to its clients in conjunction with its microfinance programme. It consists of health education, health product distribution and informal linkages with health care providers in West Bengal. The programme was developed and tested in partnership with 'Freedom from Hunger' as a part of the MAHP initiative.

Bandhan, which was established in 2002, is one of India's leading MFIs. It has received many industry awards and had a clientele of 1.9 million with outstanding gross portfolio of about $235 million (Metcalfe et al. 2010). Its portfolio-at-risk was only 0.16 per cent. From its microcredit clients, about 52,000 were members of 'Credit with Education' programme and had access to distribution of health products.

The health services programme, which was piloted between 2006 and 2009, was designed as a 'cohesive and complementary' package to determine its impact on Bandhan's clients as well as the institution, that is, Bandhan itself. As far as clients were concerned, the programme was to assess how it affected their health and financial well-being. And with regard to Bandhan, the purpose was to assess related expenses, revenues and indirect benefits to the institution.

In delivering health services, one of the important roles Bandhan played included, selecting, training and supervising health educators (also known as Health Community Organizers—HCOs). Bandhan also selected, trained and supported product distribution volunteers. It also had a full-time health manager who met with groups of HCOs and product distribution volunteers for ongoing training, health product distribution and trouble-shooting.

Bandhan purchased health products from NGOs. It provided health education along with affordable health products, that is, oral rehydration salts, paracetamol, deworming pills, antiseptic lotion, oral contraceptive pills and sanitary napkins to members of the programme. A small company owned and managed by Bandhan, staffed in part by Bandhan clients, manufactured sanitary napkins.

Under the programme, Bandhan offered health loans. After receiving a health loan application from a member, the health manager and other branch staff visit the client to verify the need for such a loan. The health loans by Bandhan carried an interest rate of 10 per cent per annum. The 10 per cent rate on health loans was close to Bandhan's own cost of funds (Metcalfe et al. 2010).

Pricing of health products are based on recommended retail price and average of local prices. Bandhan earned a margin on these products that varied from 7 to 160 per cent. The margins earned on these products were used for training and managing the volunteers. The product pricing provided a profit of about 15–25 per cent for the product distribution volunteers. Average earnings for the volunteers were reported to be less than $1 a month. The volunteers considered participation in the programme to be enjoyable and a source of enhanced sense of self-esteem and service towards their community (Metcalfe et al. 2010).

As far as underlying costs of the programme were concerned, Bandhan spent about $4,400 per branch per year in direct costs for the health programme. If one includes indirect costs such as office space, electricity and supplies are included, the cost went up to $6,700. Given the fact that in each branch about 3,200 clients were served by the programme, annual cost per client came to around $2.10 and monthly cost to around $0.17. On the revenue side, Bandhan earned about $1,172 annually per branch on the average from the sale of health products. On a net basis the cost per branch came to about $5,500, or $1.73 per client. As of June 2009, Bandhan extended the programme in five branches. Bandhan sought funding from donors to offer health services on an ongoing basis. In the light of these expenses, it is important to note that in 2008,

Bandhan had a portfolio yield of about 30 per cent, real yield on gross portfolio of 22 per cent and overall profit margin of 40 per cent. These numbers are based on 'Mix Market' data (Metcalfe et al. 2010).

All in all, it is not difficult to visualize the value proposition for the poor in having access to health services programme. On a net basis, the programme costs about $1.73 per client per year. Metcalfe et al. note that Bandhan viewed these costs to be relatively small in comparison to what the programme achieved in terms of well-being of its clients. The management viewed the cost of the programme to be an investment in the reputation of Bandhan and enhancing its image as 'more than a bank.' The health services programme is not sustainable financially. However, based on the financial strength of Bandhan, it could deliver health services programme along with microcredit to make the package attractive, in an environment of heightened competition in the microfinance industry.

BASIX: Sustainability of Livelihood Promotion Services

We have already discussed about BASIX's Livelihood Triad consisting of LFS, Ag/BDS and IDS. In order to make the Livelihood Triad centre piece of its business model, BASIX had to invest a great deal of financial and human resources in the effort (Harper et al. 2011). However, even before the 2010 Microfinance Crisis in Andhra Pradesh, the investment in the triad strategy did not result in rapid growth of BASIX in comparison to other MFIs in the region, Needless to say, most of the businesses in the region including BASIX, have experienced sharp decline in their business activities after the 2010 Microfinance Crisis in Andhra Pradesh.

Under the programme, BASIX provided livelihood interventions in such areas as cotton and groundnut farming, organic soybean growing, paddy farming, inland fish farming, chilli growing and helping to control insects in lacquer. As far as BASIX business model was concerned, most of these livelihood interventions were cash flow positive in the sense that income to BASIX minus cost to BASIX was positive. Prior to the year 2005, income and expenses of all the livelihood interventions were not consolidated. In the year 2005, it was consolidated and the earnings from such interventions were $300,000. And by 2009, the earnings reached almost $3 million, 10 times the 2005 earnings. As a part of BASIX's total earnings in 2009, these earnings were about 12 per cent. In comparison, it was 10 per cent of the total earnings in 2005 (Harper et al. 2011).

These earnings point to an important fact. That is, BASIX clients were not only paying for livelihood promotion services, the pricing of the services was such that BASIX had a positive cash flow on account of these services. And earnings went up 10-fold from 2005 to 2009. This shows that if the right kinds of livelihood promotion services are offered, the clients will be willing to pay for such services by making livelihood promotion services sustainable. It is also important to note that, without charging them for such services it would be difficult to know what services the MFI clients really value.

Conclusion

The chapter has given glimpses into how complementary non-financial services such as social intermediation, livelihood promotion and access to broader marketplace (not just access to financial services market) play critical roles in helping the poor improve their economic well-being. Poor-friendly access to quality services by the poor is also critical for the MFIs because, a client who is unsuccessful in her business is a potential credit risk for the MFIs.

Having said that, it is important to reiterate, MFIs cannot be all things to all people. As we have seen, the delivery of a wide range of financial products at the grass-root level is already challenging enough for the industry, which operates in an ecosystem of poor infrastructure and dearth of qualified professionals and management personnel. While there are those who would like the MFIs to deliver a variety of complementary services to the poor, it is believed that by collaborating with other private and public sector institutions and NGOs specialized in providing these services, the quality, cost and effectiveness of these programmes can be ensured. That would allow the MFIs to focus on their core competencies, that is, the delivery of financial products and services to the poor.

Moreover, because cost recovery in delivering these programmes is not always 100 per cent, ultimately such services have to be funded through collaborative efforts of the national government, the donors, the private sector, charitable foundations and other stakeholders. Under these circumstances, subsidy and grants could play an important role in building capacity. But at the same time, the MFIs should at least charge a nominal fee to the clients which will cover a part of the cost and in the process could ensure if the clients truly value the services being rendered. Needless to say, motivated clients normally enhance the success rate of clients being trained. Besides, successful clients could provide the basis and rationale for designing a pricing model to recover costs from offering such services. The experience at BASIX in offering livelihood promotion services shows that an appropriately designed programme has the potential to be sustainable.

Note

1. See Chapter 11 'Critiquing Microfinance,' for a discussion on related topics.

11

Critiquing Microfinance

Yunus's long-term vision is to eliminate poverty in the world. That cannot be realized by means of micro-credit alone. But Muhammad Yunus and Grameen Bank have shown that, in the continuing efforts to achieve it, micro-credit must play a major role.[1]

Press Release, The Nobel Peace Prize for 2006

At the time of its inception, very few people would have predicted that microcredit one day would become such an important financial tool for the poor that Muhammad Yunus and the Grameen Bank will share the 2006 Nobel Peace Prize. On the same vein, nobody would have predicted that business of providing access to microcredit would grow at such a rapid pace to reach over 200 million around the world at the end of 2010 (see Chapter 1). But at the same time, very few if any, would have predicted the negative consequences of commercialization of microfinance that would precipitate in the 2010 Microfinance Crisis in the state of Andhra Pradesh in India, considered the microfinance capital of India.

As the microfinance (microcredit) industry has matured, it has been the subject of great many criticisms that are the subject of this chapter. In the following, we first summarize some of the important criticisms that have been levelled against microfinance, to be followed by selectively discussing only a few of them to provide a broad perspective as to what is that ails microfinance.

- The anecdotal stories of microfinance (microcredit) in the print and the electronic media have given rise to widespread expectations that with access to microcredit, alleviation of poverty could be achieved on a mass scale. As we shall discuss in the following, recent RCT-based impact studies of microcredit point to the fact that such impact could be modest. In the same vein, many critics of microfinance question if it is not incongruous to think that millions and millions of the poor, lacking proper infrastructure, skill set and access to markets can turn into successful entrepreneurs by accessing microcredit and investing in microenterprises that lack economies of scale.

- Because funding from governmental sources and donors are usually limited, the MFIs need access to commercial capital in order to grow. However, access to commercial capital presupposes sustainability (profitability). While sustainability (profitability) is important for MFIs to be commercialized, as DBL institutions, they have to also keep their social mission at the forefront in managing their affairs. However, some of the commercialized MFIs in facing the competition and demands of the marketplace have placed profitability (sometimes too high profitability) ahead of social mission. In particular, these MFIs have been criticized for charging high interest rates and over-lending to the poor, who are predominantly vulnerable poor women. Such policies have resulted in over-indebtedness of many poor households. There have been allegations that some of the MFIs have been using coercive tactics to force their poor clients to comply with timely debt service payments. And there have been also allegations that some of these borrowers have committed suicide under duress. Many such issues and the ensuing political backlash precipitated in the 2010 Microfinance Crisis in Andhra Pradesh in India, which ruined the microfinance industry in the state. The greatest losers in the process have been the poor clients and the society-at-large.

- While EIRs charged on microloans by the MFIs are substantially lower than effective rates charged by the local moneylenders, they are much higher than the rates charged to the non-poor by the commercial banks. MFI interest rates have normally ranged between 20 and 40 per cent (Collins et al. 2009). However, there are MFIs that charge EIRs as high as 100 per cent. One such example of charging very high interest rate is Compartamos Banco of Mexico (Rosenberg 2007). Besides charging relatively high interest rates, the MFIs have been accused of lacking transparency in communicating EIRs (lending rates) to their clients. Under these circumstances, critics have described MFIs as 'loan sharks' (Lewis 2008). By charging high interest rates, some of these institutions have become quite profitable. The question that the MFIs need to wrestle with is that, is it ethical for these institutions to make exorbitant profits at the cost of their vulnerable poor clients (predominantly women) who have limited choice in accessing credit.

- Needless to say, lack of access to microsavings and microinsurance forces borrowers to substitute microcredit and other forms of credit for microsavings and microinsurance. The upshot of all this is that, mono-product world of microfinance (largely consisting of microcredit) could over-indebt borrowers (clients borrowing on their own from multiple MFIs or through over-lending by the MFIs) exposing them to increased levels of financial risk.

- Microcredit in the past enjoyed an enviable repayment record around the world. However, in their paper, 'Too Much Microcredit? A Survey of the Evidence on Over-Indebtedness,' Jessica Schicks and Richard Rosenberg (2011) discuss about high delinquency rates in countries that include Bosnia-Herzegovina, Morocco, Nicaragua and Pakistan. What is more, the delinquency rates reported to have deteriorated since then. In the paper, they also note that, on the aftermath of the 2010 Microfinance Crisis in Andhra Pradesh, debt service collections collapsed in the state. It is also important to note that timely loan repayments by MFI borrowers do not assure that the borrowers are doing well financially. What the borrowers may be doing is to tide over an inflexible cash flow situation by borrowing from the same MFI, friends and family members, other MFIs or moneylenders to repay their loans. As we noted in Chapter 1, high repayment rate on Kiva loans may be due to field partners of Kiva (i.e., the MFIs) making repayments on behalf of delinquent and defaulted borrowers to maintain high repayment standards with Kiva.

- MFIs in general have to be supportive of consumer protection. Ensuring appropriate protection of privacy, non-abusive collection practices and creation of well-functioning system to address grievances of the customers that largely consists of poor and vulnerable women is paramount. Unless complaints of clients are addressed in an orderly manner, there is always the danger that political backlash could ensue. The 2010 Microfinance Crisis in Andhra Pradesh is a prime example of minimal or lack of consumer protection by the MFIs that led to the use of coercive debt service collection practices, which in turn led to alleged suicides by some clients under duress.

Considering wide range of issues discussed above, we will focus on only a few of them in the following. To begin with, we will first discuss about four RCT-based impact assessments of microcredit that will provide insights into what one could expect with regards to microcredit impact. It will be followed by a discussion of the 2010 Microfinance Crisis in the state of Andhra Pradesh in India and a brief discussion of high levels of delinquency rates in four countries in some microfinance markets around the world. Finally, we will discuss how in spite of diminished expectations as to the effectiveness of microcredit to uplift poor people out of poverty on a large scale, it still remains an essential financial tool for the poor in managing their household and business finances.

Randomized Control Trial-based Microcredit Impact Assessment

Anyone who is familiar with anecdotal stories about microfinance in the print and the electronic media, and also depiction of successful borrowers on the websites of many MFIs, could surmise (inductively), that with access to microcredit the poor in general would have a fair chance to lift themselves out of poverty. Based on these stories, the readers could also form an impression that with extra income generated from their businesses (or through self-employment), the poor could also increase their consumption levels. What is more, many of these anecdotal stories also imply that the successful microentrepreneurs seek out improved health care for their family and education for their children. They also become socially more conscious. Last but not the least, such stories could also imply that the poor with access to microcredit can diversify their sources of income, which is one of the important ways households could reduce income volatility.

While all this may sound rather promising, the pertinent question to ask after learning all this is whether these anecdotal claims can be generalized for majority of the borrowers accessing microcredit. In this context, at the intuitive level at least, one is confronted with the following natural question, that is, given the multidimensional nature of poverty, how is it that just by streamlining access to just one input, albeit one of the most important inputs, that is, microcredit, one could expect the poor to lift themselves out of poverty on a large scale. This would also appear incongruous because to be successful in their microbusinesses, the poor have to be entrepreneurial (which is a rare trait), have to possess the necessary skills and discipline to run businesses, and have to be market-savvy in accessing inputs as well as selling their products and services. While one could acquire many of these skills, it would appear improbable that each and every client of an MFI either possess these skills or could acquire such skills in right combinations quickly to be successful in their microbusinesses.

Besides, one would expect that, the poor are risk averse, particularly when they have very minimal back stop mechanism in terms of savings and insurance. They become entrepreneurs out of necessity, because they have very minimal access to secure jobs. Besides, lack of education, skills and access to livelihood training forces them to invest in microenterprises that are clones of each other and most of these microbusinesses are not even scalable. What all this imply is that while many of the businesses that the poor invest could improve their household income, such income may not be enough to lift them out of poverty (see Chapter 4).

What is more, as many MFIs have transformed to become commercial entities, they have increasingly turned 'minimalists' by shying away from delivering other non-financial complementary services (such as livelihood and marketing training), which could help their poor clients to improve their chances of being successful in their microbusinesses. Institutions such as BRAC (see Chapter 4) that provide access to a variety of non-financial complementary services for the poor to help them succeed in their businesses are rare.

Under these circumstances, hyping microfinance by its promoters has been counterproductive for the microfinance industry to say the least.

At the same time, the pursuit of high levels of profitability to create shareholder value by some of the commercialized MFIs by over-indebting the poor has undermined the prestige of the industry. Many critics of microfinance posit that microfinance is nothing more than old style money lending that takes advantage of the fact that vulnerable poor people have very limited choice in accessing credit.

Up until recently rather limited numbers of studies on microcredit impact assessment pointed to the fact that it could produce important economic and social benefits for the poor on a large scale, such as increase in household consumption, asset acquisition, women empowerment, and improvements in such areas as education and health care. One such study, cited extensively in the field, is by Mark Pitt and Shahidur Khandker (1998). However, in 2009 David Roodman and Jonathan Morduch tried to replicate the widely quoted results of Pitt and Khandker in their paper, 'The Impact of Microcredit on the Poor in Bangladesh: Revisiting the Evidence.' (Roodman and Morduch 2009). The broad conclusion of their replication study has been summarized in the book *Economics of Microfinance* by Armendáriz and Morduch (2010, 290) as follows: 'Roodman and Morduch (2009), like Morduch (1998), do not argue that microcredit makes no difference in the lives of the borrowers; instead, they argue that the econometric set-up here is not up to the task. We need to look elsewhere for reliable evidence.'

In order to look for more reliable evidence, in recent years, there has been an increased application of RCTs for impact assessment in microfinance. As the name connotes, the use of RCTs in impact assessment applies a given treatment (such as access to microcredit or microsavings) to a group randomly selected from a large list of people and then selects another group of people from the same list randomly who are not subjected to the treatment. The first group is called the 'treatment group' and the second group is called the 'control group.' The difference between the average outcomes of the treated and the control groups provides accurate estimate of the average impact arising out of the treatment—in our case access to microcredit (Armendáriz and Morduch 2010).

While RCT-based studies provide an accurate estimate of the difference between the average outcomes of the treated and the control groups, the result does not tell anything about the median impact and the distribution of such impacts. What is more, impact estimates are context specific and difficult to generalize to other contexts. Therefore, there is need for replication of results in other settings to generalize the findings of a RCT study. Besides, moving from a small scale study (say from a pilot phase) to a larger study (say on a region-wide basis) could yield different results. In spite of these issues, RCTs have been widely used in microfinance because it provides accurate estimate of average impact (Armendáriz and Morduch 2010). The reader can find an in depth introduction to RCT methodology in the book *The Economics of Microfinance* by Beatriz Armendáriz and Jonathan Morduch (2010), including the pros and cons of using such methodology in impact evaluations.

Having described rather briefly about RCTs, we summarize below four RCT-based studies that were used to assess the impact of micro-lending in four countries, that is, South Africa, the Philippines, Sri Lanka and India. They are as follows: (1) Dean Karlan and Jonathan Zinman's study of lending by 'Credit Indemnity' in South Africa (Karlan and Appel 2012); (2) Dean Karlan and Jonathan Zinman's (2011) study of microcredit impact in the Philippines; (3) Suresh de Mel et al.'s (2008) study of productivity of additional capital in Sri Lanka and (4) Abhijit Banerjee et al.'s (2010) study of microcredit impact in Andhra Pradesh.

Impact Assessment of Lending by 'Credit Indemnity' in South Africa by Dean Karlan and Jonathan Zinman

The RCT-based study was conducted in association with 'Credit Indemnity,' a consumer lender in South Africa (Karlan and Appel 2012). The study was designed in the context of a 'marketing and interest-rate study' to understand how borrowers reacted to different interest rates.

Credit Indemnity is not an MFI. The institution does not have any social agenda like the MFIs. It did not target women or entrepreneurs. It lent only to working people. It was a for-profit consumer credit business that has a lot of similarity with payday lenders in the USA. The interest rate it charged was rather very high, around 200 per cent per annum. Credit Indemnity did not worry what borrowers did with the borrowed funds so long as they paid back the loan.

The borrowers of Credit Indemnity were quite different from the borrowers MFIs lend to. Some of the notable differences include, most of the Credit Indemnity borrowers were employed and the institution had a database about their credit history and a computer-based model was used to make lending decisions. The clients of Credit Indemnity did not borrow in a group.

Karlan and Zinman had found out that while the borrowers were sensitive to the level of interest rates, what stood out was that how the loans were marketed made a lot of difference in applying for loans. For example, 'showing one example loan in a flyer instead of four examples attracted as many applicants as dropping the interest rate by one third.' In their paper, they provide many other examples to prove that marketing triumphs over terms of lending. Besides, the borrowers were not analytical enough to apply for loans where terms of lending were favourable to them.

The design of the experiment to assess how such lending was beneficial for the borrowers of Credit Indemnity was rather ingenious. In the context of the marketing and interest-rate study, Karlan and Zinman had found out that Credit Indemnity turned away potential clients. In fact, it rejected almost 50 per cent of its applicants by classifying them to be too risky. However, Karlan and Zinman, based on their analysis of data, had surmised that clients that were borderline cases could have been profitable. With this knowledge, Karlan and Zinman modified the computer-based algorithm to randomly approve or turn down clients who were borderline cases in terms of their creditworthiness. While, credit officers had the final authority to ignore computer recommendations, even then some of the randomly selected marginally creditworthy applicants were able to receive loans.

Karlan and Zinman tracked all the applicants that were 'may be' cases for passing creditworthiness test, which also included those who received a loan randomly. After a year, what Karlan and Zinman discovered was significant: (1) those who received a loan randomly were more likely to have kept their jobs and earned significantly higher income; (2) not only the borrowers, but their families also enjoyed greater prosperity; (3) the households earned more money overall and (4) they were less likely to go to bed hungry.

How all this was possible? In rationalizing the findings, the study found the following: (1) many clients used the funds for transportation-related expenses, such as repairing cars or motor bikes or purchasing bus tickets to get to work on time and (2) clients also sent money home for relatives in need, without which they would have been compelled to leave their present job to return to their homes. All in all, the borrowed funds were used to cope with unexpected shocks. Based on the study, Karlan and Zinman observe, 'This was great news for advocates of microcredit. Actually, it was great news for advocates of payday loans.'

One more lesson from this case study may be the following: given the fact that money is fungible, how a borrower ultimately ends up using the borrowed funds for his or her benefit may be difficult to guess *a priori*. Even if the interest rates were very high, the benefits the borrowers in South Africa accrued from such borrowing were appreciably higher based on the surveys. It is true that MFI clientele are not exactly comparable to Credit Indemnity clientele. MFI interest rates are substantially lower than interest rates charged to Credit Indemnity borrowers. Given the fact that access to microcredit would increase microbusiness/household liquidity, money being fungible, can come handy to cope with unexpected shocks (such as health shocks) that a poor household may experience from time to time. Therefore, judicious use of microcredit could help poor families to absorb unexpected shocks. In fact, many MFIs provide access to emergency loans to absorb unexpected shocks.

Microcredit Impact Assessment in the Philippines by Dean Karlan and Jonathan Zinman

The objective of the study was to find out if 'microcredit mitigates market failures, spurs micro-enterprise growth, and boosts borrowers' well-being.' The study was undertaken with 1,601 clients of First Macro Bank (FMB) in the Philippines (Karlan and Zinman 2011). The average size of the loans was about $225.

FMB was lending in and around Manila and had about 7,000 clients. It exclusively lent to entrepreneurs, and it was expected that the loans were going to be exclusively used in business (Karlan and Appel 2012). The loans were given for a period of three months, and the interest rates on the loans were 63 per cent per annum. Therefore, interest rate charged by FMB was almost one-third the interest rates charged to Credit Indemnity borrowers in South Africa. The approach taken in granting loans was similar to the methodology utilized in South Africa. Karlan and Zinman modified the creditworthiness software in such a way as to approve first-time applicants, who were borderline cases (borderline cases constituted about 75 per cent of all applicants) randomly. Over the following two years, Karlan and Zinman surveyed the borrowers as well as those who did not receive any loan to find out how their lives were changed.

Many of the findings of the study are as follows: (1) net borrowing for the treatment group increased in comparison to the control group at the interest rate that was about 60 per cent per annum; (2) one-third of the borrowers in Karlan and Zinman's sample was delinquent (delinquency rate among the FMB borrowers were high); and (3) 7.4 per cent of the loans were charged off (Karlan and Zinman 2011).

As far as hypothesis that 'microcredit spurs business growth,' was concerned, the results from the experiment suggest that access to credit shrank scale of business. What this implies is that business owners who received loans consolidated their businesses, employed less number of workers. As a result, their business expenses went down and profits went up (Karlan and Appel 2012). The other important finding of the study was that male borrowers did much better than female borrowers. More specifically, male borrowers did 'three times the increase in business profits' in comparison to their female counterparts. Besides, as far as relatively wealthier half of the applicants were concerned, accessing a loan led to a 25 per cent jump in business profits. For borrowers, who were less well-off, the study was inconclusive as to the profitability of their businesses (Karlan and Appel 2012).

As far as the question about subjective well-being of clients was considered, entrepreneurs who were randomly assigned microloans, their subjective well-being did not improve, although men in the treatment group experienced increase in stress. Besides, study results suggest that access to microcredit widens the options households have to manage risk by substituting credit for insurance or 'precautionary savings,' and also through sharing risk with family and the community (Karlan and Zinman 2011).

Based on the study, Karlan and Zinman (2011) had the following observation:

> The overall picture of our results questions the wisdom of assuming that impacts are stronger for pre-existing micro-entrepreneurs and women than for "consumers," men, or aspiring micro-entrepreneurs. Money is fungible, and we find that entrepreneurs do not invest their loan proceeds in growing their businesses. Perhaps micro-entrepreneurs only increase

business investment if loan proceeds are tied to a more detailed business planning exercise or are followed by unusually close monitoring from the lender. In any case, limiting microcredit access to entrepreneurs may forgo opportunities to improve human capital and risk-sharing for non-micro-entrepreneurs.

The finding that male borrowers did three times better in terms of profits does corroborate similar findings in the case of a study in Sri Lanka by de Mel et al. to be presented next. The finding does raise the question if microfinance industry should find a better balance in terms of lending to men, which in turn would be financially beneficial for poor households. It is important to note that, in the context of the Sri Lankan study low business returns for women clients have been explained as follows: the women usually invest in businesses that require low levels of capital, have low barriers to entry (consisting of businesses such as sewing, embroidery, making handicrafts and the like) and have low margins. Besides, lack of 'intra-household' cooperation could make it difficult for the women to devote full attention to their microbusinesses whereas men may have less constraints in optimizing their efforts in running businesses.

Estimating Productivity of Additional Capital in Microenterprises: RCT-based Study in Sri Lanka by Suresh de Mel, David McKenzie and Christopher Woodruff

The study was designed to answer the question whether small and informal firms (such as the microenterprises) hold the potential for income growth or they just represent a source of subsistence income for individuals who cannot find alternative sources of work (de Mel et al. 2008). This is important because, such enterprises account for a large share of employment in the developing countries.

One of the important assumptions of microfinance is that microenterprises provide productive investment opportunities for the poor. And with access to capital, the poor potentially could enjoy higher returns. Given the fact that returns from enterprises are correlated with entrepreneurial ability of the owner, household wealth and demand shocks, the study was designed to minimize impact of such factors using RCT-based experiments, where return to capital for the average microenterprise in the sample was measured regardless of whether the owner of the enterprise applied for a loan.

Briefly, the experiments were performed as follows. From a survey of microenterprises in Sri Lanka, randomly selected subset of the firms was provided with small grants. The survey was purposefully restricted to microenterprises with less than 100,000 Sri Lankan rupees (about $1,000) in capital leaving aside land and buildings. The grants were either for $100 or $200, which was also assigned randomly. Half of the grants were 'in-kind' grants. For in-kind grants, the recipients were allowed to choose any business-related items up to the grant amount and the researchers went with the recipients to purchase the items. The other half of the grant recipients received cash, and they were free to use the funds in anything they liked.

The findings of the study were as follows: (1) real return to capital for the microenterprises were 4.6–5.3 per cent per month (i.e., 55–63 per cent per year), much higher than market interest rates; (2) returns varied based on entrepreneurial ability and household wealth, but did not vary with measures of risk aversion or uncertainty and (3) one of the surprising results was that treatment impacts were significantly larger for enterprises owned by males; in fact the researchers found no positive returns for enterprises owned by females.

About four years after the publication of the Sri Lanka study, in an interview with Tim Ogden (2012), David McKenzie observed that it was surprising to find male-owned businesses had very high increases in profits (a real return on capital of 11 per cent per month), whereas female-owned businesses had 0 per cent return. Given the fact that majority of microfinance borrowers are female, the result was not promising for female borrowers of microfinance.

In a later experiment in Ghana, David McKenzie and his collaborators wanted to replicate the same results in a different country and in a different context. They were cognizant of the fact that in South Asia, women have low labour participation rate. In Ghana, women own small business. Therefore, they purposefully chose Ghana to replicate the result. Based on their replication study in Ghana, they found that the profit went up by 20 per cent per month for in-kind grants. However, when they gave the grants in cash there was no increase in profits. Under closer examination, even in the case of in-kind grants, increase in profits materialized only in the case of top 40 per cent of women, that is, women who were wealthier and more educated in comparison to the bottom 60 per cent. The wealthier and better educated women were making $5 per day in terms of profits, whereas profits were about $1 per day for the bottom 60 per cent of the women. David McKenzie explains this by the observation that the top 40 per cent of the women might have been in business for business reasons as opposed to bottom 60 per cent who might be in business for other reasons (Ogden 2012).

In the context of 0 per cent return for females in Sri Lanka, David McKenzie had two important observations: (1) women who were in traditional female industries such as lace-making had the lowest returns and (2) the other reason for low returns could be due to a lack of 'intra-household' cooperation. He observed that women who said their husbands supported their businesses were doing better. Besides, there were indications that women did not invest optimally because they feared their profits could be captured by others. It is also possible that they did not manage themselves optimally to have enough working capital (Ogden 2012).

In his conversations with Tim Ogden, David McKenzie also discusses issues related to helping women to shift industries through business training and other related issues to increase productivity and profitability of their businesses. The key in this regard is to help them branch out of 'low barriers to entry, low capital requirements and low returns' trap. All in all, based on these discussions, it would appear that access to microcredit has to go hand in hand with other non-financial complementary services such as financial literacy, livelihood and marketing training.

RCT-based Large Scale Impact Assessment of Microcredit in Andhra Pradesh by Abhijit Banerjee, Esther Duflo, Rachel Glennerster and Cynthia Kinnan

We now describe a large-scale RCT-based microcredit impact assessment that was undertaken in the city of Hyderabad in Andhra Pradesh by Banerjee et al. (2010). The time period of the study was from 2006 to 2008. It consisted of 6,800 households in 104 communities. Out of these 104 communities, 52 were chosen at random as the treatment group by Spandana (the MFI) to access microcredit. The remaining 52 communities were used as the control group.[2] In 2005, a baseline survey was conducted in each area totalling to 2,800 households. The information collected during the survey covered the following areas: household composition, education, employment, asset ownership, decision-making, expenditure, borrowing, savings and business currently being operated or stopped during the last year.

Some of the important features of lending by Spandana were as follows: (1) the first loans by the MFI were for ₹10,000 (equivalent to about $200 based on market exchange rates) and the following loans (when everyone in the group has repaid) can be in the range of ₹10,000 to ₹12,000 (the loans could even go up to ₹20,000); (2) loans were for 50 weeks; (3) interest rate on the loans were 12 per cent (based on non-declining balance—also called the flat rate), which is equivalent to 24 per cent APR and (d) unlike other MFIs, Spandana did not require that the borrowed funds be used in a business.

What is more, Spandana, unlike Grameen Bank, did not require 'transformation' of the households by asking them to follow certain decisions (considered beneficial in fighting poverty) resolutely such as the 'sixteen decisions' (Dowla and Barua 2006) of Grameen Bank. Moreover, Spandana also did not provide livelihood and financial literacy training for its clients.

As far as households were concerned, about 69 per cent of the households had at least one outstanding loan. The average sizes of the loans were about ₹20,000 and the average interest rate was 3.85 per cent per month. The compounded annual interest rate on the loans came to about 57 per cent per annum. The sources of the loans were as follows: moneylenders (49 per cent), friends and neighbours (28 per cent), and family members (13 per cent). There was practically very little borrowing from commercial banks. Among the households, 34 per cent had savings accounts, 26 per cent had life insurance policy and almost none had any health insurance. About 60 per cent of the households had to borrow if a member of the family fell sick.

Besides Spandana, other MFIs also lent to the people in the treatment as well as the comparison areas. However, households in the treatment areas were 13.3 per cent more likely to report being Spandana borrowers. Because of Spandana's lending, the probability of accessing microcredit was about 27 per cent in the treatment area as opposed to 18.7 per cent in the comparison area. The difference of 8.3 per cent increase in the probability of microcredit access, results in about 44 per cent increase in access over the comparison area.

The households in the two groups were evaluated 15–18 months after the treatment (lending) was started by Spandana. Based on the findings of the study, the loans were used as follows: 30 per cent of Spandana loans were used for business, 22 per cent for buying stock for existing businesses, 30 per cent to repay loans, 15 per cent for buying durables for household and 15 per cent for consumption.

With the above brief outline of the study, some of the important findings of the study were as follows (Banerjee et al. 2010):

- Microcredit does have important effects on business outcomes and the composition of household expenditure.
- Existing business owners appear to use microcredit to expand their businesses by investing in durables.
- Households that did not own any business and households with low predicted propensity to start a new business, did not increase durable spending but increased non-durable spending (such as consumption on food). This might have been possible because of savings on interest by paying down expensive debt or by spending borrowed funds against future income.
- The households with high predicted propensity to start a business reduced non-durable spending. They appeared to cut back on 'temptation goods,' such as alcohol, tobacco, snacks and lottery tickets in order to conserve cash for the working capital needs of their new businesses.
- The study did not find any discernible impact on education, health and women's empowerment. It is very likely that one cannot detect any appreciable change in these areas given the fact that the treatment group had borrowed from Spandana for only about 18 months after which impact assessments were made.

Abhijit Banerjee and Esther Duflo (2011) in their book *Poor Economics* make the following overall observation based on the results of the study.

As economists we were quite pleased with these results: The main objective of microfinance seemed to have been achieved. It was not miraculous, but it was working. There needed to be more studies to make sure that this was not some fluke, and it would be important to see how things panned out in the long run, but so far so good. In our minds, microcredit has earned its rightful place as one of the key instruments in the fight against poverty.

As can be seen, the impact studies discussed above provide a mixed picture of microcredit impact. This is in comparison to some of the out-sized claims about microcredit impact that has been made in the past. Therefore, at this stage, it would be perhaps appropriate to scale down our expectations about the efficacy of microcredit until longer-term microcredit impact studies are available.

In this context, it is important to reiterate that for a long-time microfinance practitioners have observed, microcredit is necessary but not sufficient in alleviating poverty (see Chapter 10). With access to microloans the poor can only invest in microenterprises that require lows levels of capital, low barriers to entry (which allows for easy entry of other similar businesses, usually clones of the existing businesses) resulting in squeezing of margins leading to low profitability. Lack of education and livelihood training and lack of access to wider market-place also accentuate investing in businesses with low returns. For an entrepreneur, finding a niche business is not easy. Not being finan-cially literate also complicates the situation further. All in all, the dis-cussions above show microcredit is an essential tool that the poor need to have access, but from all indications it is not a panacea for alleviating poverty on a mass scale.

The 2010 Andhra Pradesh Microfinance Crisis and the Aftermath

Considering the set of complex issues that led to the 2010 Andhra Pradesh Microfinance Crisis, it would perhaps take years before full implications of the crisis for the Indian microfinance sector and the microfinance industry worldwide can be assessed. Within the confines of the present section, we present a brief account of the crisis starting with the 2006 Microfinance Crisis followed by the 2010 crisis. This section also pro-vides glimpses into some of the developments following the crisis.

Brief History of the 2006 Crisis

The confluence of events that led to the 2010 Andhra Pradesh Microfinance Crisis in India can be traced to a similar crisis in the state, but on a smaller scale, which took place in the year 2006. Prabhu Ghate (2007) in *Indian Microfinance: The Challenges of Rapid Growth*[3] provides a comprehensive analysis of complex set of interconnected issues that led to the 2006 crisis.

Based on the analysis provided by Prabhu Ghate, one of the important causes of the 2006 crisis was 'near saturation' of the microfinance market that existed in coastal Andhra Pradesh prior to the crisis. Demand conditions in the region was ideal for expansion of microfinance, which even led to dual and even multiple membership by the poor in SHGs as well as MFIs. In fact, the demand for credit was so high that many of the borrowers were also borrowing from informal lenders indicating unmet demand in the region, which was not being met by SHGs as well as the MFIs. Under these circumstances, there were no credit bureaus in the region to let the SHGs, MFIs and other lenders know if a poor borrower was overextending herself or trying to borrow from multiple MFIs.

The fact that the market was nearing saturation was indicated by the fact that borrowers were experiencing payment difficulties and some of the MFIs operating in the region had brought down loan size to tighten credit extension. But at the same time, because of tough competition in the region among the MFIs, credit standards were being lowered to capture market share. Besides, expansion of commercial bank lending to the MFIs (under the ICICI partnership model) also enabled the MFIs to expand their lending to the poor. Lending to the poor also took off because of 3 per cent per annum subsidized interest rate (subsidy was offered by the state of Andhra Pradesh) that was offered by the SHGs to their clients, while the normal interest rate on such loans hovered around 12 per cent per annum.

While the SHGs were offering loans at 3 per cent interest rate, MFI lending rates were in the range of 24–31 per cent per annum. The MFIs also charged loan processing fee, security deposit as cash collateral and a payment towards credit life insurance. No such additional fees, charges or security deposits were required by the SHGs. Under the bank-linkage programme, SHG members saved (see Chapter 4). And the borrowings from the linked bank by the SHGs, for on-lending, were a fixed multiple of their savings. As a result, how much SHGs could lend was constrained by their savings. In the case of the MFIs, there is no such implicit constraint with regard to lending and many MFIs were taking advantage of the situation by over-lending to the poor to expand market share.

It appears that over-lending by the MFIs was fuelled by competition among the MFIs to capture market share to grow rapidly and to have higher levels of profitability. In expanding market share, poaching of SHG clients by the MFIs was a major issue. Because of relatively longer maturity and substantially lower interest rate (of 3 per cent), SHG clients normally would like to borrow as much as they can from the SHGs. In fact, the borrowers were over-indebting themselves by going beyond what they could borrow from the SHGs and then some more by borrowing from the MFIs.

In spite of saturated market conditions, and much higher interest rates charged by the MFIs (that were almost 8–10 times the interest rate charged by the SHGs), lending by the MFIs in the region kept on expanding. That is not all, as we mentioned earlier, the borrowers were borrowing from the moneylenders over and above the borrowings from the SHGs and the MFIs. While it may be due to almost insatiable demand for credit that existed in the region, the MFIs, on the other hand, did not tighten their credit standards to lower lending levels. They just kept on lending, which led to over-indebtedness among their clients. Other factors that could have contributed to over-indebtedness of the clients include: (1) the borrowers were not required to post collateral to borrow, (2) lending was not capped as a multiple of voluntary savings (as in the case of the SHGs) and (3) there were no credit bureaus to check borrowers' credit standing. Compulsory savings required by the MFIs was not much of deterrence because the compulsory savings can be deducted from the loan proceeds.

Under these circumstances in order to bring down delinquency among the borrowers, some of the MFIs in the state resorted to coercive methods to collect debt service. This led to absconding by borrowers and in some cases alleged suicides by some borrowers.

The MFIs charging very high EIRs, which were almost 8–10 times the 3 per cent subsidized rate charged by the SHGs, were the subject of criticism. Besides, given the twin goals of financial sustainability and social mission, the 2006 crisis brought to fore how MFIs in the region in their quest for sustainability were paying lip service to social mission.

Undoubtedly, the MFIs were not in a position to match 3 per cent lending rate offered to SHG clients. In reality, MFIs' own cost of funds hovered around three to four times the 3 per cent rate. Under these circumstances, the MFIs were not effective in communicating to the public why their interest rates were much higher than the subsidized rates charged to the SHG clients or even rates offered by the commercial banks to the non-poor clients.

One of the important outcomes of the crisis was the approval of 'Sa-Dhan's Voluntary Mutual Code of Conduct for Microfinance' (Ghate 2007). Sa-Dhan is an association of MFIs in India. Some of the important stipulations of the voluntary code of conduct included the following: (1) MFIs will ensure to complement credit extended to the poor under the SHG-bank-linkage programme. And they will also extend service to those not adequately served by banks; (2) MFIs will avoid over-financing same household by different MFIs at the same time, this was to be achieved through informal information sharing among the MFIs and the banks that lend to the SHGs; (3) MFIs will charge reasonable interest rates based on a schedule, the schedule indicated reasonable lending rate to be in the range of 21–24 per cent per annum; (4) the voluntary code of conduct also expected the MFIs to indicate the effective lending rate as an APR and was to be computed based on declining balance method by taking into account loan processing fees and other charges and (5) as regard to collection of repayments, the code of conduct stipulated that the MFIs would strictly instruct its staff not to use abusive language or intimidation, it was also stipulated that any staff using such tactics were to be dismissed.

The 2010 Crisis

As we move forward by four years to 2010, it appears that the underlying reasons that contributed to the 2006 Andhra Pradesh Microfinance Crisis remained pretty much the same and the lessons of the 2006 crisis were not factored into the lending models used by the MFIs after the crisis. There were also enough warning signals before the 2010 crisis unfolded.

Considering the fact that the MFIs were lax in their credit standards and used coercive practices to collect debt service, the Andhra Pradesh government had constituted district-wise committees in early 2010 to monitor activities of the MFIs and to investigate complaints and grievances from the customers. The MFIs operating in the state ignored these moves by the government and assumed that it would be of little consequence and pretended that they were beyond the jurisdiction of such committees.

Prior to the 2010 crisis, access to capital by the NBFC MFIs was greatly expanded by governmental and commercial institutions such as Small Industries Development Bank of India, commercial banks (lending to NBFC MFIs by these institutions were considered priority sector lending) and access to equity investments from MIVs and mainstream private equity funds. As a result, NBFC MFIs grew at a breakneck pace of 80 per cent per annum[4] (CGAP 2010). In this context, it is important to note that these NBFC MFIs are not allowed to take any deposits, hence are largely dependent on governmental and commercial sources of funding (bank funding) to expand lending and grow.

Prior to the advent of the 2010 crisis (i.e., at the end of March 2010), the number of loan accounts per household (based on number of borrowers in SHGs and MFIs) was more than 10 (the average excluded households that were not served either by banks or MFIs). Moreover, the average outstanding loans per household (computed from average outstanding loans of SHGs with banks and MFI customers) was ₹67,000 (about $1,340 assuming $1 to be equivalent to ₹50) in March 2010 (Srinivasan 2012). The average debt of the households was over 8 times the national average of outstanding microfinance debt, which was ₹7,700 per household (CGAP 2010). All these figures do not include household borrowing from the informal sector. Based on studies, very high percentage of households in Andhra Pradesh already had contracted debt at rather high levels from the informal sector.

After one year, that is, in March 2011, the average outstanding loan (as defined above) per household reached ₹71,000 ($1,420). What is more, during the four-year period from 2008 to 2011, MFI clientele in Andhra Pradesh increased by 60 per cent and outstanding loans by 160 per cent and in the case of SHGs, the clientele went up by 108 per cent and outstanding loans went up by 138 per cent. And with explosion of lending by SHGs and MFIs, the average loans per client went up by 54 per cent from 2008 to 2011. It is important to note that, on average, about 70 per cent of the per capita microfinance debt was from the SHGs (Srinivasan 2012).

The above analysis shows the debt burden of the households in Andhra Pradesh prior to the 2010 Microfinance Crisis was already at a very high level in comparison to the national average. And based on the statistics, it is difficult to surmise how the average household in the region could service such high levels of debt comfortably (CGAP 2010).[5]

The rapid growth of the microfinance sector in the state of Andhra Pradesh was possible because of the state's support in such areas as livelihood promotion, enterprise and employment facilitations, and income enhancement through initiatives in several sectors. To top it all, the state also extended subsidized lending at 3 per cent per annum under the bank-linkage programme. In comparison, interest rates charged by the MFIs in Andhra Pradesh were in the range of 24–55 per cent per annum. It is important to note that, in spite of 'intensive handholding' and extension of complementary non-financial services, the SHGs in Andhra Pradesh recorded much higher default rates compared with the MFIs. More specifically, while the repayment rates under the government supported programmes were low, the MFIs experienced portfolio at risk of less than 1 per cent (Srinivasan 2012).

It is also important to note that profitability of some of the MFIs in Andhra Pradesh was on the high side. For example, based on data from MIX, N. Srinivasan, in his *Microfinance India: State of the Sector Report 2010*[6] comments on the ROAs of the MFIs in the region and compares it with ROAs of the commercial banks in India. Based on his analysis of 76 MFIs, of which 6 did not report on their profits, 62 had reported positive ROA and 8 had reported negative ROA. Out of the remaining 62 with positive ROAs, 6 MFIs had ROAs above 7 per cent (one among this six MFIs had an ROA of 9.41 per cent) and 35 institutions had ROAs above 2 per cent. In comparison, the banking systems had ROAs in the range of 1–2 per cent and public sector banks in 2009 had an average ROA of 0.6 per cent (Srinivasan 2010).

In an environment where borrowers were struggling with huge debt burden and EIRs, which were on the high side, many MFIs in the region were doing well in terms of profitability. In this environment, SKS Microfinance, perhaps the fastest growing MFI in the region had a successful IPO with high valuation of its shares. The market price of the shares was 98 times the face value of the shares and the original investors in SKS Microfinance shares through private placement were able to cash out a part of their shares after the IPO (Srinivasan 2012). The event attracted a great deal of media coverage and scrutiny. SKS Microfinance along with the entire microfinance sector in the region was the subject of negative publicity. Top management changes at some of the important MFIs, aspirations of other MFIs to go for IPOs with high valuations, reports of unethical practices by the MFIs in the field, levying of high interest rates on poor clients who are predominantly poor women received highly critical reporting in the media.

SKS Microfinance's successful IPO highlighted the fact that microfinance business can be highly profitable. One of the main concerns of the critics revolved around the fact that with commercialization of the MFIs, the sustainability of the MFIs had taken precedence over the sustainability of their poor clients as owners of their microbusinesses. This was particularly difficult to rationalize when many of the impact assessment studies of microcredit had been downsizing expectations with regards to the efficacy of microfinance as a poverty alleviation tool. The critics also questioned why is it that in the face of expanding loan volume and declining operating cost, the interest rates on microloans in the region were not being lowered.

As the story of SKS Microfinance's successful IPO was making headlines, there was news about alleged suicides by borrowers due to coercive debt collection practices by the MFIs in Andhra Pradesh (Lee and David 2010). Under these circumstances, the government of Andhra Pradesh in October 2010 passed an ordinance with following objectives as quoted by N. Srinivasan (2012) in *Microfinance India: State of the Sector Report 2011.*

> ... whereas these SHGs are being exploited by private microfinance institutions through high interest rates and coercive methods of recovery ... and in some cases leading to suicide, it is expedient to make provisions for protecting the interest of the SHGs by regulating the money lending transactions by money lending MFIs ....

The ordinance provided for control over the following aspects of day-to-day operations of the MFIs: how clients can be acquired, stipulations regarding number and extent of loans, rate of interest, terms of repayment, where the MFIs could meet with their clients to make business transactions, and need for prior permission by the MFIs from the state government officials at the district level before lending to anyone who is an SHG member. Later, the last stipulation was modified as follows: if in a family there is someone in the household who is currently an SHG borrower, permission will be needed if MFIs lend to any other member of the family.

The ordinance also contained such conditions as new requirements for registration of MFIs at the district level, making debt collection near local government premises and moving from weekly repayments to monthly repayment schedules. As a result, loan collections were dramatically reduced by the MFIs and lending operations almost came to a standstill. With non-repayment of loans, the MFIs in the region suffered huge losses.[7]

The Aftermath

Subsequent to the Andhra Pradesh government's ordinance, the day-to-day operations as well as financial health of the MFIs were adversely affected (Srinivasan 2012). We discuss in the following, some of the underlying reasons for the fast deterioration of financial health of the MFIs and related issues in the region (Srinivasan 2012):

- Because of the ordinance and subsequent passage of the law, the MFIs were not able to hold cluster and centre meetings where the customers were required to make repayments on loans. As a result, repayments rates that were about 99 per cent, declined precipitously to about 10 per cent. However, it is important to note that the borrowers were not prohibited from making repayments. In fact, the MFIs had issued requests and public notices to the borrowers to come over to the MFIs to make repayments. However, the customers took advantage of the fact that the MFIs practically could not hold cluster meetings or were unable to come to their residences and place of work to collect loans. In other words, there was no effective way the MFIs could enforce repayment of debt service. As far as reasons of not repaying loans were concerned, in a survey 61 per cent of the MFI clients said, they did not repay because they could not access new loans. Other reasons for not repaying to the MFIs were media reports about the crisis encouraged borrowers not to repay (37 per cent), borrowers thought nobody was repaying (32 per cent), pressure from opinion leaders discouraged repayment (24 per cent), MFI staff did not come for collecting debt service (17 per cent) and there were pressure from external agencies not to repay (12 per cent).

- Because of non-repayment of loans, financial condition of the MFIs in the region deteriorated precipitously. Because of the deteriorating financial condition, access to capital by the MFIs, that is, equity as well as loans, was substantially curtailed. This was the case because the MFIs were in the midst of cleaning up their loan portfolios on the aftermath of the crisis. Besides, some of the MFIs were not able to meet their debt service obligations and were restructuring their outstanding debt portfolios. Some of them had also already defaulted and being downgraded. Portfolio quality for the sector had deteriorated substantially. And almost 25 per cent of the loans were not performing. Needless to say, under these circumstances lenders found it risky to extend loans. As far as equity funding was concerned, equity funders had been waiting for clarity in regulatory and market environment. In a nutshell, in an environment where long-run financial health of the sector lacked clarity, flow of investment funds to the sector dried up.

- With substantial decline in repayments, the operations of the MFIs in the region languished. In October 2010, when the crisis precipitated, the borrowers owed about ₹108.9 billion (about $2.2 billion assuming $1 equivalent to ₹50) to 10 large MFIs in the region. It was estimated that over 80 per cent of the portfolio of microloans owed by the borrowers were funded by the banks and other financial institutions. Therefore, these banking institutions were exposed to the credit risk emanating from the MFIs.

- Based on surveys conducted in June-July 2011 by Centre for Microfinance, Chennai, decline in loan flows had already affected the households in the area although there were still about ₹70 billion with the MFI clients, which had not been paid back to the MFIs because of the crisis. For example, among the reporting households in the survey, financing was very difficult for 53 per cent to meet consumption expenses, 31 per cent to meet business-related expenses and 50 per cent to finance health care-related expenditures. Because of overall difficulty in financing, 85, 81 and 76 per cent of the reporting households experienced fall in regular spending for consumption, business expenses and health-related expenditures, respectively. What is more, 33, 35 and 34 per cent of the reporting households experienced large fall in consumption, business-related expenditures and health care spending, respectively. It appears that access to borrowing from the SHGs did not bridge the gap to cater to these needs.

- Because of the decline in access to loans from the MFIs, the borrowers have been already adjusting to the new situation by accessing loans from SHGs (at least in one district), which went up by 1.5 per cent (during the period from August 2010 to July 2011). Similarly, households accessing loans from moneylenders went up by 6.3 per cent. However, as to be expected, during the same period there was a reduction of 3.1 per cent borrowing from the MFIs. In this context, it is important to note that weekly loans from moneylenders in the range of ₹2,000 to ₹10,000 (about $40 to $200) carry an EIR of about 160–225 per cent per annum. Daily finance corporations for loans in the same range charge an EIR of 78–120 per cent per annum. And EIRs on loans from moneylenders (also from pawn brokers) in Andhra Pradesh range from about 30 per cent to about 120 per cent per annum.

As can be seen, the developments following the 2010 Microfinance Crisis in Andhra Pradesh have been sobering in the sense that it brought down MFI operations in the region to a standstill. As a result, clients now suffer because their access to borrowing from the MFIs has been severely curtailed and they are already starting to access credit from moneylenders and other lenders in the informal sector at exorbitant interest rates.

Even after three years of the 2010 Microfinance Crisis, while the MFI in Andhra Pradesh has yet to get back on its feet, the rest of India has slowly but surely returning to its past dynamism by overcoming the gloom and doom that shrouded the entire industry after the crisis. This can be gleaned from the fact that the industry registered 30 per cent gross loan portfolio (GLP) growth in the second quarter of FY2014 over the second quarter of FY2013. As far as funding for the industry is considered, it registered 300 per cent growth in the second quarter of FY2014 over the first quarter of 2014 (Acharya 2014a). What is more, in March 2014, the GLP for the sector stood at about ₹240 billion, which was about ₹40 billion higher than the GLP that existed prior to the 2010 Microfinance crisis (Acharya 2014b). Moreover, it is expected that the industry would register a growth rate of about 30–40 per cent in FY2014 (Acharya 2014c). To top it all, granting of 'in-principle' banking license to Bandhan by the RBI shows that India's central bank recognizes the fact that the MFIs could play an important role in delivering poor-friendly financial services at the BOP (see Chapter 6).

The poor need access to microfinance from many sources because their credit needs are varied. This is because, risk-averse borrowers like to hedge by diversifying their sources of borrowing. In an environment where the poor borrow from moneylenders, variety of government entities, trade credit and formal institutions like the SHGs and the MFIs, a level playing field is essential for these institutions to compete and thrive. Uncertainty and lack of healthy competition kills innovation, which is the driving force behind offering products and services of value at low cost to the consumers. For value-conscious consumers like the poor, SHGs and MFIs are essential. An enabling regulatory environment could help SHGs and the MFIs to compete side-by-side and complement each other. Under these circumstances, the poor can be the ultimate winner.

Learning from Over-indebtedness in Other Countries

In an exploratory paper titled *Too Much Microcredit? A Survey of the Evidence on Over-Indebtedness*, Jessica Schicks and Richard Rosenberg (2011) examine 'conceptual issues and limited empirical evidence' about over-indebtedness in microcredit markets. They note that they use 'microcredit' (microloan and microborrower) in a narrow sense to mean loans to low-income people, which has been in vogue over the last 30 years. They also note that these lenders in general provide only a fraction of the credit accessed by these households. In many countries, MFIs compete with retail credit, which provide consumer lending and merchandize finance.

While it is true that microcredit in the past enjoyed an enviable repayment record around the world, the paper by Schicks and Rosenberg considers empirical evidence of over-indebtedness by low-income people from countries such as Bosnia-Herzegovina, Morocco, Nicaragua, Pakistan and other countries in their analysis. It is important to note that delinquent loans in Bosnia-Herzegovina, Morocco, Nicaragua and Pakistan reached 7, 10, 12 and 13 per cent, respectively, in 2009. They also take into consideration the 2010 Microfinance Crisis in the state of Andhra Pradesh. They note that there was no clarity as to how much of Andhra Pradesh default was 'strategic' as opposed to inability of the borrowers to repay.

In the paper, they discuss a wide range of issues that could lead to the risk of over-indebting borrowers, which include lax lender practices in competitive markets reaching saturation point, borrower mistakes, lack of credit reporting service and lack of early warning system.

They observe that poor people often struggle to repay their loans even without microloans. In the event one finds they are struggling to repay does not necessarily imply that microloans are making these borrowers worse off. Based on the evidence, they believe, 'the evidence is too skimpy so far to draw general conclusions about the degree of microcredit over-indebtedness worldwide, but it shows that the topic needs more attention.'

Their recommendations to prevent indebtedness include the following: (1) improvements to MFI marketing and underwriting; (2) designing products that 'better match client needs and cognitive abilities' and (3) credit reporting and early warning system. They also believe that managers, loan officers as well as funders need to keep watchful eyes to the issues of over-indebtedness and more research is needed with regard to the extent and dynamics of over-indebtedness.

In the paper, Schick and Rosenberg also observe that with lower expectations, the actual benefits of accessing microcredit could be modest. They also note, 'If the quantum of benefit we expect is lower, then the potential downsides for clients that we are willing to tolerate should be lower.' This would imply, if potential downsides we are willing to tolerate have to be lower, then MFIs and its clients have to be cognizant of what are some of the potential causes of downsides (such as over-indebtedness) and guard against such causes.

In Spite of Diminished Expectations, Microcredit Remains an Essential Financial Tool for the Poor

As we have discussed in this chapter, in spite of all the promises that microcredit has shown during the last 35 years, accumulating evidence regarding the efficacy of microfinance on the ground point to the fact that the benefits of microcredit could be modest in comparison to the initial expectations. Under these circumstances, it is prudent that microfinance borrowers' propensity to absorb downside risks have to be scaled down. This has to be true not just for microcredit exposure, but other sources of debt (such as the moneylenders, payday lenders and the like) as well that poor households are exposed to.

In Chapter 4, we noted that microcredit is a powerful financial tool that can be used by the poor to smooth consumption, mitigate risk, build social and human capital, and monetize their capabilities. While we scale down our expectations regarding the benefits of microcredit that the poor could accrue on an aggregate level, the fact remains that on an individualized basis a poor client has to assess for herself the pros and cons of accessing credit. By avoiding the use of credit at any cost, a poor household could forego a good opportunity that she could leverage for economic gains by borrowing. What she has to watch out is that she is not over-indebting herself. In this regard, financial literacy training for the poor could pay rich dividends. Use of credit bureaus in the developing countries could help in this regard also. Cutting down on spurious spending and spending on 'temptation goods' could also avoid over-indebting oneself.

Leveraging balance sheets is risky, particularly fragile balance sheets of poor households. Besides, substituting credit for savings and insurance has been the modus operandi by poor households around the world—because (1) their household incomes tend to be erratic, (2) building up savings requires discipline, and building 'lump sum' savings is time-consuming, (3) there is lack of poor-friendly savings facilities for the poor, (4) there is also lack of poor-friendly and sustainable insurance providers for the poor, (5) even if poor households may sign up for insurance (say health insurance), the protection provided is not 100 per cent and the households have to have access to savings as well as credit, (6) signing up for insurance does require that the client (i.e., the household) spends from her own resources (from savings or credit) in an emergency and the household receives an insurance payout after filing a claim for the expenses, which a poor household normally finds cumbersome. Under these circumstances, when poor households are confronted with emergencies, by and large the households are forced to borrow, even if financial prudence may dictate otherwise.

In the next chapter, we will discuss about the benefits of deploying microfinance instruments and complementary non-financial services in a concerted manner. Obviously, a household has to pick and choose which instruments and which services to deploy in managing their business and household finances. In the present context, it is important to note that Grameen Bank by redesigning its Grameen I model in the early 1980s introduced microsavings (voluntary savings) intertwined with microcredit such that poor could borrow and save at the same time (Chapter 5). Under the new model, which was named Grameen II, flexibility was introduced in making loan repayments, which allowed for slower loan repayments for households experiencing financial stress. These changes have been well received by the poor. And loan recovery rate for Grameen Bank has been relatively high, which stood at 97 per cent in 2011 (Chapter 4).

All in all, the power of microcredit emanates from the fact that it injects liquid cash to households on short notice. Given the fact that money is fungible, access to microcredit provides a wide range of options for poor families. The options allow a poor family to act with self-interest, which when used wisely could benefit the entire family.

Conclusion

As we rein in our expectations regarding the benefits of microcredit, several conclusions about the industry becomes apparent: (1) delivery of microcredit to the poor may not guarantee alleviation of poverty on a large scale, although without such access, the poor will be deprived of a powerful financial tool that is essential in smoothing consumption, mitigating risk and monetizing capabilities; (2) as rapid growth combined with sustainability of many MFIs have become a reality, some of the issues related to transparent pricing, disclosure of EIRs, over-lending without regard for absorptive capacity of the clients and abusive and coercive debt service collection practices have emerged, which needs to be addressed forthright; (3) given the fact that there is diminished expectations of microcredit impact, higher levels of delinquency experience in some microfinance markets make it imperative that the MFIs remain responsible and vigilant lenders as they lend to one of the most vulnerable sections of the society; (4) while establishment of credit bureaus in the developing countries may not provide reliable credit information for the poor initially, over a period of time these institutions could build up their database and could provide an early warning system to the microfinance industry and (5) measurement of financial and social performance of an MFI have to go hand in hand, without SPM overall risk assessment of DBL-centric institutions such as the MFIs can never be complete.

Needless to say, without an enabling regulatory environment, microfinance sector cannot thrive. The poor need access to microcredit from many (informal and formal) sources that include such institutions as the MFIs, SHGs, co-operatives, trade credit, ROSCAs, ASCAs, variety of governmental entities and charitable organizations. This is because 'one-size-fits-all' approach may be suboptimal for the poor. Each of these institutions, in spite of their shortcomings, has niche products that the poor value. Based on their credit needs, they could mix and match credit products provided by these institutions. Therefore, an enabling regulatory environment in which these institutions could compete with each other on a level playing field to design and deliver niche products (that could complement each other) would be of great value for the poor.

Last but not least, while the practitioners in the microfinance industry have observed all along that microcredit is necessary but not sufficient in alleviating poverty (see Chapter 10), progress towards offering other financial instruments (besides credit) and complementary non-financial services concurrently have not kept pace with microcredit. Progress in offering these instruments and services in tandem with microcredit can go a long way in making microfinance a powerful force in fighting poverty (see Chapter 12).

Notes

1. 'The Nobel Peace Prize for 2006, Press Release, The Norwegian Nobel Committee, Oslo, October 13 2006.' Available online at http://www.nobelprize.org/nobel_prizes/peace/laureates/2006/press.html (downloaded on 28 October 2012).
2. 'Measuring the Impact of Microfinance in Hyderabad, India.' Available online at http://www.povertyactionlab.org/evaluation/measuring-impact-microfinance-hyderabad-india (downloaded on 29 December 2012).
3. Prabhu Ghate. 2007. *Indian Microfinance: The Challenges of Rapid Growth.* New Delhi: SAGE Publications, pp. 86–107.
4. 'Andhra Pradesh 2010: Global Implications of the Crisis in Indian Microfinance.' Focus Note No. 67, CGAP, November 2010.
5. 'Andhra Pradesh 2010: Global Implications of the Crisis in Indian Microfinance.' Focus Note No. 67, pp. 3, Washington, DC: CGAP. November 2010.
6. N. Srinivasan. 2010. *Microfinance India: State of the Sector Report 2010,* pp. 33–34. New Delhi: SAGE Publications.
7. 'Micro-Finance bill is anti-poor, says Andhra Pradesh government official,' Press Trust of India, May 13, 2012.

12

The Synergy

… What struck her instead was ordinariness of everything. The component parts were ordinary, and they were all based on ordinary commonsense. She discovered that the magic lies in how it all fits together, making ordinary things happen in extraordinarily difficult situations and turning the whole thing into something quite amazing.[1]

Ian Smillie

The whole is greater than the sum of its parts.

Aristotle

What is so unique about microfinance is that its pioneers visualized how poor-friendly, reliable access to microcredit on a level playing field can open up opportunities for the poor in terms of smoothing consumption, mitigating risk, building human capital and monetizing capabilities even when financial stress may be staring at their faces. Uncertainty and unpredictability kill initiatives. Reliability (and hence better predictability) in accessing credit is a sea change in the life of a poor family, which is surrounded by unpredictability. Even minimal stability (and hence predictability in cash flow) brought about by access to microcredit can encourage a poor person to act with self-confidence to improve her economic condition. Therefore, not withstanding diminished expectations of microcredit as a tool to help the poor move out of poverty on a mass scale, it remains a powerful and versatile tool, which when used with prudence could have salutary implications for a poor household.

Until now, the microfinance industry has been dominated by a single product, that is, microcredit. This is because of the versatility of micro-credit, which can be substituted for savings and insurance. While such versatility can be a boon, it can turn into a bane quickly if taken too far, that is, if the fragile balance sheets of poor households are over-leveraged (Chapter 11). While it may be easier to restrict access to microcredit to avoid downside risks associated with over-leveraged balance sheets of the poor, a better solution would be to help them take a balanced approach by providing poor-friendly microsavings facilities (Chapter 6) and microinsurance (Chapter 7) in managing specific risks that they potentially can be exposed to. The synergy emanating from such an approach could reduce the heightened financial risk that can emanate from substituting credit for savings and insurance.

As we have seen throughout the book, the challenges for microfinance industry are many. In order for microsavings, microinsurance, improved payment systems and microleasing to reach the same level of penetration amongst the poor as microcredit, it would require a great deal of hard work to say the least. Needless to say, the benefits of deploying these instruments in tandem would go beyond using the instruments in an *ad hoc* basis. For example, as we discussed in Chapter 5, the introduction of microsavings (voluntary savings) intertwined with microcredit and flex-ible repayment terms under Grameen II benefited borrowers so much so that portfolio recovery rate in 2011 stood at 97 per cent (Chapter 4). In the same vein, one would think that access to voluntary savings and flexible repayment terms by the MFI clients in Andhra Pradesh could have avoided the 2010 Microfinance Crisis. Such access also could have perhaps avoided high levels of delinquency rates in countries such as Bosnia-Herzegovina, Morocco, Nicaragua and Pakistan.

The poor usually are not financially literate. Therefore, it is impera-tive that they go through financial literacy training even before start-ing to borrow from an MFI. Particularly, they should be cautioned about the downside risks of over-borrowing and benefits of saving and insurance. Needless to say, if a family saves for the rainy days, relies on insurance for say health risk and borrows for her microbusiness, she is on a sounder financial footing than a household that substitutes bor-rowing for all these three activities. In the same vein, if a poor individual goes through a livelihood and marketing training (Chapter 10) before deciding to lease (Chapter 8) an equipment (for a niche business) will have improved potential in succeeding in her business. Needless to say, training in how all the pieces of an equipment fit together is important. The upshot of these discussions is to highlight the fact that the synergy emanating from using microfinance instruments and services in a concerted manner can deliver rich dividends for the poor.

As noted in the Prologue, the presence of microfinance industry in an economy delivers value at least on two levels, that is, at the individual level as well as at the system-wide level. Throughout the book we have discussed, how the poor could benefit from deploying microfinance instruments and complementary services in managing their business and household finances. Needless to say, there is a synergy in using these instruments and services in parallel that could deliver greater value in comparison to using these instruments in an *ad hoc* fashion. What is more, the benefits at the individual level translate to benefits at the system-wide level and there is a feedback loop between the levels. The book did not specifically highlight so far the benefits that microfinance industry could engender on a system-wide level. The present chapter is largely devoted to such a discussion.

Laying Down the Foundations of Financial Intermediation at the BOP by Transforming Small Value Finance to Formal Microfinance

The idea of small value lending to the poor on a mass scale did not emerge to the limelight until many NGO-based MFIs around the world experimented with microcredit. What has emerged during the last 35 years is that there is a huge demand for such lending because it has brought about a major revolution in the way how the poor (particularly the poor women) access credit, manage their finances, smooth consumption, mitigate specific risks and monetize their capabilities.

The prefix 'micro' in the financial products delivered by the microfinance industry captures rather succinctly the single most important feature of the financial products delivered to the poor by MFIs. The informal financial sector has traditionally delivered small value finance (basically small value credit) to the poor for ages. However, it took sometime before it was realized that it is essential for the poor to have access to formal microfinance (consisting of microcredit, microsavings, microinsurance, payment systems, and other related instruments and services) on a mass scale and on a level playing field in order to help them manage their business and household finances. It was also realized that in order to deliver these instruments, one needs to establish specialized institutions such as the MFIs, SHGs and other similar DBL institutions with financial sustainability and social mission as their goals.

Prior to the emergence of microcredit in countries like Bangladesh, Bolivia, Brazil, India and Indonesia, the poor practically did not have much access to formal sources of credit. In order to provide access to formal credit (i.e., microcredit) to the poor on a mass scale, the pioneers of microfinance had to invent formal structures (social, financial and institutional), reach out to the poor to bridge the 'last mile,' and establish linkages with major stakeholders to fund themselves in order to create the microfinance platform. In spite of many of the shortcomings of microcredit as a formal financial instrument and the institutions that deliver microcredit to the poor, one has to agree that moving from the idiosyncrasies of informal finance to build formal structures that caters in formal ways to the credit, savings, insurance and MT needs of the poor is nothing less than a quiet revolution. For example, the boldness needed to lend to the poor without collateral with group guarantee has to be revolutionary, which allowed poor women to access credit on a large scale.

In order to achieve all this, these pioneers had to demolish the age-old traditions, conventions and misgivings that were in vogue in the formal financial sector, which made it difficult for the poor to access formal financial services. It is true that, microfinance has not lived up to the hype it created for itself, and the financial instruments it has designed and delivered need constant improvement. Even then, it is only through the process of creative destruction that it has created the edifice of an industry that is slowly becoming an integral part of the financial sector around the world. The emergence of non-financial complementary services has been also possible because in the context of access to credit by the poor, the relevance of these services have been acutely felt.

Although MFIs around the world have largely remained mono-product institutions by delivering credit, there are MFIs such as Grameen Bank,

BRAC, SafeSave and others that have been delivering microsavings (voluntary savings) to the poor along with microcredit (see Chapters 5 and 6). Similarly, in order to mitigate specific risks, the MFIs and insurance providers around the world have been trying to provide microinsurance to the poor that is poor-friendly and sustainable (see Chapter 7). As far as lease finance is concerned, a limited number of MFIs have offered microleasing in the past such that the poor could access equipment and machinery (see Chapter 8). However, the instrument has yet to be adopted widely by the microfinance industry.

Financial intermediation systems ride on payment systems. While the MFIs around the world largely rely on the existing payment systems of a country, bridging the last mile to reach out to the poor depends on P2P contact, that is, either go from door-to-door to disburse loans, receive debt service payments, collect savings and the like, or use the weekly meetings for such activities. However, ITC-based payment systems such as M-PESA and FINO (see Chapter 9) and others are slowly but surely changing the scenario as to how the poor not only could transfer funds, but perform microbanking as well with ease.

The fact that microloans can make a measurable difference in the lives of the poor has empowered and is still empowering many social entrepreneurs to start small and establish MFIs for the benefit of the poor. Even Internet sites such as KIVA have emerged to source investments from socially minded investors in amounts as small as $25, which is pooled from many individuals to be lent to microentrepreneurs in different countries (see Chapter 1).[2] In India, Rang De is also an online microlending platform that collects funding (as little as ₹100, equivalent to about $2) from socially minded investors to lend for business and education (Srinivasan 2012). In other words, these institutions leverage the power of Internet to intermediate funds for the poor.

In the book, we have provided several studies that show how the MFIs are constantly experimenting to provide improved products and services for the poor. RCT-based research is also providing insights as to how improving the design of microfinance instruments could help the effectiveness of these tools. Recent innovations in product design such as commitment savings (see Chapter 6), 'lend-to-save' model P9 of Stuart Rutherford in Bangladesh and experiments such instruments as Jipange KuSave in Kenya (see Chapters 6 and 9) provide examples of how improved product design can help the poor to build savings. Similarly in microinsurance field, major insurance providers along with MFIs around the world are experimenting with different insurance products and delivery models to find ways to offer such products on a mass scale for the poor. Even if these may be small improvements in product design and delivery, cumulative impact of such developments in the long run can be profound.

The architecture of microfinance platform that is open to new ideas and inherent strengths of its financial products have allowed social entrepreneurs, the governments, the donors, the business and CSOs to cooperate for delivering financial products and complementary non-financial services for the poor. In this context, it is important to note that Michael E. Porter and Mark R. Kramer (2011) in their Harvard Business Review Article 'Creating Shared Value—How to reinvent capitalism—and unleash a wave of innovation and growth,' observe that social entrepreneurs have been instrumental in designing and deploying business models that are at the forefront of social value creation. Later in this chapter, we will briefly discuss about CSV model of Michael Porter and Mark R. Kramer and social business model of Muhammad Yunus in order to illustrate how some of the ideas inherent to microfinance are catalyzing other innovative business models to help poor fight poverty.

While the need for accessing formal financial services by the poor is a bare necessity, putting the foundations of financial intermediation from ground up at the BOP is a complex task. In order to achieve this, the MFIs had to design microfinance instruments, build institutions, formulate financial policies and reach out to the poor one-by-one by bridging the last mile. One also needs to appreciate that all these activities might have to face not so friendly regulatory environment, poor infrastructure and a cultural environment that may not allow poor women to step out of their homes to join solidarity groups and attend weekly group meetings. In this environment, building a credit culture (credit discipline) is also not easy because the poor could take advantage of opportunistic default to undermine a microfinance industry. The fact that over 200 million low-income people have accessed microcredit (see Chapter 1) under difficult circumstances is nothing less than a revolution in providing financial services to the poor.

While benefits of using microcredit may be varied, we provide below a rough estimate of interest savings by poor families around the world by borrowing from MFIs as opposed to moneylenders. Needless to say what follows are approximations based on bare assumptions. If we assume there are about 200 million active microcredit borrowers in the world, who on the average have $300 in outstanding borrowing from MFIs, then the total outstanding microcredit portfolio on world-wide basis comes to $60 billion. And if we assume the borrowers save on the average about 20 per cent per annum in terms of interest expenses (because they are borrowing from the MFIs as opposed to local moneylenders), then the yearly interest savings for these borrowers could be around $12 billion. There is no denying the fact that interest savings of $12 billion per year is substantial. The interest savings by the poor households could be viewed as extra earnings (a penny saved is a penny earned). Note that these savings are over and above the benefits the poor households could accrue from utilizing the borrowed funds in their businesses. However, following caveats need to be added. The savings could be lower if interest savings are actually lower. Besides, in the absence of MFIs, because of high interest charged by the moneylenders, the poor in general would not borrow to invest in microbusinesses.

Financial and Non-financial Instruments to Alleviate 'Unfreedoms'

If instruments (tools) are means to an end, then tools for managing one's finances and mitigating specific risks are truly useful tools that everyone should have access to. The poor have tried on their own to invent instruments such as ROSCAs, ASCAs and other financial tools to manage their finances, but these tools are no match for the power and versatility of formal financial tools.

The importance of microfinance for the poor cannot be overemphasized. If the non-poor cannot grow and prosper without access to basic financial services such as credit, savings, insurance, and reliable and efficient payment systems, then the poor cannot either. As we saw during the 2007–08 financial meltdown, when access to credit was choked, even many of the major industrialized countries around the world could not avoid severe recessions. Needless to say, the poor have been deprived of access to formal financial tools for too long. Such deprivation has forced them to use the informal financial sector, which has been one of the major reasons for their entrapment in poverty.

Before we highlight some of the important contributions of microfinance tools in helping the poor fight poverty, we discuss rather briefly how tools have been 'agents of change' from the Stone Age onwards to the digital age. In this context, the following quote from 'Computer Power and Human Reason—From Judgment to Calculation,' by Joseph Weizenbaum (1976, 18) is appropriate.

> The tool as a symbol in all these respects thus transcends its role as a practical means toward certain ends: it is a constituent of man's symbolic recreation of his world. It must therefore inevitably enter into the imaginative calculus that constantly constructs his world. In that sense, then, the tool is much more than a mere device: it is an agent of change.

If computers (digital technology), initially built for number-crunching, have profoundly changed our society in ways difficult to fathom, then financial tools such as credits, savings, insurance, derivatives and more broadly financial intermediation, banking and insurance are no less. In the same vein, one would expect access to formal financial tools by the poor would also have profound implications by putting down the roots of financial intermediation, banking and insurance at the BOP.

The introduction of these tools into the 'mental calculus' of the poor has to have profound implications in the sense that they can construct and reconstruct their world using these formal tools to manage their business and household finances little easier. Even if such improvements can be on the margin to start with, the synergy engendered by these tools can greatly help the poor in improving their financial condition as financial intermediation and banking have done for the non-poor.

While tools are designed for specific tasks, one can be creative in using tools for other purposes as well. In that sense microfinance tools are no different. For example, we discussed in Chapter 6 of an MFI client who borrowed from her MFI at an interest rate of 24 per cent per annum to save at a much lower rate (4 per cent per annum) in order to have the savings at hand at the right time. We also discussed in Chapter 6 some of the underlying reasons why a borrower would decide to take this approach to savings. What this implies is that it is difficult to comprehend *a priori* how someone would use a financial instrument for her benefit.

In the same chapter (i.e., Chapter 6), we also discussed about Stuart Rutherford's P9 'lend-to-save' model, which is an ingenious instrument to help borrowers build savings. This is helpful, given the fact that the poor lack the discipline to save. Commitment savings is another example how behavioural economics can be used to build savings instruments that could help the poor to save. Needless to say, addition of such innovative tools to the basic set of microfinance instruments provide more choices for the poor clients to find appropriate instrument for their specific needs to navigate towards financial freedom.

Needless to say, the critical innovation in delivering financial services to the poor has to be the design of microcredit, microsavings, microinsurance and payment systems that goes to the heart of how microfinance system performs. These tools have become the centre pieces around which the entire microfinance industry revolves. It is around these products that other non-financial complementary services are also delivered to help the poor improve their economic well-being. At the same time, introduction of platforms such as FINO and M-PESA around these financial instruments have added another dimension to these tools in the sense that these platforms have improved access to these instruments even in remote areas of a country.

Instruments for Alleviating 'Unfreedoms'

No one can deny that credits are double-edged swords. For example, over-indebtedness could spell disaster for a poor family. We have critiqued some of the downsides of using microcredit in Chapter 11. However, when used judiciously, it could smooth consumption, help mitigate risk and improve profit potential of microbusinesses.

Access to microcredit provides poor clients an important option (choice) to borrow without collateral and at much lower interest rates. Besides, access being on a level playing field and the borrowers having the freedom to deploy the borrowing in microbusinesses give them a great deal of opportunity to leverage their capabilities. Using borrowed funds from the moneylenders in microbusinesses (if not impossible) is difficult because of the usurious interest rates. Besides, need for collateral could restrict borrowers to go back for more credit to invest and expand business. Needless to say, having the choice to access microcredit can be viewed as a form of freedom for a poor family, which opens up many avenues to attack poverty with creativity and ingenuity. Similarly, instruments such as microsavings, microinsurance and improved payment systems also help the poor in managing cash flow, smoothing consumption and mitigating risk among other things to improve their economic well-being. In this context the following quote from *Development as Freedom* by Amartya Sen (1999, xii) is relevant.

> Development consists of the removal of various types of unfreedoms that leave people with little choice and little opportunity of exercising their reasoned agency. The removal of substantial unfreedoms, it is argued here, is *constitutive* of development. However, for a fuller understanding of the connection between development and freedom we have to go beyond that basic recognition (crucial as it is). The intrinsic importance of human freedom, in general, as the preeminent objective of development is supplemented by the instrumental effectiveness of freedoms of particular kinds to promote freedoms of other kinds.

While access to microfinance may not remove 'unfreedoms' for good, it could lessen some of these temporarily in order that the poor are empowered to act in their own self-interest. To feel free to act in one's own self-interest is rather subtle. There are many ways an individual could feel constrained to act freely. Lack of a sense of financial security steals from a poor person or for that matter anyone else, to feel free to act with confidence.

The ecosystem, in which the poor live, operates rather informally. Informality and unreliability go hand-in-hand, because in an informal world commitments are not taken seriously. As a result, informality can become bottlenecks in getting things done. Access to microfinance does create an environment where there is more reliability in terms of accessing credit and other financial instruments. Improved payment systems also increase reliability of financial transactions. All this brings about more predictability in a sea of unpredictability. More predictability in terms of their finances helps the poor to plan and improve their chances to be successful in managing their household and business finances.

Even if in small measure, access to microcredit allows leveraging two important endowments the poor have, that is, their native intelligence and physical capabilities. With access to microcredit, poor households have a wide range of options such as buy tools or inputs for businesses, retire high cost loans or deploy the funds in emergencies. Obviously access to credit is not free. It comes with strings attached, such as the need to be part of a joint-liability contract and the associated inflexibility of repayment terms (weekly repayments), no grace period (repayment starts in one week just after getting the loans) and relatively higher interest rates (in comparison to loans from commercial banks that non-poor can access). But at the same time, MFI clients should feel good that the interest rate on microcredit is much lower than the interest charged by moneylenders and there is no need to post collateral.

The temporary window during which the credit is available to a borrower is the opportunity for the poor family to invest the funds for productive purposes such that in the long run, the income generated from such investment would move the household towards attaining financial freedom. On the other hand, if the loan is used for spurious consumption, the family could end up moving on a path that could lead to over-indebtedness and even push the family deeper into poverty. In most cases, one would expect the poor households to use the funds in their self-interest such that the household could benefit.

We have long ways to go before access to microsavings facilities is available as widely as microcredit. However, the discipline to save allows a poor family to plan for the future education of their children, purchase equipment for their businesses, land for farming, savings for retirement and marriage of their daughters. As we noted in Chapter 6, GPS has been quite popular among the poor households, which provides some degree of income security in their old age. Needless to say, an annuity during old age (even if it may not fully cover the financial expenses of a poor household) can provide partial financial freedom to the household.

It is ultimately hope that drives us all. Even the poorest amongst us have dreams to achieve financial freedom. In Chapter 6, we discussed the inspiring story of Biti Rose by Nicholas Kristof (2012) in an Op-Ed in *The New York Times* titled 'Doughnuts Defeating Poverty.' The following quote from the Op-Ed is pertinent in the present context.

> Yet I think there's something going on here beyond microsavings and entrepreneurship. Esther Duflo, an economist at the Massachusetts Institute of Technology and coauthor of an exceptionally good book called

"Poor Economics," argues that outside interventions work partly when they give poor people hope. That is precisely what I've seen in many countries: Assistance succeeds when it gives people a feeling that better outcome is possible, and those hopes become self-fulfilling as people work more industriously and invest more wisely.

And in Chapter 11, we discussed about a large-scale RCT-based study of microcredit impact that was undertaken in the city of Hyderabad in Andhra Pradesh by Banerjee et al. (2010). Out of the various findings of the study, there are two important findings that are as follows:

- Existing business owners appear to use microcredit to expand their businesses by investing in durables.
- The households with high predicted propensity to start a business reduced non-durable spending. They appeared to cut back on 'temptation goods,' such as alcohol, tobacco, snacks and lottery tickets in order to conserve cash for the working capital needs of their new businesses.

While existing business owners expanded their businesses by investing in durables, what was striking about the second finding is that households with high predicted propensity to start a business reduced non-durable spending. They also appeared to cut back on 'temptation goods' such as alcohol and tobacco in order to conserve cash for working capital needs of their new businesses. What this implies is that these households with high predicated propensity to start businesses reared the hope that they can succeed and were motivated enough to cut down on temptation goods to conserve cash. Conserving cash is real savings in a poor household, more like injection of cash to do something good for the household. What this implies is that access to credit can give hope to people who are motivated to succeed. And the motivation makes them find ways to succeed and to work hard to achieve their goals.

In Chapter 5, we briefly described from a special report titled 'A Fight to Save Baby Girls in India,' by Kamala Thiagarajan (2013) that was published in *The New York Times* on 7 March 2013. The report illustrated how improving the economic status of women in Usilampatti in the state of Tamil Nadu (India), home to about 85,000 people changed the attitude of the inhabitants in the region towards women, that is, they were not considered as liabilities anymore. This led to decline of infanticide of baby girls in the region.

The change in attitude was brought about by access to microloans by women in the region, which they used to improve their economic status. The access to microloans was possible because of the presence of 300 SHGs in the region. The report highlights how women in the region as members of the SHGs improved their economic well-being by deploying these loans in microbusinesses. With improvements in women's economic status, they were no longer considered as liabilities. As a result, infanticide of the girls became a thing of the past.

All in all, the freedom to access credit, savings and insurance from MFIs not only expands choice for an MFI client to take advantage of opportunities, more importantly, there is an 'instrumental effectiveness' of this freedom, which does help to 'promote freedoms of other kinds.' The instrumental effectiveness arises because of the option a client has to use financial instruments to smooth consumption, mitigate risk and monetize her capabilities. That in turn opens the door to take advantage of other opportunities. In other words, the freedom to access financial instruments and complementary non-financial services has an expected intrinsic value. And how an MFI member ultimately utilizes this option to gain financial freedom (partially or fully) depends to a large extent on her training, experience, perseverance, motivations, hopes, aspirations, support from the family and the social and economic network she is part of.

Institutions as 'Incentive Structures': MFIs as Incentive Structures

Douglas C. North (2005), Nobel Laureate in Economic Sciences, puts the role of institutions in economies rather succinctly, 'I have placed institutions at the center of understanding economies because they are the incentive structures of economies.' The role of institutions as incentive structures is important because incentive structures are important drivers of growth and prosperity in an economy. As we shall see in this section, the MFIs provide some of the most important incentive structures for the poor by building social capital, and by providing user-friendly access to powerful financial tools. Moreover many MFIs provide access to complementary non-financial services that could enable the poor to better leverage their capabilities to be productive. Most importantly, MFIs are explicitly driven by DBL objectives of financial sustainability (profitability) and social mission to create social value. And the process of social value creation relies on creating incentive structures to help the poor work towards economic well-being.

The main thrust of this section is to show how progressive ideas that underlie the design of MFIs have been instrumental in creating incentive structures that help the poor to work towards their economic well-being. In spite of the fact that it would be difficult to measure the impact of such progressive institutions, the following quote from *Economics: A Short Introduction* by Partha Dasgupta (2007, 25) is pertinent in elucidating the role institutions play in growth and development of an economy.

> Economic historians such as Robert Fogel, David Landes and Douglas North have argued that the rich world is rich today because, over the centuries, it has devised institutions that have enabled people to improve their material conditions of life. This is a deeper explanation. It says that people in rich countries work with superior technologies, are healthier, live longer, are better educated, and produce many more productive ideas, *because* they have been able to get on with their lives in societies whose institutions permit—even encourage—the economy-wide accumulation of such factors of production as machines, transport facilities, health, skills, ideas and the fruits of those ideas. The accumulation of productive capital assets is only a proximate cause of prosperity, the real cause is progressive institutions.

If the real cause of prosperity is progressive institutions, what are some of the progressive ideas that would help institutions to bring about prosperity among the masses of the poor? In this context, the following quote from *Understanding the Process of Economic Change* by Douglas North (2005, 18) is pertinent.

> Altering the institutional framework entails changing the incentive structure and has been an essential condition for the reduction in the uncertainties of the environment over time. It has been the major tool by which humans have attempted deliberately to alter their environment. It encompasses many of the efforts in the contemporary world to improve the performance of the third world economies. Historically, institutional change has altered the pay-off to cooperative activity (the legal enforcement of contracts, for example), increased the incentive to invent and innovate (patent laws),

altered the pay-off to investing in human capital (the development of institutions to integrate the distributed knowledge of complex economies), and
lowered transaction costs in markets (the creation of a judicial system that
lowers the costs of contract enforcement).

The importance of the above quote can be gleaned from the fact that
the existence of MFIs in poor communities does change the incentive
structures for the poor in a big way because they now have the option to
borrow microloans at interest rates of 2–3 per cent per month, which is
substantially lower than the interest rates charged by the moneylenders,
which is normally in the range of 5–10 per cent per month. In fact, in
many countries, the moneylenders can charge even higher interest rates.
Besides, the borrower has to post collateral. Needless to say, these are
tangible incentives that can motivate the poor clients to take the risk of
borrowing and investing the funds in their microbusinesses. With usurious interest rates, borrowed funds from moneylenders are not suitable
in investing in businesses. Moreover, the terms of lending and customer
relationship MFIs foster a sea change from the ways the moneylenders
conduct their businesses (see Chapters 4 and 5).

Moreover, the poor can access microcredit reliably in a business-like
environment, which is a profound change from the informal world of
the moneylenders (Collins et al. 2009). Besides, under 'progressive lending' (see Chapter 4), the MFI clients have the option to borrow larger
loan amounts if they repay their loans in time. The change in the environment to access credit, because of the presence of the MFIs, empowers
the poor to manage their microbusinesses with greater confidence.

As far as legal enforcement of contracts is concerned, microfinance
by introducing joint-liability contracts has made a huge difference by
enabling millions of un-bankable poor (particularly vulnerable poor
women) to bankable status. It is true that group lending and joint-
liability contract has their downsides (see Chapter 5), and MFIs such
as Grameen Bank are not using joint-liability contracts any more, but
the fact remains, it still is one of the important innovations that MFIs
around the world utilize in lending to the poor.

Besides access to credit, access to voluntary savings (Chapter 6) and
insurance (Chapter 7) is slowly gaining ground as the poor become more
aware of these instruments and realize that the emerging synergy from
the use of these instruments in tandem can be beneficial for them than

solely relying on credit. Although microleasing (Chapter 8) has not been adopted widely by the MFIs, as an instrument it has features that can be of benefit for the clients as well as the MFIs. It could reduce financial risk for the MFIs as well as for the poor. Most importantly, it could provide access to tools and technology by the poor to pursue niche businesses to improve income potential. Therefore, by relying on a diversified portfolio of instruments, a poor household could be on a much stronger footing to immunize against risks and uncertainties of life and pursue niche livelihoods. It is important to add that in order for this to materialize on a large scale, financial literacy training for the poor is a must. In other words, financial literacy training could create the necessary incentive for the poor to use appropriate financial instruments and complementary services by poor households.

The microfinance field not only introduces new financial instruments, but also redesigns existing instruments such that the poor find the instruments better suited to achieve their desired goals. The introduction of Grameen II, which redesigned Classical Grameen model, is a prime example of such attempts (Chapter 5). Some of the efforts in the area of microsavings include introduction of commitment savings, 'P9' 'lend-to-save' model of Stuart Rutherford, retirement savings for the poor such as GPS and other such attempts that provide incentives for the poor for adopting these instruments to save. Microinsurance, being a more complex instrument, breakthroughs in designing poor-friendly instruments has been slow. Even then, insurance products in such areas as credit-life insurance, health insurance and index-based weather insurance have been attractive for the poor to use such instruments for mitigating specific risks. There have been breakthroughs in providing improved payment systems (MT) to the poor, which include M-PESA and FINO (Chapter 9). These efforts are some of the prime examples of incentive structures that the MFIs have been trying to incorporate at the institutional design stage such that microfinance instruments can be poor-friendly and help the poor in their fight against poverty.

The microfinance field realizes the importance of 'pay-off to cooperative activity (e.g., the legal enforcement of contracts),' through the introduction of joint-liability contracts in order to lend without collateral. As discussed in Chapter 5, joint-liability contracts have also helped MFIs in lowering transaction costs and contract enforcement.

Many MFIs also invest in human capital development through literacy and financial literacy training, livelihood and marketing training, and using the group meetings to keep the clients abreast of developments that can help their families in livelihoods, health, education and other areas.

Social and Economic Networks, Economic Inequality and Microfinance

Ela R. Bhatt (2006) in her book *We Are Poor but So Many* describes vividly how a populace that is illiterate cannot glean information from billboards, public notices, newspapers, bank documents, legal papers and most importantly advertisements for employment. As a result, the poor in general do not have a good grasp of what is happening around them. Consequently, they remain disconnected from reality. Their drift from one menial job to another continues. In a nutshell, disconnectedness becomes a curse.

No wonder, lacking rudimentary education, poor people even get cheated because they rely on others (say the moneylenders) to tell them how much money they owe. Because many of them are illiterate and do not have the basic understanding of arithmetic, they may not even have the requisite knowledge to question if something may be wrong in such things as financial transactions they enter into. Illiteracy and lack of knowledge of simple arithmetic do put the poor at a disadvantage in accessing financial services. Moreover, information that may be relevant and valuable to them may be held back in order to exploit them, which they may not even realize. Lack of education can be detrimental to establishing connectivity using mobile phones. For these people, sending money, paying for grocery or performing banking transactions using mobile phones can be still more difficult.

We are all imbedded inside social and economic networks. The connectivity we establish in these networks becomes an important determining factor in what kind of education we pursue, job opportunities we can access, inputs we can buy for our businesses, and products and services we can sell (Jackson 2008). The networks we establish alert us when to get inoculated to buying cheaper tickets for our travel. We benefit from the insights of members in our network that can help us in our career changes. The growth of intelligent social networks such as Google, Yahoo and Facebook is a testament to the usefulness of these networks in our daily life. It is the density, quality and effectiveness of our connectivity through networks that even determine how rich or poor we are. When one is poor, this connectivity is rather sparse.

Existence of progressive institutions like the MFIs in the midst of poor communities helps to increase the density of socioeconomic networks of poor people first through solidarity groups and group meetings and then by helping them access credit, savings and insurance. Knowledge transfers in the areas of nutrition, hygiene, sanitation, financial literacy, livelihoods and markets also deepen and expand their understanding in these areas. They also become aware of risks and opportunities that they can leverage to get ahead. The solidarity groups become support systems to help each other and gain from the insights of each other.

Establishment of businesses by the poor can expand socioeconomic networks. For example, if an MFI client starts a business to transport people from a remote village to the nearest town (say using a scooter rickshaw), it improves transportation in the locality, which not only helps the clients to earn an income, but also helps the people in the villages to go to town to buy inputs for their businesses, take family members to town to visit doctors or transport products to town for selling in the marketplace.

Slight improvements in communications and connectivity could greatly expand the envelope of social and economic networks and hence opportunities for the poor on a commensurate basis. We have already given examples of mobile phones in expanding markets for the poor. In Chapter 10, we gave the example of fishermen in Kerala who with the advent of mobile phones during the period from 1997 to 2000 were able to gather market intelligence using mobile phones in the nearby towns and travelled in their boats to those markets where they could fetch better price. As a result, fish prices stabilized across the markets. This benefited the buyers, by finding fish when they needed, and the sellers because the price of fish did not gyrate (Karlan and Appel 2012). We have also given example of M-PESA in expanding socioeconomic networks for its users in Kenya and other countries.

In an interesting article in the Harvard Business Review, 'Wealth Happens,' Mark Buchanan (2002) explores how social and economic networks play important roles in the distribution of riches in societies. In economics, Pareto distribution has been used to describe how wealth is distributed in an economy. For example, the Pareto distribution can tell if wealth is too concentrated at the top or more equitably distributed throughout the economy. What is important about Pareto distribution is that, in spite of the wide variation in the economic make-up of countries, more often than not, one finds a small fraction of the populace in an economy hold large fractions of the wealth. Ideally, one would prefer more equitable distribution of wealth to a less equitable distribution. However, stubbornness of Pareto distribution, where a small fraction of the populace hold large fraction of the wealth, has defied easy explanation.

In this article, Buchanan reports of a study by two physicists, Jeane-Philippe Bouchaud and Marc Mezard (2000) who tried to explain the stubbornness of Pareto distribution. Without going into the intricacies of this fascinating study, we quote below the lucid description of the conclusions of this study from Buchanan's article in the Harvard Business Review:

> The findings suggest that the basic inequality in wealth distribution seen in most societies may have little to do with differences in the backgrounds and talents of their citizens. Rather, the distribution appears to be something akin to a law of economic life that emerges naturally as an organizational feature of a network.

In this article, Mark Buchanan focuses on what he calls 'web of wealth.' In this web of wealth, wealth moves around when people buy and sell, that is, transact with each other. Secondly, wealth goes up and down when people invest their surplus wealth. What the paper points out is the following: even if in a society everyone starts out as equal, it is not the transactions one makes with each other but 'a string of positive returns builds a person's wealth not merely by addition but by multiplication, as each subsequent gain grows ever bigger.' In other words, it is the exponential growth of investment return that allows wealth to accumulate. Based on the study, Bouchaud and Mezard found that even if returns on investment are entirely random, huge wealth disparities could result. And one of the ways inequities in wealth can be mitigated (smoothed out) is when greater volume of money flows through an economy, that is, by money changing hands more often.

Based on these findings, one could perhaps conjecture that microfinance by planting the seeds of financial intermediation which provides poor-friendly access to credit, savings, insurance and improved payment systems such as M-PESA, FINO for MT would give rise to more economic interconnectivity and hence increased flow of funds and increased number of financial transactions. With increased flow of funds, and money changing hands more often, one would expect inequality in these communities can be lessened. It would perhaps take long time before real dent can be made in reducing such inequality, but all the same, introduction of microfinance could be considered a small but important step in the right direction. We also discussed in Chapter 4, how, based on the book by Thomas Piketty (2014) titled *Capital in the Twenty-First Century*, one could posit that the relationship $r > g$, that is, average ROR on capital (r) greater than the growth rate of the economy (g) potentially could enable a poor family to earn more from the leveraging power of microcredit, accumulate capital using microsavings and preserve capital using microinsurance and in the process fight poverty and lessen income inequality. However, we need to remember that the process could be rather slow and uneven across the poor populace, but needless to say access to microfinance could enable the poor to take advanatge of $r > g$.

In this context, it is also important to note that in a widely quoted article, 'Finance, Inequality and Poverty: Cross-Country Evidence,' the authors Thorsten Beck, Asli Demirguc-Kunt and Ross Levine (2004) provide evidence to the effect that '…financial development reduces income inequality by disproportionately boosting the incomes of the poor. Countries with better-developed financial intermediaries experience faster declines in measures of both poverty and income inequality.' Based on this evidence, one could also hypothesize, if nothing else, the presence of the microfinance industry in poor communities around the world (by putting down the foundations of formal financial intermediation) must be helping to reduce the menace of poverty and income inequality.

Microfinance and Innovations in Business Models to Fight Poverty

From an evolutionary point of view, MFIs initially piggybacked on NGOs to deliver financial services to the poor. However, based on the experience gained from the delivery of financial instruments and other non-financial services, the MFIs slowly evolved. Many of these institutions became NBFIs and later commercialized to access funding from commercial sources to attain scale and sustainability. Therefore, today we have various models of MFIs that include SHGs, NGO-based MFIs, commercialized MFIs, downscaled commercial banks lending to the poor and many other variations. There are also MFIs like Compartamos Bancos and SKS Microfinance that are listed on stock exchanges.

In this section, we will discuss about the underlying power of ideas that propelled microfinance to a world-wide movement, which has been engendering a new type of business model called 'social business.' The architect of this new model is also Muhammad Yunus of microcredit fame. He traces the origin of the ideas underlying social business model to microcredit. In fact, as we shall discuss in the following, Grameen Bank is one such business. It is important to note that, in the context of some of the criticisms that has been levelled against commercialized MFIs, the underlying philosophy of social business model requires careful consideration which is briefly discussed below.

Broadly speaking, social businesses are dedicated to solving social and environmental problems such as poverty alleviation and improving access to education, health care and livelihood training. Its goal is not to maximize profit. But at the same time, a social business will attain financial and economic sustainability. The following quote from Muhammad Yunus (2011a, 125) describes what a social business is:

> Social business is a new kind of business introduced in the market place with the objective of making a difference in the world. The goods and services created by social business are designed to provide benefits to poor people or to serve society in other ways – for example, by improving health care, cleaning the environment, or enhancing educational opportunities. Investors in social business can get back their investment money, but will not take any dividends from the company. Profits will be plowed back into the company to expand its outreach and improve the quality of its product and service. This idea is encapsulated in this simple definition of social business: 'a non-loss, non-dividend company with a social objective.'

Social businesses are not charity. This is because, in the case of charity, the funds provided do not return to the donor. As a result the funds cannot be recycled, that is, cannot be used for some other purpose. In the case of social businesses, the initial investment amount can be returned to the investor, without adjustment for inflation. As noted above, social businesses make a profit but the objective is not to maximize profit. However, the investor is not entitled to any dividends from the profit the business makes. As a result, on an inflation-adjusted basis the investors should be prepared to lose money. But at the same time, the impact of such investments would be pronounced because profits from the business are plowed back into the MFI.

Social businesses can be divided into two categories. The first type is a non-loss, non-dividend company dedicated to solving social and environmental problems; it is owned by investors who invest all profits in expanding and improving the business. This type of social businesses are called Type I social businesses. The investors in the business could take back their original amount invested in the business over a period of time that can be anywhere from one or two years to even 50 years. The time period has to be agreed to before the investment is made.

The second kind of social business, called a Type II business, is a dividend-paying company. They are similar to conventional businesses, either directly owned by poor people (its shareholders) or by a trust that invests in a set of predefined social causes. Grameen Bank is a Type II social business and is directly owned by the poor people who are its members. They receive dividends from the company. In the opinion of Muhammad Yunus, MFIs should be ideally based on Type I or Type II social business model. The investors in such MFIs do not get any dividends in return for their investments, except in the case of Type II social businesses where its members as shareholders receive dividends.

The following quote from Muhammad Yunus (2011b) provides glimpses into what social businesses like Grameen Bank can achieve:

> Grameen Bank, where I am managing director, has 2,500 branches in Bangladesh. It lends out more than $100 million a month, from loans of less than $10 for beggars in our 'Struggling Members' program, to microenterprise loans of about $1,000. Most branches are financially self-reliant, dependent only on deposits from ordinary Bangladeshis. When borrowers join the bank, they open a savings account. All borrowers have savings account at the bank, many with balances larger than their loans. And every year, the bank's profits are returned to the borrowers—97 percent of them poor women—in the form of dividends.

As we noted earlier, social business model was inspired by the experience gained from establishing and managing Grameen Bank. But at the same time, as Muhammad Yunus (2007) notes in his book *Creating a World Without Poverty: Social Business and the Future of Capitalism,* the concept of social business also emerged by establishing companies in such diverse areas as manufacturing of high-quality nutritious food products, health care, renewable energy, and systems and telecommunications industry that were focused on improving the lives of the poor.[3]

Names of some of the companies under the Grameen family of social businesses include Grameen Danone, Grameen Veolia, Grameen BASF and Grameen Reebok. As far as Grameen Danone is concerned, it is dedicated to solving the problems of malnutrition by selling fortified yogurt with micronutrients that is affordable. The company has been constantly improving the product line and in 2010 it launched a product in rural areas called 'Shakti Doi,' yogurt in squeezable pouches, which eliminates the use of spoons. The product is cheaper, has a longer shelf-life and is also more hygienic. Most importantly, 'Because it is a social business, neither Grameen nor Danone will ever take any dividend out of the company beyond recouping the initial investment. The bottom line for the company is to see how many children overcome their nutrition deficiency each year' (Yunus 2011a, 128). It is important to note that based on the success of Grameen Danone, Group Danone was involved in setting up a mutual fund called 'danone.communities,' which is publicly traded, and has been involved in financing growth of Grameen Danone. Besides, danone.communities is supporting 11 projects in eight countries around the world (Yunus 2011a, 128).

Among other major corporations that came forward to launch a social business with Grameen was Veolia, a supplier of water treatment systems and services around the world. Bangladesh has a major problem of using tube well water for drinking because water is contaminated with naturally occurring arsenic. Grameen Veolia pipes arsenic-free water to several tap points around its plant. They are planning to expand this network further. Grameen Veolia is working on a model to provide water in an affordable and sustainable way. Once the model is perfected, it will be expanded to other villages (Yunus 2011a).

The seminal ideas inherent in establishing Grameen bank were powerful enough to start the social business model, which has been adopted by Grameen family of social businesses. One could perhaps assume many of the ideas that are central to microfinance have influenced other business models such as 'CSV' model of Michael E. Porter and Mark R. Kramer. The underlying concepts of CSV model has been beautifully enunciated by Michael E. Porter and Mark R. Kramer (2011) in their Harvard Business Review Article "Creating Shared Value—How to reinvent capitalism—and unleash a wave of innovation and growth." It emphasizes how solving social and environmental problems while making economic returns has to be the goals of any business. This is because, as Porter and Kramer state cogently, '...societal needs, not just conventional economic needs, define markets,' and '...social harms or weaknesses frequently create internal costs for firms ...'.

In their paper, Porter and Kramer (2011) appropriately highlight how role played by the social entrepreneurs has been able to create shared value at the BOP.

> Businesses are not the only players in finding profitable solutions to social problems. A whole generation of social entrepreneurs is pioneering new product concepts that meet social needs using viable business models. Because they are not locked into narrow traditional business thinking, social entrepreneurs are often well ahead of established corporations in discovering these opportunities. Social enterprises that create shared value can scale up far more rapidly than purely social programs, which often suffer from an inability to grow and become self-sustaining.

In the context of commercialized MFIs going after high profitability and shareholder value creation without regard for over-indebtedness and value creation for their poor clients, social business model of Muhammad Yunus does present strikingly different philosophy that needs careful consideration by the microfinance industry.

Conclusion

In spite of the many challenges that the microfinance industry is up against, the financial instruments and non-financial complementary services offered by the industry provide a wide range of options, which the poor can leverage in a concerted manner to smooth consumption, mitigate asset depletion, build social and human capital, increase their interaction with social and economic networks, and leverage institutional capital, and in the process monetize their capabilities to fight poverty. Not all MFIs offer all the financial products. Similarly not all of them provide a wide range of non-financial complementary products as well. Large numbers of them remain minimalist institutions by offering only microcredit.

As we explored in this chapter, the benefits of microfinance is not confined to the use of specific financial instruments or non-financial complementary services. The synergy that emanate from using these instruments in parallel is greater as opposed to when households use the instruments in a piecemeal fashion. In fact a household that has some savings, health insurance and exposure to microcredit, is financially much stronger than a household that entirely relies on microcredit. Similarly, a poor person who acquires a skill through livelihood training, uses the skill in her business and knows how to market her products has a better income potential than someone who borrows from an MFI and does not possess any skill and does not know how to market her products.

On a much bigger scale, microfinance has made it possible to lay down the foundations of financial intermediation at the grass-root level that is so important for the poor in their fight against poverty. We also explored in this chapter how institutions that have been built to deliver microfinance and other complementary services give rise to social and economic connectivity, which the poor can leverage to improve their economic well-being.

None of the financial products and complementary services microfinance offers is perfect. Today we have modest expectations of microcredit impact in terms of alleviating poverty on a large scale. At the same time, in order to deliver microsavings and microinsurance a great deal of work needs to be done starting with product design to their delivery on the ground. The objectives of affordability, delivery of value for the clients, and attainment of scale and sustainability are difficult to achieve without experimentation. However, microfinance platform has a long history of experimenting with outside-the-box ideas to design and deliver products and services that the poor value. One would expect that the industry would rise up to the challenge in the coming years to provide an array of financial instruments and complementary services for the benefit of the poor that they will leverage in their fight against poverty.

Notes

1. Ian Smillie. 2009. *Freedom from Want: The Remarkable Success Story of BRAC, the Global Grassroots Organization That's Winning the Fight Against Poverty*, p. 258. Sterling, VA: Kumarian Press.
2. Jeffrey M.O. Brien, 'The Only Nonprofit That Matters,' *Fortune*, March 3, 2008.
3. Muhammad Yunus with Karl Weber. 2007. *Creating a World Without Poverty: Social Business and the Future of Capitalism*, pp. 78–82. New York: Public Affairs.

Bibliography

Abed, Fazle Hasan, Mahabub Hossain, Sussan Davis and Ron Dubtisky. 2011. 'Using Microfinance Plus Agricultural Services to Improve Rural Livelihoods and Food Security' in Sam Daley-Harris and Anna Awimbo (eds.), *New Pathways Out of Poverty*, pp. 143–83. Sterling, Virginia: Kumarian Press.

Acharya, Namrata. 2014a. 'Microfinance industry coming back to life,' *Business Standard*, 8 February, Kolkata. Available online at http://www.business-standard.com/article/printer-friendly-vrsion?article_id=114020800728_1 (downloaded on 12 June 2014).

———. 2014b. 'Bengal, Tamil Nadu usurp Andhra as new MFI hubs,' *Business Standard*, 7 March, Kolkata. Available online at http://www.business-standard.com/article/printer-friendly-vrsion?article_id=114030400482_1 (downloaded on 12 June 2014).

———. 2014c. 'Bandhan sees 37% growth in gross loan portfolio,' *Business Standard*, 19 April, Kolkata. Available online at http://www.business-standard.com/article/printer-friendly-vrsion?article_id=114041900073_1 (downloaded on 12 June 2014).

Allen, Franklin, Asli Demirguc-Kunt, Leora Klapper and Maria Soledad Martinez Peria. 2012. 'The Foundations of Financial Inclusion: Understanding Ownership and Use of Formal Accounts' Policy Research Working Paper 6290, Development Research Group, Finance and Private Sector Development Team. Washington, DC: The World Bank.

Allianz AG, GTZ and UNDP. 2006. 'India: Microinsurance Demand and Market Prospects,' Available online at http://www.undp.org/content/dam/aplaws/publication/en/publications/capacity-development/microinsurance-demand-and-market-prospects-for-india/Microinsurance.pdf (downloaded on 7 January 2013).

Alvarado, Javier and Francisco Galarza. 2003. 'ANED, Bolivia: Pioneering Rural Microleasing' in Mark D. Wenner, Javier Alvarado, Francisco Galaraza (eds.), *Promising Practices in Rural Finance: Experiences from Latin America and the Caribbean*, pp. 329–46. Lima: Centro Peruano de Estudios Sociales.

Annamalai, Kuttayan and Sachin Rao. 2007. 'E-choupals and Rural Transformation—Web-based Tools for Indian Farmers' in Deepa Narayan and Elena Glinskaya (eds.), *Ending Poverty in South Asia—Ideas That Work*, pp. 244–76. Washington, DC: The World Bank.

Armendáriz, Beatriz and Jonathan Morduch. 2010. *The Economics of Microfinance*. Cambridge, Massachusetts: The MIT Press.

Ashraf, Nava, Dean Karlan and Wesley Yin. 2006. 'Tying Odysseus to the Mast: Evidence from a Commitment Savings Product in the Philippines,' *The Quarterly Journal of Economics*, 121 (2): 673–97. New York: Oxford University Press.

Baba, Karina. 2010. 'Can Mobile Money be Profitable? We Asked Mobile Money Managers.' Blog, Washington, DC: CGAP. September 16. Available online at http://www.cgap.org/blog/can-mobile-money-be-profitable-we-asked-mobile-money-managers (downloaded on 16 January 2013).

Bailey, Ronald. 2007. 'The Secrets of Intangible Wealth,' *The Wall Street Journal*, September: 29–30. Available online at http://online.wsj.com/article/SB119103046614343129-lMyQjAxMTE0OTExODAxMzgwWj (downloaded on 19 July 2014).

Bandiera, Oriana, R. Burgess, N. Das, S. Gulesci, I Rasul and M. Sulaiman. 2012. 'Can Basic Entrepreneurship Transform the Economic Lives of the Poor?' CGAP-Ford Graduation Program, Reaching the poorest global meeting. Available online at http://graduation.cgap.org/wp-content/uploads/2012/07/ultraPoorPSlidesOBCGapJuly12.pdf (downloaded on 21 February 2013).

Banerjee, Abhijit V. 2009. 'The Game Changer,' *Hindustan Times*, November 24, New Delhi.

Banerjee, Abhijit V. and Esther Duflo. 2006. 'The Economic Lives of the Poor,' Available online at http://economis.mit.edu/files/530 (downloaded on 28 November 2012).

———. 2010. 'Giving Credit Where it is Due,' Available online at http://economis.mit.edu/files/5416 (downloaded on 30 November 2012).

———. 2011. *Poor Economics: A Radical Rethinking of the Way to Fight Global Poverty*. New York: Public Affairs.

Banerjee, Abhijit V., Esther Duflo, Rachel Glennerster and Cynthia Kinnan. 2010. 'The Miracle of Microfinance? Evidence from a Randomized Evaluation.' BREAD Working Paper No. 278, Bureau of Research and Economic Analysis of Development. Available online at http://www.ipl.econ.duke.edu/bread/papers/working/278.pdf (downloaded on 31 December 2012).

Banerjee, Abhijit V., Roland Benabou and Dilip Mookherjee (eds.). 2006. *Understanding Poverty*. New York: Oxford University Press.

BASIX. 2007. '11th Annual Report 2006–2007.' BASIX: Hyderabad, India.

Beck, Thorsten, Asli Demirguc-Kunt and Ross Levine. 2004. 'Finance, Inequality and Poverty: Cross-Country Evidence,' NBER Working Paper No. W 10979, December.

Bennett, Lynn and Carlos E. Cuevas. 1996. 'Sustainable Banking With The Poor,' *Journal of International Development*, 8(2): 145–52.

Bhatt, Ela R. 2006. *We Are Poor but So Many—The Story of Self-Employed Women in India*. New York: Oxford University Press.

Bouchaud, Jean-Philippe and Marc Mezard. 2000. 'Wealth Condensation in a Simple Model of Economy,' *Physica* 282 (2000): 536–45.

BRAC. 2013. 'Aarong: A BRAC Social Enterprise—Crafting better lives for 65,000 rural artisans,' Available online at http://www.brac.net/content/aarong (downloaded on 26 February 2013).

Bruck, Connie, 2006. 'Millions for Millions,' *The New Yorker.*

Brugmann, Jeb, C.K. Prahalad. 2007. 'Cocreating Business's New Social Compact,' *Harvard Business Review,* February.

BS Reporter. 2014. 'Bandhan to open 700 bank branches in first phase,' *Business Standard,* 2 May, Kolkata. Available online at http://www.business-standard.com/article/printer-friendly-vrsion?article_id=114050201548_1 (downloaded on 12 June 2014).

Buchanan, Mark. 2002. 'Wealth Happens—Wealth Distribution and Role of Networks,' Working Knowledge for Business Leaders, *Harvard Business Review,* April 29.

Chen, Greg, Stephen Rasmusssen and Xavier Reille. 2010. 'Growth and Vulnerabilities in Microfinance.' Focus Note No. 61. Washington, DC: CGAP.

Christen, Robert Peck, N. Srinivasan and Rodger Voorhies. 2005. 'Managing to go down market: regulated financial institutions and the move into micro-savings,' in *Savings Services for the Poor: An Operational Guide.* Bloomfield, Connecticut: Kumarian Press.

Churchill, Craig. 2006. *Protecting the Poor: A Microinsurance Compendium.* Geneva: ILO.

CGAP. 1996. 'Microcredit Interest Rates.' Occasional Paper No.1, Revised in August. Washington, DC: CGAP.

———. 2006. *Good Practice Guidelines for Funders of Microfinance,* 2nd ed. Washington, DC: CGAP.

———. 2010. 'Andhra Pradesh 2010: Global Implications of the Crisis in Indian Microfinance,' Focus Note No. 67, Washington, DC: CGAP.

Collins, Daryl, Jonathan Morduch, Stuart Rutherford and Orlanda Ruthven. 2009. *Portfolios of the Poor: How the World's Poor Live on $2 a Day.* Pinceton, New Jersey: Princeton University Press.

Colvin, Geoff. 2009. 'A CEO masters micro-credit,' *Fortune Magazine.* January 12. Available online at http://money.cnn.com/2009/01/09/magazines/fortune/colvin_barnevik.fortune/index.htm (downloaded on 20 March 2013).

Confederation of Indian Industry and the World Bank. 2005. 'National Conference on Emerging Business Opportunities at the Bottom of the Pyramid—Transforming Indian Economy through Profitability.' December 20–21.

Counts, Alex. 2008. *Small Loans Big Dreams: How Nobel Prize Winner Muhammad Yunus and Microfinance Are Changing the World.* New York: John Wiley & Sons, Inc.

Counts, Alex and Lauren Moore. 2012. 'Mobile Phones and the Rise of the Microentrepreneurs,' The Blog, Huff Post Impact. Available online at http://www.huffingtonpost.com/alex-counts//mobile-phones-microfinance_b_1881929.html (downloaded on 4 December 2012).

CRISIL. 2009. *India Top 50 Microfinance Institutions: A Financial Awareness Initiative of CRISIL.* Available online at http://www.crisil.com/pdf/ratings/CRISIL-ratings-india-top-50-mfis.pdf (downloaded on 24 February 2014).

Das, Narayan C. and Raniya Shams. 2011. 'Asset Transfer Programs for the Ultra Poor: A Randomized Control Trial Evaluation,' CFPR Working Paper No. 22. Available online at http://www.bracresearch.org/workingpapers/TUP_WP.22.pdf (downloaded on 4 December 2012).

Dasgupta, Partha. 2007. *Economics: A Very Short Introduction.* New York: Oxford University Press.

Datar, Srikant M., Marc J. Epstein and Kristi Yuthas. 2008. 'In Microfinance, Clients Must Come First,' in *Stanford Social Innovation Review*, pp. 38–45. Available online at http://www.ssireview.org/articles/entry/in_microfinance_clients_must_come_first.

Davis, Susan. 2012. 'Good News for the Ultra Poor,' CGAP. Available online at http://www.cgap.org/blog/good-news-ultra-poor/ (downloaded on 16 February 2013).

De Mel, Suresh, David McKenzie and Christopher Woodruff. 2008. 'Returns to Capital in Microenterprises: Evidence from a Field Experiment,' *The Quarterly Journal of Economics*, 123 (4): 1329–72.

De Soto, Hernando. 2000. *The Mystery of Capital—Why Capitalism Triumphs in the West and Fails Everywhere Else.* New York: Basic Books.

De Young, Robert and Ronnie J. Phillips. 2009. *Payday Loan Pricing.* Economic Research Department, The Federal Reserve Bank of Kansas City, ISSN 1936-5330, RWP 09-07.

Deelen, Linda, Mauricio Dupleich, Louis Othieno and Oliver Wakelin. 2003. *Leasing for small and Micro Enterprises: A Guide for Designing and Managing Leasing Schemes in Developing Countries.* Geneva: International Labour Organization.

Demombynes, Gabriel and Aaron Thegeya. 2012. 'Kenya's Mobile Revolution and the Promise of Mobile Savings,' Policy Research Working Paper 5988. The World Bank: Washington, DC.

Denyer, Simon. 2011. 'India's Baby Boom: Dividend or Disaster?' *The Washington Post*, October 16.

Dichter, Thomas. 2007. 'Introduction to "What's Wrong with Microfinance?"' in Thomas Dichter and Malcolm Harper (eds.), *What's Wrong with Microfinance?* Warwickshire: Practical Action Publishing.

Dowla, Asif Ud. 2004. 'Microleasing—The Grameen Bank Experience,' *Journal of Microfinance* 6 (2): 138–60.

Dowla, Asif and Dipal Barua. 2006. *The Poor Always Pay Back: The Grameen II Story.* Bloomfield, Connecticut: Kumarian Press Inc.

Drake, Deborah and Maria Otero. 1992. *Alchemist for the Poor: NGOs as Financial Institutions.* ACCION International.

Duncan, Natricia. 2014. "Crowdfunding development: 'Kiva's aim is to make microfinance easy," *Impact and Effectiveness Hub* in *The Guardian*, June 10.

Available online at http://www.theguardian.com/global-development-professionals-network/2014/jun/10/crowd-funding-for-development/print (downloaded on 12 June 2014).

Edgcomb, Elaine and Laura Barton. 1998. 'Social Intermediation and Microfinance Programs: A Literature Review,' The SEEP Network. Bethesda: Development Alternatives Inc. Available online at http://pdf.usaid.gov/pdf_docs/PNACD060/.pdf (downloaded on 18 January 2013).

ET Bureau. 2014. RBI grants 'in-principle' approval to IDFC, Bandhan for new bank licenses, *The Economic Times*, April 3, Mumbai/Kolkata. Available online at http://articles.economictimes.indiatimes.com/2014-04-03/news/48834978_1_bank-licenses-bandhan-financial-chandra-shekhar-ghosh (downloaded on 20 June 2014).

Field, Erica, Rohini Pande, John Papp, Y. Jeanette Park. 2012. 'Repayment Flexibility Can Reduce Financial Stress: A Randomized Control Trial with Microfinance Clients in India,' *PLOS| ONE*, DOI: 10.1371. Available online at http://www.plosone.org/article/info:doi/10.1371//journal.pone.00045679 (downloaded on 19 December 2012).

FINO. 2012. 'FINO Pay Tech to facilitate meaningful Financial Inclusion in Kerala,' FINO Press Release November 21. Available online at http://www.finopaytech.com/media-lounge/press-releases/news/5 (downloaded on 25 February 2013).

Flannery, Matt. 2007. 'Kiva and the Birth of Person-to-Person Microfinance,' *Innovations* (Winter-Spring issue), 2 (1–2): 31–56.

———. 2009. 'Kiva at Four,' *Innovations*, Special Edition for the Skoll World Forum 2009. Cambridge: MIT Press.

Fukuyama, Francis. 2001. 'Social capital, civil society and development,' *Third World Quarterly*, 22 (1): 7–20.

Gallardo, Joselito. 1997. '*Leasing to Support Small Businesses and Microenterprises*,' Policy Research Working Paper 1857. Financial Sector Development Department, Washington, DC: The World Bank.

Gates, Bill. 2008. 'A New Approach to Capitalism in the 21st Century,' Remarks by Bill Gates, Chairman, Microsoft Corporation, World Economic Forum 2008, Davos, Switzerland. Available online at http://www.microsoft.com/en-us/news/exec/billg/speeches/2008/01-24wefdavos.aspx (downloaded on 17 January 2013).

Ghate, Prabhu. 2006. 'Serving Migrants Sustainably—A Case Study of Remittance Services Provided by a Microfinance Institution in India,' *ADB Finance for the Poor*, 7 (1).

———. 2007. *Indian Microfinance: The Challenges of Rapid Growth*. New Delhi: SAGE Publications.

Goldberg, Mike. 2008. 'Microleasing: Overcoming Equipment Financing Barriers,' *en breve*, Number 140. Washington, DC: The World Bank.

Grameen Bank. 2011. 'Grameen Bank at a Glance, October 2011.' Available online at http://www.grameen-info.org/index.php?option=com_content&task=view&id=26&Itemid=175 (downloaded on 27 November 2012).

Gray, Abby and Sarah Bel. 2010. 'New Channels to Get Insurance to the Poor,' Microinsurance Innovation Facility, ILO. Available online at http://www.

ilo.org/public/english/employment/miffacility/download/new_channels.pdf (downloaded on 7 January 2013).

Grewal, Swati. 2012. Perspective on IRDA's proposed 'everything product'. Chennai: IFMR Trust. Available online at http://www.ifmr.co.in/blog/2012/06/18/perspective-on-irdas-propsed-everything-product/ (downloaded on 3 September 2014).

Groves, Susanna. 2012. 'Remittances Hit $534 Billion in 2012, Setting New Record'. Available online at http://diasporaalliance.org/remittances-hit-a-record-high-of-534-billion-in-2012/ (downloaded on 3 September 2014).

Gunaranjan, P. S. 2008. 'Micro insurance for protecting livelihood,' BASIX paper for Microfinance Summit, February 14-16. Kathmandu, Nepal (downloaded on 2 February 2013).

Hammond, Allen L., William J. Kramer, Robert S. Katz, Julia T. Tran, Courtland Walker. 2007. The Next 4 Billion. Washington, DC: World Resources Institute and International Finance Corporation.

Hand in Hand International. 2012. 'Results.' Available online at http://www.hihinternational.org/What-We-Do/Results.aspx (downloaded on 20 March 2013).

Harper, Malcolm. 2007. 'Microfinance and Farmers, Do They Fit?' in Thomas Dichter and Malcolm Harper (eds.), What's Wrong with Microfinance? Warwickshire, UK: Practical Action Publishing.

Harper, Malcolm, Lalitha Iyer, and Jane Rosser. 2011. Whose Sustainability Counts? BASIX's Long March from Microfinance to Livelihoods. Sterling, Virginia: Kumarian Press.

Helms, Brigit. 2006. Access for All: Building Inclusive Financial Systems. Washington, DC: CGAP, The World Bank.

Hirschland, Madeline. 2005. Savings Services for the Poor. Bloomfield, Connecticut: Kumarian Press Inc..

How We Made It in Africa. 2012. 'Kenya's Safaricom Projects Bigger M-Pesa Role in Revenue,' Business in Focus, ICT, Kenya, May 11. Available online at http://howwemadeitinafrica.com/kenyas-safaricom-projects-bigger-m-pesa-role-in -revenue/16768/ (downloaded on 24 February 2013).

IBEF (India Brand Equity Foundation). 2012. 'Networking for India's Farmers.' Available online at http://www.india-at-davos-2012.ibef.org/download/Networking—for-India-farmers.pdf (downloaded on 20 January 2013)

IFC. 'Kilimo Salama—Index-Based Agriculture Insurance: A Product Case Study,' IFC Advisory Services| Access to Finance, Ideas 42. Washington, DC: IFC (downloaded on 3 February 2013).

IFMR Trust. 2010. 'Correspondent Banking in Brazil,' IFMR Trust, July 28. Available online at http://www.ifmr.co.in/blog/2010/07/28/correspondent-bank-in-brazil/ (downloaded on 24 January 2013).

IFMR. 2011. 'Targeting the Hard-Core Poor—An Impact Evaluation,' IFMR Research, Center for Micro Finance. Available online at http://www.centre-for-microfinance.org/research-project/financial-inclusion/tarheting-hard-core-poor-impact-evaluation/ (downloaded on 16 February 2013).

India Knowledge@Wharton. 2010. 'FINO Shows a Low-cost Way out of India's Microfinance Mess'. Available online at http://knowledge.wharton.upenn. edu/india/article.cmf?articleid=4545 (downloaded on 16 January 2013).

Intermediate Technology Consultants (ITC) & Development Outcomes. 'Project Completion Report,' AG 2630 Micro Leasing for the Poor People's Enterprises, Enterprise Development Innovation Fund—DFID. Available online at http:// www.itcltd.com/microleasing/reports.htm (downloaded on 7 January 2013).

Isern, Jennifer, Rani Despande and Judith van Doorn. 2005. 'Crafting Money Transfer Strategy: Guidance for Pro-Poor Financial Service Providers,' *Occasional Paper*, No. 10. Washington, DC: CGAP.

Jackson, Mathew O. 2008. *Social and Economic Networks*. Princeton, New Jersey: Princeton University Press.

Karlan, Dean and Chris Udry. 2012. 'Impact of Village Savings and Loan Associations: Finding from Ghana,' Innovations for Poverty Action (IPA), Savings Conference, University of Ghana. Available online at http://www.povertyaction.org/sites/default/files/conference_accra_mar2012_thuysbaert_vsla.pdf (downloaded on 9 January 2013).

Karlan, Dean and Jacob Appel. 2012. *More than Good Intentions: Improving the Ways the World's Poor Borrrow, Save, Far, Lear, and Stay Healthy*. New York: Penguin Group.

Karlan, Dean and Jonathan Zinman. 2011. 'Microcredit in Theory and Practice: Using Randomized Credit Scoring for Impact Evaluation,' *Science* 332 (2011): 1278–84.

Karnani, Aneel. 2007. 'Microfinance Misses Its Mark,' *Stanford Social Innovation Review*, Summer.

Kasturi Rangan, V., John A. Quelch, Gustavo Herrero and Brooke Barton. 2007. *Business Solutions for the Global Poor: Creating Social and Economic Value*. California: John Wiley & Sons, Inc.

Kennedy, Kevin. 2010. 'The Potential of Leasing through Microfinance Institutions in Emerging Markets,' Master's Degree Dissertation in Development Finance, University of Reading. September.

Khandker, Shahidur R. 2005. 'Microfinance and Poverty: Evidence Using Panel Data from Bangladesh.' *World Bank Economic Review*, 19 (2): 263–86.

Kiva. 2012a. 'About Us.' Available online at http://www.kiva.org/about (downloaded on 30 October 2012).

———. 2012b. 'How Kiva Works, The Long Version.' Available online at http:// www.kiva.org/about/how/even-more (downloaded on 30 October 2012).

———. 2012c. 'Stats.' Available online at http://www.kiva.org/about/stats (downloaded on 30 October 2012).

Koven, Richard and Emily Zimmerman. 2011. 'Is There a Business Case for Microinsurance? A review of recent literature,' Micro Insurance Learning and Knowledge, Micro Insurance Centre. Available online at http://www. micronsurancecentre.org/.../810-is-there-a-business-case-for-microinsurance (downloaded on 7 January 2013).

Kristof, Nicholas D. 2012. 'Doughnuts Defeating Poverty,' *The New York Times*. Available online at http://www.nytimes.com/2012/07/05/opinion/dougnuts-defeating-poverty.html (downloaded on 11 March 2013).

Kumar, Kabir, Claudia McKay and Sarah Rotman. 2010. 'Microfinance and Mobile Banking: The Story So Far,' Focus Note No. 62. Washington, DC: CGAP.

Ledgerwood, Joanna. 1999. *Microfinance Hand Book—An Institutional and Financial Perspective*. Washington, DC: The World Bank.

Ledgerwood, Joanna, Victoria White, Monica Brand, Gabriela Braun, Deborah Burand, Alfred Hannig, Kelly Hattel and Marguerite Robinson. 2006. *Transforming Microfinance Institutions: Providing Full Financial Services to the Poor*. Washington, DC: The World Bank.

Lee, Yoolim and Ruth David. 2010. 'Suicides in India Revealing How Men Made a Mess of Microcredit,' *Bloomberg Markets Magazine*. Available online at http://www.bloomberg.com/news/2010-12-28/suicides-among-borrowers-in-india-show-how-men-made-a-mess-of-microcredit.html (downloaded on 3 September 2014).

Lewis, Jonathan C. 2008. 'Microloan Sharks,' *Stanford Social Innovation Review*, Summer:55-59. Available online at www.ssireview.org.

Littlefield, Elizabeth, Brigit Helms and David Porteous. 2006. *Financial Inclusion 2015: Four Scenarios for the Future of Microfinance*. Washington, DC: CGAP.

Lützenkirchen, Cédric and Christian Weistroffer. 2012. 'Microfinance in Evolution: An Industry between Crisis and Advancement,' in Current Issues: Global Financial Markets, Deutsche Bank. Frankfurt: DB Research Management.

Maes, Jan P. and Larry R. Reed. 2012. 'State of the Microcredit Summit Campaign Report 2012.' Available online at http://www.microcreditsummit.org/reports/socr/2012/WEB_SOCR_2012.English.pdf (downloaded on 20 October 2012).

Mahajan, Vijay. 2007a. 'Beyond Microfinance' in Caroline Moser (ed.), *Reducing Global Poverty: The Case for Asset Accumulation*. Washington, DC: Brookings Institution.

———. 2007b. 'From Microcredit to Livelihood Finance' in Thomas Dichter and Malcolm Harper (eds.), *What is Wrong with Microfinance*, pp. 241–49. Warwickshire, UK: Practical Action Publishing.

Maleika, Marc and Annet T. Kuriakose. 2008. 'Micro Insurance: Extending Pro-Poor Risk Management through the Social Fund Platform,' *Innovations Notes*, 5 (2). Washington, DC: The World Bank.

Mas, Ignacio. 2009. 'Reframing Micro-finance: Enabling Small Savings and Payments, Everywhere,' The Commonwealth Heads of Government Meeting, November. Available online at http://papers.ssrn.com/sol3/papers.cfm?abstract_id=1552755 (downloaded on 24 January 2013).

Mas, Igancio and Dan Radcliffe. 2010. 'Mobile Payments Go Viral: M-PESA in Kenya.' March 1. Available online at http://papers.ssrn.com/sol3/papers.cfm?abstract_id=1593388 (downloaded on 16 January 2013).

Matin, Imran, Munshi Sulaiman and M. A. Saleque. 2007. 'Imagining Microfinance More Boldly: Unleashing the True Potential of Microfinance' in

Thomas Dichter and Malcolm Harper (eds.), *What is Wrong with Microfinance*, pp. 23–34. Warwickshire, UK: Practical Action Publishing.

McKenzie, David and Christopher Woodruff. 2008. 'Experimental Evidence on Returns to Capital and Access to Finance in Mexico.' Available online at http://siteresources.worldbank.org/DEC/Resources/Experimental_Evidence_on_Returns_to_Capital_and_Access_to_Finance_in_Mexico.pdf (downloaded on 1 December 2012).

McKinnon, Ronald. 1973. *Money and Capital in Economic Development.* Washington, DC: The Brookings Institution.

Metcalfe, Marcia, Sheila Chanani and Myka Reinsch with Soumitra Datta. 2010. 'Costs of Health Education and Health Product Distribution—Bandhan's Experience in India,' Freedom from Hunger, Research Paper No. 10A. Available online at http://www.microfinancegateway.org/gm/document-1.9.47064/MAHP.CostBenefitPaper.Bandhan.Eng_.pdf (downloaded on 4 January 2013).

Meyer, Richard. 2001. 'Microfinance, Poverty Alleviation, and Improving Food Security: Implications for India,' Rural Finance Program. Columbus, Ohio: The Ohio State University.

Microfinance Gateway. 2009. 'Microfinance Now: An Interview with Vijay Mahajan.' Available online at http://microfinancegateway.org/p/site/m/template.rc/1.26.11703/ (downloaded on 4 January 2013).

Micro Insurance Network/ADA asbl. 2011. 'Commercial Insurers in Microinsurance.' Available online at http://www.microinsurancenetwork.org/publication/fichier/MiN_Commercial_insurers_2011.pdf (downloaded on 7 January 2013).

Microcredit Summit E-NEWS. 2008. Beggars, Savers and Borrowers: the 'Good Families' of Jamii Bora, (Transcription of an interview Microcredit Summit Campaign Director Sam Daley-Harris conducted with Jamii Bora founder Ingrid Munro in October 2007). Available online at http://www.microcreditsummit.org/enews/2008-03_jamiibora.html (downloaded on 25 January 2013).

Mitra, Subrata Kumar. 2009. 'Exploitative Microfinance Interest Rates,' *Asian Social Science* 5 (5): 87–93.

Mookherjee, Dilip, 2006. 'Poverty Persistence and Design of Antipoverty Policies.' in Abhijit Vinayak Banerjee, Ronald Benabou and Dilip Mookherjee (eds.), *Understanding Poverty*, pp. 231–41. New York: Oxford University Press.

Mor, Nachiket. 2006. 'Some thoughts on Access to Markets as a Strategy to Address Poverty,' Working Paper Series, Centre for Development Finance. Chennai: Institute for Financial Management and Research.

Morduch, Jonathan. 1998. 'Does Microfinance Really Help the Poor? New Evidence from Flagship Programs in Bangladesh,' Financial Access Initiative. New York: NYU Wagner Graduate School.

———. 2006. 'Micro Insurance: The Next Revolution?' in Abhijit Vinayak Banerjee, Ronald Benabou and Dilip Mookherjee (eds.), *Understanding Poverty*, pp. 337–55. New York: Oxford University Press.

———. 2007. 'Smart subsidy.' in Bernd Balkenhol (ed.), *Microfinance and Public Policy: Outreach Performance and Efficiency*, pp. 72–85. New York: Palgrave Macmillan

Muhammad, Anu. 2009. 'Grameen and Microcredit: A Tale of Corporate Success,' *Economic and Political Weekly*, XLIV(35): 35–42.

Mullainathan, Sendhil, 2006. 'Better Choices to Reduce Poverty' in Abhijit Vinayak Banerjee, Ronald Benabou and Dilip Mookherjee (eds.), *Understanding Poverty*, pp. 379–87. New York: Oxford University Press.

Mullainathan, Sendhil and Shafir Eldar. 2013. *Scarcity: Why Having Too Little Means So Much.* New York: Times Books, Henry Holt and Company.

Murphy, Ted. 2012. 'Using Microfinance to Bring Clean Water to India's Poor,' The Blog, Huff Post. Available online at http://www.huffingtonpost/tommurphy/using-microfinance-to-bri_b_1307079.html (downloaded on 10 November 2012).

Mutesasira, Leonard K., Sylvia Osinde, Nthenya R. Mule. 2001. 'Potential for Leasing Products: Asset Financing for Micro- and Small Business in Tanzania and Uganda,' *MicroSave.* Nairobi, Kenya. Available online at http://practicalaction.org/microleasing/docs/microsave%20potential%20for%20leasing.pdf (downloaded on 4 September 2014).

Mwaura, Judy Wanja and Sathirakorn Pongopanich. 2012. 'Access to Healthcare: The Role of a Community Based Health Insurance in Kenya,' *Pan African Medical Journal*, 12 (35). Available online at http//www.panafrican-med-journal.com/content/article/12/35/full/ (downloaded on 10 January 2013).

Nallari, Raj and Breda Griffith. 2011. *Understanding Growth and Poverty—Theory, Policies and Empirics.* Washington, DC: The World Bank.

North, Douglas C. 2005. *Understanding the Process of Economic Change.* Princeton, New Jersey: Princeton University Press.

O'Brien, Jeffrey M. 2008. 'The Only Nonprofit That Matters,' *Fortune*, March 3. http://money.cnn.com/magazines/fortune/fortune_archive/2008/03/03/103796533/index.htm

Ogden, Tim. 2012. 'Excerpt from Interview with David McKenzie, Part I.' Available online at http://www.philanthrophyaction.com/nc/excerpt_from_interview_with_david_mckenzie_part_i/ (downloaded on 29 November 2012).

Oikocredit. 2012. 'Offering more than microfinance in India' (downloaded from Oikocredit website on 24 February 2013).

Omwansa, Tony. 2009. 'M-PESA: Progress and Propsects,' Innovations/Mobile World Congress. Available online at http://www.strathmore.edu/pdf/innov-gsma-omwansa.pdf (downloaded on 6 January 2013).

Othieno, Louis. 'Exploring Microleasing for Poor People's Enterprises Project—Key Lessons Learnt,' Development Outcomes Ltd. Available online at http://practicalaction.org/ microleasing/docs/Lessons%20learning%20document.pdf (downloaded on 14 January 2013).

Parente, Stephen L. and Prescott Edward C. 2002. *Barriers to Riches.* Walras-Pareto Lectures, Ecole des Hautes Etudes Commerciales, Universite de Lausanne: MIT Press.

Pavoni, Silvia. 2010. 'Reaching Out to the Financially Excluded,' *The Banker*, May 28.

Peachey Stephen and Alan Roe. 2006. 'Access to Finance: What Does It Mean and How Do Savings Banks Foster Access,' Perspectives 49. Brussels: A Study for the World Savings Bank Institute (WSBI).

Piketty, Thomas. 2014. *Capital in the Twenty-First Century*. Cambridge, Massachusetts: Harvard University Press.

Pinder, Caroline. 2001. 'SELFINA (SERO Lease and Finance Company)—Tanzania.' Available online at http://sed.manchester.ac.uk/research/iarc/edais/word.../ SELFINA.doc (downloaded on 14 January 2013).

Pitt, Mark and Shahidur Khandker. 1998. 'The Impact of Group-based Credit Programs on Poor Households in Bangladesh: Does the Gender of Participants Matter?' *Journal of Political Economy*: 106 (5): 958–96.

Porter, Michael E. and Mark R. Kramer. 2011. 'Creating Shared Value,' *Harvard Business Review*, January–February.

Prahalad, C. K. 2005a. 'Democratization of Commerce.' Published in National Conference on Emerging Business Opportunities at the Bottom of the Pyramid—Transforming the Indian Rural Economy through Profitability, Confederation of Indian Industry and The World Bank, December 20–21.

———. 2005b. *The Fortune at the Bottom of the Pyramid: Eradicating Poverty through Profits*. New Jersey: Wharton School Publishing.

Putnam, Robert. 2000. *Bowling Alone, The Collapse and Revival of American Community*. New York: Simon and Schuster.

RBI. 2006. 'Financial Inclusion by Extension of Banking Services—Use of Business Facilitators and Correspondents'. Available online at http://www.rbi. org.in/Scripts/BS_CircularIndexDisplay.aspx?id=2718 (downloaded on 24 January 2013).

Ratha, Dilip. 2006. 'Leveraging Remittances for Development' in James F. Hollifield, Pia M. Orrenius and Thomas Osang (eds.), *Migration, Trade, and Development*, pp. 173–86. Dallas, Texas: Federal Reserve Bank of Dallas.

Ray, Debraj. 2014. 'Nit Piketty: A Comment on Thomas Piketty's *Capital in the Twenty First Century*,' Available online at http://www.econ.nyu.edu/user/ debraj/Papers/Piketty.pdf (downloaded on 23 June 2014).

Reddy, C. S. 2010. 'Will the Indian SHG Movement Withstand Competition from MFIs?' CGAP Blog. Available online at http://www.cgap.org/blog/ will-indian-shg-movement-withstand-competition-mfis (downloaded on 10 February 2013).

Reed, Larry R. 2013. 'State of the Microcredit Summit Campaign Report 2013.' Available online at http://www.microcreditsummit.org/reports/socr/2012/ WEB_SOCR_2012.English.pdf (downloaded on 15 August 2013).

Rhyne, Elisabeth. 2009. *Microfinance for Bankers and Investors: Understanding the Opportunities and Challenges of the Market at the Bottom of the Pyramid*. New York: McGraw Hill.

Robinson, Marguerite S. 2001. *The Microfinance Revolution—Sustainable Finance for the Poor*. Washington, DC: The World Bank; New York: Open Society Institute.

Roodman, David. 2009. 'Kiva Is Not Quite What It Seems.' http://blogs.cgdev.
org/open_book/2009/10/kiva-is-not-quite-what-it-seems.php (downloaded
on 30 October 2012).
———. 2011. 'Does Compartamos Charge 195% Interest?' in David Roodman's
Microfinance Open Book Blog. Available online at http://blogs.cgdev.org/
open_book/2011/01/compartamos-and-the-meaning-of-interest-rates.php
(downloaded on 18 December 2012).
———. 2012. Due Diligence: An Impertinent Inquiry into Microfinance. Washington, DC: Center for Global Development.
Roodman, David and Jonathan Morduch. 2009. 'The Impact of Microcredit on
the Poor in Bangladesh: Revisiting the Evidence,' Working Paper Number
174, Washington, DC: Center for Global Development.
Rosenberg, Richard. 2007. 'CGAP Reflections on the Compartamos Initial Public Offering: A Case Study on Microfinance Interest Rates and Profits,' Focus
Note No. 42, Washington, DC: CGAP.
———. 2010. 'Does Microcredit Really Help Poor People?' Focus Note No. 59,
Washington, DC: CGAP.
Rotman, Sarah. 2012. 'Savings and Credit on Mobile: The Jipange KuSave Experi-
ment.' Washington, DC: CGAP. Available online at http://www.cgap.org/blog/
savings-and-credit-mobile-jipange-kusave-experiment (downloaded on 16
January 2013).
Rotman, Sarah, Stephen Rasmussen and David Ferrand. 2012. 'Jipange KuSave
Experiment in Kenya,' CGAP. Available online at http://www.cgap.org/publi-
cations/jipange-kusave-experiment-kenya (downloaded on 6 January 2013).
Ruchismita, Rupalee and Sona Varma. 2009. 'Providing Insurance through
Microfinance Institutions: The Indian Experience.' Focus 17, Brief 13, Innovations in Insuring the Poor, 2020 Vision For Food, Agriculture and the
Environment. Washington, DC: International Food Policy Research Institute. Available online at http://www.ifri.org/sites/default/files/publications/
focus17_13.pdf (downloaded on 28 February 2013).
Rutherford, Stuart, 2000. The Poor and their Money. New Delhi: Oxford Univer-
sity Press.
———. 2005. 'What is Grameen II? Is It Up And Running In the Field Yet?' MicroSave. Available online at http://staging.microsave.net/files/pdf/MicroSave-
GB-Briefing-Note-1-Overview.pdf (downloaded on 21 February 2013).
SAMN. 2011. 'HDFC, Vodafone bring m-paisa to India's unbanked,' SAMN.
Available online at http://www.samn.eu/?q=node/698 (downloaded on 16
January 2013).
Sa-Dhan. 2012. 'Financial Inclusion: A Study on the Efficacy of Banking Correspondent Model,' Sa-Dhan. Available online at http://www.citigroup.com/citi/
microfinance/data/business_cor_study.pdf (downloaded on 23 January 2013).
Schicks, Jessica and Richard Rosenberg. 2011. 'Too Much Microcredit? A Survey
of the Evidence on Over-Indebtedness.' Occasional Paper, No. 19. Washington, DC: CGAP.

Schultz, Theodore W. 1993. *The Economics of Being Poor*. Cambridge, Massachusetts: Blackwell Publishers.

Sen, Amartya. 1999. *Development as Freedom*. New York: Knopf.

———. 2000. *Social Exclusion: Concept, Application, and Scrutiny*. Manila: Office of Environment and Social Development, Asian Development Bank.

Sharma, Ankit. 2007. 'FINO Smart Card to Drive Remittance in Rural Areas,' *Rupee Times*. Available online at http://www.rupeetimes.com/news/credit_cards/ fino_smart_card_to_drive_remittance_in_rural_areas1308.html (downloaded on 15 January 2013).

Shastri, Paromita. 2007. 'Microfinance cos Eye Untapped Local Private Remittances Market,' *Live Mint & The Wall Street Journal*. Available online at http://livemint. com/Money/WsSsPlt4F1kxnD6FOG3AiP/Microfinance-cos-eye-untapped- local-private-remittances-mark.html (downloaded on 24 February 2013).

Schumpeter, Joseph. 1975. *Capitalism, Socialism and Democracy*. New York: Harper.

Smillie, Ian. 2009. *Freedom from Want: The Remarkable Success Story of BRAC, the Global Grassroots Organization That's Winning the Fight Against Poverty*. Sterling, Virginia: Kumarian Press.

Smith, Stephen C. 2005. *Ending Global Poverty*. New York: Palgrave Macmillan.

Soros, George. 2003. *The Alchemy of Finance*. Hoboken, New Jersey: John Wiley & Sons.

SPTF. 2012. 'Universal Standards for Social Performance Management.' Available online at http://www.sptf.info/images/designed%20usspm%20manual%20 10%2015%2012.pdf (downloaded on 7 December 2012).

Srinivasan, Narasimhan. 2010. 'Crisis by Invitation,' *CGAP*. Available online at http://microfinance.cgap.org/2010/11/19/crisis-by-invitation/ (downloaded on 18 January 2013).

Srinivasan, N. 2010. *Microfinance India: Sate of the Sector Report 2010*. New Delhi: SAGE Publications.

———. 2012. *Microfinance India: Sate of the Sector Report 2011*. New Delhi: SAGE Publications.

Standard and Poor's. 2007a. *Report of the Microfinance Rating Methodology Working Group*. New York: Standard and Poor's.

———. 2007b. *Microfinance—Taking Root in the Global Capital Markets*. New York: Standard and Poor's.

Strom, Stephanie. 2009. 'Confusion on Where Money Lent via Kiva Goes,' *Global Business*, November 8.

Thiagarajan, Kamala. 2013. 'A Fight to Save Baby Girls in India,' *Asia Pacific*. Available online at http://www.nytimes.com/2013/03/08/world/asia/a- figt-to-save-baby-girls-in-india.htmal?pagewanted=all (downloaded on 11 March 2013).

Thirani, Neha. 2012. '"Yunus Was Right," SKS Microfinance Founder Says,' *India Ink, The New York Times/International Herald Tribune*. Available online at http://india.blogs.nytimes.com/2012/02/27/yunus-was-right-sks- microfinance-founder-says/ (downloaded on 12 March 2013).

Thorat, Y. S. P., N. V. Ramana, R.V. Ramakrishna, Anne Koshy and Therese Zak. 2009. 'Remittance Needs in India,' *NABARD—GTZ Technical Study.* Mumbai: NABARD.

Thorat, Y. S. P. and Howard Jones. 2011. 'Remittance Needs and Opportunities in India,' NABARD and GIZ, Mumbai and New Delhi.

Truen, Sarah, Richard Ketley, Hennie Bester, Ben Davis, Hugh David Hutcheson, Kofi Kwakwa and Sydney Mogpai. 2005. 'Supporting Remittances in Southern Africa: Estimating Market Potential and Assessing Regulatory Obstacles.' South Africa: CGAP and FinMark Trust.

Tumbe, Chinmay. 2011. 'Remittances in India: Facts and Issues'. Available online at http://papers.ssrn.com/sol3/papers.cfm?abstract_id=1780289 (downloaded on 15 January 2013).

UNCSD Secretariat. 2012. 'RIO 2012 Issues Briefs.' No. 15, RIO+20, United Nations Conference on Sustainable Development. Available online at www.uncsd2012.org.

United Nations. 2006. *Building Inclusive Financial Sectors for Development.* New York: Financing for Development Office. Available online at www.un.org/esa/ffd.

USAID. 2006. 'Rural Leasing,' RAFI Notes. Available online at http://www.ruralfinance.org/fileadmin/templates/rflc/documents/1169216602811_Rural_Leasing.pdf.

Vedantam, Shankar. 2007. 'One Thing We Can't Build Alone in Iraq,' *The Washington Post*, October 29.

Vogel, Robert C. 1984. 'Savings Mobilization: The Forgotten Half of Rural Finance.' in D. W. Adams, D. Graham and J. D. Von Pischke (eds.), *Undermining Rural Development with Cheap Credit.* Boulder: Westview Press.

Yunus, Muhammad. 2003. *Banker to the Poor: Micro-lending and the Battle Against World Poverty,* New York: Public Affairs.

———. 2011a. 'Social Business and Microfinance: Building Partnerships with Corporations and Other Entities to Speed the End of Poverty.' in Sam Daley-Harris and Anna Awimbo (eds.), *New Pathways Out of Poverty,* pp. 143–83. Sterling, Virginia: Kumarian Press.

———. 2011b. 'Sacrificing Microcredit for Megaprofits,' *The Opinion Pages* in *The New York Times*, January 14. Available online at http://www.nytimes.com/2011/01/15/opinion/15yunus.html (downloaded on 14 March 2013).

Yunus, Muhammad with Alan Jolis. 2003. *Banker to the Poor: Micro-Lending and the Battle Against World Poverty.* New York: Public Affairs.

Yunus, Muhammad with Karl Weber. 2007. *Creating a World Without Poverty: Social Business and the Future of Capitalism.* New York: Public Affairs.

Weizenbaum, Joseph. 1976. *Computer Power and Human Reason—From Judgment to Calculation.* San Fransisco: W. H. Freeman and Company.

Westley, Glenn W. 2003. *Equipment Leasing and Lending—A Guide for Microfinance.* Washington, DC: Inter-American Development Bank.

Whiting, Rob. 2009. 'BRACs? TUP Program: When Base of the Pyramid Approaches Might Not Work,' Next Billion. November 02. Available online at http://www.nextbillio.net/blogpost.aspx?blogid=1584 (downloaded on 4 December 2012).

Wiesel, Elie. 1998. *Sustaining Culture and Creative Expression in Development.* Washington, DC: The World Bank.

World Bank. 2012. 'Mobile Phone Access Reaches Three Quarters of Planet's Population.' Press Realease. Available online at http://www.worldbank.org/ en/news/2012/07/17/mobile-phone-access-reaches-three-quartres-plantes-population (downloaded on 15 January 2013).

World Bank. 'Migration and Remittances,' *News & Broadcast.* Available online at http://web.worldbank.org/WBSITE/EXTERNAL/NEWS0,,contentsMDK: 20648762~pagePK:64257043~piPK:437376~theSitePK:4607,00.html (downloaded on 15 January 2013).

Index

About the Author

Binod B. Nayak retired from the World Bank in 2001 after more than 27 years of service. During this period, he worked in the following areas: financial modeling and forecasting, financial policy and planning, and financial risk management at the corporate level. He also worked on development finance companies and project evaluations in member countries of the World Bank.

From 1999 to 2005, he was involved with a small US-based charitable organization that worked in villages of Odisha to help the villagers after the 1999 devastating 'Super Cyclone.' During this time, Binod was involved in introducing microfinance to the members of the charitable organization in order to help the villagers to join SHGs. This modest attempt opened his eyes to the need for a book to provide serious exposition of microfinance to intelligent laymen. During the last eight years, he has done extensive research in order to make this book accessible to a wider audience interested in gaining a better understanding of microfinance.

Binod has an MSc in Mathematics from IIT (Kanpur), MS in Computer Science from University of Washington (Seattle) and MBA from Robert H. Smith School of Business, University of Maryland (College Park). He also holds a CFA Charter from CFA Institute, Charlottesville, Virginia.

Currently, he is working as an Independent Researcher and Financial Consultant.